Rethinking Religion and
Radicalization

Rethinking Religion and Radicalization

Terrorism and Violence Twenty Years After 9/11

Michele Grossman and H. A. Hellyer

BLOOMSBURY ACADEMIC
LONDON • NEW YORK • OXFORD • NEW DELHI • SYDNEY

BLOOMSBURY ACADEMIC
Bloomsbury Publishing Plc
50 Bedford Square, London, WC1B 3DP, UK
1385 Broadway, New York, NY 10018, USA
29 Earlsfort Terrace, Dublin 2, Ireland

BLOOMSBURY, BLOOMSBURY ACADEMIC and the Diana logo are trademarks of Bloomsbury Publishing Plc

First published in Great Britain 2025

Copyright © Michele Grossman and H. A. Hellyer and contributors, 2025

Michele Grossman and H. A. Hellyer have asserted their right under the Copyright, Designs and Patents Act, 1988, to be identified as Editors of this work.

For legal purposes the Acknowledgements on p. xii constitute an extension of this copyright page.

Cover design by Daniel Benneworth-Gray

This work is published open access subject to a Creative Commons Attribution-NonCommercial-NoDerivatives 4.0 International licence (CC BY-NC-ND 4.0, https://creativecommons.org/licenses/by-nc-nd/4.0/). You may re-use, distribute, and reproduce this work in any medium for non-commercial purposes, provided you give attribution to the copyright holder and the publisher and provide a link to the Creative Commons licence.

Bloomsbury Publishing Plc does not have any control over, or responsibility for, any third-party websites referred to or in this book. All internet addresses given in this book were correct at the time of going to press. The author and publisher regret any inconvenience caused if addresses have changed or sites have ceased to exist, but can accept no responsibility for any such changes.

A catalogue record for this book is available from the British Library.

A catalog record for the book is available from the Library of Congress

ISBN: HB: 978-1-3503-5008-3
PB: 978-1-3503-5007-6
ePDF: 978-1-3503-5006-9
eBook: 978-1-3503-5005-2

Typeset by Integra Software Services Pvt. Ltd.
Printed and bound in Great Britain

To find out more about our authors and books visit www.bloomsbury.com and sign up for our newsletters.

Contents

List of contributors	vii
Acknowledgements	xii

Section 1 Religion and violent radicalization: Concepts and contestations

1	Introduction: Remapping the terrain of religion, radicalization and extremist violence *Michele Grossman and H. A. Hellyer*	3
2	Religion, radicalization and violence: Conceptual and interpretive issues *Lorne L. Dawson*	17
3	The racialized logic of the UK's countering extremism strategy *Tahir Abbas*	41

Section 2 Violent radicalization and the governance of religious diversity

4	The governance of religious diversity and the challenge of (violent) radicalization in Western Europe *Thomas Sealy and Tina Magazzini*	57
5	Religiously attributed radicalization and violent extremism: Policy responses and impacts on the governance of religion in South-Eastern Europe *Liliya Yakova and Rositsa Dzhekova*	77
6	The determinants of radicalization in Russia: Is religion to blame? *Marat Iliyasov*	101
7	The evolution of Salafi jihadi terrorism and state responses in Indonesia, Malaysia and the Philippines *Greg Barton*	119

Section 3 Religion and violence across extremist movements and contexts

8	A majority with a minority complex: Examining anti-Muslim violence in Sri Lanka and India *Amarnath Amarasingam and Shweta Desai*	139
9	The convergence of land- and blood-centric political theologies in Israel *Atalia Omer*	157
10	Hindu radicalization in contemporary India *Pralay Kanungo*	175

Section 4 Political mobilizations of religion on the extremist right

11 Marriage of convenience? The nexus of religious extremism and far-right militancy in Israel and the United States *Alejandro J. Beutel and Arie Perliger* 197
12 'Orthodoxy or Death': The embrace of Orthodox Christianity by the modern far right *Lydia Khalil* 227
13 Preparing for Day X: Looking into Germany's extreme right-wing radicalization *Frederic Heine and Tina Magazzini* 247
14 Mapping conspiritual radicalization: The intersection of conspiracy movements, spirituality and radicalization *Vivian Gerrand* 271

Index 289

Contributors

Tahir Abbas

Professor Tahir Abbas holds the chair in radicalization studies at the Institute of Security and Global Affairs at Leiden University in the Netherlands. He is the scientific coordinator and principal investigator of the Horizon 2020 DRIVE project, which explores the impact of social exclusion on the radicalization of Islamist and far-right groups in northwest Europe (2020–2024). His latest books are *Islamophobia and Securitisation: The Dutch Case* (with Liselotte Welten, 2022), *Countering Violent Extremism: The International Deradicalization Agenda* (2021) and *Islamophobia and Radicalisation: A Vicious Cycle* (2019). He is a Fellow of the Academy of Social Sciences.

Amarnath Amarasingam

Amarnath Amarasingam is Associate Professor in the School of Religion and is cross-appointed to the Department of Political Studies at Queen's University in Ontario, Canada. He is also Senior Fellow with the International Centre for the Study of Radicalisation. His research interests are in terrorism, radicalization and extremism, conspiracy theories, online communities, diaspora politics, post-war reconstruction and the sociology of religion. He is the author of *Pain, Pride, and Politics: Sri Lankan Tamil Activism in Canada* (2015), and the co-editor of *Stress Tested: The COVID-19 Pandemic and Canadian National Security* (2021) and *Sri Lanka: The Struggle for Peace in the Aftermath of War* (2016). He has also published around 50 peer-reviewed articles and book chapters, has presented papers at over 100 national and international conferences, and has written for *The New York Times, The Monkey Case, The Washington Post, CNN, Politico, The Atlantic* and *Foreign Affairs*. He has been interviewed on CNN, PBS Newshour, CBC, BBC, and a variety of other media outlets. He tweets at @AmarAmarasingam.

Greg Barton

Professor Greg Barton is Rector of Deakin University Lancaster University Indonesia (DLI) in Bandung, Indonesia. Prior to that he was Research Professor in Global Islamic Politics in the Alfred Deakin Institute for Citizenship and Globalisation at Deakin University, where, since August 2015, he led research on Islam and civil society, democratization and countering violent extremism (CVE). From 2007 to 2015 he was the Herb Feith Professor at Monash University, where he led research on radicalization in the Global Terrorism Research Centre (GTReC). He is Senior Fellow with the UAE-based Hedayah Center in Abu Dhabi working on CVE, and adjunct professor in the School of Global and Strategic Studies, University of Indonesia. Since 2016 he has led the Australian Department of Home Affairs Southeast Asian Network of Civil Society Organizations (SEAN-CSO), working together against extremism. He has researched and published extensively on Indonesian religion, politics and society.

Alejandro J. Beutel

Alejandro J. Beutel is a doctoral student at the University of Massachusetts Lowell, focusing on policing, homeland security and cybersecurity. He is also a Non-Resident Fellow at the New Lines Institute for Strategy, a think-tank in Washington, DC, and a Research Affiliate at the National Consortium for the Study of Terrorism and Responses to Terrorism. Alejandro previously worked as a Senior Research Analyst at the Southern Poverty Law Center's Intelligence Project. He holds a Master of Public Policy from the University of Maryland and a Bachelor of Science in International Relations and Diplomacy from Seton Hall University.

Lorne L. Dawson

Lorne L. Dawson is Distinguished Professor Emeritus in the Departments of Religious Studies, and Sociology and Legal Studies, at the University of Waterloo (Canada). He has published three books, five edited books and ninety-three academic articles and book chapters. He is the Co-Founder and Co-Director of the Canadian Network for Research on Terrorism, Security and Society (2012–23; www.tsas.ca), and his recent research has focused on such topics as foreign fighters, the role of religion in motivating religious terrorism and the social ecology of radicalization.

Shweta Desai

Shweta Desai is an independent journalist and researcher based in India and France.

Rositsa Dzhekova

Rositsa Dzhekova is a senior expert on preventing and countering violent extremism (P/CVE). She conducts research and consulting international stakeholders on P/CVE across the EU and the Western Balkans, focusing on multi-agency cooperation, disengagement programmes and strengthening the role of civil society in prevention. Between 2021 and 2024 she was Deputy Director of the International Department at the Violence Prevention Network, Germany, and contributed to the implementation of the European Commission's Radicalisation Awareness Network (RAN) as a senior staff member. Previously she was the Director of the Security Program at the Center for the Study of Democracy in Sofia, where she led EU-wide research and policy analyses on radicalization and extremism, counterterrorism, organized crime and border security.

Vivian Gerrand

Dr Vivian Gerrand is Research Fellow at the Alfred Deakin Institute for Citizenship and Globalisation at Deakin University in Australia. She was a former Max Weber Fellow and Endeavour Fellow at the European University Institute and later Visiting Fellow at the Robert Schuman Centre for Advanced Studies in her role as a chief investigator on the European Commission's Horizon 2020 BRaVE project (2019–21) and associate investigator on the GREASE project (2018–22). She is the author of *Possible Spaces of Somali Belonging* (2016).

Michele Grossman

Professor Michele Grossman is Research Chair in Diversity and Community Resilience at the Alfred Deakin Institute for Citizenship and Globalisation at Deakin University in Australia, where she is also Director of the Centre for Inclusive and Resilient Societies. Widely published as a terrorism studies scholar, Michele's research focuses on engaging communities in countering violent extremism. She is the founder and inaugural convenor of the AVERT (Addressing Violent Extremism and Radicalisation to Terrorism) Research Network; Associate Editor of the journal *Terrorism and Political Violence;* Visiting Professor at University of Huddersfield (UK); and a past Robert Schuman (Distinguished Scholar) Fellow at European University Institute in Florence (2018–22) in her role as a chief investigator and steering committee member on the Horizon 2020 GREASE project. Michele was made a Member of the Order of Australia (AM) in the King's Birthday Honours List 2023 for significant service to tertiary education through research.

Frederic Heine

Dr Frederic Heine is Lecturer at the Institute of Women's and Gender Studies of the Johannes Kepler University Linz. Frederic's research explores the interrelation between masculinities, issues of global political economy and right-wing populism, with a focus on economic crises and popular culture. Frederic holds a PhD from the University of Warwick; his research has appeared in the *International Feminist Journal of Politics* and the *Journal of Cultural Economy.*

H. A. Hellyer

Dr H. A. Hellyer is Senior Associate Fellow at the Royal United Services Institute for Defence and Security Studies (UK), and Middle East programme scholar at the Carnegie Endowment for International Peace (USA). His work in geopolitics, security studies and belief centres particularly on MENA, Europe, and Southeast Asia. He was elected as Fellow of the Royal Historical Society and the Royal Society of Arts in recognition of his scholarship, which includes seven books in his subject areas. A member of the international steering committee for the Horizon 2020 GREASE project, which produced this volume, he has held positions at Harvard University, Cambridge University, the Brookings Institution and the American University in Cairo.

Marat Iliyasov

Dr Marat Iliyasov is Visiting Assistant Professor at the College of the Holy Cross. He is an affiliate of the Wisconsin Russia Project and the Institute of Middle East,

Central Asia and Caucasus Studies at the University of St Andrews. He has researched and published on different aspects of the Russo-Chechen conflict, post-war political development in the region and migrants' identity. His latest analysis targets religious governance, radicalization and war in Ukraine.

Pralay Kanungo

Pralay Kanungo teaches at Leiden University. He was Professor at Jawaharlal Nehru University, New Delhi (2006–21); DAAD Guest Professor at Heidelberg University (2019–20); Fellow at Max-Weber-Kolleg, Erfurt (2018–19); Indian Council of Cultural Relations Chair of Contemporary India Studies at Leiden University (2013–18); Guest Professor at Sichuan University (2015–22); and Visiting Professor at Maison des Sciences de l'Homme, Paris. Kanungo has authored RSS's *Tryst with Politics* and co-edited *The Algebra of Welfare and Warfare* (2019), *The Politics of Ethnicity in India, Nepal and China* (2014), *Public Hinduisms* (2012) and *Cultural Entrenchment of Hindutva* (2011).

Lydia Khalil

Lydia Khalil is Senior Research Fellow at the Alfred Deakin Institute for Citizenship and Globalisation at Deakin University, where she convenes the AVERT (Addressing Violent Extremism and Radicalisation to Terrorism) Research Network, and Program Director, Transnational Challenges at the Lowy Institute. She began her counterterrorism and national security career after the September 11 attacks. She is a recognized expert on terrorism and extremism, having worked for the White House Office of Homeland Security, US Department of Defense, The New York Police Department, Boston Police Department and the Council on Foreign Relations. She is a frequent media commentator and has been widely published. She is the author of *Rise of the Extreme Right: The New Global Extremism and The Threat to Democracy* (2022).

Tina Magazzini

Dr Tina Magazzini is a political scientist interested in how categories of inclusion/exclusion are created and maintained across different settings in a comparative perspective. Her research focuses on tension between redistribution, recognition and representation, comparative and mixed methodologies, migration and integration policies, identity politics and the relationship between majorities, minorities and states. Currently affiliated to the Czech Academy of Sciences (Department of Mobility and Migration), she has carried out a wide range of consultancy and policy work for NGOs, UN agencies, the European Commission and the Council of Europe on ethnic, linguistic and religious minority rights.

Atalia Omer

Atalia Omer is Professor of Religion, Conflict, and Peace Studies at the Keough School of Global Affairs at the University of Notre Dame. She also served as the Dermot T. J. Dunphy Visiting Professor of Religion, Violence, and Peace Building at Harvard

University (2021–2024). She earned her PhD in Religion, Ethics and Politics (Harvard University, 2008). Her research focuses on religion, global politics and peacebuilding, with a particular focus on Palestine/Israel. Omer is the author of *Decolonizing Religion and Peacebuilding* (2023), *When Peace Is Not Enough: How the Israeli Peace Camp Thinks about Religion, Nationalism, and Justice* (2015) and *Days of Awe: Reimagining Jewishness in Solidarity with Palestinians* (2019).

Arie Perliger

Arie Perliger is Professor at the School of Criminology and Justice Studies, University of Massachusetts Lowell. Before his arrival at UMass Lowell, he was Director of Terrorism Studies and Associate Professor at the Combatting Terrorism Center and Department of Social Sciences, US Military Academy at West Point. He has engaged in extensive study of issues related to terrorism and political violence, security policy and politics, politics and extremism of the far right in Israel, Europe and the United States, Middle Eastern politics and the applicability of social network analysis to the study of political violence. His books include (with Ami Pedahzur) *Jewish Terrorism in Israel* (2009) and *American Zealots: Inside Right-Wing Domestic Terrorism* (2020), among many other publications.

Thomas Sealy

Dr Thomas Sealy is Lecturer in Ethnicity and Race in the School of Sociology, Politics and International Studies at the University of Bristol, UK. He has published journal articles and book chapters on multiculturalism, the governance of religious diversity, Islamophobia, forms of racism, converts to Islam and Simmel. His books include *Religiosity and Recognition: Multiculturalism and British Converts to Islam* (2021) (as ed.) *The Resilience of Multiculturalism* (2024), *The New Governance of Religious Diversity* (2024) and *Post-Multiculturalism, Religion, Recognition* (forthcoming).

Liliya Yakova

Liliya Yakova, PhD, works at the Centre for the Study of Democracy (CSD) Sociological Programme on projects related to public policy about ethnic minorities, vulnerable groups, radicalization and socio-economic disparity. Her areas of interest include social justice, communication and policy for social change, peacebuilding and organizational policy. Before joining CSD, Liliya was Associate Director of Operations for the Purdue Peace Project (USA), a violence prevention initiative in West Africa and Central America. She has also done research for the Hudson Institute (USA) and worked in the NGO sector as Manager of International Relations, Products and Services at the International Council for Cultural Centres (Bulgaria).

Acknowledgements

We are grateful, first and foremost, to all our colleagues on the Horizon 2020 project on Radicalization, Secularism and the Governance of Religion: Bringing Together Diverse Perspectives (GREASE), who over the project's lifespan from 2018 to 2022 provided outstanding scholarship, dialogue, research and analysis on key conceptual and empirical issues relating to the intersection of religion and radicalization in different parts of the world. Their intellectual contributions, open collaboration and personal collegiality have made this book both a possible and deeply pleasurable undertaking.

We are especially grateful for the scholarly and personal leadership and support of GREASE Coordinator Anna Triandafyllidou (then at European University Institute) and Tariq Modood (University of Bristol), with whom we collaborated intensively as part of the project's steering committee, as well as that of Tina Magazzini (also then at European University Institute) and Terry Martin (SPIA), who helped intellectually shape and pragmatically shepherd the GREASE project and its many outputs and dissemination for the life of the project.

We also want to thank those colleagues (who of necessity must remain anonymous) who provided their time and informed feedback as peer reviewers for draft chapters or for the entire manuscript. The volume as a whole is richer for the insights and guidance provided by the generosity of those who engaged constructively and thoughtfully with the ideas and the writing that appear across the chapters here.

We sincerely thank the Alfred Deakin Institute for Citizenship and Globalisation at Deakin University (Australia) and the Royal United Services Institute (UK) for their generous financial and related support in making this volume available as an open-access publication.

We are also deeply appreciative of the guidance and expertise we received from the editorial team at Bloomsbury Academic – in particular Atifa Jiwa – all of whom were unfailingly helpful and patient throughout the entire process of bringing the book to fruition.

Finally, we record our enduring gratitude to Christine Horn, our highly skilled and unflappable project manager who helped steer many aspects of this book from proposal stage to publication. Christine's support and care in managing the complex machinery of many moving parts that is an edited volume have been invaluable.

Section One

Religion and violent radicalization: Concepts and contestations

1

Introduction: Remapping the terrain of religion, radicalization and extremist violence

Michele Grossman and H. A. Hellyer

The role of religion in radicalization to extremist violence has long animated both scholarly and popular debates about how religious beliefs may intersect with violent extremist ideas, motivations and actions. This has been the case particularly since the events of 9/11, when sustained interest in the role of Islamist violent 'jihadi' activity emerged into the global spotlight, 'dominating the attention of the public, governments and academia' (Dawson, this volume).

Just over two decades later, with many subsequent developments and transformations in the global terrorism landscape, we are still exploring, and debating, how we might understand the role of religious ideas, beliefs and experiences in relation to trajectories of radicalization to violence. The chapters in this volume reflect the sustained efforts of key thinkers and scholars across disciplines – including religious studies, security studies, sociology, cultural studies, peace studies, terrorism studies and more – to explore contemporary dimensions of how and why religion and religiosity continue to feature in the ideas and actions of violent extremist individuals, groups and movements across a wide range of ideologies, regions and conflicts around the world.

How are religion and religiosity conceptualized and defined across these chapters? As Pollack and Rosta (2017: 35) note, uniform definitions of 'religion' are hard to come by because of the 'sheer diversity of religious rituals, symbols, dogmas, experiences, institutions, communities and roles' involved in religious systems, doctrines and beliefs over both time and space. They point to critiques of attempting to define 'religion' in any consistent fashion as an abstract concept that becomes of necessity divorced from its social and historical contexts, and also to the argument that what in the West is considered a consensus definition of 'religion' only emerged as part of Western Enlightenment modernity and therefore cannot be seen as either historically or conceptually legitimate in any global sense. And, of course, what both scholars, religious figures and everyday communities mean by religion – how it is defined, practised, experienced, argued over, embraced, mediated and resisted – remains an enduringly contested issue not only between religions but, more percipiently for our focus here, between the religious and non-religious.

In sketching out here our own conception of religion as a framework with which we may at least begin to think about the work appearing in the chapters that follow, we turn again to the work of Pollack and Rosta (2017: 40), who, in a reflective chapter on concepts of religion in relation to modernity, usefully retrace the elements and features of *substantive* versus *functional* definitions of religion: 'While substantive definitions seek to determine what religion *is*, functional definitions seek to determine what religion *does* and *achieves*'. They argue that the limitations of both substantive and functional models of religion mean that neither can fully capture the complexities and dynamics of religion(s) and religiosity across time and space – what they term the 'practical, ritual, emotional, ideal and communal reality' of any religious system (Pollack and Rosta 2017: 43). Knitting the two together, conceptually speaking, still might not be fully sufficient, depending on how religion is conceptualized according to various philosophical, intellectual or cultural traditions, but it is nevertheless more richly explanatory when considering the dynamics that the chapters in this volume seek to illuminate.

Religious systems are deeply concerned with how to both connect with the transcendent (as an essential distinguishing feature of any religious framework) but also make that transcendence immanent – that is, an enactment or manifestation of the transcendent in the material world. This is particularly apposite when it comes to questions of individual as well as collective religiosity, a key concern for studies of the nexus between religion, extremism and violence. Pollack and Rosta (2017: 47) identify three key dimensions of religiosity that resonate strongly with the analyses canvassed across these chapters. These are the dimensions of religious *identification or affiliation*; religious *action or practice*; and religious *experiences, beliefs and ideas*. Religious systems and the experience of religiosity right across different faith, culture and identity frameworks and dynamics thus involve questions of *belonging* or alternatively *exclusion* ('identification or affiliation'), *behaviours* ('action or practice') and the realm of the *sensory, cognitive, emotional and psycho-social* ('experiences, beliefs and ideas'). The intricate and complex interplay between these three dimensions constitutes the core of our own conceptual understanding of religion as both a system of experience, beliefs and ideas *and* a system of practices and behaviours – inextricably embedded in and both nurtured and weaponized by social and political contexts and dynamics – that can be used by, for and against the state and its citizens in various places and moments.

The specific inspiration for this collection has arisen from the European Union's Horizon 2020 Research and Innovation programme on radicalization, secularism and the governance of religion (GREASE) (www.grease.eui.eu), which was conducted from 2018 to 2022. This multinational, multi-institutional research consortium, of which both the volume's editors were steering committee members, examined key questions about how states govern religious diversity in different parts of the world, the ways in which this has changed over time, how secularism and religiosity have interacted at various levels within these societies and the impacts of these interactions on trajectories of religiously attributed or inspired violent extremism.

The book is divided into four sections that emphasize the comparative insights that may be gleaned from reading across the chapters within the volume. They chart the movement from conceptual debates to comparative empirical contextual analysis; provide comparative analyses of how significant, or otherwise, governance of religion may be in relation to the ways that different states respond to challenges around religiously attributed or inspired violent extremism; examine how religion and religiosity are harnessed to or underpin the dynamics of diverse political, national and ideological conflict settings; and, finally, explore how transformations in the global rise of the far right have witnessed the emergence of religious ideas, discourses and iconography used to promote and embed the acculturation of far-right extremist ideologies that compel a remapping of the complex ways in which religion and violent extremist movements can intersect.

In addition to our introductory chapter here, Lorne L. Dawson and Tahir Abbas, in Section I, 'Religion and violent radicalization: Concepts and contestations', deal with key debates in the current conceptual landscape surrounding the relationship between religion and radicalized violence. In Section II, 'Violent radicalization and the governance of religious diversity', contributions from Thomas Sealy and Tina Magazzini, Liliya Yakova and Rositsa Dzhekova, Marat Iliyasov and Greg Barton explore the ways in which the emergence of violent extremism can affect the governance of religious diversity – and vice versa – in a range of different regional and national contexts. In Section III, 'Religion and violence across extremist movements and contexts', chapters by Amarnath Amarasingam and Shweta Desai, Atalia Omer and Pralay Kanungo take up the ways in which religious beliefs and frameworks have been incorporated into the ideologies, narratives and actions of a diverse range of violent extremist movements across time and place. The final group of chapters in Section IV, 'Political mobilizations of religion on the extremist right', offers analyses by Alejandro Beutel and Arie Perliger, Lydia Khalil, Frederic Heine and Tina Magazzini, and Vivian Gerrand that explore the novel intersections in how religious tropes and ideas have been mobilized by far-right extremist and new spiritual movements. Below, we sketch out in greater detail some of the key themes and issues that emerge across the volume as a whole.

Contesting the role of religion in violent radicalization

The work of GREASE scholars featured in this volume has intersected with that of others who have been considering these issues in depth and over time. In a rich and informative overview of key conceptual debates around the relationship between religion and radicalization in the context of 'jihadi' terrorism, Lorne L. Dawson unpacks in this volume the ways in which the 'normative secular bias' in terrorism studies (Dawson 2018) has had pronounced impacts on the capacity of scholars and analysts to engage with the role of religiosity as a deeply felt motivation for violent extremist ideas and action, rather than as mere camouflage or superficial rationale. While religion does not cause terrorism, he argues, 'this does not mean … that many of those perpetrating acts of religious terrorism are not motivated by religion'.

In part, Dawson observes, the critical resistance offered by modern scholars to the salience of religion in violent extremist movements stems from the way in which modernist conceptions of religion per se as irrational, divisive and intolerant pit this against secular democratic liberal norms of reason and pluralist accommodation, resulting in a persistent 'hermeneutics of suspicion' (Dawson 2019) regarding the salience and authenticity of religiously inspired terrorists' accounts of their motives. The result is to either 'obscure or reject outright' the 'alternative logics of faith-based explanatory frameworks' – including those disavowing the distinction between 'religion', 'ideology' and 'politics' – that might support a more nuanced understanding of *how* religion and religiosity function within specific violent extremist matrices of meaning.

Yet if the role of ideology or religion is contestable within theories of radicalization trajectories (Hellyer and Grossman 2019), what then accounts for its persistence as an explanatory framework (Appleby 2000, Schmid 2014, Dawson 2018)? One answer to this may lie in an argument advanced by Arun Kundani, which we explore in greater detail below: that equating radicalization with Islam is itself an ideological position – one that has sought, in non-Muslim majority nations, to externalize the threat of violent extremism and to advance a construct of radicalization as a phenomenon connoting 'civilizational clash', rather than one produced by reluctance to remediate social and political inequalities or by resistance to multiculturalism in relation to national identity.

However, it is also important to acknowledge that such agendas are not exclusively deployed only by political or social discourses bent on (re)shaping narratives about the sociocultural 'other' – they can also be used by terrorists and propagandists as a form of superficial justification for violent radicalization, when in fact their motives are both more profane and more banal than this would suggest (Roy 2010, 2017). In other words, the same strategies of linking religion and radicalization can serve multiple, even competing sociopolitical purposes, and analysis must scrupulously pick these apart to examine them.

This includes the importance of critiquing the difference between the *strategic* mobilization of religion (by violent extremist actors and champions) as an attributed or explanatory pathway to/driver for radicalization, and the *felt/experienced* mobilization of radically altered religious states of consciousness/affect (by violently radicalized adherents and aspirants) (Whitehouse and Lanman 2014, McDonald 2014, 2018). As several contributors here observe, this leads to the question of whether a sufficient distinction is drawn between what might be termed 'authentic' or felt experiences of religiously inspired radicalization versus their more instrumental manipulation by extremist actors or movements, so that worldly political aspirations are dressed up in the clothes of sacred obligation in order to motivate and manage the actions of followers.

Doing justice to the conceptual and empirical complexities that emerge from these considerations and developing a meaningful analysis of how these are manifesting in new contexts and movements in the contemporary age are key aims of this book.

Conceptualizing the religion/radicalization nexus

As Arun Kundnani (2012) argued a decade ago about the conceptual underpinnings of how we approach radicalization to violence, studies on the relationship between religion and radicalization have often turned on what Kundnani calls the 'narrow question' posed in post-9/11 contexts: 'Why do some individual Muslims support an extremist interpretation of Islam that leads to violence?' (2012: 5). The emergent emphasis on theological rather than sociopolitical dynamics, he asserts, was more forcefully shaped by the needs of counter-terrorist strategists and officials to quickly fund and mount counter-radicalization offensives than by the effort to 'objectively study how terrorism comes into being' through 'scholarly understanding of the causes of terrorism' (2012).

Tahir Abbas canvasses similar points in his contribution here, arguing compellingly in relation to the UK's counter-extremism strategies that such approaches result in a reductive, essentialist and unhelpfully compartmentalized conceptualization of the relationship between religion and radicalization. He demonstrates the ways in which this helps sustain contemporary forms of Islamophobia, instrumentalizing rather than offering new insights on the role played by religious experience, doctrine and narrative in understanding and preventing violent extremist ideation and action. This aligns with Michael Barkun's (2003: 57) observation that 'references to "Islamic fundamentalism" have become so commonplace in discussions of violence that they scarcely occasion any notice', serving more often as 'an act of labelling for the purpose of condemnation, with little regard for the beliefs to which the label is attached' than as a serious analytical claim.

In part, both the secularist and the instrumentalist orientations in how Islamist-attributed or -inspired violent extremism has been treated derive significantly, as Derek Silva (2018) has suggested, from the work of Walter Laqueur (1999, 2004), who argued for a new way of theorizing radicalization that has come to be known as the 'new terrorism' paradigm. The 'new terrorism' framework privileged psychosocial and sociocultural processes over older models of analysis that foregrounded the political and structural conditions that can enable or provoke violence as a strategy for dealing with grievances and conflicts. This was in turn linked to Laqueur's conception of a new kind of terrorism that he saw as rooted not in a 'territorial dispute or the feeling of national oppression but because of a religious commandment – jihad and the establishment of shari'ah' (2004), connoting an emerging era of lethality linked to religious motivation as its primary driving force.

The 'new terrorism's' concept of radicalization – intimately bound up with its characterization as Islamist terrorism – has thus been persistently shaped by instrumentalist as well as analytical or interpretive concerns and perspectives. The focus on a break between the 'new' terrorism and the 'old' was not without its critics, however, including the terrorism scholar Martha Crenshaw, who pointed out that 'a strictly "new terrorism" viewpoint is bound to overestimate the effect of religious beliefs as a cause of terrorism and a cause of lethality' (2007: 32). Crenshaw states that the distinction between 'religious and nationalist or secular revolutionary motivations is not clearly established', with few groups able to be characterized as having other than 'mixed motives' (2007). David Rapoport's analysis of religiously inspired terrorism as the 'fourth wave' of modern terrorism (following earlier waves of anarchist, anti-colonial and New Left violent radicalization), while locating 'Islam … at the heart of the wave' (2004, 61), similarly offers a nuanced analysis of how religiously affiliated narratives and rationales for violent radicalization – both within *and* beyond Islamist contexts – intersect with critical sociopolitical and structural forces that combine to make the fourth wave a profoundly anti-democratic, rather than merely proto-religious, movement (Rapoport 2004: 65).

Nevertheless, the meaning of 'radicalization' within such analyses has often seen the term used as a conceptual byword for attempting to pin down the points at which interventions could potentially disrupt the process of mobilizing to extremist violence by turning people or groups away from religiously inflected fanatical ideologies. The focus for radicalization studies and theorizations that followed this Laqueurian turn often sought to explain violent radicalization's 'root causes' either in theological terms or – with greater sophistication and complexity – as 'an interactive process between theological and social-psychological journeys', one that 'addresses the interdependence of theology with emotions, identity and group dynamics' (Kundnani 2012: 14).

An example of this approach may be found in the work of Olivier Roy (2010, 2017), who argues that it is not so much the 'radicalism of Islam' but the 'Islamization of radicalization' that requires further analysis. He rejects the assumption that conservative Salafism should be uncritically equated with violent extremism but also asserts that hegemonic secularism, particularly in Europe, coupled with the denial or suppression of religiosity through the philosophical orientation and governance structures of states, has created a space in which the desire for spiritual meaning and transcendence can make young people in particular vulnerable to extremist narratives that appeal to this gap. The process of radicalization outlined by Roy is more aligned with the ways in which extreme forms of social and cultural alienation and grievances in specific structural contexts find expression in an urge towards redress and action that varieties of religious extremism seem better able to accommodate than secularly based frameworks.

Although 'the prevailing association between [religious] fundamentalism and violence, particularly terrorism, should not be regarded as self-evidently true' (Barkun 2003: 57), a range of scholars have nevertheless noted the entanglement of varieties of religious extremism with violence across different periods, locales and religious traditions (Barkun 2003, Juergensmeyer 2003, Pratt 2010, 2017, Pedhazur and Perliger 2011). However, treatments of how religious beliefs, concepts, histories and conflicts have become enmeshed with both established and emergent violent ideologies and movements outside of, or in addition to, concerns with 'Islamism and terrorism' have been comparatively minor by comparison. A number of contributors to this volume address this imbalance from a variety of angles across these chapters.

Reciprocal relations? Radicalization and the governance of religious diversity

As the work of the GREASE consortium attests, deep comparative analyses on how religious narratives and beliefs are mobilized by violent extremist movements across countries and regions; how state governance structures have responded to this, and the impacts of such responses on radicalization trajectories, remains vital (Sealy and Modood 2022a, 2022b; http://grease.eui.eu/policy-briefs/). Some of the alienation that Roy (2017) has addressed stems precisely from his observations concerning the ways in which certain states have either repressively governed or altogether excluded religiosity, or particular religious identities and structures, through governance frameworks. In some cases, this is related to the ways that states have chosen to deal with the increase in religious pluralism that has accompanied migration from different parts of the world; in others, it is more related to the effort to impose hegemonic ideas about national identity that position religious minorities, even though well-established in particular regions over time, as a threat to various political ideologies and regimes. In almost all cases, however, the issue of how religion is governed, and the relationship between religious governance and violent radicalization, has largely centred on the governance of religious minorities.

In this context, we need to rethink not only what the role of religion *is* but also what it is *not* in relation to religious governance/violent radicalization dynamics. In both South-Eastern Europe and Russia, the violence associated with ethnonational separatism has at times been interpreted through a religious lens, while in other cases it has been linked more to sociopolitical structural forces in which religion does not feature significantly as a variable. In Russia, for example, as Marat Iliyasov's contribution to this volume makes clear, analyses of religiously attributed or inspired radicalization in that country 'by default refer to Islamism', in part because of the shadow of Chechen resistance in the 1990s following the collapse of the Soviet Union, in part because of the way in which the 'global war on terrorism' has positioned Islamism as the key terrorist threat of the modern age and in part because 'radicalized groups and individuals linked to other religions or ideologies' are not seen as posing a similar risk to the national sociopolitical order. Iliyasov concludes that, until recent changes in the region through exposure to so-called Islamic State (IS) propaganda, 'the interaction between the state and Muslims', in which Muslim Russians recount consistent experiences of being treated as 'second-class citizens' and enduring discrimination by the state, provided sufficient cause for anti-state radicalization 'without the religious dimension' serving as a significant driver.

In the case of South-Eastern Europe, Liliya Yakova and Rositsa Dzhekova provide a comparative account of how Albania, Bosnia and Herzegovina, and Bulgaria have managed the governance of religion in response to the threat of religiously attributed violent extremism. Their analysis shows how these states have adapted their governance of religion to successive waves of policy concerned with post-communist liberalization of religious diversity, the complexities of pluralist and fundamentalist religious influences that emerged in the aftermath of this liberalization, the rise of foreign fighters spurred by the emergence of Islamic State, and the role of both the global war on terror and more localized ethno-religious conflicts. These combined factors, they suggest, resulted in restrictive measures on externally funded Muslim organizations and foundations, as well as legislative measures that responded reactively, rather than preventatively, to the perceived threats posed by religiously inspired radicalization, offset in part (except for Bulgaria) by the enhanced involvement of domestic religious institutions in prevention frameworks.

In Western Europe, Thomas Sealy and Tina Magazzini take up the central question of whether and how violent radicalization is influenced by the governance of religious diversity in Belgium, France, Germany and the UK. Framing the question of governance by distinguishing between two key modes – 'the moderate secularism of Belgium, Germany and the UK' and the 'secularist statism of France' – they ask whether there is an evidence-based relationship between modes of governing religious diversity and trends in violent radicalization, how different governance modes shape state responses to radicalized violence and the extent to which violent radicalization itself occasions shifts in the governance of religious diversity. Their comparative analysis concludes that while there is no causal relationship between mode of religious governance and trends in violent radicalization, the issue of governance mode does make a difference to state responses to violent radicalization, and that these responses in turn have implications for the governing of religious diversity more generally, including for freedom of religion.

Coalitions of hate: Religion, violence and ethnonationalism

Shifting to South and Southeast Asia, the landscape transforms yet again. Pralay Kanungo traces the ways in which both Muslim and Hindu modes of radicalism have evolved through successive phases of colonialism, communalism and nationalism in India, outlining the history of entrenched postcolonial conflict in which imperial authorities strategically deployed religious rivalry to serve the aims of empire that displaced the relatively harmonious precolonial accommodation between Muslims and Hindus. Kanungo's careful and detailed discussion of the radicalization legacies created by the emergence of this divide engages with similar themes explored in other chapters regarding the impacts of political, social, economic and religious marginalization experienced by minority Muslim communities. But he also argues the case for the emergence of reciprocal radicalization dynamics in which both Muslim and Hindu violent radicalization proceed from 'colonial and postcolonial communal politics … conditioned more by internal rather than eternal forces', albeit with pointedly uneven state responses in relation to surveillance and repression. Kanungo concludes that the momentum created for Hindutva violent radicalization following the rise of Narendra Modi's aggressive brand of majoritarian governance, with ever-increasing restrictions for Indian Muslim citizens in relation to religious freedom and citizenship, has both accelerated the regional spread of Islamist radicalization and further emboldened Hindu radicals towards sectarian violence.

Similarly, Southeast Asia's history of both ethnonationalist struggles and transnational terrorist movements – all of which have deployed religious ideologies at key points in their development – provides the focal point for Greg Barton's analysis of religiously inflected violent extremism and contrasting state responses in Indonesia, Malaysia and the Philippines. Drawing on a deep knowledge of developments in Southeast Asian terrorism and state policies over decades, he charts the ways in which military-led repression of radical Islamists in both Indonesia and the Philippines has driven the resurgence of militant Islamist violent extremism, while in Malaysia, 'a more permissive environment for extremist Islamist thought' increased the risks of extremist violence through offering more sustained opportunities for transnational terrorist influence and engagement to thrive. Barton's discussion highlights the complex ways in which states both drive and respond to simultaneously localized and transnational legacies of conflict and entanglement between religion, politics and extremist violence.

The exclusivist narratives of violent radicalization characterizing Hindu and Sinhala nationalist movements in India and Sri Lanka are taken up by Amarnath Amarasingam and Shweta Desai in their intriguing discussion of how far-right extremism and aggressive religious nationalism intersect in these countries. Drawing on Stanley Tambiah's (1986) construct of 'the majority with a minority complex' and Michael Jerryson's (2021) framework of 'religious violence as emergency mindset', Amarasingam and Desai show how anti-Muslim sentiment and violent action in India and Sri Lanka, while reflecting differences in ethnic and religious composition and history across these countries, nevertheless share common threads related to 'majoritarian extremism' that has become newly energized through contemporary manifestations of misinformation, conspiracy theories and polarization fuelled in part by the rise of social media.

As the foregoing discussion suggests, the presumed relationship between Islam and terrorism – however vigorously it has been critiqued and its founding assumptions and frameworks challenged or moderated over the last two decades – has nevertheless continued to dominate analytical treatments of the relationship between religion and radicalization. In this sense, the field has been preoccupied over a long period with how violent extremist movements have staked a claim *for* religion as a core element of their motivation – what one might call the 'yes' case for religiosity as a driving force for violent extremist mobilization.

Religion and far-right extremist movements

Far less examined by comparison, however, has been the question of how extreme far-right movements – currently dominating the security and social policy agendas of many states around the world because of the threats they pose to hard-won gains for democratic pluralism and sociocultural ethnic and religious diversity – are deploying religion and religious ideas, narratives and iconographies to promote varieties of authoritarianism, social conflict, accelerationism, xenophobia and ethnonationalism. While some far-right extremist movements may make the 'yes' case for religion – as both Atalia Omer and Pralay Kanungo explore in different national contexts here – it is also clear that in at least some instances, what is involved is not so much the 'yes' case for one's own religious identity but the 'no' case for the religious identities of others – no to Judaism, no to Islam, no to secularism or atheism. In this context, the current volume breaks new ground in offering a suite of chapters that take up what Alejandro Beutel and Arie Perliger (this volume) term 'the nexus of religious extremism and far-right militancy'.

Beutel and Perliger explore this nexus through comparative analysis of dynamics in Israel and the United States, asking whether the convergence of religion and the far-right reflects a 'marriage of convenience' or instead a more profound entanglement in which religion serves as a foundational element in how far-right extremist movements construct their identities and goals. They demonstrate that the increasing integration of religious beliefs by far-right movements can be traced through the 'specific ways in which religious sentiments, symbols, themes, and traditions are employed to (1) facilitate recruitment, (2) solidify ideological commitment and solidarity, (3) justify acts of violence by far-right actors and/or (4) gain greater social currency with wider audiences on various societal issues'. Ironically, for a broad movement often characterized by overt ideological hostility to ethnic, racial and religious diversity, Beutel and Perliger reveal the broad diversity of far-right movements' engagement with religious frameworks, including 'irreligion', varieties of Christianity, Germanic Heathen faiths and new religious movements (NRMs). They conclude that while in some instances the relationship between specific far-right movements and religious beliefs is a 'marriage of convenience', dictated more by secularist aims of establishing white supremacy, in other cases, such entanglements reflect 'deep engagement with established religious traditions'. In both cases, however, such dynamics reflect a shift towards 'the embrace [of] transnational cultural-religious identities' that arises in part from the decline of 'traditional aspects of "secular" nationalism' in favour of more regionally constructed affiliations.

In a related vein, Atalia Omer problematizes the concept of 'the secular' in her discussion of Jewish violent radicalization, noting that the secular is neither an 'empty' space nor the 'binary of the "religious"', but a distinctive formation made possible only by the modern nation-state. As such, she writes, all forms of 'religious violence' require sustained analysis within the specificity of their historical, political and structural contexts. The context Omer unpacks in her chapter focuses on how neo-biblical discourse is used to legitimate Israeli militant ultranationalism. In an extended discussion of the ultra-right militant movement of Kahanism, she illuminates the ways in which Kahanism appears to resolve a central contradiction of Zionism in its 'grounding claim for Jewish sovereignty in biblical scripts' that is then used to justify settler colonialists' violent exclusion and revenge against the enemies of ultranationalists' vision of the Jewish state. Among the contemporary legacies of Kahanism discerned by Omer are those of an emboldened Israeli far right that 'promotes unabashedly Jewish ethnoreligious supremacy with no pretense to democracy', predictably fueling increases in violence and terror in the Palestinian-occupied territories. While Omer's chapter was completed before the Israel-Gaza war erupted in 2023, its relevance in providing deep analytical context has only increased since then.

The use of religion by far-right extremist movements to prosecute their political agenda by making the 'no' case against religious others is highlighted in Frederic Heine and Tina Magazzini's consideration of extreme right-wing radicalization in Germany. Drawing on a rich range of qualitative empirical data, they chart the resurgence of recent right-wing extremist violence in Germany towards ethnocultural minorities – specifically, Muslims and Jews – as part of a broader accelerationist push to heighten sociocultural division and discord in a country still reckoning with its recent catastrophic historical past even as it grapples with contemporary tensions produced by migration policies and impacts, as well as broader shifts in European geopolitics and transnational terror networks. They find qualified cause for optimism in the recent acceptance by German authorities that far-right extremism is now Germany's biggest security threat, and signs of renewed bridging activity between state and civil society organizations across religious divides, despite evidence of continuing 'tone-deafness' by some public figures and institutions in relation to attacks perpetrated by far-right extremist actors.

From conspirituality to the Orthosphere: New configurations of religion and extremism

As we have seen, the relationship between religion and the extreme or militant right spans religious faiths and ideological orientations, including Hinduism, Christianity and Judaism. However, as Lydia Khalil argues in her distinctive contribution to the volume, our understanding of 'Christianity' in the context of far-right militancy has tended to focus on Western Christian denominations familiar to those concerned with understanding the dynamics of what she terms 'far-right white nationalist and male supremacist influencers from the Anglosphere'. This focus, she suggests, has obscured another recent trend that remains all but invisible: the growing appeal and take-up of Orthodox Christianity by the same cohort of influencers who convert to Eastern Orthodoxy 'as a political and ideological act, not just a spiritual or religious calling'. She offers a detailed analysis of the online 'Orthosphere', in which far-right extremist converts find sympathetic resonance in Orthodox Christianity's 'emphasis of the communal over the individual, its enduring values and practices in the face of modernity, the rigor of its praxis effortlessly combined with mysticism and mystery' and both doctrinal and gender hierarchy and conservatism.

It would be an error, however, to assume that these conversions represent an infiltration of far-right ideas and sentiments within Christian Orthodoxy as a religious movement; on the contrary, Khalil documents the ways in which, 'from Codreanu's Legionnaires in Romania to Greece's Golden Dawn … fascist and far-right movements have publicly embraced Orthodox Christianity as part of their exclusivist projects', supported by factions within their respective Orthodox churches. These are historical examples that serve as instructive models for contemporary far-right white nationalists in a variety of countries and regions with only weak or virtually non-existent links to Christian Orthodoxy at the level of the state. 'Steeped in the language of religion', far-right converts nevertheless acknowledge the political and ideological nature of their project, recalling Beutel and Perliger's construct (this volume) of 'marriages of convenience' between the orthodoxies of religion and politics that Khalil notes are used to 'justify, actualize and sustain' far-right political and ideological positions and actions.

In the fascinating closing contribution of the volume, Vivian Gerrand moves away from long-established religious frameworks to investigate the unlikely alliances emerging between what she terms the 'militant wellness' movement and far-right extremism. Exploring 'how conspiracy thinking has been mobilized by alternative/new religious movement (NRM) influencers during the COVID-19 pandemic' in order to map 'radicalization trajectories towards militant forms of conspiritual thinking and wellness', Gerrand sheds new light on recent trends in which 'a post-secular spiritual milieu' has generated the conspirituality movement.

While conspirituality, a portmanteau of 'conspiracy' and 'spirituality', existed prior to the advent of Covid-19, Gerrand argues this movement was accelerated significantly during the pandemic by a combination of enhanced online interactivity and perceived threats to freedom, bodily autonomy and self-agency, as well as apparent opportunities for 'awakening, planetary ascension and transformation'. These dynamics, she suggests, 'fostered increased crossover between the far right and radical action', producing a militant wellness movement that is prepared in both 'posture and action orientation' for combat and conflict against perceived global elites across both government and private sectors. Gerrand's analysis of several key online influencers within militant wellness communities demonstrates how conspiritualist and proto-fascist narratives of purification, cleansing and control have intersected and nurtured one another, in conjunction with overtly accelerationist narratives that valorize violence and conflict. As Gerrand writes, 'conspiritual trajectories of radicalization remind us that, like religion, spirituality, health and wellness may be co-opted by conspiracy thinking' in ways we have yet to fully understand or respond to in prosocial ways.

Concluding observations

J. M. Berger (2017, 2018) observes that any social collective requires the imprimatur of legitimacy to protect its identity, and that this need not be unhealthy. But – especially under perceived or actual conditions of threats to identity or integrity – the need for legitimacy can spiral out of control when identity-based groups turn towards extremisms that require harmful attitudes and behaviours towards out-groups. If unchecked by internal or external pressures, in-groups can escalate their demands for legitimacy in ways that cross the threshold from 'healthy' to 'unhealthy' forms of extremism at the expense of others.

This kind of analysis is critical because it avoids the tendency noted by Dawson (2018) to reduce religion – as one form of identity-based social collective – to the category of personal motivations for involvement in terrorism, which privileges the psychological over the political and social-structural aspects of how extremist violence may come to be embraced. Through various theoretical and empirical lenses, each of the chapters collected here compels a rethinking of the relationship between religion and radicalization that asks us to consider anew the social, political and structural contexts – within religions, between religions, between religions and states, and between established religions and new religious and sociopolitical movements – in which the intersections between ideology, religion and violence may arise and be enacted in both familiar and surprising ways. Taken together, they bring to the fore the ways in which Islam has come in for disproportionate attention in considerations of radicalization, extremism and terrorism over the last twenty years. But they also highlight that this lack of balanced perspectives tells only one part of a much broader and more complex story.

As a collection, they demonstrate – across comparative histories, geographies, ideologies, disciplines and contexts – the extent to which religion and religiosity remain a vibrant yet complex part of global trends in violent radicalization and extremism, despite the 'normative secular bias' in critical analysis discerned by Dawson with which we began this chapter. The question these chapters leave us with is not so much whether or not there is a relationship between 'religion' and 'radicalization' to violence but how that relationship is made manifest, to what ends and with what consequences for religious identities, practices, governance and freedoms, and what we need to understand in order to address the ways in which religious frameworks continue to be harnessed to the legitimation of ideologically driven violence.

References

Appleby, R. S. (2000), *The Ambivalence of the Sacred: Religion, Violence, and Reconciliation.* Lanham, MD: Rowman & Littlefield.
Barkun, M. (2003), 'Religious Violence and the Myth of Fundamentalism', *Religious Fundamentalism and Political Extremism*, 4 (3): 55–70.
Berger, J. M. (2017), *Extremist Construction of Identity: How Escalating Demands for Legitimacy Shape and Define In-group and Out-group Dynamics.* The Hague: International Centre for Counter-Terrorism, 8, No. 7.
Berger, J. M. (2018), *Extremism*. Cambridge, MA: MIT Press.
Crenshaw, M. (2007), 'The Debate over "New" vs. "Old" Terrorism', *Annual Meeting of the American Political Science Association*, Chicago: 30 August–2 September. Available online: https://www.start.umd.edu/sites/default/files/files/publications/New_vs_Old_Terrorism.pdf.
Dawson, L. (2018), 'Debating the Role of Religion in the Motivation of Religious Terrorism', *Nordic Journal of Religion and Society*, 31 (2): 98–117.
Dawson, L. (2019), 'Taking Terrorist Accounts of Their Motivations Seriously: An Exploration of the Hermeneutics of Suspicion', *Perspectives on Terrorism*, 13 (5): 74–89. https://www.jstor.org/stable/26798579.
Hellyer, H. A. and M. Grossman (2019), *A Framework for Understanding the Relationship between Radicalization, Religion and Violence*, Horizon 2020 GREASE Concept Paper. Available online: http://grease.eui.eu/publications/concept-papers/.
Jerryson, M. (2021), 'Religious Violence as Emergency Mindset', *Journal of Religion and Violence*, 9 (1): 33–49.
Juergensmeyer, M. (2003), *Terror in the Mind of God*, 3rd edn, Berkeley: University of California Press.
Kundnani, A. (2012), 'Radicalization: The Journey of a Concept', *Race & Class*, 54 (2): 3–25.
Laqueur, W. (1999), *The New Terrorism: Fanaticism and the Arms of Mass Destruction.* New York: Oxford University Press.
Laqueur, W. (2004), 'The Terrorism to Come', *Policy Review*, 126: 46–64. Available online: https://www.hoover.org/research/terrorism-come.
McDonald, K. (2014), *Our Violent World*. London: Palgrave Macmillan.
McDonald, K. (2018), *Radicalization*. London: Polity Books.
Pedhazur, A. and A. Perliger (2011), *Jewish Terrorism in Israel*. New York: Columbia University Press.
Pollack, D. and G. Rosta (2017), *Religion and Modernity: An International Comparison.* Oxford: Oxford University Press. https://doi.org/10.1093/oso/9780198801665.003.0003.

Pratt, D. (2010), 'Religion and Terrorism: Christian Fundamentalism and Extremism', *Terrorism and Political Violence*, 22 (3): 438–56.

Pratt, D. (2017), *Religion and Extremism: Rejecting Diversity*. London: Bloomsbury.

Rapoport, D. (2004), 'The Four Waves of Modern Terrorism', in Audrey Kurth Cronin and James M. Ludes (eds), *Attacking Terrorism: Elements of a Grand Strategy*, 46–73, Washington, DC: Georgetown University Press.

Roy, O. (2010), *Holy Ignorance. When Religion and Culture Part Ways*. New York: Columbia University Press.

Roy, O. (2017), *Jihad and Death: The Global Appeal of Islamic State*. Oxford: Oxford University Press.

Schmid, A. (2014), *Violent and Non-Violent Extremism: Two Sides of the Same Coin?*. The Hague: ICCT Research Paper, No. 5.

Sealy, T. and T. Modood (2022a), *State-Religion Relations in Different World Regions*, Horizon 2020 GREASE Comparative Report. Available online: http://grease.eui.eu/grease-comparative-reports/.

Sealy, T. and T. Modood (2022b), *Religious Radicalization Dynamics in Different World Regions*. Horizon 2020 GREASE Comparative Report. Available online: http://grease.eui.eu/grease-comparative-reports/.

Silva, D. M. D. (2018), '"Radicalization: The Journey of a Concept" Revisited', *Race & Class*, 59 (4): 34–53. https://doi.org/10.1177/0306396817750778.

Tambiah, S. J. (1986), *Sri Lanka: Ethnic Fratricide and the Dismantling of Democracy*. Chicago: Chicago University Press.

Whitehouse, H. and J. A. Lanman (2014), 'The Ties That Bind Us: Ritual, Fusion, and Identification', *Current Anthropology*, 55 (6): 674–95.

2

Religion, radicalization and violence: Conceptual and interpretive issues

Lorne L. Dawson

Introduction

The tragic events of 9/11 were emblematic of what David Rapoport (2004) called the fourth wave of modern (non-state) terrorism, 'religious terrorism' (1970s to the present) – preceded by the Anarchist Wave (1870s–1920s), the Anti-Colonial Wave (1920s–1960s) and the New Left Wave (1960s–1980s). The wave of religious terrorism has taken many forms (e.g. Reader 2000, Pedahzur and Perlinger 2011, Jefferis 2011) across almost all religious traditions. However, it is the threat posed by 'jihadists' – self-declared religious terrorists (i.e. those fighting a 'holy war' or *jihad* in defence, they claim, of Islam) – that has dominated the attention of the public, governments, and academia since 9/11, and is the focus of attention here. Yet after all these years, a deep suspicion persists about the role of religiosity in motivating the process of radicalization leading to this religious terrorism.

In part this is because the spectre of jihadist religious terrorism in the West has eluded full understanding, despite copious research. Our grasp of the factors contributing to the radicalization of individuals and groups in general is growing steadily, along with our appreciation of the complexity of the process (e.g. Hafez and Mullins 2015, Malthaner 2017, Dawson 2017b, Kruglanski et al. 2018, Bouhana 2019, Dawson 2023). Empirically, however, we are only beginning to piece together the elements of the perfect storm of considerations that explain why a few individuals, in circumstances shared with others, radicalize while so many do not (e.g. Allan et al. 2015, Grossman et al. 2022, Malet 2021, Stephens, Sieckelinck and Boutellier 2021). This problem of specificity, of delineating the factors that differentiate those who radicalize from others experiencing similar conditions, is the litmus test of progress in radicalization research (e.g. Taylor and Horgan 2006, Kurzman 2011, Bartlett and Miller 2012, Dawson 2014, Sageman 2014). So far, this research has shown that there are no easy answers in terms of either the background characteristics of the terrorists or the conditions impinging on them (Dawson 2019a: 152–7). It is the dynamic and diverse interactions of individuals with aspects of their environments that lead to involvement in terrorism, and in most cases a further process of secondary radicalization is required for any of those who have radicalized to become violent (Borum 2011, Horgan 2014). Consequently, while there are discernible patterns, we know that no two individuals radicalize in the same way and not everyone who radicalizes engages directly in violence (e.g. Desmarais et al. 2017, Vergani et al. 2018, Jensen, Seate and James 2020, Gill et al. 2021).

The explanatory challenge becomes even more complex with religious terrorism, and in ways that are not always well understood. The complexity stems in part from the ambiguity of religious action as a subject of social scientific analysis, and the resultant ambivalence of most social scientists in dealing with religious motivational claims. The explanatory challenge of coping with a situation where the primary datum is the actor's assertion of the role of religiosity in guiding their actions, especially ones involving mass murder and the sacrifice of one's life (i.e. through martyrdom or long imprisonment), has set off a suspicion of religious motivations that is problematic. This deep and largely unacknowledged suspicion has prompted a reliance on a series of cross-cutting conceptual dichotomies to make sense of the radicalization of religious terrorists, dichotomies which have had a distorting effect on the discourse by minimizing the etiological significance of religiosity in unwarranted ways. Researchers have striven to structure the analysis of religious terrorism in terms of a series of distinctions, between the rational and irrational, public and private, political and religious, social processes and ideology. These conceptual alternatives, however, are misleading, because they fail to adequately capture the complex reality of the situation.

Given the complexity of the situation and the different ways in which the interpretive problems are manifested in the research literature on religious terrorism, I can only take a schematic approach to delineating their presence and impact in this limited context (see Dawson 2021a, 2021b). This inevitably involves some simplification, but hopefully without adding to the distortions afflicting the debates over religious terrorism. In this regard, I first sketch the presence of two foundational perspectives influencing all discussions of religious terrorism: a religious normative bias and a secular normative bias (Dawson 2018a). Second, I reflect further on the problems posed by the dominant secular bias in the social scientific study of religious terrorism. Third, I discuss the role played by three common interpretive mistakes associated with this bias, each of which minimizes the significance of religiosity in the explanation of religious terrorism. In each case, as indicated, researchers rely on dichotomies to structure their analyses that are misleading. Fourth and finally, I argue that if we ever wish to significantly reduce the problem of specificity gripping the study of the process of radicalization leading to religious terrorism, we must recognize, in principle at least, the *sui generis* nature of religious motivations. The precise role of these motivations, or whether they are relevant at all, is something to be determined on a case-by-case basis, through appropriate empirical research. This type of research will be impaired, however, if the field of study continues to be shaped by the problematic methodological and interpretive assumptions delineated here, which tend to preclude giving such motivations serious consideration.

Before proceeding, let me stress two things. First, I am not saying religion is the cause of terrorism, in either an intrinsic or some empirical sense. Religious terrorism is exceptional. This does not mean, however, that many of those perpetrating acts of religious terrorism are not motivated by religion. Second, while my focus is primarily jihadist terrorism, I am not suggesting that Islam is uniquely culpable. On the contrary, religious extremism has often led to violence in every religious tradition (Juergensmeyer 2003, Pratt 2017).

Influence of religious and secular biases

As I have argued elsewhere, the contemporary discussion of religious terrorism is impacted by both religious and secular biases, which manifest in diverse ways (Dawson 2018a, 2018b). It is common, for example, for religious leaders (Muslim or otherwise), and politicians, to assert that jihadist terrorism has nothing to do with Islam, or religion in general. Such declarations are understandable and true to a point. We must guard against Islamophobia and recognize that most Muslims are staunchly opposed to terrorism. Violent jihadism is an abhorrent sectarian perspective held by a very small percentage of Muslims. But it is no more credible for mainstream Muslims to deny the religiosity per se of the jihadists than Christians to deny that the Jehovah's Witnesses are Christians. Such claims involve theological distinctions and are beyond the purview of the social scientific study of religious terrorism and radicalization. Unlike the religious leaders and politicians, scholars studying the links between religion and terrorism cannot simply assert that violent groups are not religious because religions are inherently peaceful and compassionate. This is a normative assertion, and one readily contradicted by the history of every major religious tradition (Jerryson, Juergensmeyer and Kitts 2013).

Likewise, it is abundantly clear that the jihadists conceive of themselves as participating in a religiously inspired and grounded movement, intent on fulminating a complete social, political and religious revolution (Murawiec 2008). In a characteristically religious way, at least for fundamentalist movements, they reject the modern Western convention of separating the religious and political. In their eyes, social and political reform begins with religious reform, and religious reform is pointless without complementary social and political reform. This means social scientists, unlike religious leaders or politicians, cannot deny the religiosity of the jihadists' self-conception simply because it contravenes their preferred political norms for the operation of religion in society.

They can and do, however, cast doubt on the sincerity of the religiosity professed by the terrorists and use this to question its primacy in their motivations. Appeals to religion, it is argued in various ways, are merely a pretext for justifying political objectives and mobilizing the ignorant to support their disguised political aspirations. Demonstrating that the religious reasons espoused for engaging in terrorism are false or simply insufficient to explain the actions taken is more methodologically challenging, though, than most of the scholars raising such questions seem to appreciate (Dawson 2021a, 2021b).

The popular proponents of the 'new atheism' (Harris 2004, Dawkins 2006, Hitchens 2007) have no problem associating religion in general, and Islam in particular, with terrorism, because they see all religions as inherently irrational and ignorant, and hence also intolerant and violent. For them, the reactionary fundamentalism undergirding jihadism is dangerous because it is a virulent contemporary manifestation of an antiqued way of life that is antithetical to the values of modern liberal-democratic societies. Scholars of terrorism may agree, but this secular bias is irrelevant to understanding the role of religion in the process of radicalization, unless one is satisfied with simply ascribing radicalization to ignorance and arguing that the position of the jihadists is not fully logical because it is antithetical to a liberal-democratic world view – something many politicians have no problem asserting.

A secular bias, however, also is present in more subtle and little understood ways in much of the mainstream scholarship on religious terrorism. The common assumption in much of the research on religious terrorism and radicalization continues to be that religiosity itself is an epiphenomenal manifestation of other latent social and psychological needs and processes. Consequently, the explanation of religious terrorism involves identifying those latent factors and largely reducing the manifest religious claims of the terrorists to them. This reductive process is understandable to a point. It is typical of the explanation of a wide array of social phenomena, but especially deviant behaviour of all types, such as criminality.

In the case of criminals, however, no one further assumes that the antecedent reasons discovered for engaging in criminal actions eliminate the relevance of the benefits of crime in the 'decisional calculus' (Taylor and Horgan 2006) of the criminals. In other words, the situation is not conceived in strictly either-or terms. Certainly, the criminal justice system does not operate with such a simple dichotomy. Individuals are held responsible for their actions, not just morally but also rationally, and other issues are taken into consideration as mitigating factors. Only rarely, when there is sufficient proof, are such other factors considered primary. Most social scientists, however, continue to associate religious commitments with irrational behaviour, either quite literally (i.e. a kind of mass psychosis) or as a result of the supposed role of other latent factors that are more primary in accounting for these commitments. This leaves such scholars with only two explanatory options, ones that have preoccupied the field of radicalization studies for some time. Either religious terrorism is rooted in mental illness, or at least psychological anomalies, and hence rationally explainable in quasi-medical terms, or somehow the actions of the terrorists must be rational in some other sense, for example, in the service of other latent motives, usually strategic, organizational or political in nature (e.g. Crenshaw 1987, Pape 2005, Berman 2009).

Considering the first explanatory option, there always has been a strong urge to say terrorists are crazy. The extremity of their actions calls for some such explanation of their repugnant behaviour. In the case of religious terrorism, the affront to conventional religio-moral sensibilities magnifies this urge. As with criminality, though, a concerted effort over many decades to associate terrorism with the presence of mental disorder has produced mixed and limited results. When initial efforts to develop a psychological profile of terrorists failed, it was reluctantly recognized, as Martha Crenshaw concluded long ago, that the most 'outstanding characteristic' of terrorists is their 'normality' (1981: 390; see also Silke 1998, Victoroff 2005).

In recent years the context of this discussion has shifted somewhat with the emergence of more sophisticated research. This research has documented the consistent presence of a history of mental illness for a significant minority of some types of terrorists (i.e. with rates of 30–40 per cent for lone actors, especially so-called single-cause ones, such as an anti-abortion extremist; see Corner and Gill 2015: 27, 31, Gill et al. 2022: 117–118). It remains clear, however, that most terrorists, and especially group-based jihadists, are decidedly 'normal' (Corner and Gill 2015: 30–1, Corner, Gill and Mason, 2016, Corner and Gill 2017, Gill et al. 2021). Consequently, once again, religious terrorism poses an explanatory challenge that necessitates rendering these actions explainable by making them rational in some regard – in terms of what is driving the actions of terrorist leaders or perhaps even many followers. This approach continues to assume that political actions are somehow intrinsically more rational, and hence explainable, than religious ones.

It also assumes that the leaders of such groups have strategically chosen to hoodwink their naïve followers into believing there is a religious justification for their actions, because religion provides a socially and psychologically advantageous ultimate justification for their actions (Juergensmeyer 2003, Pape 2005). When pressed, however, it becomes clear that this false consciousness scenario rests on limited and debatable evidence, and it depends on the imposition of the kind of rigid dichotomy of rationality and irrationality that is no longer viable in dealing with other types of deviant behaviour, with the rare exception of acts committed under the direct influence of some type of psychosis or personality disorder.

This curious assumption is largely the by-product of the secularization of Western society, a process which separated the religious from the political, and conceptually and institutionally prioritized the latter. A political motivation is thought to be more primary, and probably at the root of many religious decisions and actions. Yet we know that many political actions betray an element of irrationality, as they do not always reflect the best interests of the actors. In these and other ways, scholars of religious terrorism and the radicalization of Western jihadists have struggled, with varying degrees of reflexive awareness, with a series of interrelated and cross-cutting interpretive dichotomies: between the manifest and the latent, the religious and the political, normalcy and mental illness, the irrational and the rational, and, as we will see below, more specifically between religion and religiosity, and ideology and socio-psychological processes. It is often assumed that these conceptual dichotomies are empirically real and hence explanatorily consequential, and the various assumptions are conceptually intertwined. Unpacking any of them soon reveals the presence of the others in the discourse on religious terrorism, like nested wooden Russian dolls. Their largely unacknowledged presence has had a detrimental effect on the discourse on religious terrorism.

The dominant secular biases

In seeking to understand the role of religion in the process of radicalization, especially in the case of so-called homegrown terrorism in the West (Sageman 2008, Crone and Harrow 2011), there have been basically three interpretive options: (1) seeing jihadism, as a form of religious ideology, as central to the process; (2) seeing jihadist religious ideology as a key mediating factor, but perhaps secondary; and (3) discounting or dismissing its significance altogether. I examine instances of each in this section, but in many research studies these positions are elided as researchers slide between the positions as it suits the point they are making.

Consequently, adopting a more dimensional approach might be more accurate and advantageous. Two intersecting criteria are at play. One is the degree to which ideology, in general, is thought to effect behaviour and actions. While many studies of terrorism assume ideology plays a key role (Habeck 2006, Moghadam 2008), others largely dismiss its relevance (McCauley and Moskalenko 2011) or minimize it (Sageman 2017, Roy 2017). Thus, the relevance of ideology provides one criterion for determining the location of a theory or argument along a continuum, with poles demarcating ideology as crucial or inconsequential. Determining a precise placement is a matter of interpretation, and as indicated, some of the positions taken by researchers may shift depending on the point being addressed.

Another criterion for determining where a theory or argument is placed on a continuum is the efficacy or relevance of religiosity, which constitutes a type of ideology in the case of religious extremism. Since ideology is not relevant for some researchers (McCauley and Moskalenko 2011), neither is religiosity. For others, even if ideology is granted a significant role, religiosity per se may not be (Silke 2008). For many the relevant ideological influence is primarily political (Crone 2016). Yet for others, to varying degrees, religiosity and religious ideology are crucial (Juergensmeyer 2003, McCants 2015, Larsen 2020). Theories or arguments can be plotted on this continuum as well, with poles demarcating religiosity as crucial or inconsequential. The two dimensions, as indicated, intersect, and in ways that are too complex to delineate fully in this analysis (see Dawson 2018b, 2021c). Until recently (e.g. Holbrook and Horgan 2019), however, most discussions of these issues in terrorism studies have gravitated to the poles of these continua, presenting an overly dichotomized conception of the interpretative options, as discussed below.

Those sceptical of the influence of religion, or more generally ideology, on the actions of terrorists usually position themselves against those supposedly advocating a more naïve conception of radicalization as ideological indoctrination or brainwashing. Many experts, in this scenario, think that the struggle against terrorist radicalization, especially in its homegrown configuration, is first and foremost a war of ideas. To put things simply, as Sageman (2017) proposes, they are arguing that bad actions follow from bad ideas. In truth this was a strong orientation in public policy discussions of counter-terrorism in the wake of the 9/11 attack, and even more so after the first wave of spectacular homegrown attacks in Europe (Baran 2005, Silber and Bhatt 2007, Dawson 2010, Malthaner 2017, Mythen, Walklate and Peatfield 2017, Coolsaet 2019). Such arguments, naïve or otherwise, constitute one pole of our continuum. The ideological explanation, as framed by Sageman and others, however, is essentially a straw man. The academic scholarship on radicalization has long recognized, at least to some degree, that the extraordinary process of change involved in radicalization entails fundamental social and psychological experiences as well, ones that push persons towards extremism or cognitively open them to the pull of such ideas (e.g. Moghaddam

2005, Wiktorowicz 2005, Horgan 2005, Dawson 2010). Some of these approaches stress the key role of ideology in the onset and then successful diffusion of jihadist terrorism (e.g. Esposito 2005, Moghadam 2008, Kepel 2015, Soufan 2017), but rarely in ways that marginalize the influence of other factors or suggest a simplistic 'clash of civilizations' perspective (Huntington 1993).

The focus on jihadist ideology is almost always linked with historical analyses tracing the lineage of a tradition of thought that became identified as jihadism. The ideas constituting the narrative of jihadism have been analysed to foster understanding of the enemy, but with some appreciation for the larger geopolitical, historical and cultural contexts shaping these ideas (e.g. Habeck 2006, Wiktorowicz 2006, Bar 2006, Venkatraman 2007, Wagemakers 2013, Meijer 2013, Maher 2016, Moreno 2017). Curiously, this literature, which demonstrates the rich texture and diversity of the religio-ideological discourse of jihadism is rarely, if ever, integrated into the social scientific research on radicalization. The fields of scholarship, marked by disciplinary differences, operate in two solitudes. This situation reinforces, I suspect, the tendency for many studying radicalization to misidentify the simplistic 'jihadi narrative' promulgated in much jihadist propaganda for the substance of their full revolutionary world view. Of course, this misidentification further reflects the influence of simplistic government characterizations of the jihadist message, also for propagandistic reasons, as little more than envious and/or nihilistic opposition to the values of freedom, democracy and material prosperity. Lack of substantive engagement with the ideology has conditioned an underestimation of its possible role in positively motivating extremist actions.

In reaction to the presumed dominance of 'the ideological explanation' (Sageman 2017: 97) of jihadist terrorism, many researchers turned to the delineation of the social and social-psychological processes driving radicalization. This was a welcome development and is still progressing, with different scholars exploring insights derived from an array of interrelated theories, ranging from strain theory to social identity theory, social movement theory, sub-cultural theory and more (e.g. Wiktorowicz 2005, Schwartz, Dunkel and Waterman 2009, Agnew 2010, Cottee 2011, 2020, Hogg 2014, Pisoiu 2015, Kruglanski et al. 2018, Larsen and Jensen 2019, Bouhana 2019). Some influential scholars of terrorism, though, have swung the pendulum of reaction too far and advanced theories of radicalization that question the role of ideology altogether (and hence religious beliefs and commitments) in the aetiology of religious terrorism (e.g. McCauley and Moskalenko 2011, Sageman 2017). A push has begun to move the pendulum back to some mid-point (e.g. Bale 2013, Dawson 2014, 2017b, 2018a, 2021a, 2021b, McCants 2015, Dawson and Amarasingam 2017, Wood 2015, 2017, Cottee 2017, Kruglanski et al. 2018, Holbrook and Horgan 2019, Hellyer and Grossman 2019, Larsen 2020, 2021, Larsen and Jensen 2023; de Graaf and van den Bos 2021), but scepticism about the religious motivations for religious terrorism remains rife in the field of terrorism studies (e.g. Holmes 2005, Silke 2008, Stern 2010, Aly and Striegher 2012, Khalil 2014, Crone 2016, Perry and Hasisi 2015, Schuurman and Horgan 2016, Roy 2017, Miller and Chauhan 2017, McCauley and Moskalenko 2017, Schuurman and Taylor 2018).

Three interpretive mistakes

As I have argued elsewhere in detail (e.g. Dawson 2017b, 2021a, 2021b), the arguments for minimizing the role of religious motivations in religious terrorism are much weaker than realized. This is because they rely extensively, in different ways and combinations, on three interpretive mistakes. First, there are arguments that treat the religious background and knowledge (or lack thereof) of homegrown jihadists as an accurate indicator of their religiosity. Second, there are arguments that implicitly misapply modern Western normative conceptions of religion to homegrown jihadists. Third, there are arguments that conceptualize the relationship of social processes and ideology in the process of radicalization in an overly dichotomist manner (Dawson 2021b: 3). Let me briefly summarize the key elements of these three mistakes and their consequences.

First mistake

First, it is common to encounter government officials, academic experts and media figures inferring that jihadist terrorism has little to do with religion because many homegrown jihadists 'lack a religious background, do not have a sound grasp of the doctrines of their religion, are recent converts, or have engaged in activities prohibited by their religion' (Dawson 2021b). The prominent French sociologist of Islam Oliver Roy, for example, repeatedly argues that most of the young European Muslims who radicalize do not come from religious backgrounds. They 'are not specifically puritanical and often live or have lived the usual life of western teenagers' (Roy 2008: 5). In fact, he suggests, most have engaged in delinquency and petty crime (Roy 2008: 6, Roy 2015: 6). They neither associate with nor abide by the dictates of the Muslim communities into which they were born (Roy 2008: 5, 2015: 11–12, 2016: 4), and few have 'a past of piety'. They have not 'followed a real process of religious education' (Roy 2015: 11, 2016: 4) and most remain ignorant of theology. 'No matter what database is taken as a reference', Roy declares, 'the paucity of religious knowledge among jihadis is patent' (2017: 42, 58). In all these ways, he characteristically implies, it is a misnomer to classify them as religious terrorists.

In principle and practice, however, none of these considerations is a reliable indicator of the religiosity of the jihadists in question. Religiosity, meaning the degree and saliency of someone's religious involvement, is only partially indicated, if at all, by any of these factors. Measuring religiosity is notoriously difficult, since 'there is little consistent covariation in the variables researchers have selected, and individuals and groups can be religious in highly different ways, even within the same religious tradition' (Dawson 2021b: 3). One thing, however, is clear: as has been long recognized in the sociology of religion, there is no strong correlation between levels of religious knowledge or length of religious involvement and degree of religiosity (e.g. Stark and Glock 1968, Davidson and Knudsen 1977, Beit-Hallami and Argyle 1997).

Rarely do the social scientists commenting on the irrelevance of religious motivations specify what they mean by 'religion' – a contested concept with a history of dispute exceeding that of 'terrorism' (e.g. Wilson 1998, Droogers 2011). Implicitly, and sometimes explicitly, it is clear that they are relying on what sociologists of religion would call 'official' conceptions of religion: that is, they are mistaking the doctrinal norms of belief and practice of mainstream and legally sanctioned forms of religion for the reality of what sociologists call 'lived religion' or 'everyday religion' (e.g. Hall 1997, Ammerman 2007, McGuire 2008). The latter – religion as practised by most believers, both in the past and contemporarily – is a messy affair. Lived religion involves inconsistencies and assumptions that are sometimes transgressive vis-à-vis the 'official' conception. In other words, everyday religion is much like the religious practice observed with many jihadist terrorists. For all their fanaticism, their religiosity may be more aspirational than rigorous or correct, in terms of the official view. In terms of the realities of lived religion, though, lapses do not constitute conclusive evidence of a lack of authentic religiosity per se (Larsen and Jensen 2023).

Piety, we must remember, differs from orthodoxy, so religious deviance is not an indicator of lack of religiosity or even, as often suggested, religious knowledge. Salafism, the fundamentalist tradition undergirding jihadism, is more or less a new religious movement within Islam (Meijer 2013), deviating from mainstream views. Dying as a heretic, though, is not indicative of being irreligious or less religious. On the contrary, it usually connotes the opposite.

The evidence advanced to support the notion that many, if not most, Western jihadists are not truly religious is invariably fragmentary and indirect, and contradicted by other, often primary, sources of data (e.g. Murawiec 2008, Atran 2010, Dawson and Amarasingam 2017, Poppe 2018, Larsen 2020). The samples used in the studies casting doubt on the significance of religiosity are usually far too small and selective to support drawing any strong conclusions (Dawson 2021b: 3–6). Even those who are sceptical note, with few exceptions, that the single best indicator of jihadist radicalization is the sudden turn to intense religiosity that commonly precedes extremist commitments (e.g. Sageman 2008, Weggemanns, Bakker and Grol 2014, Roy 2017). Yet strangely, they question the authenticity and/or significance of this new religiosity, without ever investigating it seriously. I can think of no studies of this key aspect of becoming a violent religious extremist. The actual experiences of jihadists in this regard remain largely unexamined (Dawson 2021b: 4–5). Undoubtedly it would be methodologically difficult to do so, but no more than for other phenomena, such as the experience of being addicted or engaging in domestic violence.

In every case, in every way, professional judgements would have to be made as to whether, and to what degree, individuals are religiously motivated, but it is hard to see how one can avoid starting with, and substantially relying on, the testimony of the jihadists themselves. This does not mean that the professions of the jihadists must be taken at face value. On the contrary, in each case the evidence must be weighed carefully (Treadwell and Garland 2011, Altier, Horgan and Thoroughgood 2012, Nilsson 2015). But unless proven otherwise, there is no reason to be more sceptical, in principle, of claims about religious motivations than other kinds of motives espoused by jihadists or anyone else (for lengthier discussions of this issue see Dawson and Amarasingam 2017: 202–5, Dawson 2019b). Yet this is precisely what most social scientists studying jihadist radicalization do, without adequately explaining why. When pressed, the sceptics often suggest that the religious claims of the jihadists are simply the product of indoctrination, and hence unreliable indicators of their real motivations. Such an objection, however, poses problems. Their own theories turn to other kinds of social, political and psychological drivers of radicalization, after all, because they doubt the explanatory adequacy of notions of religious brainwashing or indoctrination, as advanced by the early variants of the ideological explanation of jihadist behaviour. They cast the reliance of others on such notions as naïve. Yet when they wish to dismiss the explanatory adequacy of the terrorists' religious professions, they often selectively call on the same inadequate and discredited notions to justify their approach. As the saying goes, they wish to 'have their cake and eat it'.

Second mistake

The second interpretive mistake involves implicitly misapplying modern Western normative conceptions about religion to the religiosity of homegrown jihadists. Simplifying a complex situation, the core issue is reductively interpreting the ample evidence of the public and religious commitment of jihadists as a primary motivation for their actions to personal and political factors as primary motivations.

Over and again, Western social scientists, operating with an understanding of 'religion' born of the unique history of secularized Europe, have seized on statements by Western jihadists, which mix private and public, religious and political claims, as evidence that religiosity is not the primary motive for religious terrorism (as documented elsewhere: Dawson 2021b: 7–13). In the context of the post-Reformation and post-Enlightenment West, religion was privatized and depoliticized, normatively, legally and to some extent practically. The privatization and depoliticization of religion are hallmarks of secularization of the West (Berger 1967, Bruce 2011). These developments were the product of, and a response to, the growing pluralism of these societies, with its potential for civil strife, under the conditions of capitalism, political revolution, imperialism/colonialism and globalization. Religion, the once dominant institutionally, normatively and conceptually unifying force of society, was functionally differentiated from economics, law, science, medicine, education, sexuality and, first and most importantly, politics. It was reduced to the personal sphere, becoming a matter of personal preference, a subjective experience and an individual right in the secular social orders that became dominant. With time and conquest, this secular world view and corresponding social order spread globally (to variable degrees and in different ways).

For much of the rest of the world, however, the interrelated organizing dichotomies at the heart of this new social order – the private and public, the religious and the political – bore little resemblance to everyday life, and both anti-colonialism and cultural revival movements resisted these distinctions. This was particularly true in many parts of the Islamic world (Lewis 1990, Esposito 2010, Hamid 2016). Fundamentalist revival movements worldwide have explicitly rejected these organizing principles, seeing them as detrimental to the salvation of individuals and whole societies. This is explicitly the case with the Salafi-jihadist ideology undergirding religious terrorism. So, when outside analysts choose to use the fervent claims of Western jihadists that fuse the personal, political and religious as evidence that they are not truly religious, they are applying an incorrect and significantly misleading conception of religiosity. They are assuming, rather than arguing, that the Western context of the jihadists takes precedence over the influence of the Salafi-jihadist ideology in guiding the behaviour of these individuals. Perhaps, again, this is because they are assuming that such new convictions are ephemeral. In any event, this means they are often assuming what they supposedly are seeking to demonstrate (see Dawson 2018a: 150–8, for an example).

In part, I suspect, this is because such analysts favour, as social scientists, prioritizing social processes over ideology in accounting for radicalization – the third interpretive mistake discussed below. But this may also be because, from a secular perspective, personal (i.e. largely psychological) and social or political motivations are more readily and legitimately addressed by both science and the state. In other words, there is a built-in circularity to the premises of the analysis which precludes religiosity from being consequential. Ironically, this is in part because religion and religious freedoms are still sacrosanct social goods in most secular liberal-democratic societies. They are constitutionally protected to varying degrees. In the face of a religious threat to that order, the protection of the society paradoxically necessitates defanging the threat by arguing that it is not truly religious, thereby opening the threat to public scrutiny and correction. In other words, we return, by other means, to the position adopted by most of the modern leaders of mainstream religions: real religion cannot be the source of such fundamental threats of mass violence. The grounds for this normative stance are different, since the object is to protect the liberal democratic social order and not religion per se, but the analytical result is much the same.

Third mistake

As indicated, at the core of the analysis of the process of radicalization lies the problem of specificity. No matter how we struggle to delineate the complicated set of factors contributing either directly or through their diverse interactions to this process, it remains apparent that the group of people affected remains much larger than those who radicalize. When security services in the West felt the mounting pressure to protect their citizens from the increasing threat of homegrown terrorism, they sought ways to sort out the few who might become violent from the many merely espousing extremist views. This version of the specificity issue, the talk-to-action problem, became the focal point of much radicalization research. Talk alone, it appeared, was a poor predictor of violent behaviour (Bartlett and Miller 2012, Khalil 2014, McCauley and Moskalenko 2014, Horgan 2014, Schuurman and Eijkman 2015). Drawing a distinction between cognitive (or ideological) radicalization and behavioural radicalization (Neumann 2013), some researchers went further, asserting that only the latter mattered (McCauley and Moskalenko 2009, Borum 2011). Some even argued that ideology had little role to play in radicalization (Silke 2008, McCauley and Moskalenko 2011, Crone 2016, Sageman 2017, Miller and Chauhan 2017). Violence stemmed from social and psychological processes, and ideological commitments, if they existed at all, merely served a post hoc function in justifying the violence.

Marc Sageman (2017), for example, argues that the ideological explanation for the turn to political violence should be replaced by a social-psychological explanation based on self-categorization and social identity theory (2017: 97, 111–61). Political violence, he proposes, results from 'the activation of a politicized social identity, which generates an imagined political protest community' (2017: 117). This politicized social identity emerges from the process by which all social identities form, but under conditions of social and political frustration. This not a 'pathological process' (2017: 115) per se; rather, it is rooted in the natural tendency of everyone to categorize themselves in terms of contrasting in-groups and out-groups. As experimental social psychology demonstrates, this fundamental aspect of identity formation leads to prejudice, in the form of in-group favouritism and out-group denigration. In the presence of certain social conditions, this identity formation process may lead some members of an in-group to develop a further 'martial social identity' (2017: 143). The conditions Sageman has in mind are escalating hostility between groups, the cumulative radicalization of discourse, disillusionment with peaceful means of resolving differences and mounting 'moral outrage' over the aggression of out-groups. In these circumstances the more militant members of the in-group may undergo a process of social encapsulation that heightens the boundaries between groups, narrows their horizons and escalates the hostilities. With time and under certain additional conditions (e.g. diminished social control), the resultant mutual alienation can lead to actual violence. J. M. Berger (2018) and others (e.g. Hogg 2014) have advanced similar social psychological theories of radicalization, but as noted below, Berger highlights the significant additional role of ideologues and ideology.

This process, Sageman stresses repeatedly, 'does not usually come as a conscious epiphany or a gradual evolution from careful reasoning or better understanding of an ideology' (2017: 143). Yet, as I demonstrate elsewhere (Dawson 2018b: 108–9), his account of the process points repeatedly to the instrumental role of ideology and ideologues. He dedicates no time, however, to exploring the role of ideas, beliefs and convictions in fomenting the extremism and violence.

This is curious, since his analysis has strong parallels with earlier seminal analyses of radicalization drawing on insights from social movement theory (e.g. della Porta 1988, Wiktorowicz 2005). This influence is clear in his own earlier discussions of the turn to political violence (Sageman 2011). From this perspective there is no resistance to recognizing the consequential role played by ideology in fomenting political violence, because its role is understood in terms of 'collective action frames' (Benford and Snow 2000, Snow 2004). As such, ideology, much like everyday religion, is conceived as an incomplete and evolving set of beliefs, and not some formal and codified system of ideas to which people categorically consent after careful study. Realistically, the influence of ideology on individuals is variable and the relationship between ideas and actions should be conceived in terms of degrees of influence (Guhl 2018).

In many cases we have evidence of careful study of religious and religio-political texts, and in others less. When the computers of the members of the Toronto 18 jihadist group were seized in 2006, for example, the police found a substantial library of jihadist materials. While some of the material was instrumental (e.g. about bomb building), most of it consisted of lengthy religio-political texts, filled with references to ideas from throughout the history of Islamic thought. Likewise, as Pieter Nanninga (2014) notes, Mohammed Bouyeri, who killed the Dutch filmmaker Theo van Gogh in Amsterdam in 2004, had read, and even translated, writings by Ibn Taymiyya, Muhammad ibn 'Abd al-Wahhab, Sayyid Qutb and others. Donald Holbrook (2017) found that most of the material collected by individuals seeking to carry out attacks in the UK between 2004 and 2017 involved moderate or fringe religious texts, rather than extremist or political texts. Many, if not most, jihadists display a passion for understanding why the turn to violence is warranted, and the effort displays the moral impetus underlying their actions as much as a search for convenient rationales to justify actions done for other reasons.

The impetus and goal of revolutionary ideologies, like reformist religious views, are to provoke action, not merely justify it. For the Salafist-jihadists, beliefs that are not embodied in appropriate actions are inauthentic and acting on authentic convictions is more important than ideological erudition (Qutb 2005, Manne 2016). This is the message hammered home in the call-to-action ISIS issued to Western Muslim youth to encourage them to migrate to Syria and Iraq and join the fight. The time had arrived to stop talking and act. The objective of the jihadist ideology overall is to connect the dots in a satisfying way, one which offers a simple but definitive explanation for the angst felt by many young Muslims, proposes a grand solution, targets a culprit and prescribes a course of action (Dawson 2017a: 8). The collective action frame gives a transcendent meaning to the individual's struggles. It provides an ultimate and virtuous purpose to their very being, as reflected in their extraordinary actions (Becker 1985). It places their personal troubles in solidarity with those of a whole people and in line with a divine destiny (Juergensmeyer 2003, McCants 2015).

Contrary to McCauley and Moskalenko (2011, 2017), then, I do not think separating the cognitive and behavioural aspects of radicalization is realistic or helpful. While too much emphasis may have been placed on the role of ideology in fostering extremism in the early days of research after 9/11, focusing almost exclusively on the social-psychological processes involved in radicalization simply creates an obverse imbalance. As Hellyer and Grossman (2019: 19) aptly state, social experiences and emotions 'require forms of ideological structuration to transform them into concrete platforms for action and social change, whether or not they are based on or conceptualized within religious frameworks'. In line with Holbrook and Horgan (2019), I have long advocated seeking to understand how cognitive and behavioural radicalization happens reciprocally. We need to understand the dialectic of word, thought and deed in the process of radicalization, from the earliest stages through to the last (whether that is death, imprisonment, disengagement or deradicalization). Since we are social beings, our doubts, concerns and actions may be stimulated by social experiences, but intrinsically we are also logocentric creatures – striving to make sense of our situations by constantly developing our awareness, beliefs and discourse. Again, the situation varies from person to person, but we have very little evidence of violent extremists acting on impulse alone and in the absence of any guiding beliefs (see e.g. Hirsch-Hoefler, Canetti and Eiran 2016, Reinares, Garcia-Calvo and Vicente 2017, Guhl 2018, Alonso and Delgado 2023). In fact, those striving to achieve a coherence between their beliefs and actions pose a more serious and long-term threat, as rightly recognized by those who initially turned to 'the ideological explanation' of jihadist terrorism.

Sageman's social identity theory cannot, by itself, explain why only some of the people adopting an extreme social identity turn to violence, especially the indiscriminate kind associated with jihadist attacks in the West. A few are perhaps driven by an endemic lust for power or violence, as in all social movements, and this lust conditions all manifestations of violent extremism. But there is little evidence to suggest, as some have argued (Crone 2016, Schuurman and Horgan 2016), that the primary source of the violent behaviour of jihadists is simply a history of violent behaviour. The data to support such a claim is insufficient, and the connection, when it can be established, is often circular and explanatorily sterile. Some jihadists have a history of involvement in prior violent criminal offences, but only a minority. How, though, are these offences related to becoming jihadists? Prior exposure to violence may well have a deconditioning effect, allowing individuals to act more readily. This remains an untested hypothesis, however, in the case of jihadist terrorists. Just as plausibly, and more in line with the claims of jihadists themselves, those who turn to violence may have realized that their prior violence was a response to their experiences of discrimination, marginalization and oppression, or that their prior violence reflected sinfulness and need for salvation. These realizations are not necessarily antithetical or even in tension. Both may be instrumental to radicalization occurring, and they stem from engagement with the jihadist networks so conclusively linked with the turn to political violence (della Porta 1988, Sageman 2008, Nesser 2018, Saal 2021, Klausen 2021). This engagement is both ideational and social in nature.

As J. M. Berger specifies in his own social identity model of radicalization, engagement in extremism only results in violence when a key additional factor is introduced: the belief that an in-group's success or survival depends on violent action against an out-group (2018: 44). This belief does not just evolve naturally from the state of tension generated by in-group/out-group dynamics; it is the result of ideological work. It involves framing the identity conflict in specific ways, as witnessed so graphically in the Rwandan genocide of 1994, when the Hutu majority were swayed to turn savagely on the Tutsi minority with whom they had lived peacefully for decades. In other words, we need to recognize the constitutive and mediating roles of ideology in fomenting violent extremism, and how ideology is present (in some form) throughout the personal and social journey of radicalization. Adopting an overly dichotomizing view of the social and ideological aspects of the journey is counterproductive.

Concluding thoughts

At the heart of every discussion of the role of religiosity in religious terrorism, whether acknowledged or not, is the question of motivation. Discerning the motive is fundamental in the case of terrorism, since most definitions of the phenomenon (academic, legal and administrative) hinge on differentiating terrorism from other kinds of criminal activity by attributing an ideological, political or religious motive. Of course, 'terrorism' is a social construct and a contested concept, but so is 'religion'. In either case, except for extreme epistemological relativists, most researchers do not interpret this situation to mean there is no reality to which these terms correspond, however fluidly. It does entail recognizing that our research often is more about the application and use of constructs to give analytic order to a messy reality than accessing the reality in its fullness and complexity.

All of this applies in spades to the concept of 'motives' as well. We use the language of motives, popularly and academically, to order our reality, and most particularly to impart some measure of agency and meaning to human behaviour. This statement raises enormously complicated issues that far transcend the scope of this analysis. Nevertheless, they must be broached because the debate about the religious motivation of religious terrorism boils down to the plausibility of the religious motivational claims of the terrorists. In dealing with motivational claims, we encounter the basic problem of 'other minds'. How can we ever know what someone else is thinking? To resolve this problem, epistemologically and in everyday life, we have no choice but to rely on the assumption that others are much like ourselves – that beneath our apparent differences we share a common human nature and ways of thinking. This may entail, in part, reducing us to our biology and psychology, but most often it also entails attributing a shared rational orientation. This is what makes communication across differences, linguistic, cultural or whatever, possible – in principle and in practice (Hollis 1967, 1968).

Until very recently, however, a religious grasp of the world and our meaningful place in it was an instrumental part of that shared rationality, since while this rationality is axiomatically grounded in the principles of a seemingly universal logic, like everyday religion, it is expressed in more bounded and limited ways. As Max Weber and many others argued long ago (Brubaker 1984), the kind of instrumental rationality identified with the dominant modern scientific, and disenchanted, world order (*Zweckrationalität*) remains relative, whether we commonly acknowledge it or not, to another rationality of values and ends (*Wertrationalität*). In terms of human actions, especially social ones (which constitute most), everything is relative to one's ultimate, socially conditioned convictions about the nature of reality. If those convictions rest on the premise that Allah not only exists but that achieving oneness with his intentions through obedience to His revealed teachings is the point of human existence, then there is a type of rational sense to all the actions that flow from these convictions (Wiktorowicz and Kaltenthaler 2016). In reading *Milestones*, by Sayyid Qutb (1964), for example, I found myself swayed by the force of the arguments offered in this masterful jihadist text. Yet I was barred from responding to Qtub's call to action by my inability to accept the foundational premise of everything he says – his belief in an omniscient, omnipresent and omnipotent God. As someone who has spent his life studying religion, however, I found it easy to imagine why those with faith could readily feel inspired to heed the call.

I know this statement is rudimentary, as it must be in this limited context. It is necessary, however, since most scholars studying religious terrorism are simply not willing or able to exercise the sociological imagination required to grant a measure of rational agency, based on these premises, to the religious terrorists – one that is equal to the heuristic leniency more readily accorded overtly secular political terrorists, no matter how repugnant, unconventional and incomplete their political reasoning. As stated already, the abnormality or deviance of terrorism in general poses a strong and persistent challenge for understanding, without reverting to reductive explanations that minimize agency, and this situation is significantly compounded when the actions are religious as well. In secular societies, and in social scientific disciplines exemplifying the ultimate values of such societies, it is hard to accept the sufficiency of religious rationales for actions, especially acts of public mass violence, even in the face of arguments demonstrating that a double standard exists in this regard. A latent normative secularism often short-circuits the plausibility of even seriously entertaining the significant role of anything other than non-religious motives in accounting for the extraordinary actions of religious terrorists.

References

Agnew, R. (2010), 'A General Strain Theory of Terrorism', *Theoretical Criminology*, 14 (2): 131–53.
Allan, H., A. Glazzard, S. Jesperson, S. Reddy-Tumu and E. Winterbotham (2015), 'Drivers of Violent Extremism: Hypotheses and Literature Review', London: Royal United Services Institute. Available online: https://www.gov.uk/research-for-development-outputs/drivers-of-violent-extremism-hypotheses-and-literature-review (accessed 30 September 2022).
Alonso, R. and P. Delgado (2023), 'The Radicalization of Young Jihadi Convicted of Membership of Terrorist Organization in Spain: Analysing the Pieces of the Puzzle', *Studies in Conflict and Terrorism*, 46 (5): 594–617.
Altier, M. B., J. Horgan and C. Thoroughgood (2012), 'In Their Own Words? Methodological Considerations in the Analysis of Terrorist Autobiographies', *Strategic Security*, 5 (4): 85–98.
Aly, A. and J-L. Striegher (2012), 'Examining the Role of Religion in Radicalization to Violent Islamist Extremism', *Studies in Conflict and Terrorism*, 35 (12): 849–62.
Ammerman, N. T. (2007), *Everyday Religion: Observing Modern Religious Lives*. New York: Oxford University Press.
Atran, S. (2010), *Talking to the Enemy: Religion, Brotherhood and the (Un)Making of Terrorists*. New York: HarperCollins.
Bale, J. M. (2013), 'Denying the Link between Islamist Ideology and Jihadist Terrorism: "Political Correctness" and the Undermining of Counterterrorism', *Perspectives on Terrorism*, 7 (5): 5–46.
Bar, S. (2006), *Warrant for Terror: Fatwās of Radical Islam and the Duty of Jihād*. Lanham, MD: Rowman and Littlefield.
Baran, Z. (2005), 'Fighting the War of Ideas', *Foreign Affairs*, 84 (6): 68–78.
Bartlett, J. and C. Miller (2012), 'The Edge of Violence: Towards Telling the Difference between Violent and Non-Violent Radicalization', *Terrorism and Political Violence*, 24: 1–21.
Becker, E. (1985), *Escape from Evil*. New York: Free Press.
Beit-Hallahmi, B. and M. Argyle (1997), *The Psychology of Religious Belief and Experience*. New York: Routledge.
Benford, R. D. and D. A. Snow (2000), 'Framing Processes and Social Movements: An Overview and Assessment', *Annual Review of Sociology*, 26: 611–39.
Berger, J. M. (2018), *Extremism*. Cambridge, MA: MIT Press.
Berger, P. L. (1967), *The Sacred Canopy: Elements of a Sociological Theory of Religion*. New York: Anchor.

Berman, E. (2009), *Radical, Religious and Violent: The New Economics of Terrorism*. Cambridge, MA: MIT Press.

Borum, R. (2011), 'Radicalization into Violent Extremism I: A Review of Social Science Theories', *Journal of Strategic Security*, 4 (4): 7–36.

Bouhana, N. (2019), 'The Moral Ecology of Extremism: A Systemic Perspective', Prepared for the U.K. Commission for Countering Extremism. Available online: https://assets.publishing.service.gov.uk/government/uploads/system/uploads/attachment_data/file/834354/Bouhana-The-moral-ecology-of-extremism.pdf (accessed 30 September 2022).

Brubaker, R. (1984), *The Limits of Rationality*. London: George Allen and Unwin.

Bruce, S. (2011), *Secularization*. Oxford: Oxford University Press.

Coolsaet, R. (2019), 'Radicalization: The Origins and Limits of a Contested Concept', in N. Fahil, M. de Koning and F. Ragassi (eds), *Radicalization in Belgium and the Netherlands: Critical Perspectives on Violence and Security*, 29–51, London: I B. Tauris.

Corner, E. and P. Gill (2015), 'A False Dichotomy? Mental Illness and Lone-Actor Terrorism', *Law and Human Behaviour*, 39 (1): 23–34.

Corner, E. and P. Gill (2017), 'Is There a Nexus between Terrorist Involvement and Mental Health in the Age of the Islamic State?', *CTC Sentinel*, 10 (1): 1–10.

Corner, E., P. Gill and O. Mason (2016), 'Mental Health Disorders and the Terrorist: A Research Note Probing Selection Effects and Disorder Prevalence', *Studies in Conflict and Terrorism*, 39 (6): 560–8.

Cottee, S. (2011), 'Jihadism as a Subcultural Response to Social Strain: Extending Marc Sageman's "Bunch of Guys" Thesis', *Terrorism and Political Violence*, 23: 730–51.

Cottee, S. (2017), '"What ISIS Really Wants" Revisited: Religion Matters in Jihadist Violence, but How?' *Studies in Conflict and Terrorism*, 40 (6): 439–54.

Cottee, S. (2020), 'The Western Jihadi Subculture and Subterranean Values', *The British Journal of Criminology*, 60 (3): 762–81.

Crenshaw, M. (1981), 'The Causes of Terrorism', *Comparative Politics*, 13 (4): 379–99.

Crenshaw, M. (1987), 'Theories of Terrorism: Instrumental and Organizational Approaches', *The Journal of Strategic Studies*, 10 (4): 13–31.

Crone, M. (2016), 'Radicalization Revisited: Violence, Politics and the Skills of the Body', *International Affairs*, 92: 587–604.

Crone, M. and M. Harrow (2011), 'Homegrown Terrorism in the West', *Terrorism and Political Violence*, 23 (4): 521–36.

Davidson, J. D. and D. D. Knudson (1977), 'A New Approach to Religious Commitment', *Sociological Focus*, 10 (2): 1451–73.

Dawkins, R. (2006), *The God Delusion*. New York: Bantam Press.

Dawson, L. L. (2010), 'The Study of New Religious Movements and the Radicalization of Home-Grown Terrorists: Opening a Dialogue', *Terrorism and Political Violence*, 21 (1): 1–21.

Dawson, L. L. (2014), 'Trying to Make Sense of Homegrown Terrorist Radicalization: The Case of the Toronto 18', in P. Bramadat and L. Dawson (eds), *Religious Radicalization and Securitization in Canada and Beyond*, 64–91, Toronto: University of Toronto Press.

Dawson, L. L. (2017a), 'Sketch of a Social Ecology Model for Explaining Homegrown Terrorist Radicalisation', The Hague: The International Centre for Counter-Terrorism, Report 8, no. 1, https://dx.doi.org/10.19165/2017.1.01.

Dawson, L. L. (2017b), 'Discounting Religion in the Explanation of Homegrown Terrorism: A Critique', in J. R. Lewis (ed), *Cambridge Companion to Religion and Terrorism*, 32–45, Cambridge: Cambridge University Press.

Dawson, L. L. (2018a), 'Challenging the Curious Erasure of Religion from the Study of Religious Terrorism', *Numen*, 65 (2–3): 141–64.

Dawson, L. L. (2018b), 'Debating the Role of Religion in the Motivation of Religious Terrorism', *Nordic Journal of Religion and Society*, 31 (2): 98–117.

Dawson, L. L. (2019a), 'Clarifying the Explanatory Context for Developing Theories of Radicalization: Five Basic Considerations', *Journal for Deradicalization*, 18 (Spring): 146–84.

Dawson, L. L. (2019b), 'Taking Terrorist Accounts of Their Motivations Seriously: An Exploration of the Hermeneutics of Suspicion', *Perspectives on Terrorism*, 13 (5): 65–80.

Dawson, L. L. (2021a), 'Bringing Religiosity Back in: Critical Reflection on the Explanation of Western Homegrown Religious Terrorism – Part I', *Perspectives on Terrorism*, 15 (1): 2–16.

Dawson, L. L. (2021b), 'Bringing Religiosity Back In: Critical Reflection on the Explanation of Western Homegrown Religious Terrorism – Part II', *Perspectives on Terrorism*, 15 (2): 2–22.

Dawson, L. L. (2021c), 'Terror and Violence', in R. A. Segal and N. P. Roubekas (eds), *The Wiley-Blackwell Companion to the Study of Religion*, 2nd edn, 440–50, Hoboken, NJ: John Wiley & Sons.

Dawson, L. L. (2023), 'The Social Ecology Model of "Homegrown" Jihadist Radicalization', in A. N. Awan and J. R. Lewis (eds), *Radicalisation in Comparative Perspective*, 33–56, London and New York: Hurst and Oxford University Press.

Dawson, L. L. and A. Amarasingam (2017), 'Talking to Foreign Fighters: Insights into the Motivations for *Hijrah* to Syria and Iraq', *Studies in Conflict and Terrorism*, 40 (3): 191–210.

De Graaf, B. and K. van den Bos (2021), 'Religious Radicalization: Social Appraisals and Finding Redemption in Extreme Beliefs', *Current Opinions in Psychology*, 40: 56–60.

Della Porta, D. (1988), 'Recruitment Process in Clandestine Political Organizations: Italian left-Wing Terrorism', in B. Klandermans, H. Kriesi, and S. Tarrow (eds), *International Social Movement Research*, Vol. 1, 155–69, Greenwich, CT: JAI Press.

Desmarais, S. L., J. Simons-Rudolph, C. S. Brugh, E. Schilling and C. Hoggan (2017), 'The State of Scientific Knowledge Regarding Factors Associated with Terrorism', *Journal of Threat Assessment and Management*, 4 (4): 180–209.

Droogers, A. (2011), 'Defining Religion: A Social Science Approach', in P. B. Clarke (ed), *The Oxford Handbook of the Sociology of Religion*, 263–79, New York: Oxford University Press.

Esposito, J. L. (2005), 'Terrorism and the Rise of Political Islam', in L. Richardson (ed), *The Roots of Terrorism*, 145–58, New York: Routledge.

Esposito, J. L. (2010), 'Rethinking Islam and Secularism', Association of Religion Data Archives (ARDA), https://www.thearda.com/categories/arda-papers/guiding-papers/rethinking-islam-and-secularism (accessed 30 September 2022).

Gill, P., C. Clemmow, F. Hetzel, B. Rottweiler, N. Salman, I. Van Der Vegt, Z. Marchment, S. Schumann, S. Zolghadriha, N. Schulten, H. Taylor and E. Corner (2021), 'Systematic Review of Mental Health Problems and Violent Extremism', *The Journal of Forensic Psychiatry*, 32 (1): 51–78.

Gill, P., E. Corner, A. McKee, P. Hitcher and P. Betley (2022), 'What Do Closed Source Data Tell Us about Lone Actor Terrorist Behaviour? A Research Note', *Terrorism and Political Violence*, 34 (1): 113–30.

Grossman, M., K. Hadfield, P. Jefferies, V. Gerrand and M. Ungar (2022), 'Youth Resilience to Violent Extremism: Development and Validation of the BRAVE Measure', *Terrorism and Political Violence*, 34 (3): 468–88.

Guhl, J. (2018), 'Why Beliefs Always Matter, but Rarely Help Us Predict Jihadist Violence. The Role of Cognitive Extremism as a Precursor for Violent Extremism', *Journal of Deradicalization*, 14: 192–217.
Habeck, M. (2006), *Knowing the Enemy: Jihadist Ideology and the War on Terror*. New Haven, CT: Yale University Press.
Hafez, M. and C. Mullins (2015), 'The Radicalization Puzzle: A Theoretical Synthesis of Empirical Approaches to Homegrown Extremism', *Studies in Conflict and Terrorism*, 38 (11): 958–75.
Hall, D. D. (1997), *Lived Religion in America: Toward a History of Practice*. Princeton, NJ: Princeton University Press.
Hamid, S. (2016), *Islamic Exceptionalism: How the Struggle over Islam Is Reshaping the World*. New York: St. Martin's Press.
Harris, S. (2004), *The End of Faith: Religion, Terror and the Future of Reason*. New York: W. W. Norton and Company.
Hellyer, H. A. and M. Grossman (2019), 'A Framework for Understanding the Relationship between Radicalisation, Religion and Violence', Horizon 2020 GREASE Project Concept Paper. Available online: http://grease.cui.cu/publications/concept-papers/ (accessed 30 September 2022).
Hirsch-Hoefler, S., D. Canetti and E. Eiran (2016), 'Radicalizing Religion? Religious Identity and Settlers' Behaviour', *Studies in Conflict and Terrorism*, 39 (6): 500–18.
Hitchens, C. (2007), *God Is Not Great: How Religion Poisons Everything*. New York: Random House.
Hogg, M. A. (2014), 'From Uncertainty to Extremism: Social Categorization and Identity Processes', *Current Directions in Psychological Science*, 23 (5): 338–42.
Holbrook, D. (2017), 'What Types of Media Do Terrorists Collect? An Analysis of Religious, Political, and Ideological Publications Found in Terrorism Investigations in the UK', ICCT Research Paper 11, September. The Hague: International Centre for Counter-Terrorism. Available online: https://icct.nl/publication/what-types-of-media-do-terrorists-collect-an-analysis-of-religious-political-and-ideological-publications-found-in-terrorism-investigations-in-the-uk/ (accessed 4 October 2022).
Holbrook, D. and J. Horgan (2019), 'Terrorism and Ideology: Cracking the Nut', *Perspectives on Terrorism*, 13 (6): 2–15.
Hollis, M. (1967), 'The Limits of Irrationality', *European Journal of Sociology*, 8 (2): 265–71.
Hollis, M. (1968), 'Reason and ritual', *Philosophy*, 43 (165): 231–47.
Holmes, S. (2005), 'Al-Qaeda, 11 September 2001', in D. Gambetta (ed), *Making Sense of Suicide Missions*, 131–72, New York: Oxford University Press.
Horgan, J. (2005), *The Psychology of Terrorism*, 1st ed., New York: Routledge.
Horgan, J. (2014), *The Psychology of Terrorism*, 2nd ed., New York: Routledge.
Huntington, S. P. (1993), 'Clash of Civilizations?' *Foreign Affairs*, 72 (3): 22–49.
Jefferis, J. (2011), *Armed for Life: The Army of God and Anti-Abortion Terror in the United States*. Santa Barbara, CA: Praeger.
Jensen, M. A., A. A. Seate and P. A. James (2020), 'Radicalization to Violence: A Pathway Approach to Studying Extremism', *Terrorism and Political Violence*, 32 (5): 1067–90.
Jerryson, M., M. Juergensmeyer and M. Kitts (eds) (2013), *The Oxford Handbook of Religion and Violence*. New York: Oxford University Press.
Juergensmeyer, M. (2003). *Terror in the Mind of God*, 3rd edn, Berkeley, CA: University of California Press.
Kepel, G. (2015), *Terror in France: The Rise of Jihad in the West*. Princeton, NJ: Princeton University Press.

Khalil, J. (2014), 'Radical Beliefs and Violent Actions Are Not Synonymous: How to Place the Key Disjuncture between Attitudes and Behaviours at the Heart of Our Research into Political Violence', *Studies in Conflict and Terrorism*, 37: 198–211.

Klausen, J. (2021), *Western Jihadism: A Thirty-Year History*. New York: Oxford University Press.

Kruglanski, A. W., K. Jasko, D. Webber, M. Chernikova and E. Milinario (2018), 'The Making of Violent Extremists', *Review of General Psychology*, 22 (1): 107–20.

Kurzman, C. (2011), *The Missing Martyrs: Why There Are So Few Muslim Terrorists*. New York: Oxford University Press.

Larsen, J. F. (2020), 'The Role of Religion in Islamist Radicalization Processes', *Critical Studies on Terrorism*, 13 (3): 396–417.

Larsen, J. F. (2021), 'Reinstating and Contextualizing Religion in the Analysis of Islamist Radicalization in the West', *Distinktion: Journal of Social Theory*, 22 (2): 192–209.

Larsen, J. F. and S. Q. Jensen (2019), 'Jihadism from a Subcultural Perspective', *Critical Criminology*, 27: 421–36.

Larsen, J. F. and S. Q. Jensen (2023), 'Everyday Religion and Radical Islamism – A Contribution to Theorizing the Role of Religion in Radicalization Studies', *Studies in Conflict and Terrorism*, 46 (12): 2521–37.

Lewis, B. (1990), 'The Roots of Muslim Rage', *The Atlantic Monthly*, (Sept.): 47–60.

Maher, S. (2016), *Salafi-Jihadism: The History of an Idea*. London: Hurst.

Malet, D. (2021), 'Countering Violent Extremism: Assessment in Theory and Practice', *Journal of Policing, Intelligence and Counter Terrorism*, 16 (1): 58–74.

Malthaner, S. (2017), 'Radicalization: The Evolution of an Analytical Paradigm', *European Journal of Sociology*, 58 (3): 369–401.

Manne, R. (2016), *The Mind of the Islamic State*. Collingwood, Australia: Black Inc.

McCants, W. (2015), *The ISIS Apocalypse: The History, Strategy, and Doomsday Vision of the Islamic State*. New York: St. Martin's Press.

McCauley, C. and S. Moskalenko (2009), 'Measuring Political Mobilization: The Distinction between Activism and Radicalism', *Terrorism and Political Violence*, 21: 239–60.

McCauley, C. and S. Moskalenko (2011), *Friction: How Radicalization Happens to Them and Us*. New York: Oxford University Press.

McCauley, C. and S. Moskalenko (2014), 'Toward a Profile of Lone Wolf Terrorists: What Moves an Individual from Radical Opinion to Radical Action', *Terrorism and Political Violence*, 26 (1): 69–85.

McCauley, C. and S. Moskalenko (2017), 'Understanding Political Radicalization: The Two-Pyramids Model', *American Psychologist*, 72 (3): 205–16.

McGuire, M. B. (2008), *Lived Religion: Faith and Practice in Everyday Life*. New York: Oxford University Press.

Meijer, R. (ed) (2013), *Global Salafism: Islam's New Religious Movement*. New York: Oxford University Press.

Miller, C. and L. S. Chauhan (2017), 'Radical Beliefs and Violent Behaviour', in L. Colaert (ed), *De-radicalization: Scientific Insights for Policy*, 23–45, Brussels: Flemish Peace Institute.

Moghadam, A. (2008), *The Globalization of Martyrdom*. Baltimore: Johns Hopkins University Press.

Moghaddam, F. M. (2005), 'The Staircase to Terrorism: A Psychological Exploration', *American Psychologist*, 60 (2) (Feb.–Mar.): 161–9.

Moreno, J. C. A. (2017), 'Salafism: From a Religious Movement to a Political Force', *Revista de Estudios en Seguridad Internacional*, 3 (1): 11–41.

Murawiec, L. (2008). *The Mind of Jihad*. Cambridge: Cambridge University Press.

Mythen, G., S. Walklate and E-J. Peatfield (2017), 'Assembling and Deconstructing Radicalization in Prevent: A Case of Policy-Based Evidence Making?' *Critical Social Policy*, 37 (2): 180–201.

Nanninga, P. (2014), 'Jihadism and Suicide Attacks: Al-Qada, Al-Sahab and the Meanings of Martyrdom', PhD diss., University of Groningen, Groningen, Netherlands.

Nesser, P. (2018), *Islamist Terrorism in Europe: A History*. London: Hurst.

Neumann, P. R. (2013), 'The Trouble with Radicalization', *International Affairs*, 89 (4): 873–93.

Nilsson, M. (2015), 'Foreign Fighters and the Radicalization of Local Jihad: Interview Evidence from Swedish Jihadists', *Studies in Conflict and Terrorism*, 38 (5): 343–58.

Pape, R. A. (2005), *Dying to Win: The Strategic Logic of Suicide Terrorism*. New York: Random House.

Pedahzur, A. and A. Perlinger (2011), *Jewish Terrorism in Israel*. New York: Columbia University Press.

Perry, S. and B. Hasisi (2015), 'Rational Choice Rewards and the Jihadist Suicide Bomber', *Terrorism and Political Violence*, 27: 53–80.

Pisoiu, D. (2015), 'Subcultural Theory Applied to Jihadi and Right-Wing Radicalization in Germany', *Terrorism and Political Violence*, 27 (1): 9–28.

Poppe, K. (2018), 'Nidal Hasan: A Case Study in Lone-Actor Terrorism', Program on Extremism, George Washington University. Available online: https://extremism.gwu.edu/sites/g/files/zaxdzs2191/f/Nidal%20Hasan.pdf (accessed 30 September 2022).

Pratt, D. (2017), *Religion and Extremism: Rejecting Diversity*. London: Bloomsbury.

Qutb, S. (2005), *Milestones*. Scotts Valley, CA: CreateSpace.

Rapoport, D. C. (2004), 'Modern Terror: The Four Waves', in A. Cronin and J. Ludes (eds), *Attacking Terrorism: Elements of a Grand Strategy*, 46–74, Washington, D.C.: Georgetown University Press.

Reader, I. (2000), *Religious Violence in Contemporary Japan: The Case of Aum Shinrikyo*. Honolulu: University of Hawai'i Press.

Reinares, F., C. Garcia-Calvos and A. Vicente (2017), 'Differential Association Explaining Jihadi Radicalization in Spain: A Quantitative Study', *CTC Sentinel*, 10 (6) (July): 29–34.

Roy, O. (2008), 'Al Qaeda in the West as a Youth Movement: The Power of a Narrative', Brussels: Centre for European Policy Studies, Policy Brief No. 168.

Roy, O. (2015), 'What Is the Driving Force Behind Jihadist Terrorism? A Scientific Perspective on the Causes/Circumstances of Joining the Scene', BKA Autumn Conference, International Terrorism: How Can Prevention and Repression Keep Pace? 18–19 November. Available online: https://life.eui.eu/wp-content/uploads/sites/7/2015/11/OLIVIER-ROY-what-is-a-radical-islamist.pdf (accessed 30 September 2022).

Roy, O. (2016), 'France's Oedipal Islamist Complex', *Foreign Policy*, 7 January. Available online: https://foreignpolicy.com/2016/01/07/frances-oedipal-islamist-complex-charlie-hebdo-islamic-state-isis/ (accessed 30 September 2022).

Roy, O. (2017), *Jihad and Death: The Global Appeal of Islamic State*, trans. Cynthia Schoch. London: Hurst & Co.

Saal, J. (2021), *The Dark Social Capital of Religious Radicals: Jihadi Networks and Mobilization in Germany, Austria and Switzerland, 1998–2018*. Wiesbaden: Springer.

Sageman, M. (2008), *Leaderless Jihad: Terror Networks in the Twenty-First Century*. Philadelphia: University of Pennsylvania Press.
Sageman, M. (2011), 'The Turn to Political Violence in the West', in R. Coolsaet (ed), *Jihadi Terrorism and the Radicalisation Challenge*, 117–29, Farnham, Surrey: Ashgate.
Sageman, M. (2014), 'The Stagnation in Terrorism Research', *Terrorism and Political Violence*, 26 (4): 565–80.
Sageman, M. (2017), *Misunderstanding Terrorism*. Philadelphia: University of Pennsylvania Press.
Schuurman, B. and Q. Eijkman (2015), 'Indicators of Terrorist Intent and Capability: Tools for Threat Assessment', *Dynamics of Asymmetric Conflict*, 8 (3): 1–17.
Schuurman, B. and J. G. Horgan (2016), 'Rationales for Terrorist Violence in Homegrown Jihadist Groups: A Case Study from the Netherlands', *Aggression and Violent Behaviour*, 27: 55–63.
Schuurman, B. and M. Taylor (2018), 'Reconsidering Radicalization: Fanaticism and the Link Between Idea and Violence', *Perspectives on Terrorism*, 12 (1): 3–22.
Schwartz, S. J., C. S. Dunkel and A. S. Waterman (2009), 'Terrorism: An Identity Theory Perspective', *Studies in Conflict and Terrorism*, 32: 537–59.
Silber, M. D. and A. Bhatt (2007), 'Radicalization in the West: The Homegrown Threat', New York: New York City Police Department. Available online: https://www.ojp.gov/ncjrs/virtual-library/abstracts/radicalization-west-homegrown-threat (accessed 30 September 2022).
Silke, A. (1998), 'Cheshire-Cat Logic: The Recurring Theme of Terrorist Abnormality in Psychological Research', *Psychology, Crime and Law*, 4 (1): 51–69.
Silke, A. (2008), 'Holy Warriors: Exploring the Psychological Processes of Jihadi Radicalization', *European Journal of Criminology*, 5 (1): 99–123.
Snow, D. A. (2004), 'Framing Processes, Ideology, and Discursive Fields', in D. Snow, S. A. Soule and H. Kriesi (eds), *The Blackwell Companion to Social Movements*, 380–412, Malden, MA: Blackwell Publishing.
Soufan, A. (2017), *Anatomy of Terror: From the Death of Bin Laden to the Rise of the Islamic State*. New York: W.W. Norton and Company.
Stark, R. and C. Y. Glock (1968), *American Piety: The Nature of Religious Commitment*, Berkeley, CA: University of California Press.
Stephens, W., S. Sieckelinck and H. Boutellier (2021), 'Preventing Violent Extremism: A Review of the Literature', *Studies in Conflict and Terrorism*, 44 (4): 346–61.
Stern, J. (2010), '5 myths about who becomes a terrorist', *The Washington Post*, 10 January. https://www.washingtonpost.com/opinions/five-myths-about-violent-extremism/2015/02/13/2dc72786-b215-11e4-827f-93f454140e2b_story.html.
Taylor, M. and J. Horgan (2006), 'A Conceptual Framework for Addressing Psychological Process in the Development of the Terrorist', *Terrorism and Political Violence*, 18: 585–601.
Treadwell, J. and J. Garland (2011), 'Masculinity, Marginalization and Violence: A Case Study of the English Defense League', *British Journal of Criminology*, 51 (4): 621–34.
Venkatraman, A. (2007), 'Religious Basis for Islamic Terrorism: The Quran and Its Interpretations', *Studies in Conflict and Terrorism*, 30: 229–48.
Vergani, M., M. Iqbal, E. Ilbahar and G. Barton (2018), 'The Three Ps of Radicalization: Push, Pull and Personal: A Systematic Scoping Review of the Scientific Evidence about Radicalization into Violent Extremism', *Studies in Conflict and Terrorism*, 43 (10): 854–85.

Victoroff, J. (2005), 'The Mind of the Terrorist: A Review and Critique of Psychological Approaches', *Journal of Conflict Resolution*, 49 (1): 3–42.

Wagemakers, J. (2013), 'The Transformation of a Radical Concept: Al-wala'wa-l-bara in the Ideology of Abu Muhammad Al-Maqdisi', in R. Meijer (ed), *Global Salafism: Islam's New Religious Movement*, 81–10, New York: Oxford University Press.

Weggemanns, D., E. Bakker and P. Grol (2014), 'Who Are They and Why Do They Go? The Radicalisation and Preparatory Processes of Dutch Jihadist Foreign Fighters', *Perspectives on Terrorism*, 8 (4): 100–10.

Wiktorowicz, Q. (2005), *Radical Islam Rising: Muslim Extremism in the West*, Lanham, MD: Rowman and Littlefield.

Wiktorowicz, Q. (2006), 'Anatomy of the Salafi Movement', *Studies in Conflict and Terrorism*, 29 (3): 207–39.

Wiktorowicz, Q. and K. Kaltenthaler (2016), 'The Rationality of Radical Islam', *Political Science Quarterly*, 131 (2): 421–48.

Wilson, B. C. (1998), 'From the Lexical to the Polythetic: A Brief History of the Definition of Religion', in T. A. Idinopulos and B. C. Wilson (eds), *What Is Religion? Origins, Definitions, and Explanations*, 141–62, Leiden: Brill.

Wood, G. (2015), 'What ISIS really wants', *The Atlantic*, March. Available online: https://www.theatlantic.com/magazine/archive/2015/03/what-isis-really-wants/384980/ (accessed 30 September 2022).

Wood, G. (2017), 'True Believers: How ISIS Made Jihad Religious Again', *Foreign Affairs*, September–October. Available online: https://www.foreignaffairs.com/reviews/review-essay/2017-08-15/true-believers (accessed 30 September 2022).

3

The racialized logic of the UK's countering extremism strategy

Tahir Abbas

Introduction

Considerable effort is put into figuring out the causes of radicalization by governments, think tanks, academics and community groups, but the overwhelming tendency is to view it as a function of religion, such that by moderating certain religious practices, the inclination to radicalize into violence, in particular for Muslim extremists, is likely to abate (Abbas 2011, Abbas 2021). While this seems plausible, it is also reductive and essentialist. The idea that religion has somehow a distinct role in radicalization has continued to reveal itself in the racialized logic of counter-extremism thinking. The United States, Australia and Canada have indicated a difference between religiously motivated violence and politico-ideologically motivated violence, in part to reemphasize that there is a particular pattern of extremism that emanates from the reading and practice of religion itself. Identifying religion as a separate category in finding policy solutions to questions of violent extremism is Islamophobia, however, as it represents the age-old problems of compartmentalization and essentialization. Nevertheless, there is also a challenge here, because while religion itself is important in understanding the nature of a wider experience, it cannot be reduced to the category of essential explanation or essential solution to the problems of Islamist extremism.

In critically examining the intersections of race, religion and the dynamics of power, the concepts of racialization and normalization become particularly salient. Racialization refers to the process where social relations between people are structured by the significance attached to perceived biological differences. It is backed by systems and institutions that categorize people into distinct 'races', inferring social hierarchies and inherent value based on these classifications. Normalization, on the other hand, involves shaping societal behaviours, beliefs and values in such a way that certain ideas, attitudes or practices become 'the norm'. It is a regulatory process that, when applied in the context of racialization, can perpetuate and reinforce racial hierarchies and disparities. Normalization processes are often subtle and implicit, which makes them both insidious and powerful.

A critical race and religious studies lens allow us to unpack the implications of these processes in a more nuanced manner. This area of study focuses on how race and religion intersect with power, bringing to light the structures and mechanisms that underpin racial and religious prejudices and inequalities. The normalization of racialization can lead to the internalization of racial hierarchies, both by those marginalized and by those privileged within these structures. It can create a social reality where systemic racism is not only overlooked but also perceived as a natural or inevitable condition of society. This can include the over-policing and criminalization of racialized individuals, economic inequalities and disparities in health, education and housing. The racialization of religion, an aspect often overlooked, equally merits discussion. It occurs when religious identities are collapsed into racial identities, often resulting in the stigmatization of religious minority groups. This conflation becomes a form of racialization when it serves to mark certain religious groups as 'other', justifying discrimination, exclusion and even violence against them. For example, in the post-9/11 context, the racialization of Islam has contributed to Islamophobic attitudes and policies, where Muslims are often perceived and treated as a monolithic, dangerous 'race'.

The racialization and normalization of race and religion are processes that form the bedrock of systemic racism and religious discrimination. They serve to uphold social hierarchies and maintain structures of power, often through the subtle shaping of societal norms and attitudes. Critical race and religious studies can help to deconstruct these harmful processes. This approach calls for a shift from essentialist, fixed understandings of race and religion to an understanding of these identities as social constructs that are fluid, multiple and intersecting. This perspective does not discount the very real impacts of racial and religious discrimination but rather aims to dismantle the structures that create and uphold these inequalities, and to develop a more nuanced, intersectional understanding of race and religion that disrupts their use as tools of exclusion and discrimination.

Nevertheless, the reality is that numerous governments continue to support a particular instrumentalist notion of religious extremism. The religious, or rather, the Islamic, perspective on extremism and how to deal with it is incredibly rich and distinct in the context of two decades of the 'war on terror' and the multiple attempts made to introduce broad-based edicts. However, because power is resting in the hands of state elites, this asymmetry will continue to generate further tensions on both sides of the (theoretical and conceptual) polar extremes.

This chapter provides a critical autoethnography spanning two decades relating to how the religion category has been instrumentalized as a political tool in the so-called 'war on terror' in the UK context. The aim is to outline the shifting counters of state-Muslim relations, which have yo-yoed between critical friend and entryism in more recent periods, and how these observations reaffirm ongoing patterns of societal, political and cultural Islamophobia, radicalization and othering. This will include a focus on (1) the normalization of Islamophobia, (2) the denial of racial exclusion, (3) the rise of the far right and its anti-Muslim framing and (d) the recent *New York Times* podcast on the UK Trojan Horse Affair (Reed and Syed 2022) and the response to it by the UK liberal intelligentsia.

There have been several outstanding papers and books written about the events of 9/11 and their implications for how we think about extremism and radicalization in the UK today (Hamid 2016, Sabir 2022). To contribute to the conversation, I will reflect on the continued issues associated with the global north's counter-extremism policy, as well as the implications for Muslim world disintegration and division, and the influence of European Sunni jihadism. In it, I discuss the cyclical nature of foreign policy and 'homegrown' radicalization, as well as what we might be able to do in the future to address it.

The normalization of Islamophobia after 9/11

Islamophobia was already well-established at the time of the events of 9/11 (Runnymede Trust 1997). The Rushdie Affair (which occurred at the end of the 1980s following the declaration of a fatwa by the Iranian cleric Ayatollah Khomeini against British-Indian author Salman Rushdie following the publication of his 1989 novel *Satanic Verses*) focused attention on British Muslim communities and the alleged risks associated with their integration into the mainstream (Modood 2005). Until then, integration had largely focused on minorities adhering to the laws of the country in which they reside, while states are responsible for all of their citizens (Layton-Henry and Rich 2016), including the acceptance and recognition of issues of faith, ethnicity, identity and the challenges of being a minority in a country that built its success on exploitation, appropriation and colonization (Panayi 1994). Following the events of the Rushdie Affair, there was a perception that Muslims posed a specific threat, not just to integration but also to broader security issues, such that the alternative to assimilationist acceptance into society was a risk of Islamist radicalism (Croft 2012). This approach was based on pre-existing Islamophobic tropes, but by the mid-1990s, with the emergence of the Taliban in Afghanistan, there was a much broader global Islamophobia concerning the demonization of this group, as well as the idea that intervention was necessary based on humanitarian needs and the importance of building democracy and gender equality in such societies. For many European Muslims, the Bosnian War and the resulting refugee crisis brought Islamophobia much closer to home (Kundnani 2014).

Western allies joined the fight in the 1980s against the Soviets, who were making a last-ditch effort to maintain the illusion that they were still an empire. In effect, the Soviet Union was dismantled because of the 1980s conflict in Afghanistan (Ali 2003). The Afghan mujahedeen were logistically and financially supported by information, training and military hardware provided by the United States and other Western governments (Curtis 2018). However, by the end of the 1980s, as the West withdrew, the Afghans were largely on their own, with no visible fighting to do. The battle in Afghanistan shifted inside, giving rise to the Taliban, who were later radicalized by the arrival of Al-Qa'eda in the nation. In 1998, Al-Qa'eda was able to coordinate massive terrorist strikes in Sudan and off the coast of Aden, Yemen, in both cases the objectives being the targeting of US political and military infrastructure. By the time of 9/11, foreign policy had already had a role in forming, supporting and combating Sunni Jihadi groups throughout the Middle East and South Asia. While 'Islamophobia' has become a well-accepted term in academia and among communities at home (Abbas

2019), it is unsurprising that the events of 9/11 exacerbated Islamophobia, with foreign policy interventions continuing to maintain support for Sunni Jihadi groups at the behest of Western government interests in those specific regions.

In terms of the effects of Islamophobia on radicalization and vice versa, both issues have been intensified, not mitigated, by various internal developments within the United States or the United Kingdom. This is especially the case since the events of 9/11, where the policy of advocating a positive image of Islam was expected to be led by prominent British and American Muslims to project to the Muslim world that this 'war on terror' is not a war on Islam and that, indeed, European and American Muslims are an important part of these nations' citizenry. For the Muslims steeped in these programmes, the challenge was to strike a balance between those who would condemn foreign policy and failed integration as sources of radicalization and those who would project Islam itself as out of touch with today's needs, with many calls at the time for a reformation of the religion in the same way that Christianity experienced its own reformation five hundred years ago.

This consistency of approach after 9/11 in the United States and 7/7 in the United Kingdom includes the promotion of former extremists and terrorists in the pursuit of policy measures aimed at preventing and combating violent extremism. It did, however, harm state-Muslim ties. The cynical trick of a policy aiming to rewrite the narrative weakened already low levels of societal and political confidence. It also had the effect of distancing governments from their domestic and international policies, with the ire of ordinary Muslim communities directed at former extremists, who were as vociferous and exuberant in their campaigning and advocacy to highlight the dangers of Islamist extremism as they were in emphasizing its importance before their Damascene conversion. Examples here include Ed Hussain and Maajid Nawaz, both of whom were plucked from relative obscurity and transformed into ex-radicals, promoting the dominant government rhetoric on the causes and solutions to radicalization. The UK Home Office funded these two to establish the Quilliam Foundation to deliver research and policy development along these terms. The organization folded quietly during the most intense periods of Covid lockdown in April 2021.

The global north launched fast actions in response to the events of 9/11, first in Afghanistan and then in Iraq, expecting most 'moderate' Muslims in these nations to buy into the rhetoric. Utterances by the likes of Prime Minister Tony Blair that after the events of 7/7 in 2005 'moderate Muslims are with us' while 'extremist Muslims are against us' impaired internal relations. It also resulted in additional attempts by the state to co-opt voices eager to reinforce this perspective, with these pronunciations crucial in distinguishing between 'good Muslims' and 'bad Muslims'. In fact, it further divided European and American Muslims, making it difficult for individuals and groups to organize collective reactions. It also instilled in disgruntled, furious Muslims the belief that their views were ignored and that by expressing them, they would be labelled as extremists. Such tactics had the effect of heightening the dispute while moving existing marginalized voices even further to the periphery, beyond the understanding, detection and oversight of existing Muslim groups. This Islamophobia has sown discord within Muslim communities.

While there was a clear and open endeavour to combat Sunni Jihadist extremism, Western governments were also arming, financing and facilitating numerous terrorist organizations: most recently, in the example of Sunni rebel organizations armed by Western powers to fight against the Assad regime, which eventually mutated into the Islamic State. With all of this now established as a historical reference point, what happens next in terms of Islamophobia and radicalization, whether in the Muslim world or the global north, is critical to examine.

Policymakers are increasingly appreciating the importance of broader variables that lead to radicalization, such as social exclusion, political polarization and socio-economic inequality – themes that have been discussed extensively but not completely recognized by policymakers with shorter-term agendas. There is a widespread recognition that the present terror threat is posed by far-right extremists (Miller-Idriss 2021), who are often more likely than Islamists to be involved in planning, executing and mobilizing fanaticism (Blackbourn, McGarrity and Roach 2019). Because security, policing and intelligence services have focused much of their attention and resources on Islamist extremism, the far right has only recently gained prominence. It could be argued that many far-right and extreme-right individuals and organizations are motivated by an anti-Muslim attitude fostered by the contemporary political vision of Western nation states. Simply put, Islamophobia is normal, which has led to radicalization, not only among Islamist groups but also among others who perceive their activities as a type of counter-jihad, for example.

Due to the growth of the far-right extremist threat, the intelligence services have taken over the police's responsibilities in combating far-right hate crime in the UK. Nonetheless, most Muslims' everyday lives are ones of struggle and strife, and this continues without much attention being paid to the material and lived realities of individuals and communities. With a persistent focus on religion and the idea of somehow manipulating religious principles to shift attitudes towards extremism, it has the effect of lowering trust and involvement, which is the exact opposite of the approach's intended goals. There is also far too much decision-making and planning taking place in political centres, rather than paying heed to the lessons learnt from local players engaged in local problems and local solutions. There is also the problematic reality that when prominent Muslims in the global north speak out against Islamophobia, racism and the impact of the 'war on terror', there is a tendency among some to treat these perspectives with suspicion, to the point that it is not possible to fully accept Muslim criticisms of anti-Muslim behaviour because there is likely to be some kind of agenda. This reflects Islamophobia as well. Non-Muslims' views are heard significantly more favourably when they speak out against Islamophobia. While this is a welcome area, it reflects some of the various hurdles that Muslims' voices continue to encounter around the world.

The denial of racial exclusion

Allied to the ways in which religious identity has been used to discriminate and divide is the issue of racism. The much-anticipated publication of the report of the Commission on Race and Ethnic Disparities in 2021 (known as the Sewell Report) provided a reminder of how minimally the current government views racism in society and policies associated with attempting to improve race equality (Tikly 2022). Downing

Street wanted the British public to believe that there was little to observe in terms of racism in society due to ethnic inequalities and persistent patterns of discrimination, despite the possibility that this would typically indicate that institutionalized racism is occurring. The report's problem is that, while it contains some useful sections that introduce complexity, it fails to address the core issues of racism in society – that is, how processes operating in institutions and organizations reveal outcomes that systematically discriminate against individuals and groups based on empirical observation and analysis over time. Any attempts to address these inequities are always fragmented and only serve as temporary bandages over immense fissures.

The systematic impediments that can be seen at a macro level obscure the micro-level triumphs of a few individuals who can break down racialized glass ceilings in business or governmental sectors. The reality of a few breaking through does not negate the existence of institutional racism on a larger scale. These few have suffered, jumped through hoops, had to over-perform and are often paid less than the bulk of those doing the same task, but they have made it (Khattab 2009). Class further complicates the realities of social life for people of colour. Nowhere in the world is a society more stratified than England, to the point that race and class are inextricably linked (Olusoga 2016). Historically, contemporary capitalism had a racial logic, which it still has now (Bhattacharyya, Gabriel and Small 2016). Racism is hidden in plain sight because it is hidden behind class, which is assumed. The embedding of class structure in English society parallels the embedding of race and racism in the same society (Manzoor-Khan 2022).

The Sewell Report contains useful information about schooling and the importance of appreciating how many minorities are finding (apparent) success. But, once again, this is obfuscating the reality. In actuality, ethnic minorities frequently struggle and are extremely differentiated in their outcomes. Because they understand the value of human capital for economic and social gain, middle-class South Asian parents will send their children to grammar or independent schools (Abbas 2007). Working-class South Asian parents will discover that their children struggle at local comprehensive schools, with little employment or professional possibilities for the majority (Abbas 2002). Obtaining a given degree of educational outcome, however, is not an objective in itself. Discrimination occurs much too frequently in graduate recruiting, first pay offers, promotion and retention. Minorities continue to be underrepresented in senior posts in the public sector, including the BBC, National Health Service (NHS), civil service and judiciary. Former students from the country's most well-known public schools attend Britain's elite colleges, while former students from such schools fill Britain's elite public sector positions (Tomlinson 2019). This is not to suggest that no progress has been made in recent years, but the overall picture remains bleak, including in relation to gender equality, where there remains a considerable authority gap (Sieghart 2021).

In 2017, a high-rise tower block, Grenfell Tower, covered by problematic cladding due to corners cut by local authority-appointed contractors hired to re-model these buildings, caught fire, leading to the death of seventy-two people. This was compounded by disproportionate minority mortality because of Covid, police racism, stop and search, school exclusions, disproportionate prison sentences and racial profiling in immigration services. Another example of the societal normalization of racism is the lack of participation of minorities in professional sports such as football and cricket, as well as the level of bigotry that minority athletes face daily on social media. All of these outcomes are the results of institutionally racist systems. While education, housing, health care and work are ongoing concerns, there is also the destructive reality of structural and cultural Islamophobia, which was omitted from the whole report. The word 'anti-Muslim' appears only once, in the report's introduction. The report does not appear to dispute that racism is a problem but arguing that it is not systemic is to dismiss the apparent reality that most minorities face, rendering them invisible.

Systemic racism, deeply rooted in institutions like education and law enforcement, significantly shapes minority experiences, often invisibly reinforcing societal inequalities. However, branding this systemic issue as insurmountable overlooks individuals' potential to effect change and subtly blames the marginalized victims. This belief undermines the efforts of activists and policymakers and could divert focus from proactive measures against racism. Despite its complexity, systemic racism's presence shouldn't absolve us from confronting it. Viewing it as an unbeatable barrier is not only detrimental but also a form of racism itself.

In that sense, this report is ideal for Her Majesty's Government (HMG) in that it recognizes issues, but they are not seen as institutional. Rather, it is about you (minorities) not trying harder (reminiscent of Ted Cantle and the community cohesiveness school of thought, which held that you [minorities] should endeavour to be friendlier to your neighbours and avoid 'parallel' lives). Sewell has not delivered a Macpherson (1999) or Scarman (1981) report on the state of British race relations, both of which were considered weighty for their time despite their impact registering as temporary, if at all.

One of the most challenging issues with the concept of institutional racism is that too many people of majority colour find it difficult to believe that they may be complicit in replicating patterns of systematic discrimination against people of colour or other minorities through their witting or unwitting actions. It is true that it just takes one racist in an organization to contaminate the entire organization. Even though most people in an organization are aggressively anti-racist, if one person is racist, their racism will override anti-racism. Such is the force and effect of racism. But while the allegation of racism must be taken seriously, the idea of institutional racism, as I remind my many white colleagues, is not to personalize the problem. Any attempt to better the current situation in terms of equality has the consequence of increasing objectivity and transparency for everyone. While we must all take racism seriously, the term 'institutional racism' should not be used to obstruct further discussion of problems and solutions.

Her Majesty's Government and some commentators may have expected an anti-racist outcry against the report, yet they went ahead with it nevertheless. The report contains some good ideas, but the overall goal is to kill the debate on race and racism, not advance it – and this after how Covid has exposed the dark underbelly of race, institutionalized racism and racialization, and nearly a year after twenty million Americans across all fifty states and countless millions more around the world took part in the world's largest protest movement to date, namely Black Lives Matter! Racism was at the top of the world's agenda, but this report has pushed it to the bottom. Today, numerous Conservative Party politicians have been accused of Islamophobia. Boris Johnson, former British prime minister, has referred to minorities as 'piccaninnies' with 'watermelon smiles' and has lately referred to Muslim women as 'bank robbers' and 'letterboxes' (Ali and Whitham 2021). It is also well-established that former President Donald Trump supports eugenics concepts, even applying them to his marriage relationships, implying that by mating with Eastern European ancestry, he will produce superior children (Currell 2019). All of this points to the normalization of racism and the specific logic of white supremacy.

Islamophobia and far-right extremism

Eugenicism is making a comeback in many ways. Politicians across Western Europe are becoming increasingly comfortable voicing racist sentiments. These points of view advocate the notion that there is an intrinsic distinction between various racial categories, with the majority white category at the top of the tree. People with darker skin are invariably placed at the bottom of this hierarchy. The historical motivation for these efforts was to keep the status quo in terms of slavery and later colonialism, but it later evolved into the concept of scientific racism, the apex of which was the Nazi Holocaust programme. Adolf Hitler instituted an extermination strategy aimed at Jews, communists, leftists, homosexuals and anybody else who opposed the Third Reich's ideals. The reality is that this was only the pinnacle of what had been going on in North America and Europe for the better part of a century prior.

On 19 February 2020, a horrifying attack on two shisha bars in Halle, Germany, by a far-right fanatic (see also Heine and Magazzini, this volume) raised various issues about motive, activation and implication. It was the third far-right extremist incident in nine months, and by far the bloodiest. A 43-year-old German man shot and murdered nine people and wounded nine others. The majority were Turkish and Kurdish men and women, with some Bosnian, Bulgarian and Romanians. He later returned home and shot his mother before committing suicide. This suggests a combination of issues concerning ideas of the self and the other, as well as the internalization of a specific type of racism pertaining to the belief that white groups are superior, but that they are under threat due to growing minority populations in particular areas, with their respective high birth rates and in-marrying – also known as the Great Replacement Theory (Davey and Ebner 2019).

This man's goals were to prevent the dilution of whiteness, as he perceived it. However, it is evident that the assailant had specific mental health concerns, which is common among Islamist extremist actors, despite the fact that the emphasis in media reporting on Islamist extremist attacks is on ideology and religion. For far-right aggressors who attack specific minority groups, the media emphasis is less on ideology and more on individual concerns about their mental health or other personal difficulties. This is a basic failing of reporting, particularly in the mainstream news, and despite the fact that, as examples such as Breivik in Norway in 2011 (Bjørgo and Jupskås 2021) and Tarrant in New Zealand in 2019 (Macklin 2019) suggest, it is now hard to deny a clear and obvious pattern. Tobias Rathjen, the Hanau attacker, released a manifesto in which he expressed dread of immigration (Oltermann 2020) and disdain for women.

In recent years, there has been a lot of emphasis on the idea of 'lone actor' extremists in trying to understand how far-right extremists become motivated outside of activation within an organized group, although this term has been discredited by the very people who originally promoted the concept (Bouhana et al. 2018). These are individuals who may function on the outskirts of society but are effectively on their own. Many of these attackers now have an online presence, which helps them to expand their ideological ideas as well as learn about attack methods and processes. However, while this radicalization occurs online, real-world connectedness is critical to comprehend. It is evident that we live in an era in which racism towards minorities, Islamophobia and anti-Muslim prejudice directed against a specific category of a minority, already subjected to a slew of social, cultural and political pressures, has become the new normal. This racism fuels the fires of right-wing ideologies of white supremacism, cultural superiority and exclusivity, which appear to be threatened by the reality of migration and minority settlement.

Politicians in the global north often demonize organizations supporting these ideas for political benefit, but it is clear that individuals on society's periphery are channelling these feelings into far more sinister ends. It invariably reflects on the individuals who bear the brunt of the repercussions of rapid changes in the local economy and society, and who are almost always men who no longer enjoy the recent trappings of privilege associated with their gender. It also reflects an ideology that is widely accepted in other areas of daily life. Many people in Europe will be concerned by recent developments in which random Muslims appear to be targeted where they congregate, whether in shisha bars or worshipping in mosques. These individuals are being confronted because it serves an existing agenda fuelled by bigotry, intolerance and racism. While Muslims will naturally be concerned about these issues, the vast majority will continue to live their lives.

Three variables are critical in grasping the nature of what is happening regarding far-right attacks against Muslims. First, the machinations of mainstream culture and politics provide fuel for these far-right terrorists' ideological predilections. Second, the counterterrorism and counterextremism policy frameworks that are currently receiving significant attention in the global north are ill-equipped to deal with the growing threat of far-right extremism because so much emphasis has historically been placed on the idea that the most sinister forms of extremism are only of the Islamist variety. Finally, reporting on these topics remains slanted, biased or completely absent. It is entirely incumbent on observers to report on events fairly and accurately but rarely does it happen in this way.

The Trojan Horse saga

A prime example of how such biases operate in practice is evident in the Trojan Horse Affair in the UK. The Trojan Horse scandal revolves around claims of a conspiracy to instil an 'Islamist' or 'Salafist' character in several schools in Birmingham, England. An anonymous letter given to Birmingham City Council in late 2013 described how

'Islamists' took control of a school and proposed exporting the idea to other cities. The letter was released in March 2014. At first, Tahir Alam and fourteen other teachers were permanently barred from teaching by the Department of Education in 2015, but in 2016, the courts overturned, dropped or dismissed the restrictions imposed on fourteen more teachers, including Alam. Professional misconduct complaints brought against them in October 2015 and May 2017 were dismissed owing to 'severe improprieties' on the part of the National College for Teaching and Leadership (NCTL)'s legal staff. In a January 2022 *New York Times* (*NYT*) investigative podcast (Reed and Syed 2022), it was labelled as an 'Islamophobic fabrication' and linked to The Protocols of the Elders of Zion, a historical antisemitic hoax.

The *NYT* Trojan Horse podcast has revealed various observations in addition to the immediate advantage of its critical and much-needed information. The podcast does expose the nuances underlying the Trojan Horse catastrophe, discussing the primary actors implicated and thrown aside at the end of the process. The pushback against the podcast, on the other hand, has been fascinating, particularly in how it has worked to undermine the entire notion that there was no problem at all. Rather, there was something odd going on in the city at the time, and it was a worrisome scenario that the investigations correctly uncovered. This response only adds to the problems that appeared in the first place. Too much of the reporting has been put together in London by self-selected journalists. Well-documented is Michael Gove's historical defence of his own beliefs about the Trojan Horse takeover by Islamists, as outlined in his 2006 book *Celsius 7/7* (2006). However, the efforts made to investigate several schools run counter to the widespread belief that the initial letter was a forgery. It was not that no one wanted to question it because it had been done locally and extensively, but with journalists like Andrew Gilligan, who wrote eleven articles for the *Telegraph* emphasizing the urgency of an apparent Islamist takeover, and others eager to jump on this issue because it served the sensationalist dynamic that sells well, it did not seem to matter if the letter was fake or not (Holmwood and O' Toole 2017). The truth is that far too many people were not concerned about the impact on young Muslims.

I recall these schools from the 1980s because I attended one in Small Heath, which, like many others, reeked of failure, incompetence and mismanagement. Before all of the changes, I was researching these same institutions for my doctoral thesis in the 1990s (Abbas 2004). Professional Muslims intended to transform everything in these failing inner-city schools by the late 1990s. They were successful. This achievement, however, proved to be too much for the racial class structure, and far too much for a thriving counter-terrorism industry that aimed primarily to de-radicalize Muslims in the aftermath of 9/11, 7/7 and the Lee Rigby murder. As it is now known, the Trojan Horse Affair was a precursor to the Prevent Duty (Abbas 2017, Abbas et al. 2021), which is one of the most damaging Islamophobic policies ever developed, despite recent attempts to explain it by arguing that it is relevant to the growing threat from the far right – a post hoc excuse. And therein lies the essence of the problem: far too many benefits from the Islamophobic counter-terror state (Abbas 2020).

This issue has exacerbated the polarization between Muslims and non-Muslims. Former anonymous teachers who worked at these schools speak out about safeguarding and the bullying techniques of the governing body. However, because these statements are not expressed openly, it is difficult to know for certain. Muslim women's organizations claim that young women in schools have been forced to segregate themselves and wear headscarves to avoid scrutiny. This, too, is a post hoc rationalization. Many schools have gender segregation, and research reveals that some institutions outperform others in terms of educational success. Muslim activists emphasize the inextricable relationship between institutionalized racism and Islamophobia, but this is not just about the Trojan Horse Affair. This deeper into history, specifically the late 1980s and the Rushdie Affair. The question of whether conservative Muslim males pushed anti-female practices is portrayed more fiercely than the truth. Going back to my research in the mid-1990s, I saw Muslim parents in Birmingham encouraging their schools to allow their daughters to wear headscarves to reinforce a sense of identity and to create a safe distance between them and the hypertoxic masculinity of young boys who were running amok in the same schools, and this was long before the Trojan Horse scandal.

Parents wanted Muslim governors to fulfil higher standards as they best connected with their needs and wants. The governing bodies, formed of various forms of Muslim leadership, made it happen quickly, resulting in a fundamental increase in educational standards and performance, which was what the parents intended and what the schools became proud of and were celebrated for. The schools followed all the rules. Of the investigations and hearings, only one person was found guilty of not upholding standards and was prohibited from ever serving on a governing body again (Alam 2022). This was a political choice aimed at the supposed prime motivator of the scheme. Without this single erroneous conviction, the entire incident would have gone down in history as one of the worst examples of systemic racism in the UK. Much of the liberal-conservative response is because, in part, the *New York Times* podcast not only exonerates but also portrays this person as having succeeded in his capacity to improve schools.

The Trojan Horse Affair was a watershed moment for British Muslims and their relationship with the state, yet there are still unresolved issues. Since then, it has been clear that differences are widening. This reflects, in part, a growing distrust between British Muslims and the state, but it also reflects the battle lines that British Muslims draw between themselves. Some consider the Trojan Horse Affair to be the Dreyfuss affair for British Muslims. The reality is that institutionalized racism and Islamophobia have been in the making for more than three decades – and this will continue in earnest as it divides, separates and polarizes on many different levels – but it is also clear that the same British Muslims who are living in some of the worst social and economic conditions, excluded from society and politics, will continue to be a kicking ball, not just for 'progressive' Muslims but also for parts of the liberal majority.

Concluding thoughts

The chapter's overall focus, as the title suggests, is the failure of the UK counter-extremism strategy to recognize or address its Islamophobia, as well as the way 'religion' has been incorrectly put at the centre of theories of radicalization and subsequent counter-extremism practice. The UK's counter-extremism strategy requires a different conceptualization of counter-extremism that focuses on a holistic understanding of the processes and outcomes of radicalization, including how nuanced it is, without focusing on specific communities as the primary focus of policy, but on a whole-society approach to understanding the problems and solutions of radicalization, violent extremism and terrorism.

There are more than thirty million Muslims in Western Europe, with the biggest numbers in France, Germany, the Netherlands and Britain. All of these nation states share a common history – they were all part of 'old Europe' and continue to dominate the political economy of the European Union (minus Britain) as it continues to enlarge in an attempt to compete on the global economic stage, with both the emerging economies of India and China thundering down their paths to rapid growth as the last remaining superpower, the United States, struggles to cope with its loss of supremacy, something it had in abundance in the last century. But it is in Britain, where we have over three million Muslims, that we are now faced with important questions about identity politics, social exclusion, economic marginalization and cultural relativism. Since the events of 7 July 2005, multiculturalism has come under severe attack from the right and the left, and concerns in relation to 'Muslim terrorists' fill the public imagination, pumped up by neo-Orientalist media discourses and neo-conservative political ideologies. And yet, who, apart from political philosophers, can define or imagine a genuinely multicultural society, where respect for difference is matched by a national cultural framework that is fully inclusive? Much is focused on the Muslim who is disloyal, who seeks not to integrate, women who wish to regress to wearing the face veil and a body of youth that is out of control, whether through *jihadi* sensibilities or criminological misdirection. Little attention is being paid to widening economic, social and cultural polarities.

It is critical to get beyond the notion that religion has a particular role in radicalization, which has persisted in the racialized logic of counter-extremism thought. To move forward, there is a need to focus on the domestic sphere in terms of integration, equality and diversity in order to foster social trust and engagement, thereby facilitating a sense of civic nationalism, which reflects on the concept of a nation as a whole, and where race and racialization are challenged throughout, given their historical significance and ongoing impact on polarization and social divisions. The answer is honest governmentality based on thorough independent research and evaluation, but every indicator in recent times suggests that we are far from such a vision. Indeed, experts are derived in the UK context, investigations into racial inequities are fudged, critical voices are suppressed or silenced, and a short-termist, self-selecting, elitist and conservative – and hence classed and exclusive – world view has gained hold. The pandemic has highlighted the terrible truth of societal disparities, with the UK particularly vulnerable to the social divide caused by a lack of social, physical and economic infrastructure. The pandemic's impacts will be felt for some time, but what emerges from the other side must be symbolic of a braver new future, one that is not based on perpetual economic growth and zero-sum games.

References

Abbas, T. (2002), 'The Home and the School in the Educational Achievements of South Asians', *Race Ethnicity and Education*, 5 (3): 291–316.
Abbas, T. (2004), *The Education of British South Asians*. Basingstoke: Palgrave Macmillan.
Abbas, T. (2007), 'British South Asians and Pathways into Selective Schooling: Social Class, Culture and Ethnicity', *British Educational Research Journal*, 33 (1): 75–90.
Abbas, T. (2011), *Islamic Radicalism and Multiculturalism: The British Case*. London and New York: Routledge.
Abbas, T. (2017), 'The "Trojan Horse" Plot and the Fear of Muslim Power in British State Schools', *Journal of Muslim Minority Affairs*, 37 (4): 426–41.
Abbas, T. (2019), *Islamophobia and Radicalisation: A Vicious Cycle*. New York: Oxford University Press.
Abbas, T. (2020), 'Islamophobia as Racialised Biopolitics in the United Kingdom', *Philosophy & Social Criticism*, 46 (5): 497–511.
Abbas, T. (2021), *Countering Violent Extremism: The Global Deradicalisation Agenda*. London and New York: Bloomsbury.
Alam, T. M. (2022), 'Britain's Trojan Horse: A Hoax that Still Harms Muslims', *Aljazeera Opinion*, 17 April. Available online: https://www.aljazeera.com/opinions/2022/4/17/britains-trojan-horse-a-hoax-that-still-harms-muslims.
Ali, T. (2003), *The Clash of Fundamentalisms: Crusades, Jihads and Modernity*. London: Verso.
Ali, N. and B. Whitham (2021), 'Racial Capitalism, Islamophobia, and Austerity', *International Political Sociology*, 15 (2): 190–211.
Bhattacharyya, G., J. Gabriel and S. Small (2016), *Race and Power: Global Racism in the Twenty-first Century*. London: Routledge.
Bjørgo, T. and A. R. Jupskås (2021), 'The Long-Term Impacts of Attacks: The Case of the July 22, 2011 Attacks in Norway', *Perspectives on Terrorism*, 15 (3): 2–13.
Blackbourn, J., N. McGarrity and K. Roach (2019), 'Understanding and Responding to Right Wing Terrorism', *Journal of Policing, Intelligence and Counter Terrorism*, 14 (3): 183–90.
Bouhana, N., S. Malthaner, B. Schuurman, L. Lindekilde, A. Thornton and P. Gill (2018), 'Lone-Actor Terrorism: Radicalisation, Attack Planning and Execution', in A. Silke (ed), *Routledge Handbook of Terrorism and Counterterrorism*, 112–24, Oxon: Routledge.
Croft, S. (2012), *Securitizing Islam: Identity and the Search for Security*. Cambridge: Cambridge University Press.
Currell, S. (2019), '"This May Be the Most Dangerous Thing Donald Trump Believes": Eugenic Populism and the American Body Politic', *Amerikastudien*, 64: 291–302.
Curtis, M. (2018), *Secret Affairs: Britain's Collusion with Radical Islam*. London: Serpent's Tail.
Davey, J. and J. Ebner (2019), *The Great Replacement: The Violent Consequences of Mainstreamed Extremism*. London: Institute for Strategic Dialogue. Available online: https://www.isdglobal.org/wp-content/uploads/2019/07/The-Great-Replacement-The-Violent-Consequences-of-Mainstreamed-Extremism-by-ISD.pdf (accessed 28 September 2022).
Gove, M. (2006), *Celsius 7/7*. London: Weidenfeld & Nicolson.

Hamid, S. (2016), *Sufis, Salafis and Islamists: The Contested Ground of British Islamic Activism*. London: Bloomsbury.

Holmwood, J. and T. O' Toole (2017), *Countering Extremism in British Schools? The Truth About the Birmingham Trojan Horse Affair*. Bristol: Policy Press. https://policy.bristoluniversitypress.co.uk/countering-extremism-in-british-schools

Khattab, N. (2009), 'Ethno-Religious Background as a Determinant of Educational and Occupational Attainment in Britain', *Sociology*, 43 (2): 304–22.

Kundnani, A. (2014), *The Muslims Are Coming! Islamophobia, Extremism, and the Domestic War on Terror*. New York: Verso Books.

Layton-Henry, Z. and P. B. Rich (eds) (2016), *Race, Government and Politics in Britain*. Cham: Springer.

Macklin, G. (2019), 'The Christchurch Attacks: Livestream Terror in the Viral Video Age', *CTC Sentinel*, 12 (6): 18–29.

Macpherson, W. (1999), *The Stephen Lawrence Inquiry: Report of an Inquiry by Sir William Macpherson of Cluny*. London: Stationery Office. Available online: https://assets.publishing.service.gov.uk/government/uploads/system/uploads/attachment_data/file/277111/4262.pdf (accessed 28 September 2022).

Manzoor-Khan, S. (2022), *Tangled in Terror: Uprooting Islamophobia*. London: Pluto.

Miller-Idriss, C. (2021), 'From 9/11 to 1/6: The War on Terror Supercharged the Far Right', *Foreign Affairs*, 100 (5): 54–64.

Modood, T. (2005), *Multicultural Politics: Racism, Ethnicity and Muslims in Britain*. Edinburgh: Edinburgh University Press.

Oltermann, P. (2020), 'Hanau Attack Gunman Railed against Ethnic Minorities Online', *The Guardian*, 21 February. Available online: https://www.theguardian.com/world/2020/feb/20/hanau-gunman-tobias-rathjen-railed-against-ethnic-minorities-online.

Olusoga, D. (2016), *Black and British: A Forgotten History*. Basingstoke: Macmillan.

Panayi, P. (1994), *Immigration, Ethnicity and Racism in Britain, 1815–1945*. Manchester: Manchester University Press.

Reed, B. and H. Syed (2022), 'The Trojan Horse Affair' [podcast], Serial, *New York Times*, 3 February. Available online: https://www.nytimes.com/interactive/2022/podcasts/trojan-horse-affair.html.

Runnymede Trust (1997), *Islamophobia: A Challenge for Us All*. London: Runnymede Trust.

Sabir, R. (2022), *The Suspect: Counterterrorism, Islam, and the Security State*. London: Pluto.

Scarman, L. G. (1981), *The Scarman Report: The Brixton Disorders 10–12 April 1981*. London: HMSO.

Sieghart, M. A. (2021), *The Authority Gap: Why Women Are Still Taken Less Seriously Than Men, and What We Can Do about It*. London: Penguin.

Tikly, L. (2022), 'Racial formation and Education: A Critical Analysis of the Sewell Report', *Ethnicities*, Available online: https://doi.org/10.1177/14687968211061882.

Tomlinson, S. (2019), *Education and Race from Empire to Brexit*. Bristol: Policy Press.

Section Two

Violent radicalization and the governance of religious diversity

4

The governance of religious diversity and the challenge of (violent) radicalization in Western Europe

Thomas Sealy and Tina Magazzini

Introduction

In Western Europe issues around (violent) radicalization have been pronounced features of social and political attention, debates, policies and laws since the early 2000s (for an overview of the existing analytical frameworks and definitions of 'violent radicalization' and how the concept is declined in different settings, see Hellyer and Grossman 2019). There are previous histories of political violence and radicalization which have marked current approaches, whether through laying the foundations of legislation, institutional structures, understandings, the forming of collective memory and experiences or some combination of these. Yet since the 2000s and especially in the 2010s, religiously attributed or influenced violent radicalization has been at the forefront of public and political concern in Western Europe, following a number of high-profile terrorist attacks principally associated with the violent radical Islamist groups Al-Qaèda and more recently Islamic State (IS).

A number of Western European countries have faced domestic attacks, including the UK (2005, 2017), France (2015, 2020), Belgium (2016) and Germany (2016). These have targeted civilians and have involved both high- and low-tech methods, including suicide or remote bombings, stabbings and shootings, and vehicular rammings. Several countries have also seen some of their citizens leave to fight in the wars in Iraq and Syria; although departing foreign fighters might no longer be a significant challenge, what to do with those who have returned or might return remains a contentious issue.

Further common features are forms of identitarian, populist or majoritarian backlash to such attacks. In some cases, these have given rise to further attacks by groups or individuals whose actions may not be influenced by or attributed to religion themselves, but which target a religious 'other' (see Heine and Magazzini, this volume). In Western Europe, this has predominantly come from far-right groups and has targeted Muslims – a growing concern for politicians and security bodies in several countries. Jews have also been targeted by both far-right and Islamist perpetrators.

There has also been something of a political backlash in some states. Far-right and populist political parties began to gain ground, often on explicit anti-Muslim and anti-immigrant platforms, with the so-called refugee crisis in Europe also forming an important aspect of this (Cantat, Thiollet and Pécoud 2020). However, despite the prominence of religious ideology seen in these debates, the relationship between forms of the governance of religious diversity, on the one hand, and forms of governance associated with (violent) radicalization, on the other, has been a neglected focus of study, remaining for the most part in the realm of rhetoric rather than evidence.

This chapter addresses this issue and relationship. It presents a comparative analysis of the relationship between the governance of religious diversity and (violent) religiously attributed radicalization dynamics in Western Europe, focusing on the cases of Belgium, France, Germany and the UK. In so doing, we reflect on the understandings of religiously affiliated or inspired (violent) radicalization along with state responses to it, paying particular attention to how understandings of (violent) radicalization that sit alongside ideas about state-religion connections and public religion shape these responses.

The chapter begins by outlining two distinct modes of governance of religious diversity we observe in Western Europe. We then address the question of whether we can see these modes affecting the occurrence of (violent) religiously attributed radicalization. We turn thereafter to outlining to the core understandings of radicalization operationalized by states, before examining in more detail state responses to radicalization and to what extent they are shaped by modes of governance or, conversely, to what extent modes of governance are affected by how states respond to radicalization.

In exploring the potential relationship between the governance of religious diversity and that of (violent) radicalization, we ask three main questions: First, can we see a relationship between the mode of governance of religious diversity and the occurrence of (violent) radicalization? Second, how do different modes of governance shape state responses to (violent) radicalization? Third, how does the occurrence of (violent) radicalization and states' responses to them affect the governance of religious diversity? Drawing on our four country case studies, we argue that a causal relationship of the type suggested by the first question is not evident. However, the mode of governance of religious diversity does make a difference to how states respond to (violent) radicalization, and, likewise, state responses to (violent) radicalization affect forms of governance of religious diversity in different ways, as explained in our concluding discussion.

The fieldwork for the analysis that follows was undertaken between 2019 and 2020. It involved extensive desk-based research of secondary literature and analysis of documentary sources, including government strategy and policy documents as well as reports produced by civil society organizations. It also included semi-structured interviews in each country with academic subject-matter experts, government representatives, representatives from local/regional authorities and representatives from civil society organizations who work in relevant areas, including practitioners who run prevention programmes. This research was conducted as part of the broader comparative Horizon 2020 GREASE project (2018–22), and some of the background information was also drawn from country reports on (violent) radicalization and resilience trends published by GREASE in 2020, as well as on composite indicators on radicalization levels for the selected case studies (Yakova et al. 2021).

Comparative modes of governance

There is a rich theoretical literature on secularism and models for the governance of religion in Western Europe; for instance, drawing contrasts with the United States (Madeley 2009, Ferrari 2012) or disaggregating different types of establishment and state-religion connections (Bader 2007). In considering the modes of governance of religious diversity in our country cases, we build on a particular strand in this literature and make a distinction operationalized within the GREASE project between, on the one hand, the *moderate secularism* of Belgium, Germany and the UK and, on the other hand, the *secularist statism* (or 'radical' secularism, Modood 2012) of France (see Sealy and Modood 2022a for detailed discussion of these modes and contrasts). This is the key conceptual distinction structuring our comparative analysis. We provide here a brief exposition of these two modes and their principal points of contrast, with more detailed discussion of each below. The key points of contrast between what we are calling moderate secularism and secularist statism relate to two aspects: religion understood and treated as a public good or danger, and the level of autonomy enjoyed by religions/religious organizations vis-à-vis the state.

Moderate secularism and statist secularism

Moderate secularism sees religion as a public good and is supported by the state (Modood 2017). This might include financial arrangements such as tax breaks, but there are also strong state-religion connections where religions partner and cooperate with the state. This is particularly the case in areas such as education (through provision of faith schools or religious instruction, for instance), welfare service provision and policy cooperation. Religions typically enjoy reasonable levels of autonomy from state interference (for example, in matters of doctrine or the appointment of religious leaders) within certain bounds, and even exemptions from some equality legislation, such as the ability to discriminate in employment for certain sectors or jobs. Despite variance in how these features play out in local contexts, such arrangements are all present in Belgium, Germany and the UK, and are often guaranteed in constitutions or primary legislation (Sealy 2021, Sealy and Modood 2021b, 2021c, 2021d).

By contrast, secularist statism is far more restrictive of religion, which becomes relegated to the private sphere to a much larger degree. This does not mean that state-religion connections are precluded, but that these connections serve to limit the autonomy of religions to a greater degree through state control and interference (Magazzini 2025). Having outlined our two modes of governance, we now turn to consider how they relate to issues of (violent) religiously attributed radicalization.

Links between state governance of religion and violent radicalization

In approaching this relationship in light of our three questions, we first note that inquiry into connections between the governance of religious diversity and violent radicalization is an area of research that has received scant attention (Magazzini et al. 2024). Most studies discuss links between state action and terrorism (distinct from radicalization, although not necessarily its violent manifestation) and focus on collective action responses to state violence against a group, or whether religion can be said to be a catalyst for violence (e.g. Lyall 2009, Kalyvas 2006), rather than state-religion relations as such. This does not, however, fit the kinds of attacks linked to IS and the very loose influence- or affiliation-based relations we are concerned with here.

Moreover, findings for whether a state's discrimination against religious populations provokes violence as a response are mixed. Some studies find it does (Kalyvas 2006, Akbaba and Taydas 2011, Kanungo, this volume), but others suggest that control or oppressive measures by the state can either suppress violence or simply do not lead to violence (El-Katiri 2013, Hazelton 2017), or they do both (Wang 2016). Some studies point to certain conditions that need to be present for retaliatory violence to occur (Fahmi and Meddeb 2015). These might include, for example, religious identities overlapping with other identities (such as ethnicity), political exclusion (Bassedau et al. 2016) or weak state institutions (Muchlinski 2014). There is, however, no indication of how to explain different levels of violence between similarly stable states and any possible connection to how these states govern religious diversity. How do we explain the relative absence of radical extremist Islamism in Germany compared to the UK and France, for instance, especially when previous research has found that Germany has poorer relations with its non-Christian religions than its neighbours (Großbölting 2017: 240)? There is also little written about the targeting of minorities (by groups from the majority, such as far-right attacks on Muslims, or by other minorities, such as attacks by Muslims targeting Jews), or more indiscriminate attacks targeting civilians (see Amarasingam and Desai, Beutel and Perliger, Heine and Magazzini, this volume).

Two studies that have addressed the question of governance of religious diversity more directly return mixed and ultimately inconclusive results. While Saiya (2016) finds a link between state involvement in, and restrictions on, both majority and minority religions and terrorism, Henne (2019) finds that although government measures and interference can't be said to cause instances of violence per se, when government measures of control *increase or intensify*, there is a correlative increase in deaths from terrorism. However, this only occurs in the relationship between increased government control of *majority* religious institutions and not in *minority* religions, and Henne does not look at whether the increase in violence comes from religiously influenced groups or reactions from other groups.

The increased state measures of religious control and regulation in the cases we are concerned with relate primarily to a minority rather than majority religion, albeit with some indiscriminate effects. This would suggest, following Henne, that we might not expect to see increased violence in response. Nevertheless, while there have been periods of increased violent acts, it is difficult to suggest that this is a result of changes in the governance of religion. The reverse appears just as likely to be true and other factors such as foreign policy play a role, for example, references to the shedding of Muslim blood and oppression abroad, or solidarity with IS or the Ummah.

Moreover, some attacks were carried out by recent arrivals to these countries, suggesting they were not influenced by the experience of how their countries of destination governed religion; in France, the Charlie Hebdo attacks and murder of Samuel Paty point not so much to norms of religious governance characterized by the French state's policy of *laïcité* as to cultural and narrative *laïcité* where the satirization of minorities is staunchly upheld. Furthermore, it is noteworthy that the UK and France's existing modes of governance are very different in terms of regulation and interference, as well as culturally speaking. Yet both countries have suffered more serious and higher levels of violent attacks than have Germany and Belgium. Belgium has greater degrees of interference and lower levels of accommodation of religious minorities than the UK but has faced fewer attacks. The far right has been more of a concern in Germany, but again, this can hardly be seen to emanate from state interference in how religious diversity is governed.

We find little to suggest that countries that are accommodating of religion and of religious diversity in the public sphere are more or less likely to contain religiously inspired attacks. While France's stricter approach has been a feature of discourse surrounding explanations for occurrences of violent radicalization (the latest being the murder of Samuel Paty and attack in Nice in 2020), this does not explain why the UK, with its much more open accommodations, has also witnessed attacks on a scale similar to that of France and to a much greater degree than Belgium or Germany, which both sit somewhere in between France and the UK in terms of religious accommodation.

There is likewise little to suggest that these countries are more or less likely to experience far-right radicalization. All four countries have experienced attacks on minorities (predominantly Muslims and Jews) from far-right perpetrators and all countries have seen far-right parties make political gains (although not always sustained), often on explicitly exclusionist anti-immigrant and anti-Muslim platforms, for example, in the French 2022 elections. Nevertheless, research suggests that formal accommodation of religions does act as a bulwark against populist and far-right electoral gains (Cremer 2021a, 2021b).

There is therefore little evidence to suggest such a relationship between the mode of governance of religious diversity and the occurrence of (violent) radicalization, or at least that it is of low significance when explaining violent radicalization. The remainder of this chapter turns to how the mode of governance (moderate secularism or secular statism) shapes government responses to (violent) radicalization, on the one hand, and how the mode of governance is affected by (violent) radicalization and state responses, on the other.

Conceptualizing (violent) radicalization

In terms of dominant understandings of (violent) radicalization as these are operationalized by states, we see a general emphasis on the centrality of ideology and a comparative neglect of socio-economic and socio-structural issues. This is the case even where intersectional approaches acknowledge both, but where government strategy in its rhetoric, policies and practice continues to emphasize ideological factors.

In Western Europe, Islam has come to be the focal point for religiously attributed radical ideologies, yet it is not Islam per se but rather certain forms of Islam that are seen to be particularly strict and intolerant, 'foreign' to the national context in question and therefore threatening. Distinctions are thus made between acceptable and unacceptable, 'moderate' and 'extreme', 'good' versus 'bad' Muslims. Such distinctions are drawn not only in Western Europe but also in contexts as diverse as Egypt, Morocco, Malaysia and Indonesia (Magazzini and Fahmi 2025). Important for our purposes here is how this distinction is made between groups, since which Muslim communities are seen as 'moderate' and which as 'radical' varies depending on the context. One of the main points of contrasting ideological focus to emerge in the country cases here is the Saudi-origin school of Salafism, or what is commonly referred to as Wahhabism, as a particularly problematic form of Islam (Silber and Bhatt 2007, Gartenstein-Ross and L. Grossman 2009). Successive prime ministers in the UK have referred, as David Cameron did in 2011, to 'the existence of an ideology, Islamist extremism ... [which] we must distinguish from Islam' and, as Theresa May did in 2017, to 'the single evil ideology of Islamic extremism'; the latest Prevent strategy identifies 'Salafi-Jihadi' groups with an 'inherently' violent hybrid Islamist ideology (Home Office 2018). While many Salafi groups in Germany are recognized as peaceful, they are often juxtaposed to those listed as 'Islamist extremists' by the intelligence services. Anti-Salafi campaigns have also been a significant part of Belgium's response to Islamist extremism. The idea of Salafism in different forms (e.g. as providing pre-radicalization intellectual resources or post-radicalization identification) has also been a consistent feature in France, with the government promoting the establishment of a 'French Council of the Muslim Faith' (CFCM) in 2003, even as understandings have varied and shifted. With its 2021 law on 'Guaranteeing respect for the principle of the Republic and the minimum requirements of life in society', France recently tightened its control on 'radical' religious views (Law 2021-1109 of 24 August 2021).

This focus on ideologies means that a significant part of the response of Western European states relies on the issue of shared values and ensuring that everyone can and – perhaps more emphatically from a policy perspective – does share those values. In this vein we find a general contrast to liberal values but with national expression. In Britain, the phrase 'fundamental British values', although not without precedence, first occurred in this form in the government's 2011 Prevent strategy (Home Office 2011: 62). It has since become a core part of the government's counter-radicalization framework as well as general integration rhetoric and policies. French authorities have developed and strengthened the idea of 'values of the Republic' as an antidote to radicalization. The French National Action plans of 2014, 2016, 2018 and 2019 to combat terrorism and 'prevent radicalization' all share the idea of radicalization as a form of deviance from being a 'good republican citizen' (Magazzini 2020b, 2025). The eleven measures put forward by France in 2015 to address radicalization through education were tellingly labelled 'great school mobilization for the values of the Republic', and deradicalization centres were termed 'Centres for prevention, reintegration and citizenship'. In Germany, the core strategic aims are to prevent radicalization and violence, to strengthen societal cohesion and to promote 'lived democracy' and its core values. We thus also find emphases on British, French, Belgian or German Islam, for instance, in which 'nationalized' forms of Islam are seen to be more in step with European nation states' relevant liberal-secular cultural and political values.

However, there is variance between and also within our country cases. Internally, within these same countries, the understanding of what constitutes 'radicalization' is not necessarily uniform; there can be a lack of consensus between government departments as well as between different levels of governmental authority (national and local, for example), although this is not the case everywhere. In Belgium, for instance, local authorities and the intelligence services have a more nuanced and intersectional understanding of radicalization than does regional- and national-level political discourse. While lately there has been a shift towards the concept of 'hate crime' in Germany, the counterterrorism apparatus is still largely organized around the concept of the perpetrator acting 'for a cause' rather than 'against someone' (such as a minority or a religious community). Based on the 'cause' of the attack, the police tend to use the language of 'politically motivated crimes' – differentiating between right-wing, left-wing and Islamist-motivated crimes – whereas the domestic intelligence service uses 'ideologies', and members of minority groups push to acknowledge the religious identity of the victims of Islamophobic attacks. In the UK too there is variance in how the Prevent strategy is understood, particularly between national and local levels of government (O'Toole et al. 2013, 2016), but also between government departments. Nevertheless, despite these variances, the prominence of ideology in government strategies remains highly significant in driving both understandings and policies.

This focus on ideology is further represented in some countries through shifts in understanding that have moved from a focus on violent acts to a concern with 'radicalization' framed as the process of moving towards violence, and then to a greater focus on pre-criminal extremism as beliefs associated with the radicalization process. Especially in those countries most affected by domestic attacks (notably France and the UK) the identified threat has come to include *non-violent* extremism. In 2017, the UK's Commission on Countering Extremism (CCE) (established by the UK's Home Office but independent of it), which considers extremism in wider terms, recently defined what it calls 'hateful extremism' as 'consist[ing] of a framework of behaviours, beliefs and harms [that] stands in stark contrast to pluralism and Britain's human rights, equality laws and norms' (CCE 2019: 6). As several of our study participants in both the UK and Belgium remarked, a point of criticism of this shift has been the problems created when aspects of social conservatism become conflated with radicalism. Similarly, French legislation has increasingly understood terrorism as the overlap between a 'criminal behaviour' and a 'deviant religiosity' in what has been dubbed an 'Islamization of criminal behaviour' (D'Amato 2019). In particular, the French 2018 'Prevent to Protect' strategy clearly identified as a threat even those 'radicalized' individuals who might not be themselves engaged in violence but who hold views regarded as radical (Magazzini 2020a, 2020b). Germany provides something of a contrast here, however, and it is perhaps worth reiterating that it has faced far fewer and less severe violent attacks than either the UK or France. In Germany, a key aspect of behavioural radicalization that seems to be shared across the board is the presence of violence, in contrast to cognitive radicalization, which is not directly identified as a threat.

Our country cases also reveal a more recent shift to now include the far right under the scope of radicalization, extremism and terrorism. This is not a shift away from ideological factors but rather one that acknowledges that ideological factors might be political as much as, or even rather than, religious, and that the threats posed by radicalization are not solely, or even mainly, related to radical extremist Islamists.

Overall, while flashes of something more intersectional may be present, along with the idea that extremist ideology is nurtured by alienating and dehumanizing social experience (Khosrokhavar 2013, 2017), ideology remains a central feature of how radicalization is defined and operationalized by these four states, which continue to emphasize the importance of finding antidotes to ideological influence. In this sense, intersectional nuance takes a back seat when it comes to actually constructing and implementing policy.

Radicalization and the governance of religious diversity: Responses in comparative perspective

We turn now to the question of how states respond to religiously attributed (violent) radicalization, and the relationship between the governance of religious diversity and religiously attributed (violent) radicalization. How do different modes of governance shape state responses to (violent) radicalization? And how does the occurrence of (violent) radicalization and states' responses to this affect the governance of religious diversity?

Legislative and institutional responses have strengthened and expanded existing laws and institutions as well as introduced new ones. Space constrains providing an account of all these legislative or institutional instruments. We do not, for instance, discuss in great detail broader legal and institutional instruments associated with counter-extremism, such as Prevent in the UK or EXIT Germany, and public institutions such as schools, or what has been referred to as the securitization of social services and policy (Jarvis and Lister 2013: 661, Ragazzi 2017). We are more narrowly concerned with those laws and institutional measures that have either directly addressed the governance of religion, especially in a public sense, and are bound up in justificatory discourses connected to radicalization or those that have sought to directly address radicalization and which have had effects on the governance of religious diversity. These two lines can be seen in institutional arrangements, on the one hand, and in relation to religious signs and symbols, on the other, both of which are underpinned by legislation.

In assessing state responses, this section is divided between the two governance modes referred to above: moderate secularism and secularist statism. We argue that the mode of governance of religious diversity makes a difference to how it impacts and is impacted by issues around radicalization. What we see is that although regulatory and control measures increase and intensify in both modes, this is balanced under moderate secularism by more accommodative measures, while they are unmitigated under secularist statism.

Moderate secularism: The UK, Germany and Belgium

Two types of response have been evident in the Western European countries examined here that are characterized by moderate secularism. On the one hand, there has been a more accommodationist, multicultural response, and on the other, a more 'muscular liberalism', more intolerant of such visible and audible religion in the public sphere (Modood 2019). What we can see in relation to the mode of moderate secularism is that more diversity-restricting measures such as greater interference and regulation have become more prominent, stressing liberal values and challenging the public presence of religious difference and its expression. This has not meant the severing of state-religion connections as such but rather a revising of the character and relations between state and Muslim groups/organizations.

In the 2000s and 2010s both formal and informal accommodations and connections have increased between states and their Muslim populations, and these gradual processes of institutionalization represent in some ways the institutional accommodation of religious diversity and a difference-sensitive identity recognition. In the UK, the government has since 2005 increasingly recognized and been actively involved in creating a more diversified 'democratic constellation' of the groups it engages with (Modood [2007] 2013). Germany has sought to engage with a variety of Muslim groups through the annual German Islam Conferences (*Deutsche Islam Konferenz*, DIK), with the first of these held in 2006. These were pitched in his inaugural opening speech by Wolfgang Schäuble, the then-home secretary who launched the initiative, as being 'about a genuine dialogue with Muslims in Germany, who no longer are a foreign population, but who have become an integral part of our society' (quoted in Lewicki 2014: 64). Representation has been a particular issue for both the government and for Muslims themselves, but the attempt to engage diverse groups (Großbölting 2017: 237), even acknowledging shortcomings (Lewicki 2014, Peter 2010), suggests positive efforts to engage and accommodate Germany's Muslim population. Moreover, the first Muslim groups have begun to gain public corporation status (something devolved to the *Länder*), and informal arrangements have been in place in some areas where formal connections are absent, especially in the provision of religious education in public schools. Belgium too, after a protracted process going back to 1974, has seen a representative institution established, the Belgian Muslim Executive (BME). Collaboration and partnering between local authorities and controversial Salafi groups have also more recently emerged as a policy response to combatting violence in the country (Roex and Vermeulen 2019).

If these are some of the more positive measures, such institutional accommodations and state-religion connections are also marked by contexts characterized by fears over radicalization and terrorism. In this way, measures of institutionalization have also been the instruments through which the state has sought greater interference and regulation of Muslim organizations. As we have seen above, the focus on ideology, where this relates to religion, has meant that counter-narratives to radicalization have heavily emphasized secular liberal values (such as gender equality and free speech), with extra conditions and regulations placed on Muslim organizations to ensure their adherence to these values. Moreover, these levels of interference and regulation in the affairs of Muslim organizations are often measures that are not required for other religious organizations or groups.

In the UK, Muslim organizations enjoy a politically contingent relationship with the government, where the state might pick and choose which groups it works with and which it doesn't based on the alignment of political positionings (Sealy and Modood 2021a). This has been the case, for example, with the Muslim Council of Britain, Britain's largest Muslim umbrella organization, which, alongside its successes, fell out of favour in the mid-2000s for its criticism of the invasion of Iraq and the War on Terror (Modood 2010) and has had a patchy relationship with the government since. Meanwhile, other organizations aligned with the government's position, especially in the context of perspectives on radicalization, gained greater influence. An example of this is the Quilliam Foundation (now defunct), which was a counterterrorism think tank founded by former members of Hizb ut-Tahrir. The organization was controversial among many Muslims for its support of counter-extremism measures.

In Belgium, the government played an active role in the selection of candidates for the Muslim community's representative body, the Muslim Executive, in liaison with the security services, in large part owing to security concerns, and mosques have come under greater scrutiny and regulation than other religious places of worship. In Flanders, in order to be recognized, mosques, unlike other places of worship, must have written documents evidencing their commitment to (1) their use of Dutch as their lingua operandi (with the exception of the *Khutba*), (2) their respect for the Constitution and basic rights and liberties and (3) not being involved in terrorist activities (Adam and Torrekens 2015).

Germany, shortly after 9/11, passed reforms restricting the rights of religious and ideological associations, although Germany sees significant variation across the country due to its federal model in terms of state responses in how governance of religion affects and interacts with the occurrence of radicalization. Muslim organizations have struggled to gain public corporation status, with just two having obtained this at the time of writing (one in Frankfurt and one in Hamburg) (Körs 2017, 2019), and the German Islam Conferences (DIK) have struggled with issues of representation and controversies over which groups are invited (Großbölting 2017).

A further relevant feature is the desire to 'indigenize' Islam to help foster a British, German and Belgian Islam. Many of the institutional and contractual arrangements and conditions already mentioned include this as one of their aims, and this kind of rhetoric is common among leading politicians as a direct reaction to issues of radicalization. This is a stated aim, for instance, of imam training programmes in all three countries. As another example, the Brussels attacks prompted the government to 'take back' the Grand Mosque in Brussels, which had been leased rent-free to Saudi Arabia since 1967, over concerns it was promoting radical forms of Salafism and as part of an effort to end foreign influence over how Islam is taught and preached in Belgium. The mosque's administration was handed to the Muslim Executive. This move towards 'indigenization' is not solely an aim of the state; it is also one that many Muslims and

Muslim organizations based in these countries have expressed. Nevertheless, when it comes to indigenization as a state project, this has been extremely controversial, not least because of how it is bound up with issues of security. As a result, Muslim organizations and groups have encountered difficulties in establishing themselves as 'the goal posts are constantly changing', as a civil servant in Belgium put it (Sealy and Modood 2022b).

A further set of measures adopted in Belgium, Germany and the UK relate to the restriction of religious signs and symbols in public spaces, most notably exemplified by debates over the headscarf and face-coverings. While this has been prompted by and primarily concerned with the presence of Muslims in these countries, it can have wider implications for religious diversity and public religion. This is an area, moreover, where there has not been consistency across, or even within, these moderately secular states. Unlike Belgium and Germany, in the UK such bans have not become serious political issues and no such bans exist. Belgium introduced a criminal ban on face-covering in the public sphere in 2011, provoked by the desire to outlaw the wearing of the *niqab*. Although a general ban on head coverings has not been brought in, such bans have appeared in *ad hoc* and inconsistent ways. Headscarf bans have been introduced for employees of the French-speaking Belgian Community Parliament when in contact with the public, as in other local municipalities, although a general public sector ban has not been brought in. Belgium has also banned ritual slaughter, which also affects Jews. In a recent Constitutional Court ruling, the legality of universities banning religious symbols (prompted by headscarves) for students was upheld. Nevertheless, a number of Flemish universities quickly declared that they would not be instituting such measures and bans were also lifted in schools in Wallonia. In this latter case we see a difference between strict legal terms (what is legally possible) against social sphere implementation of what is appropriate. While the law in this case only allows the possibility of bans, it does not mandate them. Therefore, how religious diversity is managed becomes an institutional matter which can thicken the law.

In Germany, bans were placed on teachers (but not pupils) wearing headscarves in some regions, following the Fereshta Ludin case in 2003. The legal debate revolved around freedom of religion, on the one hand, and an understanding of neutrality in schools where a teacher is seen as a *Beamter* (public servant, and thus a representative of the state and by proxy the common good), on the other (Schiffauer 2006: 104). In 2015 the Federal Constitutional Court again ruled against a blanket ban on the headscarf, but the door was left open for individual regions to bring in their own legislation, with varying results. Notably, the variation between them follows political lines of the *Länder* governments, with those on the left favouring general bans, and those on the right selectively targeting the Islamic headscarf, distinguishing it from Christian symbols on the basis of the former's supposed political ideology and the latter's more cultural and historical meaning (Joppke 2007: 330–1). A related recent ruling has banned civil servants in public-facing roles more broadly from displaying ideological or political signs and symbols. Although prompted by far-right tattoos, this has also come to include religious signs.

We can see from this discussion that forms of state-religion connection and dialogue have been enhanced and extended in relation to Muslims in the UK,

Belgium and Germany. There has been increased institutional recognition that has included a more multicultural set of accommodations. Yet securitization has also marked, and in some cases driven, these connections and affected their character, purpose and the conditions placed on them. Nevertheless, while these measures have affected the character and conditions of state-religion connections, they have not prevented them. The mix and ambiguity evident can be argued to reflect a moderate secularism where religion is seen as a public good, and as such is supported in the public sphere, alongside a concomitant caution over public religion, and where more targeted and restrictive measures might be brought in particular circumstances. It is ambiguous and continually contested, but the routes to do so are a feature of the arrangements themselves. In some cases, the governance of religious diversity remains relatively untouched or, alternatively, the diversity aspect can even become enhanced, notwithstanding caveats. In some cases, these measures have more to do with the governance of Islam and Muslims based on the attribution of their greater association with (violent) radicalization, rather than with religious diversity as such. That is, in some cases the measures are targeted at Muslims more narrowly with little wider effect for other religions. In other cases, religious diversity is affected more widely, as when bans conceived in general terms are brought in that have broader effects whether or not they are provoked by concerns over Islamic symbols.

This is especially the case when the discourse becomes centred on terms of secularism and notions of neutrality, for instance; there have been several high-profile cases affecting other religious faiths with mixed outcomes for public visibility of religious signs (see Human Rights Watch 2009). This can be patchy, however, and is also contextual, as suggested by previous approaches towards New Religious Movements (Richardson 2004). While particular religions may come in and out of focus for particular attention when they are seen as security threats, the general picture in which religion is seen as a public good has largely held. If moderate secularism produces this kind of ambiguity, however, things are less unclear when we turn to secularist statist France.

France: Secularist statism

France bears some similarities with the three countries discussed above, particularly in regard to aspects of institutionalization and indigenization. The question thus becomes: What difference does secularist statism make? The French state is more avowedly secular, with religion seen as a private matter to a larger degree than elsewhere in the region and the role of the state one of ensuring that freedom *from* religion has greater emphasis.

One feature of this is that in contrast, for instance, to the 'democratic constellation' in the UK or efforts in Germany through the DIK, direct work with civil society (mostly on education and employment, but also in offering specialized support for at-risk youth) tends to come through funding provided to local authorities for cultural organizations and is focused on poorer areas, rather than wider state-religion institutional connections. It also means not only that state-religion connections are more difficult but that the character of how the state relates to religious organizations is significantly different. There are state-religion connections which appear similar to those elsewhere. Nevertheless, underpinned by quite a different normative stance vis-à-vis religion, these relations are characterized by state control and interference to a much greater degree (Sealy and Modood 2022a), and the effects on Muslims in particular have been acute.

Yet because of France's general approach, these effects have also been felt in terms of religious diversity in public spaces more generally. One area in which we can see this normative difference between France and the other countries discussed is in relation to religious signs and symbols. For example, in relation to the 2004 law banning 'ostentatious religious symbols', the French state saw itself as protecting the positive liberty of girls, and positively protecting girls from themselves – that is, protecting their 'real' liberty and autonomy (Tourkochoriti 2012: 825–6, Orgad 2021). Schools, according to this vision, are a place of 'emancipation' and *mise á distance* where community identities and ties are left at the door (Kuru 2009: 125; Jansen 2013). This has also meant that laws banning 'ostentatious religious symbols' in public schools and face-coverings in public places, although targeted at Muslims, have had a wider effect. Under the 2004 law, in addition to Muslims, pupils of other faiths were also significantly affected and expelled from schools (e.g., see Howard 2012).

The effect of governing radicalization on the governance of religious diversity is here a much more centralized and restrictive affair. With the debate about violent radicalization having increasingly become a 'French' problem and no longer a 'foreign' one (as it was perceived in the 1980s and 1990s), the uneasiness of France in accommodating religious minorities has turned the public debate around radicalization into an issue that, much more than in other EU countries, foregrounds a strong identitarian-citizenship approach based on French republicanism. It is perhaps no surprise then that aspects of state control and freedom *from* religion have become much more enhanced. Part of the role of organizations such as Conseil français du culte musulman (CFCM) has been to monitor and domesticate Islam, for instance, even though they rarely achieve their stated goal (the CFCM was abolished and replaced with a grassroots-style 'forum' in 2022, after three Muslim federations refused to adopt the 2021 'charter of secularism' promoted by the government).

Following the beheading of schoolteacher Samuel Paty, the French state approved a new controversial 'anti-separatism' bill to fight radical Islamism (December 2020) and promoted a Charter outlining a brand of national 'enlightened Islam', which has been widely seen as a top-down imposition aimed at increasing the state's control over Muslims. The charter is not without precedent: Muslim associations, for instance, have long been required to sign a declaration of adherence to its principles under the Constitution, going back to the early 1990s (Cesari 2002: 341). However, these recent developments represent a significant strengthening of these types of measures. Mosques and Muslim organizations, including NGOs engaged in anti-racism work, have been shut down. Echoing some of the arguments above in relation to the schools, former French Prime Minister Jean Castex argued that the 2020 law's aim was to 'free Muslims from the growing grip of radical Islamism' (France 24 2020). In this context, an inter-ministerial committee on *laïcité* has also been established to ensure the promotion of *laïcité* by all public bodies, and 9 December has been institutionalized as the 'day of *laïcité*'. Thus, under a mode of governance already ideologically suspicious of the danger of public religion as a force for difference and disunity, which then becomes more closely and directly pinned to violence and security threats, the secular character of the state is enhanced, with a squeezing effect on religious diversity and the ability of religious organizations to operate in the public sphere.

A central contrasting issue here is the role of civil society in P/CVE initiatives and the extent to which government seeks to exert more centralized control in this sphere. In the UK, Germany and Belgium, strategies rely to a great extent on non-governmental organizations that run programmes and projects. In Germany, one of its flagship deradicalization programmes (EXIT), which was adapted for Islamist extremism from 2008, is funded by the government but independent of it. In Belgium and in the UK (under the Prevent strategy in the latter case), government funding for a wide variety of counter-radicalization programmes is administered locally; these are mostly social programmes and programmes to do with identity exploration more generally that operate autonomously. France, by contrast, has maintained greater centralized control (intensified since 2015), has exercised greater regulations targeting civil society organizations, and has partnered with them to a much lower degree. The scope and flexibility that civil society organizations have in running programmes or projects and the degree of autonomy religious organizations have from state control over these activities is significantly more pronounced in those countries characterized by moderate secularism.

Concluding remarks

Looking at these four countries in Western Europe – Belgium, France, Germany and the UK – we have been interested in understanding whether (1) we can see a relationship between the mode of governance of religious diversity and the occurrence of (violent) radicalization, (2) how different modes of governance shape state responses to (violent) radicalization and (3) how the occurrence of (violent) radicalization and states' responses to this affects the governance of religious diversity.

We find little reason to think that a particular mode of governance of religious diversity means (violent) radicalization is more likely to occur. Countries characterized by quite different modes and norms have faced issues of terrorism and violent radicalization and we have also seen that some challenges are shared across different cases. If we are to look for drivers of radicalization, we must therefore look elsewhere.

However, our analysis points to some similarities in understandings and responses to (violent) radicalization, while also noting significant differences that bear on the governance of religious diversity across the countries examined here. The centrality of ideology and a mixture of 'hard' and 'soft' measures as state responses have developed over the years are both common across the country cases. Nevertheless, there are clear and significant differences in counter-radicalization measures and how these relate to the ways in which religious diversity is governed more generally. The preceding discussion has allowed us to show that a specific mode of governance of religious diversity is not what affects *whether* (violent) radicalization will occur, but rather *how* this might take shape and the different reactions it triggers on behalf of states.

Radicalization does not cause or evolve out of any particular mode of governance of religious diversity, but how it is responded to and how such reactions affect the mode in which religion is governed will be shaped by that mode in particular ways. In short, responses to radicalization occur in specific contexts that are already shaped by particular features, tendencies and trends. In particular, different modes of religious governance contribute to defining the ways that states' P/CVE strategies are developed, which in turn affect the degree of trust and the types of collaboration possible between religious civil society and governments.

In common across all four countries, irrespective of their modes of religious governance, is that more diversity-restricting features become enhanced and emphasized in response to attacks. However, in countries characterized by moderate secularism (Belgium, Germany and the UK), while means of regulation become stronger, engagement and connections also remain intact and may even be expanded, with an emphasis on *how* religion can continue to occupy a public space in society. By contrast, in France, characterized by secularist statism, state control becomes far more pronounced and the issue of *whether* religion can continue to occupy a public space in society, with securitization becoming the main framework that spills over from countering terrorism to managing religious diversity, becomes intensified, squeezing public religious diversity in the public sphere as a result.

In France, new legislation and/or policy measures directly addressing religious diversity have been introduced following each high-profile attack of the past decade. Such policies are bound up with measures that also address (violent) radicalization (interpreted as anti-social behaviour that threatens Republican values) and exhibit increased institutional regulation, which captures how the legislation that specifically targets religious diversity is implemented in practice.

These differences are important. An issue tied to the tendency towards measures that specifically single out religious minorities is that they can create or reinforce a sense of alienation and exclusion among members of religious minorities. The traditional sectarian approach, which sees religious minorities as threatening 'cults' to be treated as a security issue itself, misses the target. Indeed, for some this is an important part of the drivers of radicalization in the first place, which questions the ideology-focused perspective of governments (although it is not wise to overexaggerate or reduce the complexities of violent radicalization to one specific driver). While terrorist events do not seem to be linked to a specific mode of governance, the degree of involvement into P/CVE programmes of religious organizations and their degree of autonomy from the state are. What becomes important in understanding the differences between states' approaches to the governance of religious diversity and its links to the governance of (violent) radicalization is whether the responses of states, and the measures and norms embedded and enhanced in those responses, can offer inclusive narratives and practices, or whether they instead rely on exclusionary measures.

References

Adam, I. and C. Torrekens (2015), 'Different Regional Approaches to Immigration Related Cultural Diversity: Interpreting the Belgian Cultural Diversity Policy Paradox',

Régionalimse et Fédéralisme, 15. Available online: https://popups.uliege.be/1374-3864/index.php?id=1526 (accessed 10 June 2022).

Akbaba, Y. and Z. Taydas (2011), 'Does Religious Discrimination Promote Dissent? A Quantitative Analysis', *Ethnopolitics*, 10 (3–4): 271–95.

Bader, V. (2007), *Secularism or Democracy? Associational Governance of Religious Diversity*. Amsterdam: Amsterdam University Press.

Bassedau, M., B. Pfeiffer and J. Vüllers (2016), 'Bad Religion? Religion, Collective Action, and the Onset of Armed Conflict in Developing Countries', *Journal of Conflict Resolution*, 60 (2): 226–55.

Cantat, C., H. Thiollet and A. Pécoud (2020), 'Migration as Crisis. Framework Paper', *HAL Open Science*, Available online: https://hal.archives-ouvertes.fr/hal-02951419/ (accessed 10 June 2022).

Cesari, J. (2002), 'Islam in France: The Shaping of a Religious Minority', in Y. Haddad-Yazbek (ed), *Muslims in the West, from Sojourners to Citizens*, 36–51, Oxford: Oxford University Press.

Commission for Countering Extremism (CCE) (2019), 'Challenging Hateful Extremism', October. Available online: https://assets.publishing.service.gov.uk/government/uploads/system/uploads/attachment_data/file/874101/200320_Challenging_Hateful_Extremism.pdf (accessed 2 June 2022).

Cremer, T. (2021a), 'Nations under God: How Church–State Relations Shape Christian Responses to Right-Wing Populism in Germany and the United States', *Religions*, 12 (4): 254. https://doi.org/10.3390/rel12040254.

Cremer, T. (2021b), 'A Religious Vaccination? How Christian Communities React to Right-Wing Populism in Germany, France and the US', *Government and Opposition*, 1–21. https://doi.org/10.1017/gov.2021.18.

D'Amato, S. (2019), 'Islamisation of Criminal Behaviour: The Path to Terrorism? Terrorist Threat and Crime in French Counterterrorism Policy-Formulation', *European Journal of Criminology*, 16 (3): 332–50.

El-Katiri, M. (2013), 'The Institutionalisation of Religious Affairs: Religious Reform in Morocco', *The Journal of North African Studies*, 18 (1): 53–69.

Fahmi, G. and H. Meddeb (2015), 'Market for Jihad: Radicalization in Tunisia', *Carnegie Endowment for International Peace*, Available online: https://www.jstor.org/stable/pdf/resrep12911.pdf (accessed 2 June 2022).

Ferrari, S. (2012), 'Law and Religion in a Secular World: A European Perspective', *Ecclesiastical Law Journal*, 14: 355–70.

France 24 (2020), 'French Government Unveils New Law Tackling Islamist Extremism', 9 December. Available online: https://www.france24.com/en/france/20201209-macron-seeks-cabinet-backing-for-new-law-tackling-islamist-extremism (accessed 10 June 2022).

Gartenstein-Ross, D. and L. Grossman (2009), *Homegrown Terrorists in the UK and UK: An Empirical Examination of the Radicalisation Process*. Washington, DC: Foundation for Defense of Democracies.

GREASE – Radicalization, Secularism and the Governance of Religion: Bringing Together Diverse Perspectives (2020), 'Country Reports and Profiles', EU Horizon 2020 Project ID 770640, Florence: European University Institute. Available online: http://grease.eui.eu/publications/country-reports-and-profiles/ (accessed 4 October 2022).

Großbölting, T. (2017), *Losing Heaven: Religion in Germany Since 1945*, trans. A. Skinner, Oxford: Berghahn.

Hazelton, J. L. (2017), 'The "Hearts and Minds" Fallacy', *International Security*, 42 (1): 80–113.
Heine, F. and T. Magazzini (this volume), 'Alternative to What? Looking into Germany's Extreme Right-Wing Radicalization', in M. Grossman and H. A. Hellyer (eds), *Rethinking Religion and Radicalization: Terrorism and Violence Twenty Years After 9/11*, London: Bloomsbury Academic.
Hellyer, H. A. and M. Grossman (2019), 'A Framework for Understanding the Relationship between Radicalisation, Religion and Violence', Horizon 2020 GREASE Project Concept Paper. Available online: http://grease.eui.eu/wp-content/uploads/sites/8/2019/05/GREASE_D1.2_Hellyer-Grossman_Final1-1.pdf (accessed 4 October 2022).
Henne, P. S. (2019), 'Government Interference in Religious Institutions and Terrorism', *Religion, State and Society*, 47 (1): 67–86.
Home Office (2011), *CONTEST: The United Kingdom's Strategy for Countering Terrorism*, July. Available online: https://assets.publishing.service.gov.uk/government/uploads/system/uploads/attachment_data/file/97995/strategy-contest.pdf (accessed 8 June 2022).
Home Office (2018), *CONTEST: The United Kingdom's Strategy for Countering Terrorism*, June. Available online: https://assets.publishing.service.gov.uk/government/uploads/system/uploads/attachment_data/file/716907/140618_CCS207_CCS0218929798-1_CONTEST_3.0_WEB.pdf (accessed 8 June 2022).
Howard, E. (2012), *Law and the Wearing of Religious Symbols: European Bans on the Wearing of Religious Symbols in Education*. Abingdon: Routledge.
Human Rights Watch (2009), *Discrimination in the Name of Neutrality. Headscarf Bans for Teachers and Civil Servants in Germany*, Available online: https://www.hrw.org/report/2009/02/26/discrimination-name-neutrality/headscarf-bans-teachers-and-civil-servants-germany# (accessed 13 April 2022).
Jansen, Y. (2013), *Secularism, Assimilation and the Crisis of Multiculturalism: French Modernist Legacies*. Amsterdam: Amsterdam University Press.
Jarvis, L. and M. Lister (2013), 'Disconnected Citizenship? The Impacts of Anti-Terrorism Policy on Citizenship in the UK', *Political Studies*, 61: 656–75.
Joppke, C. (2007), 'State Neutrality and Islamic Headscarf Laws in France and Germany', *Theory & Society*, 36 (4): 313–42.
Kalyvas, D. (2006), *The Logic of Violence in Civil War*. Cambridge: Cambridge University Press.
Kanungo, P. (this volume), 'Hindu and Muslim Radicalization in Contemporary India', in M. Grossman and H. A. Hellyer (eds), *Rethinking Religion and Radicalization: Terrorism and Violence Twenty Years After 9/11*, London: Bloomsbury Academic.
Khosrokhavar, F. (2013), 'Radicalization in Prison: The French Case', *Politics, Religion and Ideology*, 14 (2): 284–306.
Khosrokhavar, F. (2017), *Radicalization*, trans. J. M. Todd, New York: The New Press.
Körs, A. (2017), 'The Plurality of Peter Berger's "Two Pluralisms" in Germany', *Society*, 54 (5): 445–53.
Körs, A. (2019), 'Contract Governance of Religious Diversity in a German City-State and Its Ambivalences', *Religion, State and Society*, 47 (4–5): 456–73.
Kuru, A. T. (2009), *Secularism and State Policies toward Religion: The United States, France, and Turkey*. Cambridge: Cambridge University Press.
Lewicki, A. (2014), *Social Justice through Citizenship? The Politics of Muslim Integration in Germany and Great Britain*. Basingstoke: Palgrave Macmillan.

Lyall, J. (2009), 'Does Indiscriminate Violence Incite Insurgent Attacks? Evidence from Chechnya', *Journal of Conflict Resolution*, 53 (3): 331–62.

Madeley, J. (2009), 'Unequally Yoked: The Antinomies of Church–State Separation in Europe and the USA'. *European Political Science*, 8 (3): 273–88.

Magazzini, T. (2020a), 'Radicalisation and Resilience Case Study. France', Horizon 2020 GREASE Project. Available online: https://cadmus.eui.eu/handle/1814/69937 (accessed 13 April 2022).

Magazzini, T. (2020b), 'France: La République Is at War with Itself', *Open Democracy*, 26 October. Available online: https://www.opendemocracy.net/en/global-extremes/france-la-r%C3%A9publique-is-at-war-with-itself/ (accessed 4 October 2022).

Magazzini, T. (2025), 'A Self-Fulfilling Prophecy? Researching Institutional Trust Towards Muslim Minorities in France' in T. Magazzini and G. Fahmi (eds), *Causes and Consequences of the Governance of Islam and Violent Radicalisation*, London: Routledge (Studies in Extremism and Democracy).

Magazzini, T. and G. Fahmi (eds) (2025), *Causes and Consequences of the Governance of Islam and Violent Radicalisation*. London: Routledge (Studies in Extremism and Democracy).

Magazzini, T., Eleftheriadou, M. and A. Triandafyllidou (2024), *The Non-radicalisation of Muslims in Southern Europe. Migration and Integration in Italy, Greece, and Spain*. London: Palgrave Macmillan.

Modood, T. (2010), 'Moderate Secularism, Religion as Identity and Respect for Religion', *The Political Quarterly*, 81 (1): 4–14.

Modood, T. (2012), 'Is There a Crisis of Secularism in Western Europe?' *Sociology of Religion*, 72 (2): 130–49.

Modood, T. ([2007] 2013), *Multiculturalism: A Civic Idea*, 2nd edn, Cambridge: Polity Books.

Modood, T. (2017), 'Multiculturalism and Moderate Secularism', in A. Triandafyllidou and T. Modood (eds), *The Problem of Religious Diversity: European Challenges, Asian Approaches*, 52–74, Edinburgh: Edinburgh University Press.

Modood, T. (2019), *Essays on Secularism and Multiculturalism*. London: Rowman & Littlefield.

Muchlinski, D. (2014), 'Grievances and Opportunities: Religious Violence across Political Regimes', *Politics and Religion*, 7: 684–705.

Orgad, L. (2021), 'Forced to Be Free: The Limits of European Tolerance', *Harvard Human Rights Journal*, Vol. 34. Available online: https://papers.ssrn.com/sol3/papers.cfm?abstract_id=3648135 (accessed 4 October 2022).

O'Toole, T., D. Nilsson Dehanas, T. Modood, N. Meer and S. Jones (2013), *Taking Part: Muslim Participation in Contemporary Governance Report*, Bristol: University of Bristol.

O'Toole, T., N. Meer, D. Nilsson Dehanas, S. Jones and T. Modood (2016), 'Governing through Prevent? Regulation and Contested Practice in State-Muslim Engagement', *Sociology*, 50 (1): 160–77.

Peter, F. (2010), 'Welcoming Muslims into the Nation: Tolerance, Politics and Integration in Germany', in J. Cesari (ed), *Muslims in the West after 9/11: Religion, Politics, and Law*, 119–44, Abingdon: Routledge.

Ragazzi, F. (2017), 'Countering Terrorism and Radicalisation: Securitising Social Policy?', *Critical Social Policy*, 37 (2): 163–79.

Richardson, J. T. (ed) (2004), *Regulating Religion: Case Studies from around the Globe*. New York: Springer.

Roex, I. and F. Vermeulen (2019), 'Pre-Emptive Measures against Radicalisation and Local Partnerships in Antwerp', in N. Fadil, M. de Koning and F. Ragazzi (eds), *Radicalisation in Belgium and the Netherlands: Critical Perspectives on Violence and Security*, 131–67, London: I.B. Tauris.

Saiya, N. (2016), 'Religion, State, and Terrorism: A Global Analysis', *Terrorism and Political Violence*, 31 (2): 204–23.

Schiffauer, W. (2006), 'Enemies within the Gates: The Debate about the Citizenship of Muslims in Germany', in T. Modood, A. Triandafyllidou and R. Zapata-Barrero (eds), *Multiculturalism, Muslims and Citizenship: A European Approach*, 94–116, Abingdon: Routledge.

Sealy, T. (2021), 'Germany: Federal Corporatism', in A. Triandafyllidou and T. Magazzini (eds), *Routledge Handbook on the Governance of Religious Diversity*, 35–45, London: Routledge.

Sealy, T. and T. Modood (2021a), 'The Governance of Muslim Minorities in the UK', in M. Khan (ed), *Symposium on the State of Muslim Minorities in Contemporary Democracies*, June. http://doi.org/10.47816/02.001.symposium3.sealy-modood (accessed 4 October 2022).

Sealy, T. and T. Modood (2021b), 'Belgium: Devolved Federalism', in A. Triandafyllidou and T. Magazzini (eds), *Routledge Handbook on the Governance of Religious Diversity*, 13–23, London: Routledge.

Sealy, T. and T. Modood (2021c), 'France: from *laïcité* to *laïcism*?', in A. Triandafyllidou and T. Magazzini (eds), *Routledge Handbook on the Governance of Religious Diversity*, 24–34, London: Routledge.

Sealy, T. and T. Modood (2021d), 'The United Kingdom: Weak Establishment and Pragmatic Pluralism', in A. Triandafyllidou and T. Magazzini (eds), *Routledge Handbook on the Governance of Religious Diversity*, 46–56, London: Routledge.

Sealy, T. and T. Modood (2022a), 'Western Europe and Australia: Negotiating Freedom of Religions', *Religion, State and Society*, 50 (4): 362–77.

Sealy, T. and T. Modood (2022b), 'Prevention Measures of Radicalisation in Belgium', in R. Ceylan and M. Kiefer (eds), *Der islamische Fundamentalismus im 21. Jahrhundert*, 371–82, Wiesbaden: Springer.

Silber, M. D. and A. Bhatt (2007), *Radicalization in the West: The Homegrown Threat*. New York: New York City Police Department.

Tourkochoriti, I. (2012), 'The Burka Ban: Divergent Approaches to Freedom of Religion in France and in the USA', *William & Mary Bill of Rights Journal*, 20 (79): 791–852.

Wang, J. (2016), 'Islam and State Policy in Contemporary China', *Studies in Religion/Sciences Religieuses*, 45 (4): 566–80.

Yakova, L., R. Dzhekova, G. Tzvetkova, A. Triandafyllidou, T. Magazzini, M. Grossman, V. Barolsky, V. Gerrand, T. Sealy, T. Modood, E. Gemi, D. Vékony, G. Mahajan, P. Boy Zulian, Y. Taskin, E. Racius, Z. Ibrahim, I. M. Rasid, M. Lahlou, M. Zouiten, M. Iliyasov, G. Fahmi and H. Gulalp (2021), 'State-Religion Governance Indicators', Horizon 2020 GREASE Project. Available online: https://cadmus.eui.eu/handle/1814/69837 (accessed 4 October 2022).

5

Religiously attributed radicalization and violent extremism: Policy responses and impacts on the governance of religion in South-Eastern Europe

Liliya Yakova and Rositsa Dzhekova

Introduction

As the world has become more economically globalized and interconnected, it has been challenged by issues related to migration flows, growing (ethnoreligious) nationalism, extremism and violent radicalization. To varying degrees, these challenges have become intertwined with questions of religious affiliation or attribution, some of which have been framed within the context of international terrorist networks and activities (Triandafyllidou et al. 2019). Such dynamics have triggered perceptions of threats to national security and raised issues which have impacted local, national and regional political processes across the world. These include the need to develop strategies and policies for the prevention of novel security threats, a readjustment of state identities when it comes to security, and the emergence of new interpretations of the idea of sovereignty (Goetschel 2010). How the emergence of security threats linked to violent radicalization and extremism shape national policies pertaining to religion has thus become an important question.

Countries in South-Eastern Europe have both been affected by and responded to such challenges. Marked by rich ethnoreligious traditions, some of these states have been prone to radicalization and violent extremism partially or wholly tied to religion. Some have experienced a high concentration of foreign terrorist fighters (FTFs) participating in the violent conflicts in Syria and Iraq. Others have exemplified how nationalistic tendencies grounded in fear from religiously attributed or other forms of radicalization and violent extremism can shape national security responses (Prislan, Černigoj and Lobnikar 2018).

This chapter analyses how religiously attributed radicalization to violence and the emergence of violent extremism tied to religion shape state responses towards the governance of religion. We comparatively analyze this question in three countries within South-Eastern Europe – Albania, Bosnia and Herzegovina (BiH) and Bulgaria. The selection of these three states is guided by commonalities in their historical development – all were part of the Ottoman Empire and later experienced rule under a communist regime – as well as the central role of religion in their past and present sociopolitical realities. The three countries also provide a good foundation to compare and contrast how the state governance of religion is influenced by potential and existing instances of religiously attributed radicalization and violent extremism.

Albania and BiH provide examples of how states within South-Eastern Europe in which Islam is the demographically dominant religion produce responses to religiously attributed radicalization and violent extremism. These two cases also provide examples of how states within South-Eastern Europe manage religion in the face of both the FTF phenomenon and violent extremist acts executed by citizens in their homelands, as is the case in BiH. A point of contrast is offered by the case of Bulgaria, which has a Christian Orthodox majority and has been only marginally impacted by religiously attributed radicalization and extremism (Dzhekova 2020).

Relevant to our analysis here is how we operationalize the terms 'radicalization,' 'religion' and 'violent extremism'. Generally, radicalization has been defined in contested ways in both academic and policy spheres (Dzhekova et al. 2016). The Office of the United Nations High Commissioner for Human Rights defines the term as 'process through which an individual adopts an increasingly extremist set of beliefs and aspirations' which may include 'the willingness to condone, support, facilitate or use violence to further political, ideological, religious or other goals' (Human Rights Council 2016). Even though this is not always the case, radicalization can be associated with terrorist violence and/or may be linked to specific terrorist acts (UNODC 2018). The challenge of finding a common definition is further characterized by its complexity: radicalization is not a static concept or condition but a process which is contextualized and situated within certain specificities. To capture this situated complexity, we use here a definition which attends to such contextual specificities in relation to our focus on South-Eastern Europe: *Radicalization is a multi-level situational process which is framed in context 'by which people come to adopt an ideological framework that advocates for and drives action on the perceived need for fundamental transformational change in their existing socio-cultural and political order'* (Hellyer and Grossman 2019: 13).

Religion can play a role in radicalization to the extent to which it operates as an ideological inspiration or explanatory framework for radicalization (Hellyer and Grossman 2019). It is exactly in this sense that we conceptualize 'religion' in this book chapter – as a mode of 'ideology' or an 'idea' responsible for the formation and development of radicalization processes (Hellyer and Grossman 2019: 12). While embracing this definition, we are aware that the concept of 'religion' itself is more complex, having 'polythetic' meanings (i.e., belief in supernatural beings or powers, ethical norms, worship rituals and the benefits of participation for both individuals and communities in ritualistic life [Schilbrack 2022]). Religion also contains within itself structural and functional qualities, such as a system of symbols concerning the nature of things, related to specific behavioural dispositions, that may be practiced in the form of rituals and cultural performances with the goal of realizing a group's conceptions of the world (Geertz 1973).

When it comes to how the three states analysed in this chapter define 'religion,' their definition is not ideologically laden and is fundamentally untied to the notion of radicalization. In this sense, the constitutions of the three states conceptualize 'religion' in similar ways as: (1) an identity characteristic of the citizen, (2) a creed (i.e., the following of certain beliefs related to religion) and (3) a human right which needs to be respected.

At the outset of this analysis, it is important to distinguish between a demographically dominant religion and a religion dominating political realities in a state. We argue that simply because a particular religion (e.g., Islam) registers as the demographically dominant religion in a particular state does not mean that other religion(s) could not play a dominant role in determining religious identities and power distribution and struggles in that state. Indeed, as we will see in the Bulgarian case, a religion which is not demographically dominant plays a dominant role in the political agenda related to addressing (perceived) radicalization in the country. Similarly, while this chapter focuses analytically primarily on the demographically dominant religion in Albania and BiH, as we will show, the anti-radicalization responses of the two states are inscribed in realities that are broader than simply those involving the governance of a demographically dominant religion.

Importantly, the connection between radicalization and violent extremism is also complex (Dzhekova et al. 2016) since violent extremism is conceptually vague. The types of activities which constitute violent extremism can range from actions performed by legitimate reformers and activists (Awan and Blakemore 2013) to severe criminal activities such as those conducted by Islamic State, Al-Qa'eda and Boko Haram (UNODC 2018). For the purposes of this book chapter, we will use the definition proposed by Hellyer and Grossman (2019), which defines violent extremism, following J. M. Berger (2018), as a phenomenon involving an in-group's imperative to use violence against an outgroup as a constituent element of the in-group's identity as a 'defensive, offensive, or pre-emptive' measure (2018: 11).

Our discussion of Albania, BiH and Bulgaria proceeds along two lines: first, an overview of religiously attributed radicalization and violent extremism trends in these countries over the past three decades and, second, an analysis on the impacts of such trends on the governance of religion. These country-specific analyses are followed by a comparative section which brings together insights from each country to theorize about divergences and convergences. Ultimately, we argue that whereas state responses to the real or perceived threat of religiously attributed radicalization and violent extremism in these three countries have had specific impacts for the governance of religion, such responses have largely been framed within broader efforts focused on counter-terrorism policymaking.

Albania

Radicalization and violent extremism trends

Between 1967 and 1991, Albania was a communist atheistic state that denied its citizens rights to religious expression. The 1991 Albanian Constitution separated the state from religion and provided rights to religious freedoms. This led to the establishment of churches and mosques across the country, reflecting a diverse religious make-up, including Sunni Muslims (57 percent), Roman Catholics (10 percent), Orthodox Christians (7 percent) and members of the Bektashi Order (a form of Shia Sufism) (2 percent) (smaller groups of Jehovah's Witnesses, The Church of Jesus Christ of Latter-day Saints and Jews also exist) (U.S. Department of State 2021). Over the past three decades, the orientation of the largest religious community, the Muslim community of Albania, has appeared to shift from a purely patriotic outlook to one that has included the strengthening of the Islamic faith (Qirjazi and Shehu 2018).

Since the end of communism in Albania, there have been various challenges associated with religiously attributed radicalization. Some minor incidents that signified emerging radicalization trends in this context occurred in the mid-1990s; these were linked to the influence of Salafi ideologies introduced by foreign religious foundations and returning Albanians who had pursued education in Muslim-majority countries (Vurmo and Sulstarova 2018). More pronounced, however, were recent manifestations of violent extremism which occurred in Albania with the emergence of the Syrian civil war in 2011–12, primarily through the foreign fighter phenomenon (FTF). Among all the Western Balkan states, Albania ranks third in terms of its per capita number of foreign terrorist fighters (Mishkova et al. 2021). Between 2012 and 2017, 144 Albanians left for Syria and Iraq to fight for Islamic State (IS) (Vrugtman 2019). Among them, forty-five have returned to Albania, twenty-six died and seventy-three remain outside Albania (Vurmo and Sulstarova 2018, Vrugtman 2019). No recruits have been identified since 2017 (Yakova 2019), and eighteen children and six women were repatriated from the conflict by Albania in 2020–1 (Mishkova et al. 2021).

Initially, Albanian foreign fighters came from underprivileged, poor and isolated areas which were visited by unofficial imams promoting radical views and preaching. However, with the passage of time, radicalized individuals began to emerge in larger cities. Most recruits appear to have originated from specific smaller communities in certain areas where religiously attributed radicalization appeared to have a stronger influence, for example, the outskirts of Tirana, south of Elbasan and the municipalities of Librazhd, Bulqize, Kukes and Pogradec (Vrugtman 2021).

The appearance of the FTF phenomenon in Albania was driven by a number of factors. While the Muslim Community of Albania (KMSH) is Albania's official Muslim organization and is responsible for the selection and training of Albanian imams, in the 2000s, religious practices inconsistent with mainstream forms of Islam were identified (Qirjazi and Shehu 2018). In 2015, 200 of the 727 Albanian mosques were found to be in violation of the required legal compliance or KMSH regulations (some authors term such mosques as 'unofficial' in that they operate 'outside the legal standards and the Muslim community regulation' [Mejdini 2015]). Nine self-proclaimed imams (without any affiliation to KMSH) associated with the Yzberisht mosque in Tirana were arrested for supporting terrorism and recruiting foreign fighters for Islamic State (IS) (Qirjazi and Shehu 2018). Their actions resulted in the departure from Albania of seventy individuals who went on to fight for militants in the Syrian civil war. These dynamics were informed by a number of broader contextual factors, including lack of religious education for believers and clerics, disputed religious authorities, disengagement and lack of civic values, proactive religious agendas, religious disinformation by potentially malicious groups, broader cultural threats and online radicalization (Vrugtman 2021).

Violent radicalization and extremism attributed to religion have had more limited expressions in Albania's domestic context. For instance, in 2016, Albanian authorities thwarted a terrorist attack targeting a FIFA football match between Albania and Israel. The perpetrators belonged to a cell of Muslim extremists from Albania, Kosovo and North Macedonia, led by two Kosovo-Albanian IS members (Yakova 2019). Out of the nineteen people arrested, four were Albanians (Mishkova et al. 2021). In 2017, five counter-terrorism operations were conducted by Albanian authorities, resulting in the arrests of twelve individuals.

In recent years online religiously attributed radicalization appears to have increased in Albania, unregulated even among FTF returnees (Yakova 2019), a trend noted by the European Commission as well as the Balkan Investigative Reporting Network (Qirjazi and Shehu 2018). This includes a rise in Albanian-language online content promoting radicalization. Some scholars argue that individuals producing such content, though unaffiliated to particular terrorist organizations, nevertheless have the potential and capability to perpetrate domestic terrorist attacks (Mishkova et al. 2021).

Even though religiously attributed radicalization and extremism have not produced much in the way of executed attacks in Albania, such trends have become an important area of interest and concern for Albanians; currently, almost one-third (31.8 percent) of all Albanians are concerned by religious extremism (Evstatiev and Mishkova 2022). This concern has developed over time. In 2012, 12 percent of Albanian Muslims wished to make Sharia the official law of Albania, and 6 percent supported suicide bombing in support of the cause of Islam (Dyrmishi 2016). In 2018, one in ten Albanians revealed that they were aware of someone in their midst who wished to incite or support religious extremism and/or violent religious extremist action (Vurmo and Sulstarova 2018). A particularly challenging aspect for the population has been the repatriation and reintegration of returning Albanian FTFs who may still be under the influence of radical ideas (Yakova and Bogdanova 2022). Albanians are generally sceptical about the potential of these returnees to leave their radical ideology behind (Vrugtman 2021).

Policy responses and impacts on the governance of religion

In response to the perceived threats posed by religiously attributed radicalization and violent extremism, Albania, like other Western Balkan states, made changes to its national legislation. This included the government's amendment of the Penal Code in 2014 to criminalize involvement in violent conflict abroad, among other changes. It also introduced the Inter-Sectoral Strategy against Terrorism and Action Plan (2011–15), the Inter-Sectoral Strategy for fighting Organized Crime, Illegal Trafficking and Terrorism (2013–20) and eventually the National Strategy for Countering Violent Extremism (2015), followed by an accompanying Action Plan. The national strategy promotes a so-called 'whole-of-society-approach', which aims to enhance multi-partner collaboration and coordination in building resilience through community education, employment creation and policing initiatives (Vrugtman 2021). The implementation of the Strategy has proved challenging due to its cost, revealing insufficient government implementation capacity and necessitating the support of civil society organizations (CSOs) and international donors such as the European Union, the Organization for

Security and Co-operation in Europe (OSCE) and the embassies of the United States, United Kingdom and other foreign nations (Vrugtman 2021).

These responses by the Albanian state speak to the overall approach of the government to address the threat of violent extremism and terrorism. However, some of these responses, including prior to the emergence of FTFs, have had implications for the governance of religion in the country. Between the end of Communism in the 1990s and the commencement of the war in Syria in 2011, religiously attributed radicalization in Albania inspired state responses which were mostly reactive. Influenced by the events of 9/11, law enforcement became the major actor tackling religious radicalism, with little focus on prevention (Vurmo 2015).

During this period, the state took advantage of the discourse on religious harmony in Albania, which it had been promoting to enhance its potential for future EU membership (Elbasani and Puto 2017), to propound religious harmony and respect for religious diversity. Yet at the same time, it took specific steps to exert control over the influence of foreign-backed religious groups. As part of this initiative, it expelled suspected foreign-backed terrorists from the country and, in 2002, took action to block the assets of individuals and religious groups allegedly tied to foreign terrorist movements (Vrugtman 2021). The Albanian government also made promises to resolve continuing disputes tied to the restitution of religious property confiscated during communism, an issue which to date has not been fully resolved. The problem of imams who preached radical versions of Islam imported from abroad also remained unresolved (Vrugtman 2021).

Following the onset of the Syrian conflict and the recruitment of Albanian Muslims as FTFs, the state again used the religious tolerance card to promote prevention against religiously attributed radicalization and violent extremism (Vurmo and Sulstarova 2018). The government took measures to encourage religious tolerance, critical thinking and civic participation in the education system. One example of such measures was the introduction of a government education programme to prevent religiously attributed radicalization and heighten religious tolerance in schools by training relevant officials (Mejdini 2016a). To further support religious coexistence and interreligious harmony, the state also created plans to integrate religious history into the civic education curricula of schools (Yakova 2019), an initiative viewed by some imams as rather fruitless if they were not delivered by recognized institutions and experts (Qirjazi and Shehu 2018).

From 2012, resolving the challenge of 'unofficial' mosques that had supposedly intensified the growth of religiously attributed radicalization and FTF recruitment returned to the government agenda. In 2016, with the support of the KMSH, the State Agency for the Legalization, Urbanization and Integration of Informal Areas began 'legalizing' and registering 'unofficial' mosques (Mejdini 2016b). In tandem, the government took legal action against specific religious figures to prevent the further dissemination of Islamic radicalization. For example, in March 2014, nine imams held liable for the recruitment of more than seventy of Albania's FTFs during the Syrian conflict were arrested on the outskirts of Tirana (Qirjazi and Shehu 2018), an intervention that certainly had some impact in impeding further FTF recruitment (Qirjazi and Shehu 2018). However, despite these changes to the governance of religion and the tightening of scrutiny in relation to religious influencers and mosques promoting religious extremism and violence, challenges related to religiously attributed radicalization in Albania remain. These include the accommodation of religious minorities, and in particular the repatriation, deradicalization and reintegration into Albanian society of the remaining FTFs who have not yet returned to the country (Vrugtman 2021, Mishkova et al. 2021).

Bosnia and Herzegovina

Radicalization and violent extremism trends

Bosnia and Herzegovina is one of the Balkan states most severely affected by religiously attributed radicalization (Yakova and Bogdanova 2022), with strong legacies that have created ongoing challenges in this area, especially in light of the fragmented institutional structures and ethno-religious discords which the Dayton Agreement left behind (Tzvetkova and Mancheva 2019). Radicalization and violent extremism in BiH should be viewed through the lens of the particular ethnoreligious reality of the country. Around half (50.7 percent) of BiH's population is Muslim, 15.1 percent are Catholic, 30.75 percent are Christian Orthodox, 1.5 percent are 'other' and nearly 1 percent self-identify as atheists (Agency for Statistics of BiH 2016). Unresolved ethnoreligious complexities created by the legacies of the Bosnian war between 1992 and 1995, accompanied by the compromised overall post-war performance of state institutions and enduring economic insecurities, among other drivers, have shaped a sociopolitical climate that has contributed to an upswing in religiously motivated radicalization (Center for the Study of Democracy 2020). Even though, more recently, religiously attributed radicalization has emerged among minority religious groups such as Christian Orthodox Serbs and Croat Catholics (Kapidžić et al. 2020), religiously attributed radicalization in BiH has primarily been associated with Islam.

It is critical to note, however, that Islam in BiH is fluid and plays out in pluralistic ways. The majority of Muslim groups in the country adhere to the structures of the officially recognized organization governing matters for the country's broader Muslim community in BiH (Alibašić and Begović 2017). In this sense, neither association with Islam nor association with some of its stricter forms, such as Salafism, should be perceived as necessarily tied to violent extremism (Tzvetkova and Mancheva 2019). The Bosnian security institutions, for instance, distinguish between Salafists who do not generally perform violent acts and *takfirists/Kharijites* who are perceived as willing to use violence for religious goals (Bećirević 2016).

To understand the particular problematics of religiously motivated radicalization in BiH, two developments need to be analysed: first, the appearance of Arab-African mujahideen during the Bosnian war in the 1990s and, second, the departure of FTFs from BiH to Syria and Iraq after 2012 (Tzvetkova and Mancheva 2019).

The Bosnian war was a major milestone that planted the seeds of recent trends in religiously attributed radicalization in BiH. To support their Muslim brothers who had suffered abuse and atrocities in the bloody conflict between Serb and Croat nationalists,

Muslims from different places, including Syria, Sudan, Egypt, Russia, Algeria and Tunisia, arrived in BiH to answer the call to fight a jihad (Mustapha 2013). These fighters had earlier become known as the mujahideen (Islamic holy warriors) who fought for Islam during the Soviet-Afghan War (1979–89). Various sources provide different estimates on the number of *mujahideen* who entered BiH, ranging from 300 to 5,000 (Kohlmann 2004, Tzvetkova and Mancheva 2019, Erjavec 2009, Zosak 2010). Even though these mujahideen initially fought individually or in smaller groups, they soon became part of the Bosnian military and were readily welcomed by the Bosnian army (Mustapha 2013). The 1995 Dayton Peace Accords required the mujahideen to leave BiH, but many of them remained in the country and were granted citizenship (Tzvetkova and Mancheva 2019). These remaining individuals set the stage for the strengthening of Salafism in the country (Bećirević 2016).

Such foundations for Salafism were largely supported by other trends. According to Bećirević (Bećirević 2016), after the end of the communist regime, Bosnian Muslims felt disappointed and betrayed by the Western liberal regime. In their search for solidarity, they reached out to the Muslim world, which had already been supporting BiH financially through charities linked to Al-Qaèda, but also through weapons shipments and the promulgation of Salafi-style proselytizing (Bećirević 2016). These trends were complemented by funding for educational initiatives for Bosnian Muslims in Muslim states. Such developments created further grounds for the spread of rigid interpretations of Islam in BiH by students of Islam returning from Muslim-majority countries.

In more recent times, the war in Syria revealed an additional aspect of the FTF phenomenon in BiH: the categorization of foreign fighters not simply as foreign-born individuals coming out of BiH but as foreign fighters of Bosniak origin (or members of the Bosnian diaspora) who travelled illegally outside BiH to fight a war and who have been influenced by larger forces of transnational Muslim solidarity and violence (Li 2019). According to the BiH government, 217 FTFs left for Syria and Iraq by the end of 2015 (Kapidžić et al. 2020); by October 2017, the BiH Ministry of Security estimated the number at 230 (Kapidžić et al. 2020). The International Centre for the Study of Radicalization and Political Violence reports this number as 300–340 citizens (Hamidićević and Plevljak 2018). Of the 300-odd citizens who left between 2012 and 2015, 188 were men, 61 were women and 81 were children (Kapidžić et al. 2020). By January 2016, fifty men and one woman had been killed on the battlefield. The year 2016 brought fortified attempts by the BiH government to prevent and counter violent extremism, which possibly contributed to the abrupt halt of the departure of Bosnian citizens for the conflict. However, as of early 2017, there were still 220–330 BiH fighters in Syria and Iraq (Counter-Extremism Project 2022). In 2018, it was revealed that seventy-six FTFs with BiH citizenship, among whom were five women and four children, had been killed on the battlefield (Hamidićević and Plevljak 2018). By the end of the same year, it was estimated that ninety-eight adult BiH citizens (men and women) continued to conduct FTF activities while resident in Syria or Iraq (Kapidžić et al. 2020).

Significantly, 36 per cent of the Bosnian contingent who left to support Islamist militant groups are women, representing twice the numbers of women seen in other

European countries (Tzvetkova and Mancheva 2019). These women were active in managing operations, in addition to caring for their children and FTF husbands.

Relevant to the FTF phenomenon in more recent times have been the so-called *para-jamaats*. Some scholars consider *para-jamaats* to be illegal mosques – 'illegal' in the sense that they operate 'outside the jurisdiction of the (officially recognised) Islamic community', but they could also be 'any private space chosen for the purpose of a religious gathering or/and as an alternative to the religious spaces of mainstream Islam' (Metodieva 2021: 8). In this regard, some scholars also use the term 'parallel congregations' to indicate that such groups work in ways parallel to officially recognized mosques, but still lie 'outside the jurisdiction of official religious institutions' (Metodieva 2021). Even though not all such spaces were linked to violent extremism, a number of them did turn into breeding grounds for the recruitment of foreign fighters (Metodieva 2021). The *para-jamaats* managed to find a way to function outside the control of the mainstream Islamic community in BiH, with their own clergy and infrastructure (Azinović and Jusić 2016). The locations with the greatest numbers of *para-jamaats* between 2011 and 2015 were Zenica-Doboj and Sarajevo (Metodieva 2021).

Even though the FTF phenomenon in BiH constitutes a prominent manifestation of violent religiously attributed radicalization, violent acts have also occurred domestically. Since 1997 a number of terrorist attacks have occurred on BiH territory, many of them carried out by Salafists (Bećirević 2016). The 2010s brought additional instances of Salafist extremism, such as the 2010 bomb attack in Bugojno, the 2011 rifle attack on the US embassy in Sarajevo, the 2015 alleged Wahhabist attack on a police station in Zvronik and another attack in the same year in the Sarajevo suburb of Rajlovac (Tzvetkova and Mancheva 2019).

Policy responses and impact on the governance of religion in BiH

These cases of religiously attributed radicalization in BiH have provoked particular responses, primarily among international and non-governmental stakeholders. However, few of these responses have directly reflected changes in the way the BiH state governs religion. Rather, the state responses to such trends have been inscribed within BiH's broader counter-terrorism response. When it comes to specific changes relating to religious community matters, the impacts are mostly visible in the reactions of religious institutions rather than government initiatives in the governance of religion or management of religious diversity.

The BiH government's responses to cases of Islamist attributed radicalization have mainly consisted of securitizing the issue and taking measures to prevent further activity by radicalized Bosnian citizens at home and abroad. Most of its actions have involved legislative and institutional measures. For instance, in 2004 the BiH government established the Task Force for Fight against Terrorism and Strengthening Capacities for Fight against Terrorism (The Prosecutor's Office of Bosnia and Herzegovina n.d.). The Task Force operates under the Prosecutor's Office of BiH and under the supervision of the BiH Ministry of Security, the main government structure tasked with the prevention and countering of violent extremism, whose goal is to investigate crimes of terrorism. The establishment of the Task Force aligned with already existing efforts of BiH to strengthen its criminal laws since the early 2000s. In 2014, BiH amended its criminal law to counteract individuals who join and support military and parapolice organizations (Official Gazette of Bosnia and Herzegovina 2014).

Accompanying these criminal law modifications were the Strategy of Bosnia and Herzegovina for Preventing and Combating Terrorism (2015–20) and an Action Plan aiming to implement its provisions (Bosnia and Herzegovina Council of Ministers 2015). The strategy revolves around four elements. First, it aims to *prevent radicalization and terrorism* through multiple methods of targeting vulnerable individuals prone to radicalization, such as social security approaches, provision of family services and combatting misuse of the Internet. Second, it aims to *protect critical infrastructure* through guarding against cross-border movement related to terrorist activity, as well as monitoring and preventing the transportation and storage of cyber, chemical, biological and nuclear weapons. A third major facet of the Strategy is to create a framework for the *prosecution of terrorist and related acts* by aligning them with international standards. Lastly, the Strategy addresses *response/reaction to terrorism attacks* should preventive measures fail. Once the Strategy was adopted, the Council of Ministers initiated a so-called Supervisory/Monitoring Body, acting under the umbrella of the BiH Ministry of Security and comprising members of the Ministry of Justice, Ministry of Human Rights and Refugees and Ministry of Foreign Affairs. This body was charged with the development and coordination of radicalization and violent extremism prevention, as well as with monitoring and implementation of the Strategy. In 2018 and 2019 the Supervisory/Monitoring Body initiated local counter-terrorism programmes which focused on local capacity-building (Center for the Study of Democracy 2020).

An updated "Strategy of Bosnia and Herzegovina for Prevention and Combating Terrorism (2021–26)" was published in 2022 (Council of Ministers of BiH 2022). The cite by Kuloglija can be taken out as it is no longer relevant to the current reality. Regarding the previous strategy, various stakeholders have criticized it for a number of reasons, including equating radicalization with violent extremism and terrorism, providing the BiH government with pre-emptive powers, the insufficient participation of some stakeholders (e.g., CSOs) in the design of the Strategy, as well as scant funding and capacity for local implementation (Center for the Study of Democracy 2020). Institutional approaches have also characterized the BiH response, including capacity-building for security and intelligence services between 2014 and 2016, which resulted in the adoption of tools used by the European Union and the United States in fighting radicalization (Center for the Study of Democracy 2020).

BiH has also become involved in resilience-building initiatives in collaboration with members of religious communities. However, such positive developments have been overshadowed by criticisms against the state's initially hard-line approach to tackling the risk of religiously attributed radicalization and violent extremism through the actions of security and intelligence agencies. One example was Operation Ruben in Republika Srpska, one of the constitutive entities of BiH with a majority population of ethnic Serbs. Operation Ruben was implemented by Republika Srpska's law enforcement agencies and involved the public arrests of thirty-two Bosnian Muslims, who were eventually released. This operation was considered excessive and to have contributed to escalating ethnic and political tensions in BiH (Jukic 2015). Later in 2015, another set of specialized actions targeted Bosnians suspected of being connected to terrorists and terrorist groups. During these special operations law enforcement stormed into private homes and places of religious gatherings alleged to be promoting radical ideas (Džidić 2015). As was the case with Operation Ruben, this special action did not result in any actual indictments of persons suspected of having links to international terrorist organizations. Such approaches have been controversial, given that they have prioritized and politicized religiously attributed radicalization while setting aside a focus on non-religious threats such as right-wing radicalization (Center for the Study of Democracy 2020).

The measures taken by BiH in response to religiously attributed radicalization and violent extremism do not specifically correspond to changes in policies relevant to the governance of religion and religious diversity. However, the impacts of radicalization and violent extremism on the governance of religion have been more clearly present in BiH through the actions of the Interreligious Council (IRC) and the Islamic community of BiH, rather than on behalf of the state. The IRC, for example, organized local counter-radicalization efforts encouraging local religious dialogue. The Islamic community, with strong encouragement from the BiH government (Toé 2016), took steps to incorporate the *para-jamaats* into its structures, thus altering the country's Islamic religious landscape (Lilyanova 2017, Preljević 2017). It is important to consider the impacts of religiously attributed radicalization on how religion is governed through the prism of non-state actors who transform the way they run their own religious institutions and activities, and not merely through the lens of the state itself.

Bulgaria

Radicalization and violent extremism trends

Bulgaria, with a majority Christian Orthodox population, has been only marginally affected by religiously motivated radicalization. With 10 percent of the population identifying as Muslim according to the latest national census (National Statistical Institute 2021), Bulgaria is the EU member state with the largest autochthonous Muslim community, formed over centuries following the Ottoman conquest at the end of the fourteenth century. As such, Bulgarian society has inherited centuries of experience in interactions between Christian majority and Muslim minority populations. Islam is the religion of three historical minorities whose understanding and practice of Islam developed under the influence of the Ottoman Empire: Turks, Roma and Bulgarian-speaking Muslims (Zhelyazkova 2014). Members of the Roma community share different religious affiliations, including Orthodox Christianity, Evangelism and Islam (Mancheva 2019), with religious conversions being a common practice (Benovska-Sabkova and Altanov 2010).

Against this background, Bulgaria has been affected by violent manifestations of Islamist attributed radicalization and extremism to a limited extent. In 2012, Bulgaria was targeted for the first time by a terrorist attack, which was plotted externally and committed against Israeli citizens visiting the country for holidays. Five Israelis and one Bulgarian were killed together with the perpetrator himself, with another thirty-five injured. On 5 February 2013, the Bulgarian government officially named Hezbollah as the perpetrator of the terrorist act (Lalov 2013). Since the onset of the Islamic State-related conflict in Syria and Iraq, the country has become a transit route for FTFs from Europe on their way to and from combat zones (Dzhekova 2020). Arrests and prosecutions of foreign nationals for terrorist-related offences have also increased as a result (Dzhekova and Stoynova 2018). However, only a few isolated cases of Bulgarian citizens connected to Islamist extremist networks have been registered. Examples include a man of Syrian descent with a Bulgarian passport apprehended in 2017 on suspicion of being a high-ranking member of Islamic State and of financing its activities through trade in illegal tobacco products (Novinite.com 2017). In 2018, a Bulgarian citizen was sentenced to seven years in jail by an Austrian court for the preparation for terrorist activity after returning from Syria, together with an Austrian citizen of Bulgarian and Turkish descent who was sentenced to eight years in jail for recruiting people to join IS (Bulgarian National Radio 2018). In June 2017, a Bulgarian court sentenced a dual Australian-Bulgarian citizen to four years imprisonment on charges of training for terrorist activity in Bulgaria under Art. 108a (4) of the Penal Code following his return from Syria (Spassov 2017). In 2019, a sixteen-year-old boy from Plovdiv was detained after police found handmade bomb components in his home (Nikodimov 2019); he had reportedly fallen under the influence of IS online.

The risks of so-called home-grown Islamist radicalization are most often associated in Bulgaria with the arrival of Salafi interpretations of Islam and their subsequent adoption by some Bulgarian Muslim communities (Shentov, Todorov and Stoyanov 2015). Salafism is not typical in Bulgaria and is often considered to be at odds with the traditional Hanafi Sunni Islam professed by the majority of Bulgarian Muslims (Zhelyazkova 2014). Even though Salafi interpretations of Islam have been rejected by the majority of Bulgarian Muslims, Salafism has managed to reach Muslims in Bulgaria through four main channels: foreign missionaries; foreign charities from Jordan, Egypt, Saudi Arabia or Kuwait; young Bulgarian Muslims who receive education at prestigious religious universities in Egypt, Jordan and Saudi Arabia; and, finally, migration to Western European countries leading to encounters with local immigrant Muslim communities (Shentov, Todorov and Stoyanov 2015).

The spread of Salafism is limited to a small number of Bulgarian-speaking Muslim villages and Roma settlements. While Salafi interpretations of Islam should not be equated with radicalization, in some isolated instances, the adoption of Salafism has been manifested through endorsement of radical Islamist organizations and their ideas by some small segments of Bulgaria's highly heterogeneous Roma communities (Shentov, Todorov and Stoyanov 2015, Mancheva and Dzhekova 2017). The first visible indication appeared in 2003 when a flag with the declaration 'The state is a Halifat' was displayed above two houses in Pazardjik in the Roma Quarter of Iztok, where followers of the banned Islamist organization Halifat were gathering (Nikolov 2004). About ten years later, in cities like Pazardjik, Plovdiv and Asenovgrad, acts demonstrating sympathy with organizations such as Al-Qa'eda in Iraq and later IS were observed (Mancheva and Dzhekova 2017). In 2015 a criminal trial was launched against Ahmed

Musa, an informal Islamic preacher in the Pazardjik Roma quarter. Musa had been previously convicted in 2004 and 2012 on similar charges, and thirteen of his followers from the local Salafi Roma community were also charged with anti-democratic propaganda, religious hatred and inciting war (Shentov, Todorov and Stoyanov 2015, Mancheva and Dzhekova 2017, Dzhekova and Stoynova 2019). The defendants were reportedly involved in disseminating IS-inspired propaganda and calls for jihad, as well as allegedly providing logistical support to foreign fighters transiting to Syria (Mancheva and Dzhekova 2017).

However, these incidences of radicalization have not manifested in violent incidents. Further analysis suggests that a differentiation needs to be made between the underlying drivers of, first, the adoption of Salafism and, second, proselytism and endorsement of terrorist organizations and their ideas (Mancheva and Dzhekova 2017). A study on the root causes and the social meaning of the latter phenomenon among Roma from the Iztok neighbourhood in the city of Pazardzhik found that, while the adoption of Salafism in this community did play a role, additional factors need to be considered. These factors include the role of IS online propaganda as an external pull factor, the rise of a charismatic spiritual leader and an informal local mosque, contacts with radical Islamist circles abroad and group encapsulation as the result of increased negative public, and media attention following a much publicized trial on 'radical Islam' (Mancheva and Dzhekova 2017). Deficiencies in the government and institutional approach towards Islam as a religious denomination, and responses to the perceived threat of home-grown radicalization in particular, have been emphasized by various scholars (Ivanova 2019, Shentov, Todorov and Stoyanov 2015). Field research on attitudes among Muslim communities has found that encapsulation and alienation are strongly associated with responses to the rise of Islamophobia and nationalism, rather than with increased religiosity per se (Ivanova 2017).

The fact that a small segment of a local Roma community was associated with the most widely publicized case of Islamist radicalization in Bulgaria has led to an undue focus on this community as a potential breeding ground for extremism (Ivanova 2020, Stojlova 2016). Another trend in public and policy debates is the conflation of religious resurgence based on orthodox interpretations of Islam with Islamist radicalization (Shentov, Todorov and Stoyanov 2015). The lack of nuanced understanding (and research) on Islam as a religion and social practice, and the role of religious resurgence in identity dynamics (Mancheva and Dzhekova 2017), coupled with hostility towards Islam in Bulgarian national discourse arising from opposition to the Ottoman Empire's legacy (Evstatiev 2006), are important contextual factors that have bearing on these debates.

Policy responses and impact on the governance of religion in Bulgaria

By the mid-1990s, the uptake of Salafi interpretations of Islam among some segments of Bulgarian Muslim communities prompted security institutions to impose a more restrictive regime on proliferating externally funded Muslim religious organizations. This involved rejecting registrations or renewals, as well as launching investigations and deporting foreign nationals seen to pose a threat to national security (Troeva 2012,

Nikolov 2004). The 9/11 terrorist attacks in 2001 and attacks in Europe in the early 2000s increased awareness about jihadi terrorism and intensified the Bulgarian security services' approach to foreign vectors of potential Islamist radicalization in the country (Öktem 2010). Control over and prosecution of Islamic organizations in Bulgaria tightened further from 2008, when a National Plan for Combating Terrorism was adopted (Council of Ministers of the Republic of Bulgaria 2008).

The 2012 terrorist attack in Burgas prompted further counter-terrorism legislative changes, enhanced information exchange, coordination and intelligence monitoring (Shentov, Todorov and Stoyanov 2015). The threats to society posed by radicalization and violent extremism became the subject of more intensified political debate in 2015, mainly in light of global and EU-wide responses to terrorist recruitment by Islamic State and Al-Qaëda, as well as the issue of FTFs using Bulgaria as a transit zone (Shentov, Todorov and Stoyanov 2015). The Bulgarian Criminal Code was amended in June 2015, expanding its scope in relation to terrorism by criminalizing, among other things, assistance rendered within Bulgaria to foreigners for committing terrorist acts abroad. This resulted in an increased number of prosecutions.

A milestone in Bulgaria's preventing and countering violent extremism (P/CVE) approach was the 2015 Strategy for Countering Radicalization and Terrorism (2015–20), accompanied by an annually updated implementation plan (Council of Ministers 2015, (2016–19), Shentov, Todorov and Stoyanov 2015, Dzhekova 2020). As did other EU countries, the Strategy envisioned a more comprehensive approach to countering radicalization, violent extremism and terrorism, including a primary prevention pillar and the involvement of a wide array of institutions including non-security actors, civil society and religious community organizations.

In practice, however, security actors such as the Ministry of Interior, the State Agency for National Security and the Prosecution Office have dominated the institutional response, while prevention measures addressing drivers have lagged significantly (Stoynova, Ralchev and Dzhekova 2021). One reason for this is the absence of harmonization and cross-integration between P/CVE measures with other key policy areas such as education, social policy, child protection, crime prevention, minority integration, countering hate crime and discrimination. Consequently, the role of non-security actors such as social services, educational professionals, CSOs and religious organizations in the implementation of soft measures aimed at building societal resilience to radicalization has been marginal (Stoynova, Ralchev and Dzhekova 2021).

Alongside this securitised P/CVE approach, there has been a disproportionate focus on tackling the (perceived) threat of Islamist radicalization, despite Bulgaria's country-specific dynamics. Research on what shapes the understanding of radicalization and P/CVE responses among different stakeholders clearly shows major differences between the perceptions of state institutions on the one hand and civil society on the other. State institutions place excessive focus on the perceived threat from Islamist radicalization, while civil society underlines far-right and nationalist risks of violent extremism as being more pressing yet systematically ignored threats (Stoynova, Ralchev and Dzhekova 2021).

In recent years, there have been several examples of attempts in Bulgaria to more restrictively govern religion, mostly initiated by far-right political parties in government relying on increased threat perceptions of the rise of 'radical Islam' (Ivanova 2019). In particular, the heightened public attention to the 2015 court trial of Ahmed Musa contributed to a series of resolutions enacted by local municipal councils in several Bulgarian cities to prohibit the full-face veiling of women (Mancheva 2019, Ivanova 2019). By 2016, this process had culminated in the adoption of the Act to Limit the Wearing of Clothing Partially or Completely Covering the Face. Other municipal councils of the cities of Pazardzhik, Stara Zagora and Burgas followed suit. On 4 May 2018 a Project Law for Revision of the Denominations Act in Bulgaria was submitted to the National Assembly. The proposed revisions were justified by the need to impose stricter state control by the Directorate of Denominations at the Council of Ministers over the financial and religious activities of Bulgaria's denominations as a means to prevent and combat religious radicalization (Mancheva 2019). The overarching objective was to tackle 'radical Islam' by imposing strict control over the activities of Muslim denominations. The proposal faced concerted opposition by all religious denominations within the country; although it was not adopted, it demonstrates the vulnerability of religion to instrumentalization by political actors with populist agendas (Mancheva 2019).

These developments occurred at a time of increased social hostilities to ethnic and religious minorities in the aftermath of the 2015 European refugee crisis (Alpha Research 2020) and rising far-right sentiments in society and politics (Center for the Study of Democracy 2021, Todorov 2021). Another important factor was the deepening prejudice against Muslim Roma, who were seen as 'at risk' of radicalization by default (Stoynova, Ralchev and Dzhekova 2021). Some have argued for a direct relationship between an increase in Muslim communities' religious zeal and its visibility and the degree of pressure exerted by society and the state as a consequence (Ivanova 2019). This in turn risks deepening social divisions and hostilities, as well as radicalization.

Comparative insights

Based on the analyses for each of the country cases, several benchmarks emerge that support the assessment on comparisons and contrasts across these countries. One benchmark pertains to the contexts influencing the emergence of religiously attributed radicalization and violent extremism. In all three countries there were similar developments influenced by the ending of communism and the liberalization of different aspects of each nation's sociopolitical realities. In all the cases, the end of communist regimes saw an end to the complete banning of religion. Similarly, following the end of communism, all three countries established secular principles that separated the state from religious affairs, also opening the door to greater religious freedom. In each case, the state took a step back from exerting control over religion, which created opportunities for foreign religious influences to enter without much initial state oversight. This allowed for the free dissemination of various interpretations of religious doctrine, in particular stricter interpretations of Islam. An important aspect of convergence between the three countries in this regard is that for all three countries, religiously attributed radicalization became an especially hot topic in the context of 9/11 and subsequent events around the world. These events brought to the fore the need for prevention and implementation of policy instruments to combat radicalization and violent extremism which eventually would have implications for the governance of religion.

When it comes to contextual influences for religiously attributed radicalization, BiH stands out as a peculiar case because its ethnoreligious war produced implications for future manifestations of religiously attributed radicalization and violent extremism. Whereas Albania and Bulgaria were not affected by a bloody internal conflict after the end of communism, BiH suffered a war which had significant and ongoing implications for the character of ethno-religious relations in the country from the mid-1990s onwards. Although military actions ended with the Dayton Peace Accords, in practice, true reconciliation between the opposing sides of the conflict, driven along ethno-religious lines, has not eventuated. Unresolved tensions from the war, combined with continuing socio-economic challenges, have contributed to a volatile ethnoreligious environment in the country which has opened space for the emergence of violent extremism, in some cases attributed to religious motivations or influences (Center for the Study of Democracy 2020).

A second benchmark of comparison between Albania, BiH and Bulgaria concerns the nature of the perceived or genuine threat of violent radicalization. In this regard, Albania and BiH converge, as the FTF phenomenon reflects a form of religiously attributed radicalization with implications for the governance of religion in both countries. In both cases citizens left these countries by the hundreds to fight in foreign lands. By contrast, the FTF phenomenon in Bulgaria has not been that salient, since Bulgaria has instead served primarily as a place of transit rather than as a source country for foreign fighters. Domestic religiously motivated radicalization in Bulgaria is mostly associated with several isolated groups of Roma Salafi communities, which has not resulted in violent incidents. The threat landscape in Bulgaria therefore differs from that in Albania and BiH.

A third comparative benchmark concerns government responses to perceived or genuine religiously attributed radicalization and violent extremism, as well as the impacts of these responses on the governance of religion. In all three cases, government responses have been initially reactive, with less emphasis on preventive measures. Reactive responses emerged in the 1990s with the introduction of restrictive measures imposed on externally funded Muslim organizations and foundations in all three countries. When it comes to addressing the FTF phenomenon and domestic cases of religiously attributed violent radicalization, reactive measures have also been expressed in the forms of special operations, detention and court cases against suspects, and in the case of Bulgaria, in the deportation of Muslim foreigners considered a threat to national security (Mancheva 2019). A different aspect in the case of Bulgaria has been the focus on the monitoring and interception of transiting transnational fighters or other foreigners suspected of having ties to terrorist groups. Irregular migrants and asylum seekers have also been the subjects of law enforcement attention in Bulgaria (Mancheva 2019). Such measures have not been strictly related to changes in the governance of religion in the respective countries. Rather, they have been inscribed within the general counter-terrorism policy frameworks of the countries. Religious matters have been significant in the extent to which suspects have been typically associated with a specific religious group.

Responses in the three countries have also involved legislative measures tailored to the countering and prevention of violent extremism and terrorism more broadly, in the form of counterterrorism strategies and accompanying action plans, changes in the criminal law framework and in some cases the creation of special coordinating bodies (as is the case in BiH) tasked with the strategies' implementation. The Bulgarian case provides two examples of how far legislative measures went to prevent an alleged threat of Islamic radicalization: first, through the enactment of local-level prohibitions on women's face veiling and, second, through the effort to change the Denominations Act and impose strict measures over the activities of Bulgarian Muslims. These measures instrumentalized religion through the interventions of political actors with populist agendas, accompanied by a security-led institutional approach that stigmatized Muslim Roma communities as being at risk by default and further enhanced their social encapsulation.

In Albania and BiH there are genuine instances of civil society intervention by local religious communities through the activities of these countries' major Muslim institutions, which have respectively worked to mitigate the threats coming from vulnerable areas such as *para-jamaats* in BiH and unofficial mosques in Albania. In Albania, the government collaborated with the Islamic community of Albania to integrate unofficial mosques that had supported the growth in FTFs. In BiH, the government has strongly encouraged the Islamic community to incorporate the *para-jamaats* into its structures. In this sense, the participation of religious institutions in the response to and prevention of religiously attributed radicalization is a main component of the impacts of radicalization on religious governance, including self-governance, in Albania and BiH.

Concluding remarks

Religiously attributed radicalization and violent extremism have played a crucial role in the post-communist sociopolitical realities of Albania and BiH and to a lesser extent in Bulgaria. Whether as a threat or an actual event, such radicalization has inevitably shaped the policy frameworks of these states and their overall political discourses regarding religion. This analysis suggests a number of overlapping tendencies in terms of the impacts of radicalization and violent extremism on the governance of religion, including specific contextual influences as well as the major courses of action taken by the governments in these countries.

Overall, we observe more similarities than divergences in these impacts. A major point of divergence is the presence of an ethno-religious conflict in BiH, which has continuously maintained volatility to radicalization. Another point of divergence concerns the perceived nature of the threat – in Albania and BiH, the threat has been mostly in the form of FTFs, whereas in Bulgaria, it has been couched domestically in relation to specific ethnic minority communities. Religious institutions in Albania and BiH have had a strong impact on the governance of religious structures perceived as vulnerable to radicalization. All in all, this analysis suggests that the majority of the responses to religiously attributed radicalization in these South-Eastern European countries have been tied more to general counter-terrorism policy frameworks than to changes in policies governing religion.

References

Agency for Statistics of Bosnia and Herzegovina (2016), *Census of Population, Households and Dwellings in Bosnia and Herzegovina, 2013 Final Results* Available online: https://dataspace.princeton.edu/handle/88435/dsp0176537424z (accessed 29 June 2022).

Alibašić, A. and N. Begović (2017), 'Reframing the Relations between State and Religion in Post-War Bosnia: Learning to Be Free!', *Journal of Balkan and Near Eastern Studies*, 19 (1): 19–34.

Alpha Research. (2020), *Majority and Minority 2020*, Available online: https://alpharesearch.bg/post/965-mnozinstvo-i-malcinstva.html?lang=bg (accessed 30 June 2022).

Awan, I. and B. Blakemore (eds) (2013), *Extremism, Counter-Terrorism and Policing*, 1st edn, London: Routledge.

Azinović, V. and M. Jusić (2016), 'The New Lure of the Syrian War: The Foreign Fighters' Bosnian Contingent', Atlantic Initiative, Available online: https://www.rcc.int/swp/download/docs/The%20New%20Lure%20of%20the%20Syrian%20War%20%20The%20Foreign%20Fighters%20Bosnian%20Contingent.pdf/b5594b3a54e94a5f8596053b0d35db5c.pdf (accessed 15 June 2022).

Bećirević, E. (2016), *Salafism vs. Moderate Islam: A Rhetorical Fight for the Hearts and Minds of Bosnian Muslims*. Sarajevo: Atlantic Initiative, Centre for Security and Justice Research. Available online: http://www.helsinki.org.rs/doc/Edina%20Becirevic%20-%20Salafism%20vs.%20Moderate%20Islam.pdf (accessed 30 June 2022).

Benovska-Sabkova, M. and V. Altanov (2010), *Working Paper: Evangelical Conversion Among Roma in Bulgaria: Between Capsulation and Globalization*, New Bulgarian University, 21 August. Available online: http://eprints.nbu.bg/id/eprint/440/ (accessed 30 June 2022).

Berger, J. M. (2018), *Extremism*. Cambridge, MA: MIT Press.

Bosnia and Herzegovina Council of Ministers (2015), *Strategy of Bosnia and Herzegovina for Preventing and Combating Terrorism (2015–2020)*, Available online: https://polis.osce.org/file/347/download?token=iM9lAER- (accessed 30 June 2022).

Bulgarian National Radio (2018), 'Bulgarian National Sentenced to 7 Years in Prison in Austria', 29 November. Available online: https://bnr.bg/en/post/101051289/bulgarian-national-sentenced-to-7-years-in-prison-in-austria (accessed 30 June 2022).

Center for the Study of Democracy (2020), *Radicalization and Resilience Case Study: Bosnia and Herzegovina*, Horizon 2020 GREASE Project: Radicalization, Secularism and the Governance of Religion: Bringing Together European and Asian Perspectives. Available online: http://grease.eui.eu/wp-content/uploads/sites/8/2021/01/WP4-Report_BiH.pdf (accessed 15 June 2022).

Center for the Study of Democracy (2021), 'Overcoming Youth Vulnerabilities to Far-Right Narratives', 21 June. Available online: https://csd.bg/publications/publication/overcoming-youth-vulnerabilities-to-far-right-narratives/ (accessed 30 June 2022).

Council of Ministers of the Republic of Bulgaria (2008), *National Plan for Countering Terrorism*, Available online: https://www.strategy.bg/StrategicDocuments/View.aspx?lang=bg-BG&Id=497 (accessed 30 June 2022).

Council of Ministers of the Republic of Bulgaria. (2015), *Strategy for Countering Radicalization and Terrorism (2015–2020)*, Available online: https://www.strategy.bg/StrategicDocuments/View.aspx?lang=bg-BG&Id=979 (accessed 30 June 2022).

Council of Ministers of the Republic of Bulgaria (2016–2019), *Implementation Plans and Implementation Reports 2016–2019*, Available online: https://www.strategy.bg/StrategicDocuments/View.aspx?lang=bg-BG&Id=979 (accessed 30 June 2022).

Council of Ministers of BiH. (2022), *Strategy of Bosnia and Herzegovina for Prevention and Combating Terrorism, 2021–2026*, Available online: https://msb.gov.ba/PDF/010620234.pdf.

Counter-Extremism Project (2022), *Bosnia & Herzegovina: Extremism & Counter Extremism*. Available online: https://www.counterextremism.com/countries/bosnia-herzegovina-extremism-and-terrorism (accessed 15 June 2022).

Dyrmishi, A. (2016), *Radicalization and Religious Governance in Albania*, The Centre for the Study of Democracy and Governance, Available online: http://csdgalbania.org/wp-content/uploads/2017/08/Radicalisaon-and-Religious-Governance-in-Albania-.pdf (accessed 15 June 2022).

Dzhekova, R. (2020), *Country Reports: National Approaches to Extremism – Bulgaria*, CONNEKT Country Reports, 21 December. Available online: https://h2020connekt.eu/wp-content/uploads/2021/01/Bulgaria_CONNEKT_Approaches_to_extremism.pdf (accessed 15 June 2022).

Dzhekova, R. and N. Stoynova (2018), 'From Criminals to Terrorists and Back?', *Quarterly Report, GLOBSEC*, 30 May. Available online: https://www.globsec.org/publications/criminals-terrorists-report-2018-bulgaria/ (accessed 30 June 2022).

Dzhekova, R. and N. Stoynova (2019), 'From Criminals to Terrorists and Back? Bulgaria, Vol. 2', *Quarterly Report, GLOBSEC*, Available online: https://www.globsec.org/wp-content/uploads/2019/08/GPI-bulgaria-QUARTERLYREPORT.pdf (accessed 30 June 2022).

Dzhekova, R., N. Stoynova, A. Kojouharov, M. Mancheva, D. Anagnostou and E. Tsenkov (2016), *Understanding Radicalization: Review of Literature*, Center for the Study of Democracy, 18 March. Available online: https://csd.bg/publications/publication/understanding-radicalization-review-of-literature/ (accessed 15 June 2022).

Džidić, D. (2015), 'Bosnia Terror Suspects "Planned New Year Attack"', *Balkan Insight*, 23 December. Available online: https://balkaninsight.com/2015/12/23/arrested-wahhabis-in-bosniasuspected-of-planning-terror-act-12-23-2015/ (accessed 26 February 2022).

Elbasani, A. and A. Puto (2017), 'Albanian-Style Laïcité: A Model for a Multi-Religious European Home?', *Journal of Balkan and Near Eastern Studies*, 19 (1): 53–69.

Erjavec, K. (2009), 'The Bosnian War on Terrorism', *Journal of Language and Politics*, 8 (1): 5–27.

Evstatiev, S. (2006), *Public Islam on the Balkans in a Wider European Context*, Open Society Institute. Available online: http://pdc.ceu.hu/archive/00003105/01/simeon_evstatiev_final.pdf (accessed 30 June 2022).

Evstatiev, S. and D. Mishkova (2022), *Policy Brief Summarizing Lessons Learnt on the EU's Measures to Prevent Violent Extremism in the Region*, Prevex: Prevent Violent Extremism. Available online: https://www.prevex-balkan-mena.eu/wp-content/uploads/2022/01/D5.6-Policy-Brief_WB.pdf (accessed 26 February 2022).

Geertz, C. (1973), *The Interpretation of Cultures*. New York: Basic Books.

Goetschel, L. (2010), 'Globalization and Security: The Challenge of Collective Action in a Politically Fragmented World', *Global Society*, 14 (2): 259–77.

Hamidićević, S. and B. Plevljak (2018), 'Bosnia and Herzegovina', in A. Orosz (ed), *Returning from Violence: How to Tackle the Foreign Fighters Problem in the Western Balkans*, 56–67, Budapest: Institute for Foreign Affairs and Trade.

Hellyer, H. A. and M. Grossman (2019), *Concept Paper: A Framework for Understanding the Relationship between Radicalisation, Religion and Violence*, Horizon 2020 GREASE Project – Radicalization, Secularism and the Governance of Religion: Bringing Together European and Asian Perspectives, 2019. Available online: http://grease.eui.eu/wp-content/uploads/sites/8/2019/05/GREASE_D1.2_Hellyer-Grossman_Final1-1.pdf (accessed 26 February 2022).

Human Rights Council (2016), 'Report on best practices and lessons learned on how protecting and promoting human rights contribute to preventing and countering violent extremism', *United Nations Human Rights*, 21 July. Available online: https://ap.ohchr.org/documents/dpage_e.aspx?si=A/HRC/33/29 (accessed 15 June 2022).

Ivanova, E. (ed) (2017), *Muslims in Bulgaria: Dynamics and Attitudes*. Sofia: New Bulgarian University.

Ivanova, E. (2019), 'Lawmaking as an Experiment', Балканистичен Форум, 2: 277–94.

Ivanova, E. (ed) (2020), *Religion as a Crime – Bulgaria's Islamic State*. Sofia: New Bulgarian University.

Jukic, E. (2015), 'Bosnian Serb Police Sweep Alleged Terrorist Cells', *Balkan Insight*, 7 May. Available online: https://balkaninsight.com/2015/05/07/bosnian-serb-police-tackle-alleged-terrorist-cells/ (accessed 12 February 2022).

Kapidžić, D., A. Dudić, V. Kadić and S. Turčalo (2020), *National Approaches to Extremism: Bosnia and Herzegovina*, CONNEKT Country Reports, 21 December. Available online: https://h2020connekt.eu/wpcontent/uploads/2021/01/Bosnia_CONNEKT_Approaches_to_extremism.pdf (accessed 1 April 2022).

Kohlmann, E. F. (ed) (2004), *Al-Qaida's Jihad in Europe: The Afghan-Bosnian Network*. Oxford: Berg Publishers.

Kuloglija, N. (2022), 'Bosnian Counter-Terrorism Strategy Delayed by Dispute over "Right-Wing"', *Balkan Insight*, 27 January. Available online: https://balkaninsight.com/2022/01/27/bosnian-counter-terrorism-strategy-delayed-by-dispute-over-right-wing/ (accessed 12 February 2022).

Lalov, N. (2013), 'Bulgaria Officially Convicted Hezbollah for the Attack in Burgas', *Mediapool*, 5 February. Available online: https://www.mediapool.bg/bulgaria-ofitsialno-obvini-hizbula-za-atentata-v-burgas-news202505.html (accessed 30 June 2022).

Li, D. (2019), *The Universal Enemy: Jihad, Empire, and the Challenge of Solidarity*. Stanford: Stanford University Press.

Lilyanova, V. (2017), 'Saudi Arabia in the Western Balkans', European Parliamentary Research Service, 17 November. Available online: https://www.europarl.europa.eu/thinktank/en/document/EPRS_ATA(2017)614582 (accessed 15 June 2022).

Mancheva, M. (2019), *Country Report: Bulgaria*, Horizon 2020 GREASE Project – Radicalization, Secularism and the Governance of Religion: Bringing Together European and Asian Perspectives. Available online: http://grease.eui.eu/wp-content/uploads/sites/8/2019/11/Bulgaria-Report.pdf (accessed 30 June 2022).

Mancheva, M. and R. Dzhekova (2017), *Working Paper: Risks of Islamist Radicalization in Bulgaria: A Case Study in the Iztok Neighbourhood of the City of Pazardzhik*, Center for the Study of Democracy, 28 February. Available online: https://csd.bg/publications/publication/risks-of-islamist-radicalization-in-bulgaria-a-case-study-in-the-iztok-neighbourhood-of-the-city-of/ (accessed 30 June 2022).

Mejdini, F. (2015), 'Uncontrolled Mosques Proliferate in Albania', *Balkan Insight*, 17 December. https://balkaninsight.com/2015/12/17/state-slams-albanian-muslim-over-uncontrolled-mosques-12-17-2015/ (accessed 8 October 2024).

Mejdini, F. (2016a), 'Religious Education Plan Worries Albania's Teachers', *Balkan Insight*, 12 April. Available online: https://balkaninsight.com/2016/04/12/religion-in-public-schools-sparks-debates-in-albania-04-11-2016/ (accessed 15 June 2022).

Mejdini, F. (2016b), 'Albania Starts to Legalize Unofficial Mosques', *Balkan Insight*, 2 September. Available online: https://balkaninsight.com/2016/09/02/albania-starts-the-muslim-properties-legalisation-09-01-2016/ (accessed 15 June 2022).

Metodieva, A. (2021), 'The Radical Milieu and Radical Influencers of Bosnian Foreign Fighters', *Studies in Conflict & Terrorism*, https://doi.org/10.1080/1057610X.2020.1868097.

Mishkova, D., S. Evstatiev, E. Bećirević, S. Doklev, K. Gashi, M. Ignjatijević, S. Kelmendi, P. Petrović, A. Sadiku, R. Shehu and E. Stanchev (2021), *Working Paper on Enabling Environments, Drivers, and Occurrence/Non-occurrence of Violent Extremism*. PREVEX: Preventing Violent Extremism, 31 December. Available online: https://www.prevex-balkan-mena.eu/wp-content/uploads/2021/12/D5.2-final.pdf (accessed 26 February 2022).

Mustapha, J. (2013), 'The Mujahideen in Bosnia: The Foreign Fighter as Cosmopolitan Citizen and/or Terrorist', *Citizenship Studies*, 17 (6–7): 742–55.

National Assembly of the Republic of Bulgaria (2015), *Constitution*, Available at: https://www.parliament.bg/en/const (accessed 23 May 2023).

National Statistical Institute (2021), *Census 2021*, Available online: https://infostat.nsi.bg/infostat/pages/module.jsf?x_2=338 (accessed 4 November 2024).

Nikodimov, I. (2019), 'A 16-Year-Old Was Preparing a Terrorist Attack in Plovdiv', *BNT News*, 8 June. Available online: https://bntnews.bg/bg/a/16-godishen-podgotvyal-atentat-v-plovdiv (accessed 30 June 2022).

Nikolov, Y. (2004), 'The Emissaries Come First', *Capital*, 14 August. Available online: https://www.capital.bg/politika_i_ikonomika/bulgaria/2004/08/14/227488_purvi_idvat_emisarite/ (accessed 30 June 2022).

Novinite.com (2017) 'The police arrested a commander from Islamic State in special operation in Sofia (video)', 13 October. *Novinite.com*. Available online: https://www.novinite.com/articles/184264/The+Police+Arrested+a+Commander+from+Islamic+State+in+Special+Operation+in+Sofia+%28Video%29 (accessed 20 November 2024).

Official Gazette of Bosnia and Herzegovina (2014), *Law Amending the Criminal Code of Bosnia and Herzegovina*, Available online: http://www.ohr.int/ohr-dept/legal/laws-of-bih/pdf/New2015/BH%20Law%20Amending%20the%20CC%2047-14.pdf (accessed 17 February 2022).

Öktem, K. (2010), *New Islamic Actors after the Wahhabi Intermezzo: Turkey's Return to the Muslim Balkans*. Oxford: European Studies Centre, University of Oxford.

OSCE –Albania (1998), *1998 Constitution of the Republic of Albania*, Available at: https://www.osce.org/albania/41888?download=true (accessed 23 May 2023).

Preljević, H. (2017), 'Preventing Religious Radicalization in Bosnia and Herzegovina: The Role of the BiH Islamic Community', *Journal of Muslim Minority Studies*, 37 (4): 371–92.

Prislan, K., A. Černigoj and B. Lobnikar (2018), 'Preventing Radicalization in the Western Balkans: The Role of the Police Using a Multi-Stakeholder Approach', *Revija za kriminalistiko in kriminologijo*, 4: 257–68.

Qirjazi, R. and R. Shehu (2018), *Community Perspectives on Preventing Violent Extremism in Albania*, Berghof Foundation and Institute for Democracy and Mediation. Available online: https://berghof-foundation.org/library/community-perspectives-on-preventing-violent-extremism-in-albania (accessed 15 June 2022).

Refworld (1994), *Constitution of the Federation of Bosnia and Herzegovina*, Available at: https://www.refworld.org/docid/3ae6b56e4.html (accessed 23 May 2023).

Schilbrack, K. (2022), *The Concept of Religion*, Stanford Encyclopedia of Philosophy. Available online: https://plato.stanford.edu/entries/concept-religion/ (accessed 23 May 2023).

Shentov, O., B. Todorov and A. Stoyanov (2015), *Radicalization in Bulgaria: Threats and Trends*, Center for the Study of Democracy, 15 November. Available online: https://csd.bg/publications/publication/radicalization-in-bulgaria-threats-and-trends/ (accessed 30 June 2022).

Spassov, T. (2017), 'What Is behind the "First Terrorism Sentence" in Bulgaria?', *Dvenik*, 7 June. Available online: https://www.dnevnik.bg/bulgaria/2017/06/07/2984042_kakvo_se_krie_zad_purvata_prisuda_za_terorizum_u_nas/ (accessed 30 June 2022).

Stojlova, Z. (2016), 'Roma and the Radicals: The Alleged Bulgarian Support of IS', *Balkan Insight*, 11 January. Available online: https://balkaninsight.com/bg/2016/01/11/romite-i-radikalite-predpolagaemata-b-lgarska-podkrepa-za-idil-01-10-2016/ (accessed 30 June 2022).

Stoynova, N., S. Ralchev and R. Dzhekova (2021), *Connekt Country Papers on Macro-Level Drivers: Bulgaria*, CONNEKT Country Reports, July. Available online: https://h2020connekt.eu/wp-content/uploads/2021/09/Bulgaria_CONNEKT_Macro_Drivers.pdf (accessed 30 June 2022).

The Prosecutor's Office of Bosnia and Herzegovina (n.d), *Task Force for Fight against Terrorism and Strengthening Capacities for Fight against Terrorism*. Available online: https://tuzilastvobih.gov.ba/?opcija=sadrzaj&kat=3&id=7&jezik=e (accessed 30 September 2022).

Todorov, A. (2021), *Radicalization of the Non-Acceptance: Group Hatred and Extremist Far-Right Sentiments in Bulgaria*, Friedrich Ebert Stiftung. Available online: https://bulgaria.fes.de/fileadmin/user_upload/documents/publications/2021/Grupova_omraza_i_djasno-ekstremistki_naglasi_v_Bulgaria_WEB_BG.pdf (accessed 30 June 2022).

Toè, R. (2016), 'Bosnia Struggles to Control "Rebel" Mosques', *Balkan Insight*, 26 April. Available online: https://balkaninsight.com/2016/04/26/bosnian-islamic-community-struggling-to-control-parallel-mosques-04-25-2016/.

Triandafyllidou, A., H. Gülap, M. Iliyasov, G. Mahajan and E. Racius (2019), *Concept Paper: Nation and Religion – Reflections on Europe, the MENA Region and South Asia*, Horizon 2020 GREASE Project – Radicalization, Secularism and the Governance of Religion: Bringing Together European and Asian Perspectives. Available online: http://grease.eui.eu/wp-content/uploads/sites/8/2019/05/GREASE-concept-paper_D1.3_Nation-and-Religion_30May2019_FINAL1-2.pdf (accessed 15 June 2022).

Troeva, E. (2012), '"Traditional" and "New" Islam in Bulgaria', *Bulgarian Folklore*, 3–4: 5–23.

Tzvetkova, G. and M. Mancheva. (2019), *Country Report: Bosnia and Herzegovina*, Horizon 2020 GREASE Project – Radicalization, Secularism and the Governance of Religion: Bringing Together European and Asian Perspectives. Available online: http://grease.eui.eu/wp-content/uploads/sites/8/2019/11/Bosnis-and-Herzegovina-Report.pdf (accessed 20 June 2022).

UNODC (United Nations Office on Drugs and Crime) (2018), '*Radicalization*' and '*Violent Extremism*'. Available online: https://www.unodc.org/e4j/zh/terrorism/module-2/key-issues/radicalization-violent-extremism.html#:~:text=Some%20commentators%20have%20suggested%20that,7%2D8 (accessed 15 June 2022).

U.S. Department of State (2021), '*2021 Report on International Religious Freedom: Albania*'. Available online: https://www.state.gov/reports/2021-report-on-international-religious-freedom/albania/ (accessed 17 May 2023).

Vrugtman, L. (2019), *Future Challenges of Violent Extremism in the Western Balkans*, PREVEX: Preventing Violent Extremism. Available online: https://www.prevex-balkan-mena.eu/future-challenges-of-violent-extremism-in-the-western-balkans/ (accessed 29 June 2022).

Vrugtman, L. (2021), *The EU and Other Stakeholders' Prevention Strategies towards VE in Albania*, PREVEX: Preventing Violent Extremism. Available online: https://www.prevex-balkan-mena.eu/wp-content/uploads/2021/01/Prevex-Policy-Paper-PCVE-in-Albania-final-for-web-2.pdf (accessed 26 February 2022).

Vurmo, G. (2015), *Religious Radicalism and Violent Extremism in Albania*, Institute of Democracy and Mediation. Available online: https://idmalbania.org/wp-content/uploads/2021/11/Religious-Radicalism-Albania-web-final.pdf (accessed 15 June 2022).

Vurmo, G. and E. Sulstarova (2018), *Violent Extremism in Albania: A National Assessment of Drivers, Forms and Threats*, Institute for Democracy and Mediation. Available online: https://idmalbania.org/wp-content/uploads/2021/11/Study_Violent-Extremism-in-Albania-2018-web-1.pdf (accessed 15 June 2022).

Yakova, L. (2019), *Country Report: Albania*, Center for the Study of Democracy, Available online: http://grease.eui.eu/wp-content/uploads/sites/8/2019/11/Alb%D0%B0nia-Report.pdf (accessed 26 February 2022).

Yakova, L. and V. Bogdanova (2022), *Preventing Religiously Motivated Radicalization: Lessons from South-Eastern Europe*, Horizon 2020 GREASE Project – Radicalization, Secularism and the Governance of Religion: Bringing Together European and Asian Perspectives. Available online: https://cadmus.eui.eu/bitstream/handle/1814/74548/QM-AX-22-012-EN-N.pdf?sequence=1&isAllowed=y (accessed 15 June 2022).

Zhelyazkova, A. (2014), 'Bulgaria', in J. Cesari (ed), *Oxford Handbook of European Islam*, 565–616, Oxford: Oxford University Press.

Zosak, S. (2010), 'Revoking Citizenship in the Name of Counterterrorism: The Citizenship Review Commission Violates Human Rights in Bosnia and Herzegovina', *Northwestern Journal of International Human Rights*, 8 (2): 216–32.

6

The determinants of radicalization in Russia: Is religion to blame?

Marat Iliyasov

Introduction

'We pledge our allegiance …' starts a childish voice behind a camera. Four boys with knives in their hands stand in front of a yellow wall and repeat after the group's leader, who can't be seen: 'To the Amir of true believers Abu Bakr Al Baghdadi' (Caucasian Knot 2018). The youngest of the teenagers is only eleven years old and the oldest eighteen. The video became public only after members of the group knife-attacked police officers in different locations in Chechnya on 20 August 2018. Four of the attackers were killed on the spot, and the fifth was wounded and died in hospital. Before being taken down, the boys managed to wound five police officers.

Three months before this, shouts of 'Allah Akbar' (Arabic for 'God is great') and gunshots interrupted the calm service at the Orthodox Church of Archangel Mikhail in Chechnya's capital Grozny. Only the quick reaction of the priest, Father Sergiy, and a member of the congregation prevented a bloodbath. They managed to close the heavy door of the church, saving those attending liturgy. Two police officers and a civilian were killed, while several others were wounded. Special forces units eventually arrived and gunned down the shooters. The attackers were eighteen- and nineteen-year-old inhabitants of Chechnya and Ingushetia with an arsenal of ten Molotov cocktails, a sawn-off shotgun, knives and small axes (BBC 2018). 'They were very young, did not even have beards', said Father Sergiy to journalists (Svoboda 2018). Law enforcement treated this as a terrorist attack, assigning responsibility for it to the Islamic State (IS).

This was the second attack on an Orthodox church in the North Caucasus in 2018. The first one happened in the Dagestan town of Kizlyar, where a 22-year-old man killed five women. He also left behind a video address with a reference to IS (BBC 2018). A fourth attack of this kind occurred on 31 December 2019. Some hours before New Year's Eve celebrations, three young men rammed police officers with their car at the entrance of Ingushetia's capital Magas. They then jumped out of the vehicle and attacked nearby police officers. The officers opened fire, killing two attackers immediately and heavily wounding one. IS claimed responsibility for this attack (Novaya Gazeta 2021).

All four attacks occurred within two years in the mostly Islamic region of the North Caucasus. They were all treated as terrorist acts, the most common expression of radicalization in the region. In each case, the attackers targeted either Orthodox Churches or police forces, both these institutions representing Russia in the minds of the attackers, which some North Caucasians perceive as a foreign and hostile state. Drawing on analysis of the historical and socio-economic context and semi-structured interviews with experts, mullahs and ordinary inhabitants of the North Caucasus, this chapter examines whether Islam contributes to radicalization in the region. First, it explains why the focus of this research concentrates on the North Caucasus. After that, the chapter turns to how the term 'radicalization' is conceptualized and describes the research methodology used in the study on which this discussion is based. The final section of the chapter analyses the factors of radicalization identified by other scholars and interviewees. I conclude that the threat of Islamist radicalization in Russia up until the rise of Islamic State in 2014 was mostly determined by the consequences of the Russo–Chechen war, even though other factors also played a role.

Why the North Caucasus?

The North Caucasian Federal District of Russia is worthy of analysis in thinking about the relationship between religion and radicalization in Russia for five reasons. First, the region is largely Muslim, which, in the context of global trends, makes it more vulnerable to security concerns about Islamist radicalization in the eyes of the state. The district consists of seven units, six of which are national republics. In five of them, ethnic Muslims constitute most of the population. In total, there are approximately seven million inhabitants in the region who profess Islam (see Table 6.1), making up roughly half of Russia's Muslim population and 70 per cent of the total population of the North Caucasus (RosStat 2022). In comparison to other Muslim republics in Russia (Tatarstan and Bashkortostan), the North Caucasians are more devout. Much of the population practised Islam even under atheist Soviet rule (Akhmadov, Bowers and Doss 2001). In other words, there is only a small percentage of people who can be identified as 'ethnic' Muslims – those born into Muslim families but who do not observe the religious commands. After the dissolution of the Soviet Union in 1991 and the revival of religion, the region became even more overtly Islamized (Halbach 2001). The majority practices Sufi Islam, which is apolitical and is adapted to the local traditions.

The second factor is the significance of the two Russo–Chechen wars of 1994–1996 and 1999–2009. A recent study by Klimentov (2021) established the connection between these wars and radicalization. According to Klimentov (2021), the peaks of terrorist activities in Russia correspond to the most active phases of these wars (1995–1996 and 2000–2004, respectively). These wars radicalized a part of the Chechen population, who then fell under the influence of foreign fighters and missionaries who supported politically radicalized interpretations of Salafi Islam, such as Sheikh Fatkhi or Amir Khattab (Al-Shishani 2006, Moore and Tumelty 2008).

Table 6.1 The units of Russian Federation with significant muslim populations

Federal Unit	Ethnic Muslims (%)	Others (%)
Moscow	364,667 (3.08%)	11,503,501 (96.92%)
Dagestan (N. Caucasus)	2,793,179 (95.97%)	117,070 (4.03%)
Chechnya (N. Caucasus)	1,241,377 (97.82%)	27,612 (2.18%)
Ingushetia (N. Caucasus)	408,625 (99.05%)	3,904 (0.95%)
North Ossetia (N. Caucasus)	62,496 (8.77%)	650,484 (91.23%)
Kabardino-Balkaria (N. Caucasus)	633,993 (73.72%)	225,946 (26.27%)
Karachaevo-Cherkessia (N. Caucasus)	315,820 (66.09%)	162,039 (33.91%)
Bashkortostan	2,306,392 (56.63%)	1,765,900 (43.37%)
Tatarstan	2,064,877 (54.53%)	1,721,611 (45.47%)

Source: Russia Census (2010) Due to the corrupt nature of the Russian census of 2020, updates are not available.

The third factor is related to the number of terrorist attacks in the North Caucasus or attacks committed by those from the region elsewhere in Russia. Many agree that since 1991, terrorism in Russia has largely emanated from the North Caucasus. As Sinai (2015: 96) puts it, 'Russia's primary terrorist threats originate in the turbulent North Caucasus's republics of Chechnya, Dagestan, Ingushetia, and Kabardino-Balkariya, where extremist ethnonationalist and Islamist militants have been waging an insurgency for the past decades against Russian rule.' Indeed, according to Klimentov's (2021) calculations, North Caucasians committed ninety-nine deadly terrorist attacks on Russia's territory outside of the North Caucasus between 1992 and 2018.

The fourth factor is the commonly assumed connection between the North Caucasus and terrorism in Russia. This link was firmly established by Russian media and politicians from the beginning of the second war in Chechnya in 1999. Following the official discourse, Russia's media largely framed that military campaign as anti-terrorist. Today, it is difficult to find a study that mentions terrorism in Russia without linking it to the North Caucasus and in particular to Chechnya (e.g. Klimentov 2021, Moore 2007, Yarlykapov 2017).

The fifth factor is related to the appearance and spread of Salafism, also commonly known as Wahhabism, in Russia. Since its first appearance in Russia in the early 1990s, this type of political Islam spread mostly in the North Caucasus and to some extent facilitated the radicalization of the local population during the wars in Chechnya. However, the popularity of Salafism did not overtake traditionally practised Sufi Islam in the region. Many followers of Salafism participated in the last Russo-Chechen war of 1999–2009, even taking over the leadership of the Chechen resistance movement around 2006. The emergence of Salafism in other North Caucasian republics helped the Chechen resistance to reconceptualize the war from a conflict representing the

Chechen fight for independence from Russia into jihad (i.e. a religious war against infidels), which aimed to attract volunteers from the neighbouring republics. Today, with the North Caucasus largely pacified, both types of Islam cohabit in the region and in Russia, even if the followers of each despise each other. Russian officials and the leadership of the institutionalized, officially registered religious groups still perceive Salafism as a potential threat to the existing political system and governance of religion in the country, which sometimes results in the persecution of Salafism followers.

These five factors help contextualize why the Muslim population of the North Caucasus is the primary focus of scholarly research on terrorism and radicalization in Russia. Other reasons that may contribute to this focus include the perceived threat of Islamism often reiterated by journalists, politicians and experts around the world, foregrounding the risks and impacts of jihadist-inspired or attributed radicalization.

Conceptualizing radicalization

To analyse the phenomenon of radicalization, it is necessary to outline the exact meaning of the term. Besides the general need to define concepts, there are two specific problems that make such clarification necessary: the concept's elusiveness, and the diverse understandings of radicalization across states and societies. Both issues have existed at least since the term entered everyday usage between 2005 and 2007 (Sedgwick 2010). The concept's elusiveness stems in part from related problems in defining other adjunct phenomena like extremism and terrorism. It is more often the contexts and political agendas of entities such as international organizations, states, non-government organizations (NGOs) that determine the ways in which radicalization is defined, described or understood (Kundnani 2012, Rae 2012). Besides the variety of definitions that different institutions or political organizations adopt, every individual has their perceptions and understanding of the concept, as Coolsaet, Ravn and Sauer (2019) note. This diversity of definitions and perceptions can result in confusion and disagreement rather than clarity and consensus.

Bearing in mind that a universally accepted definition is nearly impossible, this chapter draws on the solution suggested by Ramsay (2015), who advocates for using *ad hoc* definitions designed for specific cases. This approach narrows down the analysis to one or two facets of the phenomenon, avoiding complications and ambiguities associated with generalization and inclusivity. There are indeed some characteristics that are commonly agreed on by scholars who have attempted to define radicalization.

The first characteristic of radicalization is that it is a process. Rapidly changing realities or an individual's search for self-identity often serve as a trigger for initiation of the process (Della Porta 2018, Doosje et al. 2016, Tkhostov and Surnov 2005). The second characteristic that scholars agree on is that radicalization processes take a long time, undergo different stages and do not necessarily result in obvious violent or other action (Doosje et al. 2016, Sedgwick 2010). In other words, radicalization may be manifested only verbally or remain completely unexpressed. The third point of agreement is that radicalization's action may or may not involve violence (Coolsaet, Ravn and Sauer 2019, Moskalenko and McCauley 2009). Githens-Mazer (2012) uses the example of protest movements, where organized rallies express radical ideas but do not resort to violence. This brings up the fourth point, which is the lawfulness of expressions of radicalization. Indeed, some radical expressions can be completely legal depending on a country's legislation (Githens-Mazer 2009). The fifth and final characteristic is that radicalization may be informed by a cultural-psychological disposition that can be politically, ideologically or religiously shaped or charged (Coolsaet, Ravn and Sauer 2019, Kundnani 2012).

These characteristics demonstrate the difficulty of pinpointing causal factors for radicalization and of identifying radicalized individuals if they do not speak or act out. This problem is especially true in the context of authoritarianism, where free expression is severely limited. Therefore, this chapter focuses exclusively on radicalized individuals' physical actions, rather than statements or narratives, in Russia. Moreover, the context of authoritarianism necessitates the exclusion of all legal and non-violent actions from the analysis, leaving in focus only those classified as terrorism in Russia. Keeping in mind these characteristics and the focus of the analysis, this chapter defines radicalization as a process which is informed or impacted by different (personal, societal, structural, cultural) factors that encourage an individual to commit a terrorist attack in order to undermine the authority, power or legitimacy of an existing political and/or social order.

Having defined radicalization for the purpose of this analysis, it is also important to understand how it happens. Scholars have different ideas about how the process of radicalization evolves, what its components are and what motivates people to radicalize. For instance, Borum's (2011) model refers to four stages of radicalization that often result in terrorism. According to this model, an individual develops a grievance about a personal predicament. After that, they start comparing their situation with that of others and decide their predicament is unfair. In the third stage, they identify a wrongdoer – usually a group or organization whom they believe is the cause of their suffering. In the final stage, an already radicalized individual dehumanizes and demonizes the 'enemy', legitimating their own violent action.

Doosje, Loseman and Van Den Bos (2013) identified four components that define radicalized individuals. The first component is their perception of authorities wielding illegitimate power (Loza 2007). The second component is related to their idea of the superiority of the in-group (Mazarr 2004). Third, radicals perceive a great distance between themselves and those who live differently (Doosje, Loseman and Van Den Bos 2013). Fourth, radicalized individuals feel societal disconnectedness, meaning that they do not consider themselves to be part of society (Mazarr 2004).

According to Hogg (2021), radicalization is more likely to happen when a person is in circumstances of uncertainty, whether financial, social or other. While an individual may see religion as an answer to their grievances, it does not necessarily inspire them to commit a terrorist attack. Kruglanski et al. (2014) specified that a person's inclination towards violence might depend on cultural factors such as high or low fatalism, strong or weak punishment for deviation from norms, collectivism versus individualism, high or low gender egalitarianism, and distance from a position of power. Collective cultures of high fatalism with strong social norms, low gender egalitarianism and greater distance from power are likely to increase the probability of radicalization and terrorism (2014).

This brief discussion demonstrates there are many variables and reasons behind radicalization. Scholars who analyse these factors agree that it is usually a complex mix of variables that propels radicalization and results in terrorism (Janeczko 2014). Following a brief section on the methodology used to gather the empirical data discussed here, I will return to examine the most commonly cited factors of radicalization in Russia.

The empirical study: Methodology

Many of the issues pertinent to the study of radicalization mentioned above inform the methodology of this research. As it is noted, it is difficult to identify a radicalized person in an authoritarian setting until they commit an act of violence. Even then, as Tikhonova et al. (2017) argue, the reasons behind a person's radicalization may not be so clear. A possible non-speculative source that could be used to determine the contours of radicalization process would be a statement left by an individual before committing an attack or, if available, a confession after the fact. However, without access to such data or to the attackers themselves, we are often left to identify and analyse the factors that may have facilitated radicalization in the North Caucasus drawing on secondary sources and expert interviews. Accordingly, the methodology here uses provisional hypotheses based on the existing literature about the factors salient to radicalization in Russia in the absence of such primary data from radicalized violent actors themselves.

To identify these factors, I first collected and analysed a range of scholarly and media-based secondary sources. Second, I conducted a total of twenty-three semi-structured interviews between January 2019 and May 2021, averaging about one hour and twenty minutes each, with experts and inhabitants of the North Caucasus. All interviewees consented to participation and were informed about their right to withdraw at any point. Stringent measures were adopted to protect identities, ensure anonymity and guarantee the security and encryption of stored data. Seven of the interviewees were experts affiliated with either independent non-government organizations or with Russian state universities.

I also interviewed five inhabitants from Dagestan, seven from Chechnya and four from Ingushetia. For almost twenty years, these three republics have been regarded as the cradle of religiously inspired terrorism in Russia. The interviewees from these North Caucasus republics were males aged between thirty-five and fifty-seven years old. All had either witnessed or participated in the Russo–Chechen wars. Because of cultural and religious sensitivities and the nature of the research topic, access to female informants in the region proved limited; due to this limitation, I interviewed only two female experts, both of whom were external to the region. In each republic, I interviewed one person who was working for or otherwise affiliated with the local government, one who represented institutionalized (i.e. officially registered and supported by the state) Islam, and one who represented non-institutionalized Islam. The remaining interviewees were representatives of the local intelligentsia (scholars, journalists and writers) recommended to me by gatekeepers.

All interviewees were asked to describe radicalization as they understood the phenomenon and to name the factors that can inform processes of radicalization in Russia. The experts external to the region, both men and women, identified the state's suppressive and discriminatory policies as a primary reason for radicalization. They defined the state's understanding of radicalism as people's readiness to participate in an action against the ruling power. Among such actions, they mentioned different forms of protests (rallies, strikes, road blockades, etc.), ethnic and religious clashes, and terrorism. Referring to the North Caucasus, they mostly described violent attacks as acts of despair rather than expressions of radicalism. They defined radicalization as a process that results in violent action against the state or an ethnic and/or religious group that is inspired by a political or religious ideology.

The representatives of the local authorities and of institutionalized Islam had a different perspective, saying that radicalization occurs due to the spread of Salafism and the missionary activities of the adherents of this branch of Islam in the North Caucasus. Radicalization for them, by definition, is associated with terrorism oriented against the state. They consider every adherent to Salafism to be a potential terrorist. To a large extent, the opinions of representatives of non-institutionalized Islam and the intelligentsia coincided with those of the external experts. They blamed state policies for radicalization but defined it mostly as a violent action against the state without referring to ideological background or context.

Factors of Islamist radicalization in Russia

Russo–Chechen wars

As mentioned above, the current wave of radicalization in the North Caucasus is usually associated with the Russo–Chechen wars of 1994–6 and 1999–2009. Scholars agree that the first war Islamized Chechnya and the second war radicalized its population (Hertog 2005, Radnitz 2006). The Russian military's harsh methods were, according to Toft and Zhukov (2012), an apparent factor for the radicalization of locals and the surge in terrorism. The phenomenon of female suicide bombings was one consequence of this conflict (Speckhard and Akhmedova 2006), demonstrating the desperation of people losing their families at the hands of the Russian military (Kurz and Bartles 2007). As Wilhelmsen (2005) argues, the wars, which spilled over the borders of Chechnya, also influenced radicalization trends in the neighbouring North Caucasian republics. Meanwhile in Chechnya, Russia's Chechenization policy, whereby a government loyal to Moscow was established during the second war, also provided a strong impetus for radicalization because of the state's heavy-handed suppression of dissent (Russell 2008, Souleimanov 2015). In other words, it was not religious ideology per se but loss and grievances that primarily encouraged people to join the armed resistance and resort to suicidal terrorist attacks (Speckhard and Akhmedova 2006). The following excerpt from a project interviewee echoes this conclusion and suggests the war itself radicalized people, whereas jihadists simply provided them with the means to retaliate:

It depends on what kind of radicalization you are talking about and in what period. The radicalization and terrorism in the late 1990s and the early 2000s were connected to the Chechen wars. It is questionable if religion played an important role, though. The motivation might have been different. Many people who joined Chechen jihadism were driven by the grief that they felt due to the loss of loved ones. It was easy to recruit them to commit a terrorist attack, even if suicidal. However, the true motivation of these people was probably revenge, or incapability to cope with trauma.

(Interview with expert, Moscow, 2019)

Other experts expressed similar opinions. They also attributed the rise of radicalism in the regions to the two Russo–Chechen wars and the suppressive policies of the state, which they thought pushed individuals to commit terrorist attacks or join the resistance out of despair. The opinion expressed by adherents of non-institutionalized Islam (Salafists) and local intelligentsia largely coincided with the position of the experts presented above. In contrast, representatives of Russia's institutionalized Sufi Islam community followed official propaganda in blaming Salafism and the West for radicalizing the population:

It is all because of Wahhabism [Salafism]. Do you remember, in the 1990s, many foreign mullahs came to the North Caucasus to teach us Islam? They were agents sent by the West, which wanted to repeat the same [thing in Russia] they did to the Soviet Union. Their influence grew much stronger during the first war [Russo–Chechen war of 1994–6] and then they almost took over the power in Chechnya. If not for Russia, they were ready to overthrow [Aslan] Maskhadov [president of Chechnya from 1997] and then to move on. They attacked Dagestan and started a new war in Chechnya, then they announced their goal to create an Islamic Emirate of the Caucasus.

(Interview with institutionalized cleric, Chechnya, 2020)

These comments also reflect, to a large extent, the opinions of the public. Many Chechens, especially those who are not connected to the current elite, assign responsibility for radicalization in the North Caucasus to the Russo–Chechen wars, blaming either the state or the spread of Salafism.

Domestic politics and legislation

Dannreuther (2010) provides a comprehensive analysis of Russian domestic politics and factors that may have potentially facilitated Islamist radicalization in Russia. However, as Verkhovski (2010) argues, it is unlikely they would result in mass radicalization without the Russo–Chechen wars, which prompted marginalization and persecution of Salafists (Hughes 2013, Johnston and Alimi 2012, Kroupenev 2009). Adherents of Salafism were considered the only political and religious movement that could challenge the power of regional authorities between 2007 and the early 2010s. The decision to sanction their persecution, however, opened up another opportunity for abuses of power and encouraged further radicalization of the population. Two experts and three inhabitants of the North Caucasus who were interviewed said that law enforcement often abused their power for personal gain:

> Who is an extremist in Russia today? An extremist is the one who was assigned this label. It is up to *siloviki* [the law enforcers] to make one an extremist if they want to. The[ir] reasons might be different. Maybe they did not like what you have written on your Facebook page, or maybe they just wanted to show the efficiency of their work, which means another star on their epaulets and more money. In either case, no one is guaranteed that tomorrow he will not appear on the list of the wanted. Of course, people are upset with this situation, and having in mind the Caucasian 'hot blood', it is possible to understand why the youth are taking up arms so willingly.
> (Interview with inhabitant of Dagestan, 2019)

The negative attitude towards Muslims who belong to Salafist non-institutionalized organizations or groups was similar all over Russia in the early 2000s but has more recently improved significantly in Moscow and the Volga region (Tatarstan and Bashkortostan) since 2010. There were even attempts to incorporate Salafist Muslims into official Islamic institutions in some places, but not in the North Caucasus, where relations between the authorities and non-institutionalized Muslims remain tense (Sokirianskaia 2019). By the early 2010s, policies softened even in the North Caucasus. The regional authorities in the North Caucasus relied on the formula that the practice of Salafi Islam is not forbidden as long as it is not public or political:

> You are free to do what you want, to pray as you want, as long as you do not spread your ideas or do not blame the officials in being the followers of incorrect Islam. Do what you do silently, without advertising it, and you will be alright.
> (Interview with institutionalized cleric, Chechnya, 2020)

This observation suggests that what authorities are most sensitive to is Salafism's political edge. When blunted, they do not see it as a serious threat to power.

Foreign politics

In terms of foreign politics, as Dannreuther (2010) reminds us, Russia has, through the legacy of the Soviet Union, supported some Islamist movements in the Middle East (e.g. Hamas, Hezbollah) but also waged an 'anti-Islamic' war in Afghanistan (1979–89). This legacy could conceivably have produced mixed feelings among Russian Muslims. However, none of my interviewees referenced Soviet foreign politics. Nor is this factor often raised in public discourse, making it questionable whether foreign politics is in fact an important contributor to radicalization in Russia. As the previous analysis suggests, the radicalization of Russian Muslims acquired an Islamist component only after the initial experience of personal grievance or loss. Were this not the case, the suffering of the *ummah* (Arabic for the world's Muslim community) would be sufficient motivation to take up arms or resort to terrorism, which did not initially occur in

Russia. Only later, with the appearance of IS on the world scene, did this become a significant factor. Dannreuther (2010) notes that under Boris Yeltsin's presidency (1991–9) there was little evidence that Russian Muslims were considered vulnerable to Islamic radicalization. Moreover, even during the Chechen wars, radicalization was not linked to religion (Wilhelmsen 2005). In other words, the interaction between the state and Muslims was upsetting enough to radicalize people without the religious dimension playing a role.

This situation began to change in 2014, however, when the Islamist-turned-armed-resistance in the North Caucasus pledged its allegiance to IS (Sagramoso and Yarlykapov 2020). The rise of IS opened a new avenue for the resistance, which had been losing ground. This change can be attributed in part to the initial military and administrative success of IS and its propaganda campaign (Al-Tamimi 2014). The movement of Caucasian fighters (and civilians unhappy with Russia's politics) to the Middle East was also encouraged both by IS's successful propaganda (Sagramoso and Yarlykapov 2020) and by Russia's military involvement in the Syrian conflict. Both factors contributed to the idea that Russia, like most other non-Muslim countries, is waging war against Islam. This perception of Russia was common across some of the interviewed North Caucasians and non-institutionalized clerics from the region:

> Russia hates Muslims. Look what [Russians] do in Idlib [a province of Syria]. They do not even try to distinguish the civil population from the rebels. They bomb everyone. They pretend to be anti-American, anti-Western, or anti-Semites, but in fact, all that they do indicates the opposite. All their policies in the Middle East are in line with the general Judeo-Christian vision, which aims to suppress Muslims.
> (Interview with an inhabitant of Chechnya, 2020)

Until the appearance of IS on the world stage, it was questionable whether the radicalization of Russia's Muslims was religious in any essential way. However, after 2014, the religious element became more salient in understandings of transnational radicalization processes. The desire to be a part of the IS project and to avenge the *ummah*, coupled with extant personal grievances, can be said to have contributed to radicalization without being identified as a primary cause.

Socio-economic and psychological factors

In addition to the factors covered above, there are a number of other factors that can be attributed to people's psychological states and socio-economic realities of the region. For instance, one of the most important drivers of radicalization identified by North Caucasian participants is the feeling of being second-class citizens in Russia:

> It is difficult to live in Russia, especially for people from other places. Russians are very xenophobic. They label us as 'black-ass' and Central Asians as 'narrow-eyed', let alone more humiliating names for Armenians, Azerbaijanis, etc. They hate others and do not consider them as humans. Even if I am a Russian citizen, I do not feel at home in Russia, because I am from the Caucasus and because I

am Muslim. The only option for me is to answer aggression with aggression. I do not expect justice from the Russian police. They have the same attitude. They do not even investigate if a person from the Caucasus or Central Asia dies.
(Interview with an inhabitant of Chechnya, 2019)

This assessment from a male in his fifties cannot be taken as wholly representative of all ethnic, professional, gender or age groups in the North Caucasus. However, such views are reasonably widespread and find support in scholarly analyses of hate crimes in Russia (Arnold 2015), which skyrocketed between 2004 and 2009 (Tarasov 2006, Verkhovskiy, Kolstø and Blakkisrud 2018). Although the number of hate crimes began to steadily reduce after 2009, recent data suggest that xenophobic attitudes are still widespread in Russia (Light 2010, Vendina 2013). In 2012, as many as 65 per cent of Russians supported the campaign to 'stop feeding the Caucasus' (Holland 2016). Such popular slogans capture a widespread attitude. As Judah (2013) observes, a majority of Russians view Chechens, Dagestanis and other North Caucasians as foreign immigrants, rather than fellow Russian citizens. This produces a counterreaction, leading to protests and troublesome public behaviour (Molodikova and Watt 2014: 135). The result is a spiral of escalation that can lead to radicalization and violence.

North Caucasians' sense of ostracism also stems from their unsatisfied demand for justice. The region's authorities and law enforcement are infamous for abusing power. In this context, the paradigm proposed by IS, which promises a return to the golden age of Islam with just rulers, may seem worth fighting or even dying for. People in the region also claim that the local tradition of vendetta contributes to spread of violence, but it is sometimes confused with radicalism (Kurz and Bartles 2007). For instance, one of Starodubrovskaya's (2013) respondents argues:

Today my father may be killed, somebody else's father may be killed, the same thing over and over, and people think of revenge, what to do. They would need arms. Where? Where to go? To the woods. People are driven to the woods by despair, because of what has been done – the impermissible and the forbidden – with their honour and dignity ... They have realized that those who did it to them represent this country, they will fight against this country and destroy everything it has. In other words, they don't even realize what consequences it might lead to.

In his narrative, this respondent Dagestan depicts how radical attitudes are formed. The arbitrariness of law enforcement denies people a dignified life, while the local tradition of vendetta drives either those directly humiliated or their relatives to revenge. By joining existing resistance groups, they gain access to weapons for retaliation. An individual seeking personal vengeance is automatically labelled a Salafist, which transforms them a *de facto* enemy of the state. The reflections of Staradubrovskaya's informant echo the observation of NGOs that much of the unrest in the region stems from the rampant violation of human rights, a climate of violence and the impunity of law enforcement to practice abuses of power (Human Rights Watch 2016). Dagestani expert Ruslan Gereyev observes further that North Caucasian youth would have found another channel to express their frustration with injustice, corruption, unemployment and nepotism if there was no Salafi ideology through which to frame their grievances (Aliyev 2013: 12).

According to recent research by Sokirianskaia (2020), the children of those who were involved in the Russo–Chechen conflict or were arrested for alleged terrorist activities are especially vulnerable. They are the primary target of the police and often suffer discrimination (2020: 1). Bearing in mind the collectivist culture and strong kinship networks of the North Caucasus, such targeting and discrimination can also contribute to the radicalization of their immediate family, relatives, friends and others in their local community networks (Molodikova and Watt 2014: 133).

Nepotism, corruption, high unemployment and low standards of living are also frequently cited factors influencing radicalization in the region. For instance, in 2014, the level of unemployment was 48.8 per cent in Ingushetia and 36.7 per cent in Chechnya (Trukhachev et al. 2014). As Holland (2016) documents, residents identify the economic situation as their primary concern. Economic deprivation often leads to social marginalization and political grievances, which, according to Aliyev (2013), motivates young men to join the regional insurgency. This problem has even been acknowledged by Russia's leadership (Holland 2016). However, neither significant investment in the region nor anti-corruption measures have helped to uproot radicalization. Indeed, recent data on recent terrorist attacks suggest some violent actors come from wealthy families or even from the families of officials, suggesting, in the words of Russian radicalization expert Akhmet Yarlykapov, that violent radicalization in Russia 'is not the terrorism of the poor anymore' (Dzhalilov 2020).

In summary, the foregoing analysis suggests that a range of socio-economic and psychological factors contributed to creating a sociopolitical environment that played a key role in facilitating radicalization in the North Caucasus. These factors include xenophobia, ethnic hatred, corruption, unemployment, social marginalization, discrimination and nepotism that Muslims from the North Caucasus face in Russia proper and from the power institutions in the region. Other factors at a broader population scale also come into play. These issues include the socio-ethnic homogenization of the region (Holland 2016), which gives people few opportunities to socialize and develop tolerance for other cultures; a rate of comparatively fast population growth and density in the North Caucasus, which increases competition for limited structural resources (Starodubrovskaya 2013, Iliyasov 2019); and the impact of structural changes undergone by both the state and society in Russia following the dissolution of the USSR (Starodubrovskaya 2013).

Conclusion

Researchers and policymakers generally agree there is a complex and unique mix of factors that determine the radicalization of each individual (McGilloway, Ghosh and Bhui 2015). Attempts to profile radicals or terrorists have proven futile (Fiala 2003, Schbley 2003, Rae 2012). However, this does not mean it is impossible to discern salient factors contributing to radicalization in particular contexts or settings, particularly in relation to broader social-ecological dynamics that can influence radicalization vulnerabilities. In the case of the North Caucasus, we may conclude the following. First, to a large extent, radicalization in the region is an outcome of the two Russo–Chechen wars, which produced a wide range of grievances among the local population. Second, up until the appearance of IS on the world stage, religion played only a minor (if any) role in the process. Later, the spread of Salafism in Russia facilitated radicalization by highlighting an unjust state system, the persecution of the believers and the promise of justice in this life or the next. Third, the appearance of IS propelled and inspired the terrorist action orientation of already radicalized individuals. Fourth, the upsurge of radicalization and terrorism in the North Caucasus is largely related to personal grievances and sense of injustice in relation to state law enforcement institutions, corruption, nepotism and economic factors. Finally, most of these grievances are linked, directly or indirectly, by radicalized individuals to the Russian state or its representatives in the region, as suggested by the fact that the main targets of terrorist attacks in this region are aimed at local police, politicians or Orthodox clerics and churches.

Even if the impact of social and psychological factors may appear less obvious than those connected to political or economic factors, their significance is nevertheless clear. Social and psychological factors are recognized by Russian media and were repeatedly mentioned by the project's interviewees. Feeling like second-class citizens or experiencing discrimination can be powerful drivers of radicalization. Indignation is also fuelled by knowing people who have suffered at the hands of the 'enemy', by the phenomenon of guilt by association for those with older relatives who collaborated with the state, by having relatives who participated in the resistance and died or were arrested and by the heroization of resistance and those who lead it, including those who resorted to terrorism.

All these factors, which do not emphasize religious motivation per se – despite, in the post-IS context, being framed by the promises and narratives of Islamist propaganda – have had a clear impact on radicalization in the North Caucasus. Yet the effects of Islamic State's rise and the consequences of this have also been made clear, among other things, by the number of combatants from the North Caucasus who fought in Syria and Iraq; Barrett (2017: 13) claims that at least 3,400 Russian citizens were recorded as fighting for IS in 2016. The struggles of the local resistance in the North Caucasus appear to have left few options for radicalized individuals to cope with their grievances beyond joining the global jihad.

How these interacting and complex factors will influence radicalization patterns in the Northern Caucus in the future is difficult to determine. But staying attuned to available evidence, remaining cognisant of the challenges of identifying potential pathways to radicalization and – crucially – looking at how such factors and dynamics manifest in specific geopolitical and religious contexts, remains an ongoing project for scholars and other actors working to counter violent radicalization in Russia.

Acknowledgement

I am immensely grateful to colleagues from the University of St. Andrews who read and commented on earlier drafts of this chapter. My biggest thanks go to Orts Lamroe for an amazing job of proofreading.

References

Akhmadov, Y., S. R. Bowers and M. T. Doss Jr. (2001), 'Islam in the North Caucasus', *The Journal of Social, Political, and Economic Studies*, 26 (3): 569.

Aliyev, H. (2013), 'Socio-Political and Socio-Economic Causes of Conflict Escalation in the North Caucasus', *Ethnopolitics*, 25, June: 1–31.

Al-Shishani, M. B. (2006), 'The Rise and Fall of Arab Fighters in Chechnya', in Howard, G. E. (ed), *Volatile Borderland: Russia and the North Caucasus*, 265–93, Washington, DC: Jamestown Foundation.

Al-Tamimi, A. J. (2014), 'The Dawn of the Islamic State of Iraq and Ash-Sham', *Current Trends in Islamist Ideology*, 16 (5): 5–15.

Arnold, R. (2015), 'Systematic Racist Violence in Russia between "Hate Crime" and "Ethnic Conflict"', *Theoretical Criminology*, 19 (2): 239–56.

Barrett, R. (2017), *Beyond the Caliphate: Foreign Fighters and the Threat of Returnees*. New York: The Soufan Center. Available online: https://thesoufancenter.org/wp-content/uploads/2017/11/Beyond-the-Caliphate-Foreign-Fighters-and-the-Threat-of-Returnees-TSC-Report-October-2017-v3.pdf (accessed 6 October 2022).

British Broadcasting Corporation (BBC) (2018), Napadenie na pravoslavnyi khram v Groznom, est' pogibshi, 19 May. Available online: https://www.bbc.com/russian/news-44183929 (accessed 20 June 2022).

Borum, R. (2011), 'Radicalization into Violent Extremism II: A Review of Conceptual Models and Empirical Research', *Journal of Strategic Security*, 4 (4): 37–62.

Caucasian Knot (2018), Video prisyagi IG chechenskih podrostkov opublikovano v Internete, 22 August. Available online: https://www.kavkaz-uzel.eu/articles/324457/ (accessed 12 June 2020).

Coolsaet, R., S. Ravn and T. Sauer (2019), 'Rethinking Radicalization: Addressing the Lack of a Contextual Perspective in the Dominant Narratives on Radicalization', in N. Clycq, C. Timmerman, D. Vanheule, R. Van Caudenberg and S. Ravn (eds), *Radicalisation: A Marginal Phenomenon or a Mirror to Society?*, 21–46, Leuven: Leuven University Press.

Dannreuther, R. (2010), 'Islamic Radicalization in Russia: An Assessment', *International Affairs*, 86 (1): 109–26.

Della Porta, D. (2018), 'Radicalization: A Relational Perspective', *Annual Review of Political Science*, 21: 461–74.

Doosje, B., A. Loseman and K. Van Den Bos (2013), 'Determinants of Radicalization of Islamic Youth in the Netherlands: Personal Uncertainty, Perceived Injustice, and Perceived Group Threat', *Journal of Social Issues*, 69 (3): 586–604.

Doosje, B., F. M. Moghaddam, A. W. Kruglanski, A. De Wolf, L. Mann and A. R. Feddes (2016), 'Terrorism, Radicalization and De-radicalization', *Current Opinion in Psychology*, 11: 79–84.

Dzhalilov, R. (2020), Analytiki ukazali skhozhest ataki v Magase s drugimi napadeniyami pod brendom IG, 4 January. Available online: https://www.kavkaz-uzel.eu/articles/344290/ (accessed 23 February 2020).

Fiala, I. J. (2003), 'Anything New? The Racial Profiling of Terrorists', *Criminal Justice Studies: A Critical Journal of Crime, Law and Society*, 16 (1): 53–8.

Githens-Mazer, J. (2009), 'Causal Processes, Radicalization and Bad Policy: The Importance of Case Studies of Radical Violent Takfiri Jihadism for Establishing Logical Causality', American Political Science Association Annual Meeting, Toronto, September 3–6.

Githens-Mazer, J. (2012), 'The Rhetoric and Reality: Radicalization and Political Discourse', *International Political Science Review*, 33 (5): 556–67.

Halbach, U. (2001), 'Islam in the North Caucasus', *Archives de Sciences Sociales des Religions*, 115 (3): 93–110.

Hertog, K. (2005), 'A Self-fulfilling Prophecy: The Seeds of Islamic Radicalisation in Chechnya'. *Religion, State and Society*, 33 (3): 239–52.

Hogg, M. A. (2021), 'Self-uncertainty and Group Identification: Consequences for Social Identity, Group Behavior, Intergroup Relations, and Society', in Gawronski, B. (ed), *Advances in Experimental Social Psychology*, Vol. 64, 263–316, Cambridge, MA: Academic Press.

Holland, E. C. (2016), 'Economic Development and Subsidies in the North Caucasus', *Problems of Post-communism*, 63 (1): 50–61.

Hughes, J. (2013), *Chechnya: From Nationalism to Jihad*. Philadelphia: University of Pennsylvania Press.

Human Rights Watch (2016), 'Human Rights Violations in Russia's North Caucasus', Statement for the Legal Affairs and Human Rights Committee of the Parliamentary Assembly of the Council of Europe, 28 January. Available online: https://www.hrw.org/news/2016/01/28/human-rights-violations-russias-north-caucasus (accessed 6 October 2022).

Iliyasov, M. (2019), 'Chechen Demographic Growth as a Reaction to Conflict: The Views of Chechens', *Europe-Asia Studies*, 71 (10): 1705–33.

Janeczko, M. (2014), '"Faced with Death, Even a Mouse Bites": Social and Religious Motivations behind Terrorism in Chechnya', *Small Wars & Insurgencies*, 25 (2): 428–56.

Johnston, H. and E. Y. Alimi (2012), 'Primary Frameworks, Keying and the Dynamics of Contentious Politics: The Islamization of the Chechen and Palestinian National Movements'. *Political Studies*, 60 (3): 603–20.

Judah, B. (2013), 'Russia's Migration Crisis', *Survival*, 55 (6): 123–31.

Klimentov, V. A. (2021), 'Bringing the War Home: the Strategic Logic of "North Caucasian Terrorism" in Russia', *Small Wars & Insurgencies*, 32 (2): 374–408.

Kroupenev, A. (2009), 'Radical Islam in Chechnya', *International Institute for Counter Terrorism (ICT)*.

Kruglanski, A. W., M. J. Gelfand, J. J. Bélanger, A. Sheveland, M. Hetiarachchi and R. Gunaratna (2014), 'The Psychology of Radicalization and Deradicalization: How Significance Quest Impacts Violent Extremism', *Political Psychology*, 35 (S1): 69–93.

Kundnani, A. (2012), 'Radicalization: The Journey of a Concept', *Race & Class*, 54 (2): 3–25.

Kurz, R. W. and C. K. Bartles (2007), 'Chechen Suicide Bombers', *Journal of Slavic Military Studies*, 20 (4): 529–47.

Light, M. (2010), 'Policing Migration in Soviet and Post-Soviet Moscow', *Post-Soviet Affairs*, 26 (4): 275–313.

Loza, W. (2007), 'The Psychology of Extremism and Terrorism: A Middle Eastern Perspective', *Aggression and Violent Behavior*, 12 (2): 141–55.

Mazarr, M. J. (2004), 'The Psychological Sources of Islamic Terrorism', *Policy Review*, 125: 39–60.

McGilloway, A., P. Ghosh and K. Bhui (2015), 'A Systematic Review of Pathways to and Processes Associated with Radicalization and Extremism amongst Muslims in Western Societies', *International Review of Psychiatry*, 1: 39–50.

Molodikova, I. and A. Watt (2014), *Growing up in the North Caucasus: Society, Family, Religion and Education*. London: Routledge.

Moore, C. (2007), 'Combating Terrorism in Russia and Uzbekistan', *Cambridge Review of International Affairs*, 20 (2): 303–23.

Moore, C. and P. Tumelty (2008), 'Foreign Fighters and the Case of Chechnya: A Critical Assessment', *Studies in Conflict & Terrorism*, 31 (5): 412–33.

Moskalenko, S. and C. McCauley (2009), 'Measuring Political Mobilization: The Distinction Between Activism and Radicalism', *Terrorism and Political Violence*, 21 (2): 239–60.

Novaya Gazeta (2021), Участник нападения на пост ДПС в Магасе в 2019 году приговорен к 27 годам, 29 September. Available online: https://novayagazeta.ru/articles/2021/09/29/uchastnik-napadeniia-na-post-dps-v-magase-v-2019-godu-prigovoren-k-27-godam-zakliucheniia-news (accessed 20 June 2022).

Radnitz, S. (2006), 'Look Who's Talking! Islamic Discourse in the Chechen Wars', *Nationalities Papers*, 34 (2): 237–56.

Rae, J. A. (2012), 'Will It Ever Be Possible to Profile the Terrorist?', *Journal of Terrorism Research*, 3 (2): https://research-repository.st-andrews.ac.uk/handle/10023/3986.

Ramsay, G. (2015), 'Why Terrorism Can, But Should Not Be Defined', *Critical Studies on Terrorism*, 8 (2): 211–28.

RosStat (2022), *The Preliminary Estimate of the Population Size in the North Caucasus*, PrPopul2022_Site.xls (accessed 11 March 2022).

Russell, J. (2008), 'Ramzan Kadyrov: The Indigenous Key to Success in Putin's Chechenization Strategy?', *Nationalities Papers*, 36 (4): 659–87.

Russia Census of 2010 (2010). Available online: http://www.demoscope.ru/weekly/ssp/rus_etn_10.php?reg=0 (accessed 8 May 2022).

Sagramoso, D. and A. Yarlykapov (2020), 'Political, Social and Economic Factors', in G. M. Yemelianova and L. Broers (eds), *Routledge Handbook of the Caucasus*, 273–87, London: Routledge.

Schbley, A. (2003), 'Defining Religious Terrorism: A Causal and Anthological Profile', *Studies in Conflict and Terrorism*, 26 (2): 105–34.

Sedgwick, M. (2010), 'The Concept of Radicalization as a Source of Confusion', *Terrorism and Political Violence*, 22 (4): 479–94.

Sinai, J. (2015), 'The Terrorist Threats Against Russia and its Counterterrorism Response Measures', *Connections*, 14 (4): 95–102.

Sokirianskaia, E. (2019), *Mozhno li predotvratit novye volny radikalizatsii na Severnom Kavkaze? Radikalizatsia I ee profilaktika v Chechne, Insushetii, Dagestane i Kabardino-Balkarii*, Centr Analiza i predotvrashcheniia konflikto.

Sokirianskaia, E. (2020), 'Deradicalisation Tacticis in the North Caucasus Can Serve as a Lesson and a Warning', 12 February, Conflict Analysis and Prevention Center.

Available online: https://cap-center.org/de-radicalisation-tactics-in-the-north-caucasus-can-serve-as-a-lesson-and-a-warning/ (accessed 6 October 2022).

Souleimanov, E. (2015), 'An Ethnography of Counterinsurgency: Kadyrovtsy and Russia's Policy of Chechenization', *Post-Soviet Affairs*, 31 (2): 91–114.

Speckhard, A. and K. Akhmedova (2006), 'Black Widows: The Chechen Female Suicide Terrorists', in Y. Schweitzer (ed), *Female Suicide Bombers: Dying for Equality*, 63–80, Tel Aviv: Jaffee Centre for Strategic Studies.

Starodubrovskaya, I. (2013), 'A Cure for Fear: What Kind of Policy Can Ease the Conflict in the North Caucasus of Russia', *Economic Policy*, Moscow, 2, 12 November. Available online: https://papers.ssrn.com/sol3/papers.cfm?abstract_id=2353349 (accessed 5 October 2022).

Svoboda (2018), 'Malaya krov'. Svideteli napadeniya na xram v Groznom ne veryat vlastyam, 22 May. Available online: https://www.svoboda.org/a/29241385.html accessed 12/06/2020 (accessed 20 June 2022).

Tarasov, A. (2006), 'Meniashchiesia subkul'tury. Opyt nabliudeniia za skinkhedami', *Svobodnaia mysl'* 5, May: 19–32.

Tikhonova, A. D., N. V. Dvoryanchikov, A. Ernst-Vintila and I. B. Bovina (2017), 'Radicalization of Adolescents and Youth: In Search of Explanations', *Cultural-Historical Psychology*, 13 (3): 32–40.

Tkhostov, A. S. and K. Surnov (2005), 'Influence of Modern Technologies on the Development of the Individual and the Formation of Pathological Forms of Adaptation: The Reverse Side of Socialization', *Psychological Journal*, 26 (6): 16–24.

Toft, M. D. and Y. M. Zhukov (2012), 'Denial and Punishment in the North Caucasus: Evaluating the Effectiveness of Coercive Counter-Insurgency', *Journal of Peace Research*, 49 (6): 785–800.

Trukhachev, V. I., E. I. Kostyukova, E. I. Gromov and A. N. Gerasimov (2014), 'Comprehensive Socio-ecological and Economic Assessment of the Status and Development of Southern Russia Agricultural Regions', *Life Science Journal*, 11 (5): 478–82.

Vendina, O. G. (2013), 'Migrants in Russian Cities', *Russian Politics & Law*, 51 (3): 48–65.

Verkhovsky, A., P. Kolstø and H. Blakkisrud (2018), 'The Russian Nationalist Movement at Low Ebb', in P. Kolstø and Blakkisrud, H. (ed), *Russia before and after Crimea. Nationalism and Identity 2010–17*, 142–62, Edinburgh: Edinburgh University Press.

Wilhelmsen, J. (2005), 'Between a Rock and a Hard Place: The Islamisation of the Chechen Separatist Movement', *Europe-Asia Studies*, 57 (1): 35–59.

Yarlykapov, A. (2017), *Terrorism in the North Caucasus*. Berlin: Dialogue of Civilizations Research Institute.

7

The evolution of Salafi jihadi terrorism and state responses in Indonesia, Malaysia and the Philippines

Greg Barton

Introduction

Violent extremism involving religion has had a persistent but uneven presence across Asia for decades, going back to the middle of the twentieth century and the emergence of independent postcolonial states (Hellyer and Grossman 2019). Sectarianism, communal conflict and violence in the name of religion have a much longer history, with the origins of modern violent extremism movements being substantially bound up with nationalist struggles (Stepanova 2008). By definition, they have been concerned with, or at least justified by, narratives of political power, identity, equity and representation in the modern nation state.

Inasmuch as it is used to define and shape group identity, religion has frequently figured in violent extremist movements across the region. Some movements, however, such as the Liberation Tigers of Tamil Eelam (LTTE) in Sri Lanka, the Khalistan movement in northern India, the Gerakan Merdeka Aceh (GAM – Free Aceh Movement) in the north-west of Indonesia and the Patani movement in southern Thailand have been predominantly ethno-nationalist in nature, whereas groups such as the Abu Sayyaf Group (ASG) in Thailand, Jemaah Islamiyah (JI) in Indonesia, Malaysia, Singapore and the Philippines, and more recently Jemaah Ansharut Daulah (JAD) in Indonesia have been linked to the global jihadi movements of Al-Qa'eda and Islamic State in Iraq and Syria or ISIS, also known as ISIL, Islamic State of Iraq and the Levant, which, after declaring a caliphate on 29 June 2014, rebranded simply as Islamic State (IS). In West Asia – particularly in Pakistan and Afghanistan – the problem of jihadi violent extremism has been a much greater problem, at times constituting an existential threat. By comparison, in Southeast Asia, terrorist networks have been less extensive and attacks have generally smaller and less frequent. In this chapter, I focus on the issue of contextual factors and policy responses to jihadi violent extremism in Indonesia, Malaysia and the Philippines, with extended consideration of Indonesia in particular because of its sheer size and centrality to jihadist movements in Southeast Asia.

Indonesia

The Darul Islam (DI) movement

With a population of 280 million people, Indonesia is the world's fourth-largest nation and third-largest democracy. With around 87 per cent of citizens identifying as Muslims, it is also the world's largest Muslim-majority nation. Islam, Islamic leaders and Islamic social movements have long played a prominent role in shaping Indonesian society (Hefner 2011, Kersten 2015, Hadiz 2016, Pepinsky, Liddle and Mujani 2018).

The Indonesian nationalist movement, beginning in the late 1920s and contributing to the achievement of independence two decades later, owes much to the energetic and visionary contribution of Islamic leaders and the communities that back them. This contribution is largely constructive and frequently progressive in nature. Nevertheless, Indonesia has long had an energetic extremist religious fringe. Proto-Islamist groups competed with progressive pro-democracy forces within the nationalist movement, and over time a sense of being excluded or cheated out of playing a larger role has contributed to a sense of deep resentment both on the part of moderate Islamists and to those who would become more radical and violent. Violent radical Islamist movements in Indonesia are a direct legacy of the Darul Islam, or Islamic State, insurgency that controlled pockets of West Java, southern Sulawesi and Aceh from 1949 to 1962 (Ramakrishna 2014).

The Darul Islam (DI) (literally, the 'abode of Islam') movement originated in West Java in January 1948, when local Sundanese militant Kartosuwirjo led a breakaway insurgency as the leader of one of the many nationalist militia outfits resisting efforts by the Dutch military to retake control of their former colony (Barton 2004, 2009, 2010, Solahudin 2013). Unhappy with the lack of recognition that he and his militia were receiving from nationalist leaders, in August 1949 Kartosuwirjo declared the mountainous territory in West Java controlled by his fighters to be 'Negara Islam Indonesia' (NII – the Islamic State of Indonesia). In 1952, Kartosuwirjo's fledgling Darul Islam NII in the highlands of West Java was joined by a like-minded insurgency in the jungles of Southern Sulawesi led by Abdul Kahar Muzakkar. Muzakkar's local insurgency in Southern Sulawesi began as a regional dispute but mutated into an Islamist cause. Both insurgencies used the support of local communities, reinforced by an enhanced sense of religious justification, to retain control of their rugged, heavily wooded domains for more than a decade. In 1962, Kartosuwirjo was arrested and put on trial. Three years later, in 1965, Muzakkar was killed by the Indonesian military. Their micro-religious states were doomed from the outset, but they endured long enough to build resilient communities of 'true believers', and their influence and social networks have persisted for seventy years.

The origins of Jemaah Islamiyah

In 1977, a decade after coming to power, President Suharto initiated a campaign to address the latent threat posed by the residual DI network. This resulted in the arrest of 185 people, most with DI connections, on the pretext that they were alleged to belong to a violent extremist organization known as Komando Jihad. It soon became clear that these mass arrests were part of an elaborate sting operation orchestrated by Indonesian army intelligence General Ali Murtopo, who led special operations at the time. Murtopo was alleged to have persuaded influential former DI leaders to reactivate their movement in order to counter a resurgent communist threat.

Two radical DI preachers from central Java, Abu Bakar Ba'asyir and Abdullah Sungkar, were charged with leading Komando Jihad and were sentenced to nine years in prison, with their sentences subsequently reduced to three years and ten months. After they were released, the two men focused on rebuilding the DI network. When it seemed likely that they would be rearrested and returned to prison, the two leaders made a strategic retreat, or *hijra*, to Malaysia (Barton 2004, 2009, 2010, Solahudin 2013).

Ba'asyir and Sungkar had long been the key leaders for DI in Central Java, based in the city of Surakarta (also known as Solo). Their main activities there had been running a pirate radio station promoting jihadi ideas. They also established an Islamic boarding school, or *pesantren*, which unlike the vast majority of Indonesia's 28,000 plus *pesantren* took a narrow Salafist approach to teaching. This *pesantren* in the Surakarta neighbourhood of Ngruki, known as Pesantren al-Mukmin, produced many of Indonesia's most influential terrorists, including the team behind the 2002 Bali bombing, discussed in greater detail below.

From 1985, Ba'ashir and Sungkar operated out of Malaysia's capital Kuala Lumpur and from the southernmost state of Johor, where they established a radical *pesantren*. From Malaysia they recruited hundreds of people to support the *mujahideen* in Afghanistan fighting Soviet military occupation. An estimated 300 to 400 Southeast Asians, mostly Indonesians but also Malaysians and Filipinos, responded to the call to join the *mujahideen* in Afghanistan during the late 1980s and early 1990s, where training continued along the Afghanistan-Pakistan border even after the Soviet withdrawal.

In 1993 Ba'asyir and Sungkar declared that they were breaking ranks with DI and forming a new group, which they named after a militant faction of the Egyptian Muslim Brotherhood calling itself simply the community of Islam, or Jemaah Islamiyah (JI). Most of the Southeast Asians who had followed Ba'asyir and Sungkar to Afghanistan under the auspices of DI formally switched allegiance to the new group. Following the Soviet withdrawal in 1989, JI activity shifted to the main training camp in Peshawar across the Pakistan border. By 1996, a shift in policy by the Pakistan military led to this camp being closed. At this point, many of the JI members returned to Malaysia, but some of the key leaders and trainers went on to the southern Philippines island of Mindanao, where they established a new training camp called Camp Abubakar.

Immediately after the sudden resignation of Suharto in May 1998, Ba'asyir, Sungkar and many of their followers relocated to Surakarta. Their focus at this point was on consolidating the JI community and taking advantage of the changed political landscape's planning and elections in 1999. The official position of JI at this point was that post-Suharto Indonesia was neither the place nor the time to engage in violent jihad.

The emergence of Jemaah Islamiyah and Islamic State terrorism

A key turning point occurred with the October 2002 bomb attacks in Bali. These came after a string of smaller attacks in 2000 and 2001 that, at the time, were not well understood. Post-blast forensic investigation revealed the Bali bomb attacks to be linked to JI. Although the network was by no means new or unknown, up until the 2002 Bali bombing it was assumed that JI lacked both the capacity and the intent to carry out a major terror attack. The extent to which elements within JI had been inspired and enabled by Al-Qa'eda had been underestimated and overlooked, even though it was clear that the core leadership of JI had been formed in Al-Qa'eda camps in Afghanistan and Pakistan in the 1980s and early 1990s.

On the night of Saturday 12 October 2002, a powerful improvised explosive device (IED) packed into a minivan produced an explosive fireball that devastated the Sari Club in the popular tourist district of Kuta on the Indonesian island of Bali. Moments earlier, a smaller IED carried in a backpack had been detonated by a suicide bomber in the nearby Paddy's Bar, sending patrons onto the street in front of the Sari Club. The combined bomb attacks killed 202 people and injured dozens more.

When JI leaders and activists had returned to Indonesia following the collapse of the Suharto regime in May 1998, there were no immediate signs that JI would be involved in a campaign of terror attacks. Indeed, the larger portion of the JI network genuinely believed that there was no immediate need for a campaign of violent jihad in post-Suharto Indonesia. Some returnees disagreed with the argument for restraint, however, and took it upon themselves to plan and execute a series of attacks involving improvised explosive devices and suicide bombers. This reached a peak of insurgent violence in and around the city of Poso in central Sulawesi in 2007 (Karnavian 2014, IPAC 2015). This precipitated a rare intervention by the Indonesian military and police that broke the back of the regional insurgency and saw JI turn away from high-profile attacks to focus on quietly rebuilding over the longer term.

A fresh wave of terrorist attacks, this time linked not to Al-Qa'eda and JI but to the Islamic State (IS) movement and its caliphate project in Syria and Iraq, commenced in Indonesia in 2015. Although now somewhat diminished, IS continues to pose a threat not just in Indonesia but also in the Philippines and Malaysia. These two distinct waves of terrorism point to the influence that a relatively small number of foreign fighters travelling to a conflict zone can have on their source communities. It is not just those who travel to fight who become directly involved in violence but also those who are frustrated at not being able to travel who resort to carry out attacks at home.

Radicalization and social networks in Southeast Asia

The experience in Indonesia since the 1950s, as well as the Philippines and Malaysia, demonstrates that violent extremism is very much a social network phenomenon. And because these social networks have proven to be resilient, and constantly regenerating, violent extremism is also very much an intergenerational phenomenon. A direct line can be drawn from the early DI militancy of the 1950s through to the formation of JI and its Afghan alumni, continuing on to those inspired by the formation of IS.

Intermarriage and cross-regional collaboration have further generated extensive and enduring networks of jihadi extremists that extend beyond three generations (Barton 2004, 2009, Jones 2007, 2010, Solahudin 2013), despite the global rivalry between Al-Qa'eda and IS reflected in contemporary jihadi networks in Indonesia. Many, including most activists associated with JI, align with Al-Qa'eda, but a substantial number of militants in newer groups such as Jemaah Ansharut Tauhid (JAD) have sworn allegiance to IS.

Indonesian police have now arrested more than 2000 alleged terrorists. Despite this sustained level of tactical success, the threat of radicalization to violent extremism continues unabated. In 2021, for example, a total of 370 terrorism suspects were arrested, representing a significant increase from the 232 suspects arrested in 2020. With relatively rare exceptions, Indonesia's specialist counter-terrorism unit Detachment 88 has been consistently successful in intercepting and disrupting terrorist plots. The success of police counterterrorism units disrupting larger terrorist plots means that the majority of terrorist attacks are lone-actor attacks, or at the very least involve small family groups operating autonomously.

Yet partly for this reason, media reporting about lone-actor attacks in Indonesia creates a general impression that religiously inspired radicalization is very much an individual phenomenon. Loose talk of 'self-radicalization' contributes an impression that radicalization largely revolves around individual choices. While individual choices are important, this does not mean that radicalization is best understood as individuals making bad decisions. It is, in fact, extremely rare for individuals to radicalize in complete isolation; in the vast majority of cases, the process involves recruitment into a new social group (Atran et al. 2017, 2018, Hwang and Schulze 2018, Vergani et al. 2018).

In general, it is social relationships, a sense of belonging and engaging with a new community that drive the process of violent radicalization. Internalizing core narratives and moving deeper into extremist literature tend to follow a natural desire to fit in and be accepted, but social networks and relationships tend to proceed cognitive radicalization, or at least closely accompany and bolster it (Horgan 2008, Schmid 2013, Coolsaet 2016, IPAC 2017a, Schuurman and Taylor 2018).

In the Indonesian context, this is borne out by the fact that intergenerational jihadi families feature prominently in Indonesian extremist groups and networks, often reinforced through intermarriage and schooling. As is the pattern elsewhere in the world, there are a number of families who have connections with both the conflict in Afghanistan in the 1980s and the Islamic state caliphate project in Syria and Iraq after 2013.

It is not family networks alone, however, that contribute to the social networks facilitating radicalization. For example, Hwang and Schulze (2018) assembled a normalized data set of 106 Indonesians who joined militant Islamist groups between the mid-1980s and 2014 in order to understand the pathways and processes involved in their radicalization. Their research confirmed that social relationships formed through a variety of sources and settings including kinship circles but also schooling Islamic study sessions and involvement in local conflicts were important elements in the radicalization of these individuals. In general, as new social bonds are consolidated, a process of gradual separation from mainstream society takes place and deeper associations with groups involved in risky and antisocial behaviour come to dominate. This is a familiar pattern that broadly fits with what has been observed elsewhere around the world in radicalization into violent extremism (Atran et al. 2017, 2018, Vergani et al. 2018).

Chalmers (2017), for example, interviewed twenty former Indonesian extremists in depth to understand, based on their personal biographical narratives, the processes and pathways that shaped their radicalization experience. He identified a jihadi subculture that supports and enables jihadist ideas and normalizes extremist narratives in a community of like-minded people.

Jihad in Ambon and Poso

The election of the progressive Islamic leader Abdurrahman Wahid as president of Indonesia in October 1999 was met with deep displeasure and misgiving by conservative elements and radical Islamists across Indonesia as well as by key elements of the Suharto-era elite, particularly in the military. One way in which this manifested was in the support of radical Islamist fighters who travelled to the eastern island of Ambon to fight against local Christians in intercommunal conflict.

Thousands of mujahideen travelled from Java to Ambon under the auspices of a group calling itself Laskar Jihad. This occurred despite orders from President Wahid for the fighters who had been training openly in Java to be stopped from departing from the East Java port city of Surabaya. Nevertheless, with the support of key elements of the military, around 7,000 members arrived in Ambon, where they were also well supplied with military-style weapons (Barton 2002, 2004, Noorhaidi 2006, Sholeh 2006). A smaller group that was initially not well documented called itself Laskar Jundullah. This group, unlike Laskar Jihad, was linked to JI.

Laskar Jundullah was much more effective militarily on the ground and had a disproportionately larger impact. This was, in large part, because it involved many who had had training in Afghanistan. Laskar Jihad, despite its name, was not a global jihadist group but rather a Salafist group with links to key Salafi state clerics in Saudi Arabia. The surge of fighters from Java to Ambon represented an opportunistic response to an outbreak of communal violence. At the same time communal violence was also erupting in the central Sulawesi city of Poso. When concerted efforts by the Philippines military resulted in the closure of camp Abubakar in Mindanao, many of the JI leaders relocated to Poso.

Communal unrest and fighting in Ambon and Poso led to tens of thousands of people being displaced and more than 9,000 lives lost. At the time, reporting focused on Laskar Jihad, which had sent as many as 7,000 fighters to Ambon. But in October 2002 the leader of Laskar Jihad, Jafar Umar Thalib, abruptly shut down the organization. This appears to be a direct result of a *fatwa* by Sheikh Rabi'i ibn Hadi al-Madkhali, one of the seven *ulama* in Saudi Arabia who had previously provided endorsement for Laskar Jihad's campaign in Ambon (Umam 2006). Significantly, this order came just five days after the Bali bombing of 12 October 2002. It seems likely that there was a desire to distance Laskar Jihad and its involvement in communal violence in eastern Indonesia from jihadist terrorism.

JI splinter bombings

In August 2000 Abu Bakar Ba'asyir organized a three-day open congress in Yogyakarta, Central Java, to which he invited radical Islamist groups from all over Indonesia. He used this congress to declare the formation of a group called Majelis Mujahideen Indonesia (MMI) (the Indonesian Mujahideen Council), declaring it to be dedicated to preparing the way for the establishment of a new international caliphate. At the congress he had himself declared as the commander of MMI's governing council. Many within Jemaah Islamiyah were confused and even annoyed by Ba'asyir's approach to open engagement with mainstream forces.

Shortly after Ba'asyir and Sungkar had moved back to Surakarta, Sungkar died of natural causes. Abu Bakar Ba'asyir replaced Abdullah Sungkar as the leader of Jemaah Islamiyah. But importantly, whereas Sungkar was seen as a natural charismatic leader who commanded wide respect and commanded natural authority, Ba'asyir was regarded as being much less authoritative. In establishing MMI, Abu Bakar Ba'asyir was seen by many within Jemaah Islamiyah to be deviating from the pure path of jihad. Although it was not clear at the time, a significant number of younger leaders decided to take matters into their own hands and orchestrate a series of violent attacks. This involved a number of mysterious attacks throughout 2000, including a bombing at the Jakarta stock exchange and a series of coordinated bombings on Christmas Eve that occurred nearly simultaneously across the archipelago.

Terrorist attacks occurred throughout Indonesia, and also in the Philippines, in 2000, 2001 and 2002, including an assassination attempt on the Philippines ambassador in Jakarta and a bombing at a shopping mall as well as an attack on a public ferry in Manila's harbour (ICG 2002, Barton 2004, Sholeh 2006, 2010, Solahudin 2013, Karnavian 2014, IPAC 2017b, 2020). It was not until after the Bali bombings of October 2002, however, that it became clear that JI, or at least breakaway splinter factions impatient with Abu Bakar Baasyir's leadership, represented a substantial terrorist threat in Indonesia.

In addition to the Bali bombings of 12 October 2002 there was an attack on the JW Marriott hotel in Jakarta in 2003 and a vehicle-borne IED attack outside the Australian Embassy in 2004, followed by further bombings in Bali in 2005 and a second attack on the JW Marriot and twinned Ritz-Carlton hotels in Jakarta in 2009. These attacks took place despite the fact that the Indonesian police had greatly increased counterterrorism capacity, including establishing Detachment 88, also known as Densus 88 (a contraction of Detasemen Khusus), and had arrested hundreds of alleged terrorists.

IS and the split with JI

Abu Bakar Ba'asyir was never successfully prosecuted for involvement in the Bali bombing of 2002 but was subsequently found guilty of immigration offences and jailed. When released from jail in 2008, he established the organization Jemaah Anshrut Tauhid (JAT). JAT operated openly but also it conducted some activities in a clandestine fashion. In 2010, Abu Bakar Ba'asyir was involved in establishing a large 'cross-functional' training camp for jihadist fighters in Aceh, but local villagers reported the activities to the authorities and the camp was quickly locked down. This led to the arrest and eventual prosecution of Abu Bakar Ba'asyir and a number of other JI leaders. This time, the charges involved fundraising and preparation for acts of terror. The rapid demise of the ill-advised training camp in Aceh saw JI drop from public attention, with the network turning away from the provocative activities that brought it into contention with authorities. Instead, JI focused on teaching and on establishing religious fundamentalist, exclusivist communities (Chalk 2019).

With the declaration of the Islamic State caliphate in 2014, however, the flow of foreign fighters to support the caliphate project accelerated, ultimately including over 800 from Southeast Asia (Schulze 2018). From his prison cell, Ba'asyir videoed a declaration of support for IS. This immediately resulted in a split in JAT, with the faction opposed to IS and aligned with Al-Qa'eda forming Jamaah Ansharusy Syariah (JAS). As IS became increasingly popular in Indonesia, radical Islamist groups banded together to form a new organization called Jamaah Ansharut Daulah (JAD), led by cleric Aman Abdurrahman. Other smaller groups also formed in support of IS, while many in JI and in other jihadist groups remained loyal to Al-Qa'eda, choosing to back the original jihadist group in its now open rivalry with IS.

Several veteran observers of Islamist extremism in Indonesia, such as Sidney Jones (IPAC 2017b), have argued that in the longer run JI may be the most dangerous of jihadist groups in Indonesia. It is clearly playing the long game and planning patiently for a time in which it can be more directly active. Nevertheless, ever since the declaration of the IS caliphate, it has been the IS movement and groups affiliated to it, such as JAD, that have been responsible for the majority of terrorist attacks in Indonesia.

The 17 July 2009 bombings of the twined JW Marriott and Ritz-Carlton hotels in Jakarta were the last large-scale terrorist incidents in Indonesia up until 2016, when militants inspired by IS commenced a series of both successful and attempted attacks in Indonesia. Most often affiliated with JAD, IS-inspired terrorists conducted a series of attacks against police forces and civilians (especially Christians) in Jakarta (January 2016), Samarinda (November 2016), Jakarta (May 2017), Medan and Jakarta (June 2017), Depok detention facility, Surabaya and Riau (May 2018). Tragically, a new development with these attacks was the involvement of women and children as suicide bombers (IPAC 2017a, 2017c, 2018, 2020, Schulze 2018, Barton 2020a, 2020b).

Malaysia

A persistent but contained threat

There has only been one terrorist attack in Malaysia linked to an international jihadist group, a failed effort involving IS militants and a hand grenade lobbed into a Movida sports bar in the Puchong district of the capital Kuala Lumpur on 28 June 2016, wounding eight patrons. The fact that there have been no significant jihadist terrorist attacks in Malaysia does not gainsay numerous attempts to carry out such attacks, however. Like the Indonesian police Detachment 88 counterterrorism unit, the Special Branch of the Royal Malaysia Police has been extraordinarily successful in detecting terrorist cells and intercepting and disrupting terrorist plots.

With a population of around 33 million, compared with Indonesia's 280 million, Malaysia is just one-eighth the size of Indonesia. Nevertheless, the proportional level of threat it has faced has been comparable to that faced by Indonesia. Up until the beginning of the Covid-19 pandemic in 2020 Special Branch had foiled more than 26 planed terror attacks in the preceding seven years and arrested more than 460 terrorism suspects. Significantly, these arrests have involved a large proportion of international militants, with 131 suspected terrorists from the Philippines and Indonesia arrested up until late 2019 (Chew 2019a). By July 2019, the number of arrests had risen to 519 and in the three years since there has been a steady pattern of interrupted terror plots (Rodzi 2019).

Just as Filipinos and Indonesians have figured prominently in jihadi circles in Malaysia, so too Malaysians have been active in the Philippines and Indonesia (Chew 2019b, 2019c; Rodzi 2019). The series of bombings in Indonesia in the 2000s linked to JI involved a number of prominent Malaysians, including the bomb maker Azahari Husin and the charismatic recruiter Noordin Mohammad Top. More recent attacks have also involved Malaysian militants. For example, in a suicide bombing attack at a security check point outside the town of Lamitan on the island of Basilan, the bodies of six Malaysian fighters were recovered from the wreckage of the explosive-packed vehicle used in the attack (Yusa 2018).

Support for Islamic State in Malaysia

Social surveys in both Indonesia and Malaysia reveal a disturbingly significant level of support for jihadist violence, with the level of public support in Malaysia appearing to be significantly higher than that of Indonesia. In a 2019 survey, for example, 21 per cent of Muslim university students responded by saying they felt that terrorism represented 'an effective strategy to achieve an objective' and half of those surveyed acknowledged that they could 'possibly develop radical ideas that might result in violent acts' (RSIS 2019).

Since 2014, as has been the case in Indonesia, the focus of concern in Malaysia has been with those inspired by the Islamic State movement. It's not known precisely how many Malaysians travelled to Syria to support IS and other groups. Official figures acknowledge that, since 2013, more than 102 Malaysians travelled to Syria to support jihadist groups, including those aligned with Al-Qa'eda. Of these, at least forty are thought to have been killed in combat, including up to nine dying as suicide bombers (RSIS 2019). Significantly, unlike most of the source countries for foreign terrorist fighters (including almost all Western democracies), Malaysia has been ready and willing to repatriate and process its foreign fighters. This process of prosecution and attempted rehabilitation is, for understandable reasons, not subject to public scrutiny, but it is clear that Malaysian authorities have invested considerable efforts in rehabilitation and have seen significant positive results.

Concern about IS supporters is not confined to those who have travelled to Syria and Iraq and who might possibly return, including, worryingly, those who might return undetected. There are also concerns with those who wanted to travel to Syria but for various reasons have been unable to do so. Malaysia, even more so than Indonesia, struggles to manage extremist influences in a social environment rife with sectarian sentiment openly promoted in religious lectures and study circles. In this context, the dominant themes of *takfiri* judgementalism in IS narratives, especially those promoting anti-Shia, anti-mainstream Muslim and anti-Christian sentiment, find ready acceptance in a febrile environment of radical and sectarian rhetoric (Liow 2009, 2017, 2021).

Malaysia has long had an open-door policy facilitating the free movement of people from across the Muslim world. At the same time the dominant party in government, UMNO (the United Malays National Organisation), has since independence been locked in fierce competition with PAS (Parti Islam Se-Malaysia), the Islamist Malay majority party, to prove itself an equally worthy defender of Islam and Muslims. This has resulted in a destructive race to the bottom which has contributed to the government being reluctant to crack down on radical Islamist preachers, including influential figures from the Middle East and South Asia (Ramakrishna 2021).

The charged social and political environment in Malaysia has meant that the Special Branch counterterrorism police unit has faced a very difficult challenge in of trying to cut through the noise to detect the 'signal' of jihadist terrorist activity. In particular, the focus of IS supporters on anti-Shia sectarian narratives is broadly echoed across Malaysians' society by significant numbers of radical preachers and study circles that use anti-Shia language to bolster their claim on a deeper commitment to Sunni Islam.

In May 2019, Special Branch revealed that they had foiled a planned wave of large-scale terror attacks, including assassinations, directed towards so-called 'anti-Muslim' figures (Chew 2019d). Special Branch said that these interrupted attacks were planned by 'IS wolf packs' with the intention of being executed during the fasting month of Ramadan. Those arrested initially included one Indonesian and one Burmese national. Eventually sixteen suspects were arrested, twelve of whom were Indonesians, three Malaysians and one Indian, all alleged to have been acting in the name of Islamic State. On 24 May 2019, two more men were arrested and alleged to making IEDs using TATP (Rodzi 2019).

These arrests were part of a total of eighty suspected terrorist arrests over the span of twelve months (Chew 2019d). In addition to this, a larger structural concern involving radicalization to violent extremism involves international links and travel between the East Malaysian state of Sabah and the neighbouring islands of the Philippines in the Sulu archipelago that span the shallow waters between Mindanao and Borneo and link the two nations. More recently, there are concerns that jihadist groups largely based in the Philippines are establishing networks across Sabah and playing into communal tensions.

The Philippines

IS and the siege of Marawi

For decades, extremism in the Philippines has been predominantly a home-grown phenomenon. But the rise of the Islamic State movement and the declaration of the caliphate in mid-2014 in particular led to a new alliance between four leading jihadi groups, the most prominent of which was the notorious Abu Sayyaf Group (ASG), best known for its kidnapping-for-ransom crimes. The rise of IS provided these groups with a new sense of discipline and purpose (Liow 2017, Ramakrishna 2021). This has manifested in a series of terrorist attacks over the past ten years, most dramatically in a protracted siege in the Philippines' largest Muslim-majority city of Marawi that broke out on 23 May 2017 and continued for five months, culminating in the virtual physical destruction of the city.

The siege of Marawi saw at least 930 militants killed, including 44 foreigners, with 165 security personnel and 87 civilians also losing their lives. The largest of the militant groups involved was ASG, acting in the name of IS. Although the militants were ultimately defeated, the liberation of Marawi came at an enormous price. Frustrated by difficulties in breaking the siege, the Philippines Armed Forces resorted to launching artillery and aerial barrages, the impact of which was indiscriminate, or at least inaccurate. The physical destruction of much of the city saw more than 350,000 people displaced and, years later, tens of thousands continue to live in poor quality temporary housing.

The ongoing failure to resolve the suffering and sense of persecution experienced on the ground in Marawi, particularly on the part of younger people, is likely to have ongoing impacts resulting in recruitment to violent extremism, whether in the name of Islamic State or under the auspices of local groups dissatisfied with the government's response to the crisis and its aftermath. When the siege of Marawi commenced, the Armed Forces of the Philippines declared confidently that they would have the situation resolved within days. The fact that it took five months and came at the price of massive urban and infrastructure destruction and population displacement significantly undermined the legitimacy and authority of the central government and security forces.

The siege of Marawi also resulted in many IS-aligned leaders being killed or arrested, but many succeeded in escaping the city before the siege concluded. In the five years since, a series of suicide attacks have taken place. Historically, the contested lands of western Mindanao and the Sulu Archipelago have been subject to innumerable attacks using small arms and kidnapping for ransom. The region is awash with small arms, including military issue assault rifles and handguns, many of which have clearly come out of military stocks and have either been captured or sold to militants.

The use of suicide bombs and improvised explosive devices, however, is a relatively new development in the Philippines and closely follows a pattern of IS attacks in the Middle East. Indeed, many of the tactical methods used in the siege of Marawi replicated methods used by IS in cities such as Mosul in Iraq and Raqqa in Syria where IS militants were involved in protracted conflict. And just as the IS conflict in Syria and Iraq attracted a stream of foreign fighters, so too comparatively large numbers of foreign militants travelled to join the conflict in Marawi. More than 100 foreign fighters have made their way to the region, often coming via the Malaysian state of Sabah to join IS forces in the jungles of Western Mindanao and the islands of the Sulu Archipelago.

Despite decades of communal conflict, insurgency and extremist and criminal violence in the southern Philippines, suicide bomb attacks were unknown prior to 2018. This devastating mode of attack arrived in July 2018 when an explosive-packed van driven by a Moroccan extremist was detonated at a security checkpoint in the town of Lamitan on the island of Basilan, a stronghold of the ASG, resulting in the death of the driver and ten others, including, as noted above, six Malaysians. Six months later, on 27 January 2019, another devastating suicide attack occurred at the Cathedral of Our Lady of Mount Carmel on the island of Jolo. This attack occurred just one week after the holding of a plebiscite to determine support for the creation of the Bangsamoro Autonomous Region, a conflict resolution approach rejected by IS-aligned jihadists.

Even though the people of the Sulu Archipelago are all too familiar with insurgent and criminal violence, this attack on the cathedral was still extraordinarily shocking, not least because it involved suicide bombers. The attack killed 22 people and wounded more than 100. Post-blast forensic tests, including DNA analysis, confirmed earlier reports that the suicide bombers involved an Indonesian husband-and-wife couple linked to JAD. Rullie Rian Zeke and Ulfah Handayani Saleh had reportedly travelled to Turkey in 2016 in an unsuccessful attempt to enter Syria and join the Islamic state caliphate but were arrested by Turkish authorities and repatriated to Indonesia in 2017 (Paddock and Gutierrez 2019). Despite having participated in a rehabilitation programme in Indonesia, they were able to make their way to the Philippines. They represent one of the first cases known of Indonesian deportees from the Middle East being involved in a major terrorist attack.

The New People's Army

As is the case with Indonesia, global Salafi jihadism represents the immediate primary threat in the Philippines, with most of the violent extremist groups in the country now aligned with IS. It is important to remember, however, that jihadists linked to IS, or even jihadi extremists acting independently in the name of local causes, are not the only form of violent extremism to threaten the Philippines. It is easy to overlook the fact that for decades the Maoist New People's Army (NPA) has had thousands of political supporters and fighters across the Philippines Archipelago, including in the capital Manila. Indeed, the NPA has found support wherever there are communities struggling with poverty and a sense of injustice, which is to say in virtually every major urban centre in the Philippines. The retired chief of staff of the Armed Forces of the Philippines, General Ray Carreiro, claimed that the NPA commands as many as 3,700 fighters (RSIS 2019). The NPA has been conducting violent attacks in the Philippines for more than fifty years. As is the case with many jihadist groups and attacks over the decades, many of these attacks have been linked to intimidation and revenue-raising. While in recent years the NPA has not been involved in major incidents of violence, the fact that it continues to show resilience and has large support across the country, much like Jemaah Islamiyah in Indonesia, suggests that it has the potential for future violent extremist activity.

Conclusion

Salafi jihadism continues to represent the dominant violent extremist threat in Southeast Asia. It has very limited appeal but deep roots and resilient, intergenerational social networks. It is a product of globalization, inasmuch as the global networks of Al-Qaʾeda and Islamic State have forged alliances with regional networks and local grievances. But its origins in Indonesia lie well beyond the emergence of global Salafi jihadism, having evolved out of a radical Islamist reaction, in the form of the Darul Islam movement, to the dominance of pluralist, non-sectarian nationalism.

The violent nature of the Darul Islam insurgency meant that it was met with a firm response from the Indonesian military. The resilient nature of what remains an expansive if secretive movement now encompassing four generations speaks to the fact that while the 'hard' approach may have succeeded in curtailing militancy, it has not destroyed the larger social movement. Given the very substantive contribution that the Darul Islam community has made to subsequent jihadi terrorist groups such as JI and JAD, this represents a significant failure.

Nor is the problem confined to Salafi Jihadi violent extremism. The heavy-handed approaches taken by both the Sukarno and Suharto regimes to limiting the political activism of Islamist leaders and parties produced lasting resentment that continues to play out in post-Suharto democratic Indonesia. And while there is considerably more freedom for an open contest of ideas in twenty-first-century Indonesia, with radical Islamist political parties such as the Egyptian Muslim Brotherhood-inspired PKS (Partai Keadilan Sejahtera – the Prosperous Justice Party) emerging as a significant political force, resentment persists.

Radical Islamists take issue with the non-sectarian state philosophy of Pancasila, arguing that Indonesia should be an Islamic state based on Sharia law. And while they, along with other mainstream actors, reject violence, they look to religious populism to advance their cause. At the same time, they push the limits of local government power in districts that they rule to impose Sharia-based local bylaws that have them impact of eroding the rights of women. The Indonesian national government has largely sought to avoid open confrontation with the Islamists but has doubled down on using the language of Pancasila to advocate for tolerance.

In Malaysia, which is formally described as being an Islamic nation, the federal government is much less willing to advocate for minority rights and to criticize Islamist aspirations and hard-line ideas. PAS-ruled states have been allowed to impose Sharia-based legislation. And for decades, the circulation of books and ideas linked to progressive Islamic thinkers from Indonesia (who, dialect differences aside, use the same language as Malaysians) has been restricted and 'liberal' approaches to Islam demonized. It is a significant development, then, that beginning in 2023 the government of Prime Minister Anwar Ibrahim has advocated for a Madani (or civil) approach (borrowing the language of the late progressive Indonesian Islamic intellectual Nurcholish Madjid) to shaping Malaysia as a 'progressive nation'.

The current progress of the Bangsamoro peace process in the Philippines provides a way for the national government to distance itself from decades of policy seen to be hostile to the nation's small (6.4 per cent) Muslim minority, based largely in Mindanao.

As former militant groups, such as first the MNLF and then the MILF, have entered into the peace process, there has been greater recognition of the role of Islam. The government of President Ferdinand Marcos Junior has, so far, continued to build on the rapprochement with Muslim communities initiated by earlier governments.

In the Philippines, ethno-nationalist grievances, which impacted deeply on the Muslim minority in the south, generated a multitude of local insurgent groups, while in Malaysia, global Salafi jihadist thought, arriving primarily via Indonesia, captured the imagination of a small but significant element of Muslim society. The mujahideen struggle in Afghanistan against Soviet military occupation in the 1980s saw several hundred would-be mujahideen travel to Al-Qa'eda camps in the mountains between Afghanistan and Pakistan. These camps, which continued until 1996, gave birth to groups such as Jemaah Islamiyah and the Abu Sayyaf Group, and laid the foundations for the recruitment of new generations of fighters drawn to the caliphate project of Islamic State.

Mistaken state responses and associated failures contributed most obviously to the emergence of violent extremist movements in the Philippines, but also played a role in Indonesia and Malaysia. In Indonesia, military-led repression of radical Islamists under the presidencies of Sukarno and Suharto not only failed to eliminate the problem but ultimately contributed to its re-emergence, while in Malaysia a more permissive environment for extremist Islamist thought opened the doors more widely to transnational influence and engagement.

These three large states of maritime Southeast Asia have a long history of circular migration and transnational social networks. Porous borders and small boat transits continue to represent a continuing challenge to policing criminality. The continuing development of transnational cooperation in intelligence and training has been a significant factor in containing the threat of violent extremism in the region. But the threat is resilient and the cycle of radicalization and recruitment to jihadi violent extremism cannot be addressed through law enforcement alone. The steady stream of terrorism detainees exiting the prison system as they complete their sentences, together with returning foreign fighters and their families, represents a challenge to rehabilitation and prevention that goes beyond detection and policing.

While the Taliban takeover in Afghanistan in 2021 has not yet resulted in an observable flow of mujahideen from Southeast Asia to Al-Qa'eda and IS camps, it would be foolish to ignore the lessons of history and discount the possibility of this cycle recommencing over the course of the decade. Whatever the combination of local, regional and global circumstances that develop, the threat of Salafi jihadism is certain to be as resilient and adaptive as the ideas and social networks that sustain it.

References

Atran, S., R. Axelrod, R. Davis and B. Fischhoff (2017), 'Challenges in Researching Terrorism from the Field', *Science*, 355 (6323): 352–4.

Atran, S., H. Waziri, A. Gómez, H. Sheikh, L. López-Rodríguez, C. Rogan and R. Davis (2018), 'The Islamic State's Lingering Legacy among Young Men from the Mosul Area',

CTC Sentinel, 11 (4): 15–22. Available online: https://ctc.westpoint.edu/islamic-states-lingering-legacy-among-young-men-mosul-area/ (accessed 14 August 2022).

Barton, G. (2002), *Abdurrahman Wahid: Muslim Democrat, Indonesian President: A View from the Inside*. Sydney: UNSW Press.

Barton, G. (2004), *Indonesia's Struggle: Jemaah Islamiyah and the Soul of Islam*. Sydney: UNSW Press.

Barton, G. (2009), 'The Historical Development of Jihadi Islamist Thought in Indonesia', in S. Helfstein (ed), *Radical Islamic Ideology in Southeast Asia*, New York: Combating Terrorism Center at West Point. Available online: https://www.hsdl.org/?view&did=718972 (accessed 14 August 2022).

Barton, G. (2010), 'Indonesia', in B. Rubin (ed), *Guide to Islamist Movements*, New York: M.E. Sharpe.

Barton, G. (2020a), 'Salafist-Jihadism in Southeast Asia', in I. Kfir and J. Coyne, (eds), *ASPI Counterterrorism Yearbook 2020*, 43–51, Canberra: Australian Strategic Policy Institute. Available online: https://www.aspi.org.au/report/counterterrorism-yearbook-2020 (accessed 14 August 2022).

Barton, G. (2020b), 'The Historical Context and Regional Social Network Dynamics of Radicalisation and Recruitment of Islamic State Foreign Terrorist Fighters in Indonesia and Its Southeast Asian Neighbours', in L. Waha (ed), *United by Violence, Divided by Cause: A Comparison of Drivers of Radicalisation and Violence in Asia and Europe*, 117–39, Baden-Baden: Nomos/KAS. Available online: https://www.nomos-elibrary.de/10.5771/9783748905738.pdf (accessed 14 August 2022).

Chalk, P. (2019), *Jemaah Islamiyah: an Uncertain Future*, ASPI, Canberra, 21 March 2019. Available online: https://www.aspi.org.au/report/jemaah-islamiyah-uncertain-future (accessed 14 August 2022).

Chew, A. (2019a), 'Top Malaysian Police Officer Warns of Suicide Attacks as Isis Fighters Return Home', *South China Morning Post*, 18 June 2019. Available online: https://www.scmp.com/week-asia/politics/article/3015087/facebook-fail-top-cops-warning-isis-fighters-return-malaysia (accessed 14 August 2022).

Chew, A. (2019b), 'Why a Resurgent Jemaah Islamiah in Indonesia Is Also Bad News for Malaysia and Singapore', *South China Morning Post*, 7 July. Available online: https://www.scmp.com/week-asia/society/article/3017465/why-resurgent-jemaah-islamiah-indonesia-also-bad-news-malaysia (accessed 14 August 2022).

Chew, A. (2019c), 'Southeast Asia on Alert for Isis "Grand Agenda" as Escaped Indonesian Jihadists in Syria Eye the Region', *South China Morning Post*, 19 October. Available online: https://www.scmp.com/week-asia/politics/article/3033658/southeast-asia-alert-isis-grand-agenda-escaped-indonesian (accessed 14 August 2022).

Chew, A. (2019d), 'Islamic State "Wolf Pack" in Malaysia Planned Wave of Terror Attacks, Police Say after Detaining Four Suspects in Sting Operation', *South China Morning Post*, 13 May. Available online: https://www.scmp.com/news/asia/southeast-asia/article/3010061/islamic-state-wolf-pack-malaysia-planned-wave-terror (accessed 4 October 2022).

Chalmers, I. (2017), 'Countering Violent Extremism in Indonesia: Bring Back Jihadists', *Asian Studies Review*, 41 (3): 331–51.

Coolsaet, R. (2016), *All Radicalisation Is Local: The Genesis and Drawbacks on an Elusive Concept*, Egmont Paper 84. Available online: https://www.egmontinstitute.be/all-radicalisation-is-local/ (accessed 14 August 2022).

Hadiz, V. (2016), *Islamic Populism in Indonesia and the Middle East*. Cambridge: Cambridge University Press.

Hefner, R. W. (2011), *Civil Islam: Muslims and Democratization in Indonesia*. Princeton: Princeton University Press.

Hellyer, H. A. and M. Grossman (2019), *A Framework for Understanding the Relationship between Radicalisation, Religion and Violence: Concept Paper*, Horizon 2020 GREASE Project, European University Institute. Available online: http://grease.eui.eu/publications/concept-papers/ (accessed 14 August 2022).

Horgan, J. G. (2008), 'From profiles to Pathways and Roots to Routes: Perspectives from Psychology on Radicalization into Terrorism', *The Annals of the American Academy of Political and Social Science*, 618 (1): 80–94.

Hwang, J. C. and K. Schulze (2018), 'Why They Join: Pathways into Indonesian Jihadist Organizations', *Terrorism and Political Violence*, 30 (6): 911–32.

International Crisis Group (ICG) (2002), 'ICG Asia Briefing, Al-Qaeda in Southeast Asia: The Case of the "Ngruki Network" in Indonesia', 8 August. Available online: https://www.crisisgroup.org/asia/south-east-asia/indonesia/al-qaeda-southeast-asia-case-ngruki-network-indonesia (accessed 14 August 2022).

Institute for Policy Analysis of Conflict (IPAC) (2015), *Indonesia's Lamongan Network: How East Java, Poso and Syria Are Linked*, IPAC Report No. 18, April. Available online: https://understandingconflict.org/en/publications/Indonesias-Lamongan-Network (accessed 14 August 2022).

Institute for Policy Analysis of Conflict (IPAC) (2017a), *The Radicalisation of Indonesian Women Workers in Hong Kong*, IPAC Report No. 39, 26 July. Available online: https://understandingconflict.org/en/publications/The-Radicalisation-of-Indonesian-Women-Workers-in-Hong-Kong (accessed 14 August 2022).

Institute for Policy Analysis of Conflict (IPAC) (2017b), *The Re-emergence of Jemaah Islamiyah*, IPAC Report No. 36, 27 April. Available online: https://understandingconflict.org/en/publications/The-Re-emergence-of-Jemaah-Islamiyah (accessed 14 August 2022).

Institute for Policy Analysis of Conflict (IPAC) (2017c), *Mothers to Bombers: The Evolution of Indonesian Women Extremists*, IPAC Report No. 35, 31 January. Available online: https://understandingconflict.org/en/publications/Mothers-to-Bombers-The-Evolution-of-Indonesian-Women-Extremists (accessed 14 August 2022).

Institute for Policy Analysis of Conflict (IPAC) (2018), *The Surabaya Bombings and the Future of ISIS in Indonesia*, IPAC Report No. 51, 18 October. Available online: https://understandingconflict.org/en/publications/Extremist-Women-Behind-Bars-in-Indonesia (accessed 14 August 2022).

Institute for Policy Analysis of Conflict (IPAC) (2020), *Extremist Women behind Bars in Indonesia*, IPAC Report No. 68, 21 September. Available online: https://understandingconflict.org/en/publications/Extremist-Women-Behind-Bars-in-Indonesia (accessed 14 August 2022).

Jones, S. (2007), 'Inherited Jihadism: Like Father, Like Son', *Australian Financial Review*, 4 July. Available online: https://www.crisisgroup.org/asia/south-east-asia/indonesia/inherited-jihadism-father-son (accessed 14 August 2022).

Jones, S. (2010), 'Darul Islam's Ongoing Appeal', International Crisis Group, 18 August. Available online: https://www.crisisgroup.org/asia/south-east-asia/indonesia/darul-islam-s-ongoing-appeal (accessed 14 August 2022).

Karnavian, M. T. (2014), *Explaining Islamist Insurgencies: The Case of Al-Jamaah al-Islamiyyah and the Radicalisation of the Poso Conflict 2000–2007*. London: Imperial College Press.

Kersten, C. (2015), *Islam in Indonesia: The Contest for Society, Ideas and Values*. Oxford: Oxford University Press.
Liow, J. (2009), *Piety and Politics: Islamism in Contemporary Malaysia*. Oxford: Oxford University Press.
Liow, J. (2017), *Religion and Nationalism in Southeast Asia*. Cambridge: Cambridge University Press.
Liow, J. (2021), 'Malaysia's Creeping Islamization – and Dimming Prospects for Convenantal Plurism', *The Review of Faith & International Affairs*, 19 (2): 1–13.
Noorhaidi, H. (2006), *Laskar Jihad: Islam, Militancy and the Quest for Identity in Post-New Order Indonesia*. Ithaca, NY: Cornell University Press.
Paddock, R. and J. Gutierrez (2019), 'Indonesian Couple Carried Out Philippines Cathedral Bombing, Police Say', *New York Times*, 23 July. Available online: https://www.nytimes.com/2019/07/23/world/asia/philippines-bombing-deportees-isis.html (accessed 14 August 2022).
Pepinsky, T. B., R. W. Liddle, and S. Mujani (2018), *Piety and Public Opinion: Understanding Indonesian Islam*. Oxford: Oxford University Press.
Ramakrishna, K. (2014), *Islamist Terrorism and Militancy in Indonesia: The Power of the Manichean Mindset*. Singapore: Springer.
Ramakrishna, K. (2021), *Extremist Islam: Recognition and Response in Southeast Asia (Causes and Consequences of Terrorism)*. Oxford: Oxford University Press.
Rodzi, N. (2019), '16 Terror Suspects Nabbed in Malaysia', *Straits Times*, 27 September. Available online: https://www.straitstimes.com/asia/se-asia/nine-suspected-militants-arrested-by-malaysia-amid-fears-of-large-scale-attacks (accessed 14 August 2022).
Rajaratnam School of International Studies (RSIS) (2019), 'Malaysia', *Counter Terrorism Trends and Analyses*, January. Singapore: RSIS. Available online: https://www.rsis.edu.sg/wp-content/uploads/2020/01/CTTA-Annual-Threat-2020.pdf (accessed 14 August 2022).
Schmid, A. (2013), *Radicalisation, De-Radicalisation, Counter-Radicalisation: A Conceptual Discussion and Literature Review*, ICCT Research Paper. The Hague: International Centre for Counter-Terrorism. Available online: https://icct.nl/publication/radicalisation-de-radicalisation-counter-radicalisation-a-conceptual-discussion-and-literature-review/ (accessed 14 August 2022).
Schulze, K. (2018), 'The Surabaya Bombings and the Evolution of the Jihadi Threat in Indonesia'. *CTC Sentinel*, 11 (6): 1–6. Available online: https://ctc.usma.edu/surabaya-bombings-evolution-jihadi-threat-indonesia/ (accessed 14 August 2022).
Schuurman, B. and M. Taylor (2018), 'Reconsidering Radicalization: Fanaticism and the Link Between Ideas and Violence', *Perspectives on Terrorism*, 12 (1): 3–22.
Sholeh, B. (2006), 'Jihad in Maluku', in A. T. H. Tan (ed), *A Handbook of Terrorism and Insurgency in Southeast Asia*, 152–4, Cheltenham: Edward Elgar.
Solahudin (2013), *The Roots of Terrorism in Indonesia: From Darul Islam to Jemaah Islamiyah*, trans. D. McRae, Sydney: UNSW Press.
Stepanova, E. (2008), *Terrorism in Asymmetrical Conflict: Ideological and Structural Aspects*. Stockholm International Peace Research Institute, Research Report No. 23. Oxford: Oxford University Press.
Umam, S. (2006), 'Radical Muslims in Indonesia: The Case of Ja'far Umar Thalib and the Laskar Jihad', *Explorations in Southeast Asian Studies*, 6 (1): 1–26.
Vergani, M., M. Iqbal, E. Ilbahar and G. Barton (2018), 'The 3 Ps of Radicalization: Push, Pull and Personal. A Systematic Scoping Review of the Scientific Evidence about

Radicalisation into Violent Extremism', *Studies in Conflict & Terrorism*, 43 (10): https://doi.org/10.1080/1057610X.2018.1505686.

Yusa, Z. (2018), 'Six Malaysians Were Involved in Basilan Suicide Bomb Plot, Expert Says', *The Defense Post*, 24 December. Available online: https://www.thedefensepost.com/2018/12/24/malaysian-involved-basilan-suicide-bomb-plot/ (accessed 14 August 2022).

Section Three

Religion and violence across extremist movements and contexts

8

A majority with a minority complex: Examining anti-Muslim violence in Sri Lanka and India

Amarnath Amarasingam and Shweta Desai

Introduction

With the start of Ramadan in 2022, recognizable instances of radical Hindu nationalists provoking members of the Muslim community in India became commonplace. In early April 2022, when Muslims in the Rajasthan town of Karauli were going about their day, 'Hindu worshippers on motorcycles draped in saffron scarves arrived' and began playing a hugely popular song by Sandeep Chaturvedi, a member of the Hindutva youth movement (Dua 2019). The lyrics are not subtle: 'The day the Hindus wake up, the consequence will be/that the skull-cap wearer will bow down and say victory to lord Ram/the day my blood boils, I wish to show you your place/then I will not speak, only my sword will' (Iyer 2022). Some Muslims watched in fear and panic, but others decided to defend themselves: they picked up stones and flung them at the motorcycles. Once again, communal violence, this time short-lived, descended on an Indian town.

Narratives like this are increasingly common in South Asian countries like India, Sri Lanka and Myanmar, where majoritarian radical Buddhists or Hindus have come to see minorities among them – most often Muslims – as a sinister fifth column that must be alienated and attacked. Extremism researchers have often bemoaned the fact that much of the literature in the field is related to non-state actors, and relatively less attention has been paid to how communal violence, racism and hate speech have been mainstreamed and sanctioned by those in power. This chapter provides a deep dive into anti-Muslim violence in Sri Lanka and India over the last decade or so in particular. While the ethnic and religious make-up and history of both countries are indeed different and long running, this chapter argues that common threads are nevertheless clear. We focus here not only on majoritarian extremism, which stretches back several decades in each of these countries, but also examine the ways in which social media has made these fault lines worse through misinformation, conspiracy theories and polarization.

Majority populations, demographic panic and the emergency mindset

In 1986, in what he called his 'engaged political tract' on Sri Lanka, respected anthropologist Stanley J. Tambiah wrote that the Sinhalese community in the country suffers from a 'majority with a minority complex' (Tambiah 1986: 92). This is, he argued, partly due to the island's minuscule size but also because of its proximity to South India, where the state of Tamil Nadu makes the Sinhalese feel like they are a minority in the region even if they are a majority on the island. This notion of a 'majority with a minority complex', while written with Sri Lanka in mind, has been used by other scholars and writers as a useful analytical frame to think about communal dynamics in Myanmar (Foxeus 2019), India (Guha 2019) and far-right politics in Europe (Fisher and Taub 2019), as well as extremist movements and their notion of 'white genocide' and 'the great replacement theory' (Galloway et al. 2022). These false ideas, increasingly prevalent among majority populations – that they are being overrun, outbred and replaced – have been brought about by a kind of demographic panic that can 'make majorities feel as if their dominance is endangered, leading to fear of – and sometimes attacks on – minorities whose very existence is perceived as an existential threat' (Fisher and Taub 2019).

Under certain conditions, in other words, individuals can start to believe that their ingroup is under grave danger of being 'overrun, overbred, and replaced', and that drastic measures are required to rectify this situation. As the late Michael Jerryson noted in his discussion of the 'emergency mindset' (2021), emergencies are scenarios when normal kinds of behaviour can legitimately be set aside. When an individual is driving a car, they may normally not speed or run red lights, but if they are transporting someone who is injured or about to give birth, then the normal rules no longer apply. As Jerryson (2021: 41) writes, 'if the emergency is not localized in a person or place, but rather a worldwide emergency, it impacts more than one type of behaviour; it realigns a person's worldview'. When individuals come to adopt an emergency mindset, according to Jerryson (2021), 'nuances are lost and the world is dominated by the duality of good and evil – and good is under threat'.

J. M. Berger, in his book *Extremism* (2018), attempts to make sense of hatred and extremism of all kinds, not simply those of a particular ideological variety. To his credit, he clearly sees how his framework becomes immediately relevant for understanding not only non-state actors like Al-Qa'eda or far-right groups but also majoritarian communal hatreds like those found in Myanmar, India, China or Sri Lanka. He defines extremism as 'the belief that an in-group's success or survival can never be separated from the need for hostile action against an out-group' (2018: 44). As Berger (2018: 46) notes, whether this hostile action is discrimination, segregation, attacks or genocide, and whether such action is seen by the in-group as defensive, offensive or pre-emptive, the key element of the framework is inseparability. The in-group, according to Berger (2018: 55), consists of: (1) beliefs, such as shared creed, values, as well as overall worldview; (2) traits, including physical, mental, social or spiritual attributes; and (3) practices, which include the past history of the group, the behaviour of the group today, as well as notions of the group's destiny.

With respect to the out-group, its mere existence is not enough to result in hostile action. Rather, the out-group must be similarly constructed through a description of their beliefs, traits and practices (Berger 2018: 57). As he rightly notes, and as will become clear below, descriptions of the out-group tend to naturally rely less on personal experience and facts, and more on interpretation, fiction and conspiracies. Berger's Crisis/Solution framework is also important for making sense of our discussion below. Members of the in-group see the out-group as presenting a crisis in several ways: impurity (there is something about the out-group that is corrupting the identity and integrity of the in-group), conspiracy (the out-group is involved in a sinister and secretive plot to harm the in-group), existential threat (the in-group is in danger of being wiped out imminently) and apocalypse (the out-group is literally bringing about the end of civilization, and the in-group must stop them) (Berger 2018: 75–94). Solutions available to the in-group, according to Berger, have varied: harassment, discrimination, segregation, hate crimes, terrorism, oppression, war and genocide (2018: 99–100).

For our purposes, each of these broader frameworks – majority with a minority complex, emergency mindset and extremist violence – is quite similar, although most usefully detailed by Berger. Using the framework, we now turn to a discussion of how these dynamics have played out most recently in Sri Lanka and India. For our Sri Lanka case study, we examine some key elements in the development of Sinhala nationalism, the various anti-Muslim riots prior to the Easter attacks in 2019 and the violence that followed. For India, we explore the rise of Hindu nationalism in the country and look closely at the Delhi riots, the anti-Muslim conspiracy theories related to the Covid pandemic, and conspiracy theories related to how Muslims are secretly converting Hindu women to Islam.

Anti-Muslim violence in Sri Lanka

Sri Lanka has a population of approximately 20.3 million people, according to the 2012 island-wide Sri Lankan census (the first since 1981), and this population is fairly ethnically and religiously diverse. According to the 2012 census, the majority ethnic group in Sri Lanka is the Sinhala (75 per cent), the vast majority of whom are Buddhist (around 90 per cent). The Tamil community in Sri Lanka, roughly 15 per cent of the total population, consists of Sri Lankan Tamils (11.2 per cent of the total population) and Indian Tamils (4.2 per cent). The vast majority of the Tamil population in Sri Lanka are Hindu (around 80 per cent), but there are a significant number of Christians (8 per cent).

The Moors of Sri Lanka (Muslims) are also an important ethnic group and make up about 9 per cent of the population. They are called Moors not because they have any direct connection to the people of North Africa but because the 'Portuguese gave this name to all the Islamic communities they encountered on the Indian Ocean littoral' (De Silva 1997: 3–5). The smaller ethnic groups (1 per cent in total) consist of the Burghers (descendants of European settlers), the Malays (descendants of settlers from the Malay Peninsula, arriving during the Dutch and British colonial period) and the Veddas (the indigenous peoples of Sri Lanka).

For over 400 years, all or parts of Sri Lanka fell under the control of successive European powers: the Portuguese (1505–1658), the Dutch (1658–1796) and the British (1796–1948). For our purposes, the British colonial period is most significant in providing a context for the Hindu and Buddhist revivals of the nineteenth century. Indeed, as de Silva (1997: 198) notes, 'the Buddhist revival is perhaps better described as the Buddhist reaction to the missionary onslaught'. The Buddhist revivalists of the late nineteenth and early twentieth centuries were convinced that they were recovering a lost ideal from the Anuradhapura period (377 BCE–1017 CE).

According to the Sinhala, the *Mahavamsa*, a historical poem about the great kings of Sir Lanka compiled in about the fifth century, testifies to the fact that they were the original inhabitants of the island, and much attention is paid to the account of one monarch in particular, Dutthagamini. His story encourages the view that the Sinhala and Tamil people are long-standing enemies (DeVotta 2004: 26), and it centres on his defeat of the Chola king, Elara, who ruled Sri Lanka from the ancient capital of Anuradhapura. In this account, Dutthagamini is not at peace with himself following the brutal defeat of the Chola king, and eight arahants are sent to provide comfort and ease his mental anguish. They do so by convincing him that he went to war 'not for personal glory but for the sake of the Buddhist religion' (Kent 2008: 19–20).

In other words, the point of the story, as Grant (2009: 48) notes, is that the 'overthrow of the Tamil king is required first and foremost because Sri Lanka cannot be united unless the monarch is Buddhist'. For many contemporary Sinhala-Buddhist nationalists, then, the Dutthagamini epic is not a thing of the past. Modern activist bhikkhus have uncritically called on the story of Dutthagamini to justify their actions and so, as Grant (2009: 49–50) makes clear, 'the ghost of Dutthagamini has lived on, reclothed in modern dress – and now also equipped with modern weapons'.

An important later figure in the Sinhala-Buddhist revival was Anagarika Dharmapala (1864–1933). He was a fierce opponent of colonialism and sought to articulate the deep-seated fears of the Sinhala population. Dharmapala looked to the *Mahavamsa* to confirm the intimate and historical relationship between the Sinhalese people and Buddhism. His writings are a mixture of ethnic supremacism, anti-colonialism and Buddhist glorification. Given historical realities, his anti-colonial tirades may be justified. However, as DeVotta (2004: 31–2) points out, 'his rhetoric, whether intended to do so or not, legitimated extremism and helped catalyze the chauvinism that followed. It was jingoist and exclusivist and showed no regard or tolerance for non-Buddhists'.

Walpola Rahula (1907–97) also had a significant influence on Sinhala-Buddhist nationalism in the early twentieth century. Rahula was an internationally respected scholar of Buddhism, but his book *The Heritage of the Bhikku* ([1946] 1974) was a 'virtual manifesto for Sinhala Buddhist nationalism, linking the identity of the Sinhalas with the land and religion, and declaring a willingness to resort to violence to defend the Sinhala interest' (Grant 2009: 81). He argued that prior to colonization the Sangha (a Buddhist monastic community) was revered and socially engaged. Under the British, they had lost much of their social influence and had become reclusive, a plight that can only be corrected by gaining independence from colonial rule (Seneviratne 1999: 168–88). Rahula ([1946] 1974: 95) was also highly critical of some Sinhalese, who, having internalized a Western notion of private religion, thought that bhikkhus should stay out of politics.

While the intellectual groundwork had been laid for Sinhala-Buddhist majoritarianism, its full consequences would not be felt until after independence in 1948. While the full story of anti-Tamil policies and the resultant civil war in Sri Lanka is beyond the scope of this chapter, it is important to note that the Muslim community of Sri Lanka came to be victimized by both Tamil militancy and Sinhala militancy over the next several decades leading up to the end of the civil war in 2009.

After the war ended in 2009, Sinhala-Buddhist extremist groups, like the Bodu Bala Sena (BBS) and its supporters, aided by social media conspiratorialism, turned on the Muslim community and began to see them as demographic and economic threats to the Sinhalese community. This resulted in several years of sporadic riots, destruction of mosques and killings (Amarasingam and Bass 2016). In September 2011, a 300-year-old Muslim shrine in Anuradhapura was destroyed by a mob of 100 people, led by Buddhist religious leaders, who argued that the shrine was 'on land given to Sinhala Buddhists 2000 years ago' (Centre for Policy Alternatives 2013: 51). In April 2012, thousands of people forcibly entered a mosque in Dambulla and destroyed everything inside. The then prime minister, to the shock of many, ordered that the mosque be moved to another part of town since the area it was currently located was considered 'sacred to Buddhists' (Sarjoon et al. 2016: 5). BBS attacks against the Muslim community escalated in subsequent years and peaked around two events in 2014 and 2018.

In June 2014, the towns of Aluthgama, Dharga Town, Valipanna and Beruwela – cities on the southwestern coast of Sri Lanka – saw several days of communal violence (Haniffa et al. 2014). The violence seems to have been sparked by a local altercation between three Muslim youths and a Buddhist monk. As the situation grew tense, meetings between the police and religious leaders were convened to try and establish calm. On 15 June 2014, the BBS held a meeting in Aluthgama laced with racism, hate speech and suggestions of violence. Crowds streamed out of the meeting and started confronting Muslims they saw on the streets. Both sides started to throw stones. Violence began in surrounding villages as well, and several businesses and homes were attacked and burnt.

While the role of social media in spreading misinformation and conspiracy theories in Sri Lanka, which often spurred on this kind of communal violence, has been well documented (Samaratunge and Hattotuwa 2014), platforms like Facebook and WhatsApp played a particularly destructive role in subsequent violent episodes in the country (Rajagopalan and Nazim 2018). Bizarre rumours have long existed online and have played into Sinhala nationalist fears of losing their majority status on the island. The 2013 violence against Muslim-owned businesses like Fashion Bug, for instance, was spurred on by rumours that Muslims were selling Sinhalese women underwear laced with sterilization cream in order to stifle the community's population growth (Francis 2013).

In late February 2018, an altercation started in Ampara, a small town in the Eastern province, when a Sinhala patron began berating a Muslim restaurant owner about something he found in his meal (Borham and Attanayake 2018). Prior to this encounter, conspiracy theories had been circulating on Facebook that 23,000 sterilization pills had been seized from a Muslim pharmacist. The viral rumour seemed to confirm long-running fears among some in the Sinhalese community that Muslims were secretly plotting to demographically supplant them in the country. In a shaky cell phone video, the customer yells at the store owner in Sinhala, 'You put in sterilization medicine, didn't you?' The store owner, who does not understand Sinhala, just nods in agreement to the questions being shouted at him (Taub and Fisher 2018). The crowd that had gathered then beat the store owner and set fire to a nearby mosque. As Taub and Fisher (2018) rightly point out, 'in an earlier time, this might have ended in Ampara', but as the cell phone video was posted to Facebook and spread, communal tensions started to simmer.

The anger around the sterilization rumours would converge with the death of a Sinhalese man, who had been beaten by several Muslim youths after a traffic dispute, in Kandy on 3 March 2018. The violence began in Kandy and surrounding areas on 4 March and would finally cease on 9 March 2018. At the end of the violence, two people lay dead and around 20 mosques, 224 houses and 119 businesses were either damaged or destroyed (Zubair et al. 2018). The government, as it would after the Easter bombings, temporarily blocked social media platforms in order to prevent further attack planning and spreading of disinformation (Amarasingam and Rizwie 2020).

The Muslim community in Sri Lanka, which had been facing waves of anti-Muslim violence since the end of the war against the Liberation Tigers of Tamil Elam (LTTE) in 2009, rarely put up any coordinated resistance. Yet researchers who have conducted fieldwork in these communities note that Muslims were worried this was just going to continue indefinitely, whenever it was politically expedient to rile up the Sinhala nationalist base – and they would eventually need to stand up for themselves. Given the level of anti-Muslim violence, though, it is perhaps surprising that the country did not witness some level of militant Islamist – let alone jihadi – mobilization in all these years. While reports suggest that around thirty-two individuals left Sri Lanka to join the Islamic State since 2013, there has been no evidence of local plots in Sri Lanka until 2019 (Aneez 2016).

In April 2019, a series of seven coordinated suicide bomb attacks in popular hotels and historical churches occurred across the capital city of Colombo, other coastal cities in the west and towns in the east of the country, killing hundreds as they gathered for Easter (for more on the Easter attacks, see Amarasingam 2019). Two days later, Islamic State claimed the attacks via its Amaq news agency, stating the attackers were 'Islamic State fighters' and had 'targeted citizens of coalition states and Christians in Sri Lanka'. The Easter attacks immediately set off a wave of retaliatory attacks and anti-Muslim animus that was unique in its intensity.

Within hours of the bombings, a Muslim-owned shop was burnt to the ground (Gettleman and Bastians 2019). The violence reached fever pitch on Monday, when mobs reportedly armed with gasoline bombs swept through western Sri Lanka, destroying 500 Muslim shops, houses and mosques, and in some cases carrying out brutal assaults on Muslims themselves (Aneez and Ulmer 2019, Shah and Jayasinghe 2019). Residents of the affected towns reported dozens of injured, and one man was killed (Ahmed and Griffiths 2019). In one particularly graphic video, police appear to comply with rioters' instructions to drag a severely injured man along the road rather than take him to the hospital in a trishaw. Dozens of everyday Muslims were rounded up and held in detention; heart-breaking instances of Tamil and Sinhalese families pulling their children out of classrooms run by Muslim teachers, even though they had been their child's teacher for years, were also prevalent.

Anti-Muslim violence in India

Hindu nationalism, also known simply as Hindutva, refers to ethno-religious and nationalist political attitudes in India. While the movement has roots in earlier organizations like the Arya Samaj (Jaffrelot 1993: 11), contemporary currents of Hindu nationalism harken back to the thinking and writing of Vinayak Damodar Savarkar (1883–1966). During the First World War, Indians put enormous pressure on the British colonial power for increased self-rule. The British were at war with the Ottoman Caliphate, and sections of the Indian Muslim leadership scoffed at the idea of allying with colonial forces against a Muslim power. With the carving up of the Ottoman Caliphate after the war, the Khilafat movement led by Shaukat Ali and Mohammad Ali arose in protest, demanding that the caliphate be preserved (Qureshi 1999).

For individuals like Savarkar, these kinds of transnational loyalties held by some Indians were a cause for concern. His book *Hindutva: Who Is a Hindu?* – written in 1922 while in prison – is the clearest articulation of Hindu nationalist identity building. For Savarkar, some Muslims in India are a threat to Hindu national unity because, as was clear with the Khilafat movement, their loyalties lie elsewhere, with pan-Islamic ideals. As Savarkar wrote, 'Mecca to [the Indian Muslims] is a sterner reality than Delhi or Agra' (Jaffrelot 1993: 26).

Some contemporary commentators, taking the term 'Hindu nationalism' in its literal sense, often assume that it is fundamentally a religious movement. This largely misses the point. For Savarkar and contemporary Hindu nationalist organizations, religion was only one aspect of the 'Hinduness' they envisioned. For Savarkar, the territory of India was fundamentally linked to Hindu racial identity and culture – one aspect of which was religion. But it was much more than that. Savarkar rejects some of the pillars of Western forms of nationalism built on ideas like social contract and citizenship. Rather, for him, everyone in the territory of India is bonded together by 'blood'.

Savarkar draws a distinction between the religions that originated in India – Hinduism, Buddhism, Jainism and Sikhism – and the ones that have followers in India but originated elsewhere (namely, Islam and Christianity). During the colonial period, the British Empire applied a Western notion of 'religion' to the Indian subcontinent, trying to separate the religions that originated in India into distinctly separate entities. Some Indians began to feel as though this separation was forcing them to compartmentalize what was actually mutually dependent. As Arvind Sharma (2020: 43) writes, 'Indian followers of these four members of the Indic religious tradition did not treat their own relationship to these traditions necessarily in exclusive terms prior to the British intervention.' In the Indian understanding of religious life, a follower could be part of more than one tradition at a time and draw from the broader cultural repository as needed. The term 'Hindutva' was meant to signify this fluidity of membership by talking about 'culture' instead of religion. Hindutva followers 'claimed that although these four religions were four different religions according to the British census, all four of them share a common culture. What the word "religion" had divided, the word "culture" united' (A. Sharma 2020: 43).

After independence from the British, the Rashtriya Swayamsevak Sangh (RSS, the National Volunteer Corps) became the most important and politically successful organizational expression of Hindu nationalist ideology. It has grown to about 20,000 branches (*shakhas*) and has a regular membership of several million volunteers in India. The RSS considers itself the foundational organization of the 'family' (Sangh Parivar) of affiliated organizations and movements that make up Hindu activism. In 1948, the RSS formed its student wing to combat 'polluting' influences in the education system (Bhatt 2001: 114). In 1952, the RSS started work among tribal communities in order 'to integrate them into the Hindu mainstream' and launch reconversion campaigns to 'combat the influence of "foreign" Christian missions' (Bhatt 2001). They work in the education system to establish RSS textbooks that extol Greater India 'as the Aryan homeland and the birthplace of humanity, and from whom the Persians, Greeks, Egyptians, and Native Americans and indeed Jesus (said to have roamed the Himalayas) gained their knowledge and wisdom' (Bhatt 2001). The RSS also has an international wing, Sewa International, which organizes welfare activities outside India and raises funds for projects in India (Bhatt 2001).

The Bharatiya Janata Party (BJP, the political arm of the RSS) champions Hindu nationalism by centring its politics on a Hindutva agenda and advocating for the reestablishment of the Hindu order (Vaishnav 2019). It promotes Hindu supremacy and ultra-nationalism by projecting minorities as the hostile 'other', often at the cost of communal violence and deepening religious schisms. Communal tensions, vigilante lynching, violence against minorities and hate speech have been on the rise under BJP rule (Mallapur 2019). The roots of the BJP's earliest political success lay in the Ram Janmabhoomi movement in the 1980s, which led to the demolition of the sixteenth-century mosque constructed over the alleged birthplace of Lord Rama in Ayodhya, Uttar Pradesh (The Wire Staff 2021). The destruction of the Babri mosque was pivotal in the rise of majoritarianism and cultural nationalism (Ghadvalpatil and Varma 2017).

The BJP has consistently projected Islam and Muslims as an internal enemy of the Hindus through propaganda, fearmongering and manipulation (Mander 2019). To exemplify these trends, we now take a deep dive into two recent cases of anti-Muslim hate speech and violence: 'corona jihad' conspiracy theories related to the Covid pandemic and the 'love jihad' legislation. Both paint a clear picture of the ways in which the Muslim community in India is seamlessly woven into conspiratorial narratives and seen as inherently suspect.

The broader backdrop to Indian anti-Muslim sentiment and violence after 2020 was the controversy and protests that erupted with respect to the Citizenship Amendment Act (CAA). In December 2019, large-scale protests broke out against the Indian parliament's passing of the contentious CAA, providing conditional fast-track citizenship to persecuted religious minorities including Hindus, Sikhs, Christians,

Jains, Parsis and Buddhists from Afghanistan, Bangladesh and Pakistan who arrived in India before 2015. The Act wilfully excludes Muslims and persecuted groups in the region such as Hazara Shias, Ahmadis, Rohingyas and Tibetans. The main opposition to the legislation came from the provision selectively granting citizenship on religious grounds in violation of the secular guarantees of the Constitution.

The initial student-led demonstrations in the university campuses in Uttar Pradesh, Delhi and by the indigenous Hindu populations in the northeast border region of Assam snowballed into nationwide protests, predominantly helmed by the Muslim communities. They feared the CAA, combined with the proposed all-India National Register of Citizens (NRC) (India Today Web Desk 2019), would be used to disenfranchise Muslims and other marginalized groups unable to provide documented evidence of their citizenship, enabling the state to hoard them in detention centres. The National Register of Citizens is an official record of citizens in India that was first prepared after the 1951 Census, but it has thus far only been implemented in the state of Assam. When the process was carried out in Assam in 2015, around 1.9 million people failed to provide the adequate documentation to make the NRC list. When Home Minister Amit Shah proposed that the NRC be implemented across India as a measure to target 'illegal immigrants', many feared that tens of millions of people, including many Muslims, would be left off the list, given what happened in Assam. Widespread protests erupted.

The landmark feature of these demonstrations was the sit-in protests in the Muslim-dominated localities of Shaheen Bagh and Jamia Milia Islamia, both located in Delhi, where protestors occupied public roads around the clock. By January, as the protests strengthened nationally and the Shaheen Bagh women refused to vacate the road until the Modi government repealed the Act, the BJP in Delhi began to denounce the anti-CAA protesters as anti-nationals and traitors (TNN Staff 2020). With upcoming Delhi state assembly elections slated for February 2020, the BJP leveraged the anti-CAA protests, making them part of its prime election agenda (Bhatnagar 2020). From 23 to 27 February 2020, violence engulfed several parts of Delhi's sprawling northeast suburbs densely inhabited by Hindu and Muslim communities. Of the fifty-three people killed during the chaos, forty were Muslim.

CoronaJihad

On 25 March 2020, India imposed one of the largest lockdowns in history (Umachandran 2020), confining its 1.3 billion citizens for over a month to contain the spread of the novel coronavirus (Covid-19) (Miller and Jeffrey 2020). By the end of the lockdown's first week, reports started to emerge that there was a common link among a large number of the new cases detected in different parts of the country: many had attended a large religious gathering of Muslims in Delhi. Hindu nationalist groups began to see the virus not as an entity spreading organically throughout India but as a sinister plot by Indian Muslims to purposefully infect the population. #CoronaJihad thus began trending on Twitter. Even as the Indian government struggled to provide food and transport for millions of stranded migrant labourers (Associated Press 2020), failed to address access to clean water and healthcare in densely populated slums and tried to respond to the virus without adequate testing kits, ventilators or personal protective equipment (Iyer 2020), large parts of the country still maintained that the true drivers of the health crisis were a shady cabal of extremist Muslims.

From 13 to 15 March, the Tablighi Jamaat – an Islamic reformist movement founded in 1927 whose followers travel around the world on proselytizing missions – held a large gathering for preachers from over forty countries at its mosque headquarters in Delhi, known as the Nizamuddin Markaz. The mosque is situated in a densely populated neighbourhood near the famous Sufi shrine, Nizamuddin Auliya. According to media reports, this gathering became a 'hotspot' for dozens of new cases, as attendees left the gathering and returned to their respective homes in India (N. Sharma 2020). Subsequently, the Indian government declared the mosque to be an infection hotspot, and Delhi police filed a first information report under the Epidemic Diseases Act and sections of the Indian Penal Code against members of the Tablighi Jamaat for disobeying government lockdown orders (Express Web Desk 2020). The Ministry of Home Affairs revoked the visas of and blacklisted foreign Islamic preachers who attended the event, and the health ministry traced several cases of the virus in India back to the gathering (V. Singh 2020).

Hindu nationalists and pro-government news channels in India latched on to components of the story and used it to feed a variety of anti-Muslim narratives (Jha and Dixit 2020). Unsurprisingly, this has led to an increase in incendiary hate speech, false claims and vicious rumours intended to encourage violence and ostracize the Indian Muslim community. The steady flood of anti-Muslim content in WhatsApp groups, TikTok and Facebook videos, Twitter posts, panel discussions on news media and official government briefings was astonishing. There were three main themes of anti-Muslim propaganda related to Covid that made the rounds: that Muslims believe they are immune from Covid, that Muslims believe Covid is divine punishment and that Muslims are deliberately spreading the virus.

In a video clip of anti-CAA protests in Shaheen Bagh, Delhi, from 20 March, a protestor opines, 'There is no corona here at Shaheen Bagh. We know that. They might be afraid of the corona. Corona emerged from the Quran. What is Corona? Deadlier diseases that corona will come. God willing, we will remain unscathed from those diseases. However, it is a matter of concern for them. They should be worried' (OpIndia Staff 2020a). This video received much media coverage and commentary on social media.

Related to the second theme, a wave of videos, allegedly by Muslim Indians, claimed that Covid-19 was a gift from Allah to punish the enemies of Islam and those who support the National Registration of Citizens. A fourteen-second TikTok clip that circulated widely on Facebook, Twitter and WhatsApp around 2 April showed three Muslim men taking turns to say, 'Welcome to India, coronavirus. To the ones who were for our NRC, my God (Allah)'s NRC is now being implemented. Now only He will decide who will stay and who will go' (OpIndia Staff 2020b). A video from 2 April uploaded to TikTok by @sayyedjameel48 that also caused outrage and spread panic featured its creator calling the coronavirus divine punishment while licking and wiping his nose with currency notes: 'There is no treatment for a disease like corona. It is a greeting by Allah, for you people.' The creator of the video was later arrested by the Maharashtra police (Press Trust of India 2020). Such content gave fuel to right-wing extremists, who took these videos as proof that Indian Muslims are intentionally driving the Covid-19 pandemic.

Related to the third theme, a five-minute video compilation heavily circulated on WhatsApp and Telegram groups starts with the following question and statement: 'Why are Muslims Spreading Coronavirus? Why Muslims of India are threatening to spread the virus?' It is followed by a recorded voice that declares, 'We Muslims of India have taken a vow and are united to bring coronavirus in India and have decided to spread it around. Look at our ghettos, no one is following social distancing, we will not sit at home'. Next, the disembodied voice claims that Muslims were incited to spread the virus, as the Tablighi Jamaat congregation did. It ends with more clips of Muslims licking fruits and currency notes and the message, 'India right now stands at 3000 corona cases, with 647 linked to Muslims from Tablighi Jamaat. In just 2 days. Rise above this hatred for Hindus and Hindustan'.

Following sensational reports that Tablighi Jamaat members had been sneezing, spitting and urinating publicly to spread the virus, several videos began circulating allegedly showing Indian Muslims spitting on other people or food to intentionally spread Covid-19. Unlike the videos described above, which were explicitly attributed to the Tablighi Jamaat, these videos generally were not (though some commentators still made a link to Tabligh members). A video that actually depicted a situation in Thailand went viral on Twitter on 3 April, supposedly portraying an infected Indian Muslim spitting on a healthy man at a railway station (OpIndia Staff 2020c). In a since-deleted tweet, the account @TheShaktiRoopa posted the video (with 65,000 views) with the caption, 'Is this not #CoronaJihad !!!?' (Poovanna 2018). Another old video from 2019 which had already gone viral in the United Arab Emirates, Singapore and Malaysia, showing a Muslim man at a fast-food stall blowing into food containers before delivering them, was shared in Indian social media circles with claims that an Indian Muslim delivery man was spitting on the food (Mehta 2020).

Love Jihad

Less than six months after Muslims were targeted in the Delhi riots and blamed for deliberately spreading the Covid-19 virus, the Muslim community was again at the centre of a raging storm related to accusations of them waging 'Love Jihad'. The term was devised by right-wing Hindu nationalist organizations and refers to the conspiracy that Muslim men honey-trap unsuspecting Hindu women into marriages to convert them to the fold of Islam. The idea was to oversaturate the level of threat presented by love jihad to justify anti-Muslim violence, thus designating the Muslim man as a dangerous threat. Two BJP-ruled states, Uttar Pradesh (The Leaflet 2020) and Madhya Pradesh (R. P. Singh 2020), both passed anti-conversion legislation with penalties and jail time for forceful and deceitful interfaith marriages as a preventative measure against love jihad. In West Bengal and Kerala, where the BJP was eyeing upcoming state elections, local leaders promised to legally protect the honour of Hindu women from 'jihadis'.

The term 'love jihad' has its origins in a 2009 judicial order by Kerala High Court to describe several cases of Muslim boys pretending to fall in love with Hindu or Christian girls and converting them to Islam. The issue itself has prevailed for centuries, deriving its origins from the conquests of Islamic invaders who forcefully converted the masses in then-newly occupied Hindu territories. In the 1920s, nationalist and radical Hindu organizations whipped up communal frenzy (Gupta 2009) against Indian Muslims using similar tropes of love jihad. Post-independence, RSS and its affiliated organizations attacked Christian missionaries for evangelizing among indigenous and Dalit communities.

The term was thereafter picked up by Hindutva organizations for whom fighting against religious conversions is a raison d'etre. In Kerala, the VHP has found an unusual ally among traditional opponents – some Catholics and Protestant Christians – who say that 'love jihad' is a reality (Ananthakrishnan 2009). Catholic groups have taken cues from the likes of Hindu groups to prevent girls from their community falling prey to Islamic designs by issuing guidelines for solemnizing interfaith marriages, particularly with Muslims, and setting up helplines to fight 'love jihad' (Babu 2017).

Right-wing organizations mounted concerted awareness campaigns on the reality of love jihad. Bajrang Dal, Hindu Janajagriti Samiti and VHP, including its women's wing Durga Vahini, issued advisories in schools and colleges, published leaflets and pamphlets and organized camps for parents and young girls (Poovanna 2018). They set up hotlines to report any suspicious cases of love jihad, formed anti-Romeo squads on the ground to act on the complaints and continued publicizing campaigns such as *Bahu Lao, Beti Bachao* (bring home a Muslim daughter-in-law, save a Hindu daughter) (Khanna 2014). The concerns about love jihad gained renewed attention in mainstream discussions nationally around September 2020 after the Vishva Hindu Parishad, a Hindu right-wing organization, released a love jihad special issue publishing an alleged list of 147 cases of Hindu love jihad victims, deeming love jihad a 'demographic war' that must be neutralized by the timely action of police, government and society (Vishva Hindu Parishad 2020).

Public furore, trends on social media and politicization of this issue from around September 2020 provided ideal timing for the BJP-ruled state governments in Uttar Pradesh and Madhya Pradesh to introduce legislation against conversion that specifically targeted love jihad at the provincial level. To enforce the law, police in Uttar Pradesh conducted surprise raids at wedding venues and registration offices where Hindu–Muslim interfaith couples were tying the knot; they stopped traditional wedding ceremonies midway, arrested bridegrooms and registered criminal cases. This anti-religious law, under the guise of preventing love jihad, is now being used to settle past personal scores against Muslim men or to incarcerate them in prison as punishment for indulging in romantic relationships (Kumar 2021).

Love jihad became an attractive and easy way for the right wing to victimize minority Muslim communities by propagating their so-called dangerous intentions. The conspiracy has enabled the Hindu right wing to fan the popular Islamophobic myth of 'demographic invasion' that Muslims will eventually outnumber the majority Hindu population. Love jihad is another weapon in the arsenal of Indian Muslims, the argument goes, to seduce gullible Hindu girls for sexual exploitation and convert them through fraudulent marriages in order to destroy the source of Hindu lineage and increase its demography.

Conclusion

As is clear from the discussion above, in the era of social media, age-old anti-Muslim animus in India and Sri Lanka is accelerating and spreading in unprecedented ways. Minor disagreements that in previous eras may have been contained as local disputes now spread nationwide and are recorded as existential threats to majority communities. The Covid-19 pandemic has also gone a long way in providing Islamophobes in India and Sri Lanka with fresh conspiracy theories to peddle. While this chapter focused on historical and recent developments in India and Sri Lanka, similar dynamics are present in Myanmar with the Rohingya population, in China with the Uighurs, and in the Western world with Muslim and Mexican immigrants and refugees. In many parts of the world, some individuals in majority communities are experiencing a kind of demographic panic – a minority complex – wherein they see, at best, a slow attack on the majority status of their in-group through natural population shifts or, at worst, a sinister plot to unseat, oppress or overrun them.

Political leaders in countries like India and Sri Lanka are using this demographic panic to push electoral platforms that are tugging at the fault lines of intercommunal harmony by passing legislation that specifically targets Muslim and other minorities and reinforces Sinhala nationalist and Hindu nationalist sentiments. For extremism researchers, it is important to continue to centre the ways in which these in-group/out-group dynamics come not only from non-state actors but also from those in power. Keeping this consistently in mind has important consequences for how we think about individual radicalization to violence and the blind spots in countering violent extremism (CVE) and counter-narrative programming, as well as ongoing debates related to the role of social media companies in platforming hate speech and extremist content. Left unchecked, Hindu nationalists in India and Sinhala-Buddhist nationalists in Sri Lanka will continue to exacerbate existing ethno-religious and cultural cleavages that tear apart the social fabric of both countries.

References

Ahmed, I. and J. Griffiths (2019), 'One Dead as Sri Lanka Town Gripped by Another Bout of Anti-Muslim Violence', *CNN World*, May 14. Available online: https://edition.cnn.com/2019/05/14/asia/sri-lanka-muslim-violence-intl/index.html (accessed 10 April 2022).

Ananthakrishnan, G. (2009), '"Love Jihad" Racket: VHP, Christian Groups Find Common Cause', *The Times of India*, 13 October. Available online: https://timesofindia.indiatimes.com/india/Love-Jihad-racket-VHP-Christian-groups-find-common-cause/articleshow/5117548.cms (accessed 2 April 2022).

Aneez, S. (2016), 'Sri Lanka Says 32 "Elite" Muslims Have Joined Islamic State in Syria', Reuters, 18 November. Available online: https://www.reuters.com/article/us-mideast-crisis-syria-sri-lanka-idUSKBN13D1EE (accessed 10 April 2022).

Aneez, S. and A. Ulmer (2019), 'Sri Lanka Says Hardline Buddhist Groups Likely to Blame for Anti-Muslim Attacks', *Reuters*, 15 May. Available online: https://www.reuters.com/article/us-sri-lanka-blasts-unrest/sri-lanka-says-hardline-buddhist-groups-likely-to-blame-for-anti-muslim-attacks-idUSKCN1SL15H (accessed 9 April 2022).

Amarasingam, A. (2019), 'Terrorism on the Teardrop Island: Understanding the Easter 2019 Attacks in Sri Lanka', *CTC Sentinel*, 12 (5): 1–10. Available online: https://ctc.usma.edu/terrorism-teardrop-island-understanding-easter-2019-attacks-sri-lanka/#reference51 (accessed 9 April 2022).

Amarasingam, A. and D. Bass (eds) (2016), *Sri Lanka: The Struggle for Peace in the Aftermath of War*. London: Hurst and Co.

Amarasingam, A. and R. Rizwie (2020), 'Turning the Tap Off: The Impacts of Social Media Shutdown after Sri Lanka's Easter Attacks', *International Centre for Counter-Terrorism Report*, October 20. Available online: https://icct.nl/publication/social-media-shutdown-after-sri-lankas-easter-attacks/ (accessed 30 March 2022).

Associated Press (2020), 'Indian Migrants Walk Hundreds of Miles to Return Home Amid COVID-19 Lockdown', *HuffPost*, 1 April. Available online: https://www.huffpost.com/entry/indian-migrants-coronavirus-walk-lockdown_n_5e843f87c5b65dd0c5d68b49 (accessed 30 March 2022).

Babu, R. (2017), 'BJP Man in Kerala Sets up Christian Helpline to Fight "Love Jihad"', *Hindustan Times*, 14 June. Available online: https://www.hindustantimes.com/india-news/christian-helpline-in-kerala-next-to-fight-so-called-love-jihad/story-XBtmb2ZF47gc5mAWsxJ0EP.html (accessed 3 April 2022).

Berger, J. M. (2018), *Extremism*. Cambridge, MA: MIT Press.

Bhatnagar, G. V. (2020), 'Shadow of Anti-CAA protests Looms over Delhi Assembly Polls', *The Wire*, 13 January. Available online: https://thewire.in/politics/anti-caa-protests-delhi-assembly-polls (accessed 30 March 2022).

Bhatt, C. (2001), *Hindu Nationalism: Origins, Ideologies, and Modern Myths*. New York: Berg.

Borham, M. and D. Attanayake (2018). 'Tension in Ampara after Fake "Sterilization Pills" Controversy' *Sunday Observer*, 4 March. Available online: http://www.sundayobserver.lk/2018/03/04/news/tension-ampara-after-fake-%E2%80%98sterilization-pills%E2%80%99-controversy (accessed 30 March 2022).

Centre for Policy Alternatives (2013), *Attacks on Places of Religious Worship in Post-War Sri Lanka*, March. Available online: https://s3.amazonaws.com/f.cl.ly/items/3L2T1z0A1G1f3o0m2H3g/Attacks%20on%20Religious%20Places.pdf (accessed 30 March 2022).

De Silva, C. R. (1997), *A History of Sri Lanka*. Colombo: Vijitha Yapa Press.

DeVotta, N. (2004), *Blowback: Linguistic Nationalism, Institutional Decay, and Ethnic Conflict in Sri Lanka*. Stanford, CA: Stanford University Press.

Dua, M. (2019), 'Sound and Fury: The Voices Creating Aggressive Hindutva's Soundtrack', *The Indian Express*, 22 January. Available online: https://indianexpress.com/article/express-sunday-eye/aggressive-hindutva-soundtrack-fury-internet-5545915/ (accessed 11 April 2022).

Express Web Desk (2020), 'Nizamuddin Congregation: Delhi Police Registers FIR against Maulana Saad, Others', *The New Indian Express*, 31 March. Available online: https://www.newindianexpress.com/cities/delhi/2020/mar/31/nizamuddin-congregation-delhi-police-registers-fir-against-maulana-saad-others-2124002.html (accessed 30 March 2022).

Fisher, M. and A. Taub (2019), '"Overrun", "Outbred", "Replaced": Why Ethnic Majorities Lash Out over False Fears', *The New York Times*, 30 April. Available online: https://

www.nytimes.com/2019/04/30/world/asia/sri-lanka-populism-ethnic-tensions.html (accessed 2 April 2022).

Foxeus, N. (2019), 'The Buddha Was a Devoted Nationalist: Buddhist Nationalism, Ressentiment, and Defending Buddhism in Myanmar', *Religion*, 49 (4): 661–90.

Francis, K. (2013), 'New Fears in Sri Lanka amid Anti-Muslim Campaign', *Associated Press*, 7 April. Available online: https://www.irrawaddy.com/news/asia/new-fears-in-sri-lanka-amid-anti-muslim-campaign.html (accessed 30 March 2022).

Galloway, B., J. Noulty and A. Amarasingam (2022), 'The Great Replacement and the Far-Right Music Scene', *GNET Insights*, 31 May. Available online: https://gnet-research.org/2022/05/31/the-great-replacement-and-the-far-right-music-scene/ (accessed 11 April 2022).

Gettleman, J. and D. Bastians (2019), 'Sri Lanka's Muslims Face Angry Backlash after Easter Sunday Attacks', *The New York Times*, 24 April. Available online: https://www.nytimes.com/2019/04/24/world/asia/sri-lankas-muslims.html (accessed 10 April 2022).

Ghadyalpatil, A. and A. Varma (2017), 'How Babri Masjid Demolition Redefined Politics of Social Identity', *Mint*, 6 December. Available online: https://www.livemint.com/Politics/DMH9dZ2cO44c0g9hZ7zGwO/How-Babri-Masjid-demolition-redefined-politics-of-social-ide.html (accessed 30 March 2022).

Grant, P. (2009), *Buddhism and Ethnic Conflict in Sri Lanka*. Albany: SUNY Press.

Guha, R. (2019), Social Media Post, *Twitter*, December 13. Available online: https://twitter.com/ram_guha/status/1205701773324779521 (accessed 30 March 2022).

Gupta, C. (2009), 'Hindu Women, Muslim Men: Love Jihad and Conversions', *Economic and Political Weekly*, 44 (51): 13–15.

Haniffa, F., H. Amarasuriya, V. Wijenayake and G. Gunatilleke (2014), 'Where Have All the Neighbors Gone? Aluthgama Riots and Its Aftermath', *Law and Society Trust*. Available online: https://www.academia.edu/10331700/Where_Have_All_the_Neighbours_Gone_Aluthgama_Riots_and_its_Aftermath (accessed 31 March 2022).

Iyer, K. (2020), 'Mumbai Washes Its Hands of Lakhs, Do's & Don'ts Don't Matter Here', *The Indian Express*, 20 March. Available online: https://indianexpress.com/article/coronavirus/mumbai-slums-coronavirus-6321068/ (accessed 30 March 2022).

Iyer, A. (2022), '"The Day My Blood Boils": How Songs Incited Hate at the Navratri Rally in Rajasthan's Karauli', *Scroll.in*, 11 April. Available online: https://indianexpress.com/article/express-sunday-eye/aggressive-hindutva-soundtrack-fury-internet-5545915/ (accessed 11 April 2022).

Jaffrelot, C. (1993), *The Hindu Nationalist Movement in India*. New York: Columbia University Press.

Jerryson, M. (2021), 'Religious Violence as Emergency Mindset', *Journal of Religion and Violence*, 9 (1): 33–49.

Jha, N. and P. Dixit (2020), 'A Cluster of Coronavirus Cases Can Be Traced back to a Single Mosque and Now 200 Million Muslims Are Being Vilified', *BuzzFeed News*, 3 April. Available online: https://www.buzzfeednews.com/article/nishitajha/coronavirus-india-muslims-tablighi-jamaat (accessed 30 March 2022).

Kent, D. W. (2008), 'Shelter for you, Nirvana for Our Sons: Buddhist Belief and Practice in the Sri Lankan Army', PhD diss., University of Virginia, Charlottesville. Available online: https://thecarthaginiansolution.files.wordpress.com/2011/08/buddhist-belief-practise-in-sl-army.pdf (accessed 11 April 2022).

Khanna, T. (2014), 'Bajrang Dal to Launch "Bahu Lao, Beti Bachao" Campaign to Counter "Love Jihad": Report', *Zee News*, 27 December. Available online: https://zeenews.india.

com/news/india/bajrang-dal-to-launch-bahu-lao-beti-bachao-campaign-to-counter-love-jihad-report_1521139.html (accessed 4 April 2022).

Kumar, A. (2021), 'Is the "Love Jihad" Bogey Being Used to Settle Scores in UP?', *Newslaundry*, 1 March. Available online: https://www.newslaundry.com/2021/03/01/in-up-is-love-jihad-bogey-used-to-settle-scores (accessed 3 April 2022).

Mallapur, C. (2019), '28% Rise in Communal Incidents under NDA, Short of UPA high', *India Spend*, 8 February. Available online: https://www.indiaspend.com/28-rise-in-communal-incidents-under-nda-short-of-upa-high-58126/ (accessed 20 March 2022).

Mander, H. (2019), 'Over Five Years, BJP Has Consistently Sought to Marginalise Muslims', *The Indian Express*, 4 May. Available online: https://indianexpress.com/article/opinion/columns/muslim-marginalisation-bjp-rule-narendra-modi-5709640/ (accessed 30 March 2022).

Mehta, A. (2020), 'Fact Check: Old Video of Muslim Man Spitting on Food Goes Falsely Viral', 4 April. Available online: https://thewire.in/media/fact-check-old-video-muslim-man-spitting-on-food-goes-falsely-viral-covid-19 (accessed 30 March 2022).

Miller, A. and H. Jeffery (2020), 'Coronavirus Puts Over 1 Billion People in India on 21-Day Lockdown to Combat Spread', *CNBC*, 26 March. Available online: https://www.cnbc.com/2020/03/26/coronavirus-puts-over-1-billion-people-in-india-on-21-day-lockdown-to-combat-spread.html (accessed 30 March 2022).

OpIndia Staff (2020a), 'Corona Emerged from Quran, Nothing Will Happen to Us: Shaheen Bagh Protester', *OpIndia*, 20 March. Available online: https://www.opindia.com/2020/03/shaheen-bagh-quran-corona-covid-19-anti-caa/ (accessed 29 March 2022).

OpIndia Staff (2020b), 'Coronavirus: Islamists on TikTok Refer to Contagion as NRC of "God"', *OpIndia*, 2 April. Available online: https://www.opindia.com/2020/04/tiktok-islamists-coronavirus-tablighi-jamaat-maulana-saad-nrc-of-god/ (accessed 29 March 2022).

OpIndia Staff (2020c), 'Coronavirus Positive Man in Thailand Spits on a Person, Later Dies in Train', *OpIndia*, 3 April. Available online: https://www.opindia.com/2020/04/viral-video-coronavirus-positive-spit-on-person-die-train-thailand/ (accessed 29 March 2022).

Poovanna, S. (2018), 'Right-Wing Outfits Campaign in Karnataka against "Love Jihad"', *Mint*, 4 January. Available online: https://www.livemint.com/Politics/T4DS9yZjZVOIDSH4xHTc1M/Rightwing-outfits-campaign-in-Karnataka-against-love-jihad.html (accessed 29 March 2022).

Press Trust of India (2020), 'Nashik Man Arrested after TikTok Video of him Licking Notes Goes Viral', *NDTV.Com*, 3 April. Available online: https://www.ndtv.com/india-news/coronavirus-nashik-man-arrested-after-tiktok-video-of-him-licking-notes-goes-viral-2205845 (accessed 29 March 2022).

Qureshi, N. (1999), *Pan-Islam in British Indian Politics: A Study of the Khilafat Movement, 1918–1924*. Leiden: Brill.

Rahula, W. ([1946] 1974), *The Heritage of the Bhikku*. New York: Grove Press.

Rajagopalan, M. and A. Nazim (2018), '"We Had to Stop Facebook": When Anti-Muslim Violence Goes Viral', *Buzzfeed*, 7 April. Available online: https://www.buzzfeednews.com/article/meghara/we-had-to-stop-facebook-when-anti-muslim-violence-goes-viral (accessed 29 March 2022).

Samaratunge, S. and S. Hattotuwa (2014), 'Liking Violence: A Study of Hate Speech on Facebook in Sri Lanka', Centre for Policy Alternatives, 24 September. Available online: https://www.cpalanka.org/liking-violence-a-study-of-hate-speech-on-facebook-in-sri-lanka/ (accessed 3 April 2022).

Sarjoon, A., M. A. Yusoff and N. Hussin (2016), 'Anti-Muslim Sentiments and Violence: A Major Threat to Ethnic Reconciliation and Ethnic Harmony in Post-War Sri Lanka', *Religions*, 7 (10): 125. Available online: https://doi.org/10.3390/rel7100125 (accessed 9 April 2022).

Seneviratne, H. L. (1999), *The Work of Kings: The New Buddhism in Sri Lanka*. Chicago: University of Chicago Press.

Shah, S. and U. Jayasinghe (2019), 'Buddhist Mobs Target Muslims in Sri Lanka Following Deadly Easter Bombings', *Wall Street Journal*, 14 May. Available online: https://www.wsj.com/articles/buddhist-mobs-target-muslims-in-sri-lanka-11557854344 (accessed 10 April 2022).

Sharma, A. (2020), 'On the Difference between Hinduism and Hindutva', *Education about Asia*, Spring. Available online: https://www.asianstudies.org/publications/eaa/archives/on-the-difference-between-hinduism-and-hindutva/ (accessed 15 May 2023).

Sharma, N. (2020), 'A Religious Congregation in Delhi could be the Coronavirus Hotspot India was trying to Escape', *Quartz*, 31 March. Available online: https://qz.com/india/1828919/delhis-tablighi-jamaat-event-becomes-indias-coronavirus-hotspot/ (accessed 20 March 2022).

Singh, R. P. (2020), 'MP Cabinet Approves "Love Jihad Law", Forced Conversion Will Invite 10-Year Jail Term, Penalty', *India Today*, 26 December. Available online: https://www.indiatoday.in/india/story/mp-govt-okays-freedom-of-religion-bill-against-forced-conversion-1753278-2020-12-26 (accessed 1 April 2022).

Singh, V. (2020), 'Home Ministry Asked States to Identify 824 Foreign Tablighi Members', *The Hindu*, 31 March. Available online: https://www.thehindu.com/news/national/home-ministry-to-blacklist-800-tablighi-preachers-from-indonesia-for-violation-of-visa-rules/article31214048.ece (accessed 30 March 2022).

Tambiah, S. J. (1986), *Sri Lanka: Ethnic Fratricide and the Dismantling of Democracy*. Chicago: The University of Chicago Press.

Taub, A. and M. Fisher (2018), 'Where Countries Are Tinderboxes and Facebook Is a Match', *New York Times*, 21 April. Available online: https://www.nytimes.com/2018/04/21/world/asia/facebook-sri-lanka-riots.html (accessed 10 April 2022).

The Leaflet (2020), 'UP Cabinet Approves "Love Jihad" Ordinance to Punish Interfaith Marriages without Informing District Magistrate', *The Leaflet*, 24 November. Available online: https://www.theleaflet.in/up-cabinet-approves-love-jihad-ordinance-to-punish-interfaith-marriages-without-informing-district-magistrate/ (accessed 1 April 2022).

The Wire Staff (2021), 'Basri Masjid: The Timeline of a Demolition', *Wire*, 6 December. Available online: https://thewire.in/communalism/babri-masjid-the-timeline-of-a-demolition (accessed 27 September 2022).

TNN Staff (2020), 'Shaheen Bagh, Jamia Are a Plot to Destroy Harmony: PM Modi', *The Times of India*, 4 February. Available online: https://timesofindia.indiatimes.com/india/shaheen-bagh-jamia-are-a-plot-to-destroy-harmony-pm-modi/articleshow/73917319.cms (accessed 30 March 2022).

Umachandran, S. (2020), 'Blame It on the Virus, It's the Largest Lockdown in History', *Mint*, 25 March. Available online: https://www.livemint.com/news/india/blame-it-on-the-virus-it-s-the-largest-lockdown-in-history-11585159348758.html (accessed 30 March 2022).

Vaishnav, M. (2019), 'Religious Nationalism and India's Future – the BJP in Power: Indian Democracy and Religious Nationalism', Carnegie Endowment for International Peace, Available online: https://carnegieendowment.org/2019/04/04/religious-nationalism-and-india-s-future-pub-78703 (accessed 30 March 2022).

Vishva Hindu Parishad (2020), Social media post, Facebook, 25 September. Available online: https://www.facebook.com/VHPDigital/posts/2970710169701676 (accessed 11 April 2022).

Zubair, L., C. Malge, F. Shakira, T. Hadgie, S. Rameez and A. Nijamdeen (2018), 'Is the State Grossly Underestimating the Losses from the Mob Violence in Kandy?' *Groundviews*, 24 June. Available online: https://groundviews.org/2018/06/24/is-the-state-grossly-underestimating-the-losses-from-the-mob-violence-in-kandy/ (accessed 29 March 2022).

9

The convergence of land- and blood-centric political theologies in Israel

Atalia Omer

Introduction

'The Temple Mount belongs to us. We own the place. We want to clean the Temple Mount from all the terrorists and anti-Semites and give it back to the Jews so we can build the Third Temple.' These words were uttered by Baruch Marzel, a radical Jewish activist seeking ethnic cleansing, in an interview with *Middle East Eye* (Cohen 2015). On another occasion, he said: 'It's a religious war. And they believe they have to destroy us ... to kill us ... And we believe that ... they can't stay here' (cited in Hanania 2019). Marzel, like others involved in various manifestations of the Third Temple movement, conveys in these quotations both a genocidal intent to erase Palestinian presence and a related rhetorical transference of the Jewish experience of antisemitism into the indigenous Palestinian population, who are labelled as both antisemites and terrorists. The apparent religious argument Marzel makes not only depends on state violence but also conceals how ('secular') Zionist ideological formations produced him.

The word 'secular' is in scare quotes because, together with a familiar scholarly genealogy in religious studies (e.g. Asad 1993), I do not presume the 'secular' is an empty space, or a binary of the 'religious'. They are mutually constitutive and are implicated both in the modernist projects of nationalism and in colonial and epistemological forms of violence, as scholars of religion and coloniality have exposed (Maldonado-Torres 2014). This chapter examines the question of Jewish 'radicalization' by tracing the impossibility of investigating this question outside the modern nation state. The case of Jewish violence exemplifies why the analysis of such a thing as 'Jewish violence' cannot happen in abstraction from historical, political and structural contextual factors. This is the case for all other forms of 'religious violence' too.

'Secular' Zionism has operated rhetorically for a long time at the intersection of claims to ontological antisemitism on the one hand, in which Jewish victimhood is interpreted as an essence, not an outcome, of contextual configurations and, on the other hand, Orientalist erasures of Palestinian humanity. This rhetoric has also underpinned a supposedly realist narrative about self-defence to justify aggressions and land thefts. The weaponization of antisemitism and the ahistorical rhetorical stuck-ness in 1933

Berlin at the moment of Hitler's rise to power through democratic means constitute the key ingredients in the official Israeli narrative. Marzel's grotesque Manichean rhetoric is only an inch away from the official narrative that Israel promotes around the world in an effort to spin the 'telegenically killed' (Kenizor 2014); the phrase was Benjamin Netanyahu's in describing the rows of dead Gazans that dared to ethically enrage (some of) the world, as a necessary cost for Jewish security. For Netanyahu, the victims of Israeli aggression, the scores of dead Gazans, constitute a PR challenge, not a mass atrocity.

Subverting the Jewish tradition

A Jewish radical, Marzel was a disciple of the American-born Rabbi Meir Kahane, who was assassinated in 1990 in Manhattan. Kahane preached racist hate, Jewish supremacy, apocalyptic zeal and a genocidal world view, glorifying Jewish power and vindictive domination over its enemies. Merzel 'distinguished' himself through the Jewish colonization of the Palestinian city of Hebron and terrorized the Palestinian residents there while cosying up with the Israeli Defence Force (IDF) and inviting troops to his home for meals. He is one of the leaders of the notorious anti-miscegenation gang Lehava, which eventually morphed into parliamentary form in the shape of various political parties, including Otzma Yehudit or Jewish Power. Otzma Yehudit was established in 2012 and has gained force and substantial presence in the Knesset, partly due to coalition-building games orchestrated by Netanyahu, but also due to the fact that Kahanist ideas have permeated the sociopolitical space, converging with and reinforcing religious Zionist entitlement to pursue an ongoing process of the Zionist colonization of historical Palestine.

While Marzel is a violent radical, the president of Israel, Isaac Herzog (incubated in liberal Zionism), decided in 2021 to conduct an official Hanukah candle-lighting ceremony in Hebron to mark the Hasmonean victory over the Greeks. Hebron, a Palestinian town, is now emblematic of Jewish supremacist policies. Herzog lit the candles surrounded by the most violent settlers, including Merzel and Itamar ben Gvir (another inheritor of Kahanist ideology), whom I will examine later. These two embody the convergence of land- and blood-centric Jewish radical currents.

The land-centricity of the earlier settlement movement of Gush Emunim, or Block of the Faithful, launched in 1974, focused on the commandment to settle the biblical land in anticipation of the messianic moment. Perceiving this moment to already be unfolding and thus the time as extraordinary, this demands the elevation of the one commandment to settle the land over the other 612 commandments. Unlike the narrative of redemption underlying messianic land-centricity, blood-centricity conveys a sense of ontological un-safety in which Israel is also a project of racial purity sanctified by a neo-biblical apocalyptic logic of revenge, wrath and genocide. The 'neo-biblical' label, as I show below, in effect denotes an anti-traditional and ahistorical stance.

That Herzog chose to light Hanukkah candles in Hebron, surrounded by Jewish terrorists, indicates the mainstreaming of such radicalism. This mainstreaming signals a consistency between 'moderate' and 'secular' Zionism and its radical expressions. Herzog's office justified this act as a unifying gesture. However, the Iranian-Israeli journalist, translator and political activist Orly Noy (2021) names the violence of Herzog's symbolic act in this way: 'In a society that has transformed the right to oppress and crush another people into a consensus, unity is a dangerous value, and certainly not some essential dynamic to be sanctified. More appropriate would be to promote justice, equality and liberty – all the values being trampled upon daily in Hebron.' Justice, equality and liberty are exactly in tension with a political and cultural project that was intent on establishing a Jewish democracy, glossing over the contradictions inherent in this construct and without acknowledging that the fulfilment of Jewish self-determination in Palestine has relied on settler colonial logic (see Barakat 2018). Indeed, thinking about the justice, equality and liberty that Noy pleads for would require a lucid analysis of how the dispossession of Palestinians relates to the Jewish story of 'return'.

One of the key motifs of settler colonialism is the focus on land and the ongoing processes of elimination and replacement of the natives, as well as the indigenization of the settlers (Wolfe 1988). The radicalization of Jewish politics exposes the weakness of 'secular' categories such as national self-determination to authorize acts of state terrorism that Israel is inflicting on Palestinians, which can also be described in terms of Achille Mbembe's concept of 'necropolitics' (Shalhoub-Kevorkian 2020).

Reading such a violent process of elimination as a necessary act sanctioned divinely through apocalyptic and messianic scripts certainly adds a layer of combustibility apparent in the escalations at the Haram al Sharif/Temple Mount, which signals the site's political power. This sacred site is no longer an *axis mundi*, a site of hierophany or divine interruption, but a place from where one can glimpse a human-made apocalypse. On the surface, conflicts between Jews, Muslims and Christians in this site of concentrated sacredness produce the appearance that what is at stake is no longer a question of political control but instead a religious war that invites civilizational claims rather than norms of international law. The distance is short, however, between the brutal desecration of al-Aqsa mosque by Israeli security forces during Ramadan days in May 2021 and again in April 2023 (under the banner of 'security' on both these and many other occasions) and the bands of Third Temple Jews provocatively seeking to ritually slaughter at the Temple Mount during Ramadan when coinciding with Passover. An even shorter distance exists between the ritual slaughter of a pascal lamb at the Temple Mount and the annual display of Jewish supremacy during the Jerusalem Day Flag March as it progresses through the Muslim Quarter in occupied East Jerusalem to mark the 'reunification' of the city in 1967. The march involves a sea of Israeli flags and genocidal chants such as 'death to Arabs'.

The increasingly visible assault on Occupied East Jerusalem, which one Palestinian scholar (Shalhoub-Kevorkian 2017) aptly referred to as the 'occupation of the senses', is also gendered, as it is accompanied by threats about rape and claims for the protection of Jewish girls and women from 'pollution'. These displays of nationalism constitute an expression of Jewish Israeli racial theopolitics. They are about claiming the space as a Jewish space in which non-Jewish native people are marked for elimination. The claim is ultimately based on biblical narratives, even if such narratives are expressed through 'secular' registers. The Judaization of space, or *yihud*, in Israeli Hebrew, also increasingly entails policing the ways in which people interpret what being Jewish means. Hardly an issue in Israel, the fear-mongering rhetoric against miscegenation plays on the persistent ethos of (in)security where material and physical fears of annihilation shift to fears of discontinuity through assimilation, a persistent diasporic anxiety relocated to the 'Jewish home'. This ontological insecurity is telegraphed in Merzel's invocation of a generic enemy of 'antisemites and terrorists'.

The radicalism of a Merzel connects centrally to a mainstream Jewish Israeli nationalist discourse, which explains why Herzog, an Ashkenazi Labor Zionist establishment politician, thought it was wise to accept the invitation to be hosted in Hebron by Marzel and his friends for Hanukkah's candle lighting. This mainstreaming is evident in how the quest for Jewish sovereignty over the Temple Mount has become integrated into the political platform of the Likud Party, as well as the financial support of successive Israeli governments for the Temple Institute (established in 1983) by way of various Ministries ranging from Culture, Science and Sports to Education (see also Persico 2017). Indeed, the neo-biblical obsession with claiming political control over the Temple Mount has a secular rather than religious (Halakhic) genealogy, rooted in ultra-nationalist proponents of the Greater Eretz Yisrael (or a maximalist vision of the territory) and the pre-state Jewish militias.

In the 1960s, at least two decades before some segments of religious Zionism turned their gaze to the idea of the Third Temple (revealing the erosion of Halakhic concerns and the augmentation of an ethnocentric drive), a 'secular' group known as Ne'manei Har Habayit (Temple Faithful) operated at the margins, sharing elective affinities with what Tomer Persico calls 'underground messianism' (2017: 109). The fixation on the Temple Mount as the emblem of Jewish redemption and/through power is more indicative of an ethnocentric project than a religious discourse (2017), which has clearly articulated the need for distance rather than contact with the site of the holiest of holy. Like the Flag Parades in occupied East Jerusalem, expressions of sovereignty over the Haram al Sharif/Temple Mount such as flying the Israeli flag on top of the mosque convey an intimidating and potentially apocalyptic show of force that is aided by the infrastructure of state power. Even though Marzel and other religious Jews frame their desire to worship at the site where the Temple once stood in religious neo-biblical terms and also through the human rights idiom of 'religious freedoms', this aspiration nevertheless signals a shift from Halakhic sensibility to ethnocentric consciousness (2017: 112).

Anti-tradition neo-biblicalism

This shift marks the point where neo-biblicalism is also anti-tradition. Traditional rabbinic accounts of return to the land were articulated over millennia of rabbinic interpretive praxis as an event outside of ordinary history, an unfolding in messianic time, not human but divinely initiated. Likewise, actual physical presence on the site of the holiest of holy in Jerusalem is forbidden due to an inability of contemporary Jews to maintain purity laws dictated by the ancient prescriptions of the era of the Temple in Jerusalem. The presence of the Third Temple activists on the Temple Mount as well as their insistence on their right to worship there, as in the days of the ancient Temple and in violation of traditional rabbinical authoritative prohibitions against an intrusion into the holiest of holy, is not the expression of spontaneous aspiration to worship but an outcome of the subversion by Zionism of traditional Jewish views regarding Jewish presence on this very site. This subversion happened within Zionism's ideological framing, in which reliance on 'secular' principles of self-determination and democracy increasingly eroded when faced with the realities involved in sanctifying and legitimating the control of another group of people. This legitimization therefore increasingly doubles down on religious claims of ownership, a neo-biblical grammar that has always underpinned 'secular' Zionism. One example of 'secular' Zionism's neo-biblicalism is its fascination with Hebraism, the book of Joshua, and the land conquest narratives, as well as the ethos of the negation of exile, which devalues millennia of Jewish diasporic flourishing. One need not go further than the language of the Israeli Declaration of Independence (1948), often heralded as an embodiment of an original 'secular liberalism': 'The Land of Israel was the birthplace of the Jewish people', the Deceleration reads. 'Here', it continues, 'their spiritual, religious and political identity was shaped. Here they first attained statehood, created cultural values of national and universal significance and gave to the world the eternal Book of Books'. The reliance on keeping the tradition to preserve the political dimensions of Jewish peoplehood is captured by the words:

> After being forcibly exiled from their land, the people kept faith with it throughout their Dispersion and never ceased to pray and hope for their return to it and for the restoration in it of their political freedom ... Impelled by this historic and traditional attachment, Jews strove in every successive generation to re-establish themselves in their ancient homeland. In recent decades they returned in their masses.

The motif of the negation of the Jewish diaspora and Jewish histories and traditions is conveyed through their reduction to neo-biblicalism.

It's political

Rotating back to 2022 and the volatile convergence of Passover, Ramadan and Easter, the provocative effort of violent Jewish Third Temple extremists to ritually slaughter a pascal lamb seemed designed to prime a regional war. But it is not exactly correct to frame what sounds absurd (recreating ancient Temple rituals as if through the erasure of time, not only the erasure of people) as merely the actions of some outliers. Perhaps not everyone is intent on undergoing ritual slaughter, but this act is an expression of decades of messianic, apocalyptic and ethnoreligious-centric politics and an instrumentalist back-and-forth between 'secular' and religious interpretations of Jewish security and redemption.

Zionism is not an abstract idea but a concrete political programme that has unfolded historically. Its unfolding has entailed a settler colonial project from the perspective of indigenous Palestinian communities. As a political movement, Zionism was about gaining control of the land of Palestine and 'returning' to it because of a presumed land title inscribed in biblical scripts. This is regardless of the framing of such claims to the land of historic Palestine in terms of 'history', 'culture' and other forms of inheritance. Undoubtedly, the 'return' was instigated by rising antisemitism in Europe and the eventual genocide committed against the Jews. It produced the Nakba (the Palestinian catastrophe of 1948) as an ongoing erasure of Palestinian lives, landscapes and political aspirations. Support for the Zionist project in Palestine also facilitated 'repentance' for the crimes against the Jews, but this 'repentance' came on the backs of Palestinians (e.g. Ellis 2020).

In addition, investment in chauvinistic efforts to establish Jewish sovereignty over the Haram al Sharif/Temple Mount, or even to instigate the demolition of Muslim structures therein as a conduit of an apocalyptic end-time theological moment, is also heavily channelled from Christian Zionists, especially from the United States ('*Til Kingdom Come* 2020). Hence, Jewish violent radicalization needs to be interpreted within this matrix of geopolitical and theological agendas. Indeed, the case of 'Jewish radicalization' in Israel cannot be interpreted outside its ideological discursivity. The next part of this chapter is accordingly devoted to discourse and framing. I then turn to examine the convergences of land- and blood-centric varieties of Jewish radicals.

Hasbarah and discursive violence

Usually, the discussion of religious violence and, in this chapter, Jewish violence points to obvious instances of violence, such as the Jewish Underground's failed plot on 2 June 1980 to blow up the Al-Aqsa Mosque or the attempt in 1984 of the Lyfta Gang of 'lone wolves' youth to explode the mosques (Pedahzur and Perlinger 2009: 140–5). These 'underground messianic' actors believed their actions were necessary to hasten redemption. In this they only took the more establishment settlement movement's notion of *hatkhalta de'Geula* (dawn of redemption) by way of settling the biblical land one step further in preparation for the establishment of the Kingdom of Israel. The 'underground messianic' actors expressed frustration with the King David Accords of 1979, which resulted in peace with Egypt, a return of Sinai and the dismantling of settlements therein. I will return to this legacy of an obvious manifestation of violence in the next section. Here, I highlight the less obvious discursive forms of violence.

One site of nested discursive violence is Hasbarah (Hebrew: explaining). Hasbarah refers to concentrated financially and politically dedicated efforts to control the narrative about Israeli 'secular' aggressions against Palestinians as the expression of Jewish self-defence. As Edward Said famously said in 'Permission to narrate' (1984), it erases the validity of Palestinian narratives of the ongoing Nakba: ethnic cleansing, displacement, and replacement as well as fragmentation in which those Palestinians within the 1948 borders are also targets of a racialized citizenship discourse (Tatour 2019). Hasbarah elevates Jewish survival by way of Jewish force (tanks, bombs, surveillance infrastructures) as a sacred conversation stopper. Concurrently, this sacralization of Israeli state violence and Jewish 'safety' has continuously denied Palestinian lives and political aspirations. Quite literally, the supposed right of self-determination of one group means the denial of another. And when Palestinians express their claims for humanity, they are accused of antisemitism and terrorism. This constitutes a violent discursive constellation, which has taken shape in efforts to criminalize the nonviolent tactics of boycott, divestment and sanctions by rendering them antisemitic, as reflected in the International Holocaust Remembrance Alliance 'definition' of antisemitism (for a critical engagement, see Stern-Weiner 2021).

Ontological un-safety

One of the key tools of Hasbarah's discursive violence is an appeal to the memory of Jewish un-safety through what many interpreters refer to as the 'weaponization of antisemitism' (Goldberg et al. 2021). Accusations of antisemitism have become a site of discursive violence intent on controlling the narrative of Jewish self-defence and existential threat, an ahistorical argument that assumes the identity of the Jew-qua-victim as an essence rather than something situated contextually. This ahistorical account of Jewish un-safety resonates with Kahane's ontological account of antisemitism, or what Shaul Magid (2021) calls Kahane's 'Judeo-pessimism'. The Kahanist grammar sits in close proximity to Hasbarah. The harder it is to spin aggression as self-defence, the closer Hasbarah comes to a Kahanist gloss. Certainly, ontological and ahistorical claims of Jewish victimhood constitute key components of Hasbarah, regardless of the empirical realities of Jewish power.

The Hasbarah mechanism thrives on other forms of Orientalist discursive violence to control a narrative that posits Israel as a 'villa in the jungle', as a former Israeli prime minister once referred to Israel (Avnery 2002). Here, 'pinkwashing' – the branding of Israel as progressive on sexual and gender issues in supposed contrast to its 'neighborhood' – is a notable tool of a civilizational reductive discourse that erases a serious analysis of violence and oppression. The Orientalist branding of Israel as existing in a constant state of ontological un-safety concocts a simple formula of redirection from empirical reality: it is about terror, not territory (*Occupation of the American Mind* 2016). Hasbarah draws on the assimilation of (white) Jews into 'Judeo-Christian' discourse as a weapon, the victims of which are Palestinians, who have lived under Israeli domination for decades. According to many reputable human rights organizations, the entire geopolitical space of Palestine/Israel demonstrates that Israel commits the crime of apartheid, regardless of the differentiation between 1948 and 1967 Palestinians. Apartheid here means that Zionist supremacy dictates realities throughout the entire space from the Jordan River to the Mediterranean Sea (Amnesty International 2022). Hence, relegating the label of 'Jewish radicalization' to a few 'lone wolves' obscures the Jewish radicalism of the 'secular' regime itself.

A relational approach

One cannot analyse Jewish violence without analysing the Palestinian experiences of such violence, which is what I mean by the relational approach to the question of both Jewish 'radicalization' and Jewish 'self-defence'. They are interlinked. Invoking sacred warrants augments the sacralization of the security discourse (i.e. security for Jews only). The more Israel needs to justify its aggressions against the Palestinians, the more it needs to rely on ontological accounts of anti-Jewish hate and the more dependent Hasbarah becomes on neo-biblical, eschatological and messianic sources. The resulting onto-theological narrative cross-fertilizes with a global semiotic landscape central to the so-called 'war on terror' that is infused with Orientalism (Said 1978). This dialectical and relational prism clarifies the trajectory of mainstreaming neo-Kahanist racism. If, over the decades, Israel fancied itself as 'Jewish and democratic', a trope integral to its self-perception as a 'villa in the jungle', the realities of entrenched occupation and apartheid also demonstrate a greater level of comfort with dropping the 'democratic' part of the construct of 'Jewish democracy'. This is where 'radicalization' occurs in dialectic relation to Palestinian resistance.

Settler land-theology

Messianic land-centric ideology is associated with Rabbis Avraham Isaac Kook (1865–1935) and Zvi Yehuda Kook (1891–1982), as well as their Merkaz HaRav Yeshivah in Jerusalem. I thus refer subsequently to religious Zionist ideology as Kookism. Propelled initially by the elder Avraham Isaac Kook's aspiration during the pre-state period to sanctify the Zionist project through a combination of mystical kabbalism and a Hegelian account of history, Kookism understands the moment of Jewish 'return' and 'ingathering' in the land as signalling the dawn of redemption (*athalta de'geula*), requiring Jews to settle the biblical geography in anticipation of an interlaced Jewish and cosmic redemption. Later, in the statist context of Israel, Avraham Isaac Kook's son, Rabbi Zvi Yehuda Kook, articulated a less mystical, universalistic and cosmological account of redemption and a more ethnocentric vision of the end-time. Accordingly, religious youth who sought political belonging, and for whom Zionism is religiously significant rather than subversive of the Jewish tradition's prohibition against hastening the messianic moment, found in Kookism a synthesis of their religiosity and their Zionism. The religious youth who could not subscribe to the iconoclastic and atheistic (even if biblical or Hebraic) secularity of Ben Gurion found a theology that allowed them to express themselves politically as belonging within a Zionist framework. The secularity of political Zionists, therefore, is tolerated for its instrumentality in the sacred process of redemption. Where the usefulness of the state appears to erode is where the marriage of convenience ends.

Initially instrumentalized as a useful mechanism for territorial expansion of Jewish control into the territories occupied in 1967, the religious Zionist settlers have transformed the political map completely. In the West Bank, settlers' lawlessness allows the government to do things it otherwise does not want to appear to be doing directly, but rather offer 'reluctantly', after the fact – a stamp of approval, as when illegal hilltop settlements are eventually recognized out of a purported inability to control the settlers. It is the case, however, that not just settler violence but the settlers' insistence on inserting themselves into the hearts of Palestinian spaces (armed with both actual weapons and biblical geography and/or martyrology) assists the general policies of Israel, which have been to increase territory and reduce or eliminate Palestinian presence in the land. This is the replacement and eliminative dimensions of settler colonialism that co-constitute the Zionist project.

In its inception in a European context defined by colonialism, imperialism, nationalism, racism and antisemitism that named the Jews as a problem, Zionism emerged as a solution that drew on all these vocabularies. Hence, both the focus on Jewish power, survival and purity, associated with the legacy of Kahane, and the romantic reclaiming of the biblical landscape through settlement to bring about the messianic arrival, associated with the Rabbis Kook, are all motifs constitutive of secular political Zionism. This continuity of Jewish violent radicals with, rather than departure from, a mainstream discourse was made clear in 2018 with the Knesset's passing of the Jewish Nation-State Law, enshrining through legislation what had been the practice all along: Israel is a state for Jews and Jews only.

I alluded above to the vigilante gangsterism of neo-Kahanist groups who preach the 'purification' of Jewish bodies and spaces. Indeed, like 'secular' Zionism itself, Kookism and Kahanism are not mutually exclusive. Both rely on settler colonial mechanisms of displacement, elimination of the natives and their replacement with indigenized settlers whose indigenization relies on biblical scripts and the mechanisms of biblical archaeology (Abu El-Haj 2001). However, there are important differences, highlighted below, that relate to a focus on a land theology and cosmological redemptive vision for Kookism through a more capacious view of the relationship between Jewish redemption and a broader *tikkun olam* (repair of the world). This more cosmological outlook, as noted, has been significantly diminished as the torch passed from Kook the father to Kook the son and then to the movement and multiple generations of being enabled as 'lords of the land' (Zertal and Eldar 2007), but also enablers of an Israeli 'secular' expansionist 'ongoing Nakba'.

Messiah's donkey

The Gush Emunim movement underwritten by Kookism deployed an instrumental approach to the Israeli nation state. It sanctified institutions such as the military for their usefulness in an end-time theology. This sanctification of secular political Zionism was not acceptable for Kahanism's focus on power and Jewish blood purity, which involved policing the spiritual, religious and physical boundaries of the Jewish people and 'perfecting it' as a precondition for ethnocentric (rather than universal) redemption and as a necessity against Hellenization. Hellenization is a concept harkening back to the revolts of the Hasmonean era and reflects a Kahanist neo-biblical eschatological outlook. If Rav Kook famously thought of the secular Zionists as the yeast in the making of the wine or the 'Messiah's donkey' (a metaphorical reference to the image of the messiah's arrival on a donkey) – a necessary but ultimately discarded agent of redemption – this changed drastically with the so-called 'disengagement' from Gaza in 2005, when a 'Jewish army' evacuated the settlements in the Gaza Strip. This was not unlike the 'radicalization' in the aftermath of the evacuation from Sinai, which was also propelled through the previously mentioned attempts to blow up the Haram al-Sharif. In 2005, for many who experienced the evacuation as a traumatic uprooting from a sacred topography, the yeast was no longer useful nor sacred.

The 2005 moment signals a turning point for the convergence between Kookism, with its focus on land and messianic promise, and Kahanism, with its focus on Jewish racial supremacy and ontological insecurity. They both, however, share elective affinities with and expose political Zionism's incoherence. The 'Judaization' of space *is* the project of Zionism. From Zionism's inception at the point of turning from the Ottomans to the British Mandate, leaders of the Zionist movements used the theological categories of 'return' and Aliyah (or assent) to authorize the settler colonial move at a time when settler colonialism was still acceptable in Europe. Zionism also utilized a secularized yet theological notion of 'redemption' to label and purchase land in Palestine (when land was purchased by the Jewish National Fund, it was considered 'redeemed'). *Geulat Haadama,* or redeeming the land, has been a tenet of political Zionism's 'secular' registers, which explains why explicitly religious registers appear to bring this theopolitical ambiguity to its logical (though not inevitable) conclusion.

Over decades of Israeli history, a marriage of convenience has been formed between the security ethos and messianic religious Zionist ideologies. The latter rekindled a drive to settle/colonize 'the frontier', where settlement practice has always worked strategically to enhance security capabilities. If the earlier Zionists settled/colonized Palestine – deploying secularized conceptions of Jewish identity and history as well as, in some instances, socialist/utopian ideals and other modernist political principles such as self-determination – the religious Zionists of Kookism were driven by their interpretation of the moment as messianic and urgent. Critically, the instrumentalization of the messianic drive translated into enabling policies such as subsidies, which subsequently expanded the demographics of illegal settlements (according to international laws of occupation) to include 'economic settlers', often Mizrahi, Ethiopian and other marginalized communities, who were then incubated within settler ideology. As in all marriages, no party to the union remains untransformed by the relationship. In this case, a relational lens can illuminate how the Third Temple movement and other such radicalized publics constitute but an expression (even if particularly grotesque) of the most ethnocentric motifs of secular and 'moderate' (meaning not 'radical') forms of Zionism.

Zionism as a political movement has always exhibited tensions between Judaism and Hebraism – a reclaiming of the Jew as the New Hebrew, the 'muscular' binary of the 'sickly' and passive diasporic Jew. This ethos of the negation of exile reveals an internalized discourse of racial antisemitism at the heart of political Zionism. It is the same form of internalized antisemitism that undergirds Kahane's Judeo-pessimism or the notion of hatred of Jews as an ontological truth that can only be responded to with force and Jewish domination (Magid 2021). This Judeo-pessimism then relates to his neo-biblical apocalyptic account of Jewish self-defence against Amalek, the biblical Manichean designation of the enemy of Israel.

Indeed, when stated simply through rhetoric about Zionist Jewish supremacy, Kahanism sounds like a radical departure from 'moderate' Zionism. It also, however, brings to fruition Zionism's most toxic constitutive elements. As noted, when Israel uses the concept of *yihud* (literally, Judaization) to describe the 'redemption' of spaces formerly inhabited by Palestinians, what is meant rather is the Zionization of such spaces. However, despite its departure from tradition, Zionism's hegemonic control over the narration of Jewish meaning, identity and history has made it increasingly difficult to extricate Jewishness from the political project of settler colonialism, occupation and apartheid. This is where the weaponization of antisemitism and the sanctification of Jewish safety/security/redemption constitute a discursive form of violence that defends Israeli state terrorism, ethno-religious-centric nationalist projects and ongoing settler colonial processes, as if such a defence means taking a principled stance against antisemitism. I now turn to examine Kahanism for the movement's racial preoccupation with ontological antisemitism, Jewish survival and the project of Jewish power and purity.

Kahanism and the politics of Jewish purity

In Magid's (2021) tracing of the evolution of Kahane's thought as the latter transitioned from the United States and the Jewish Defense League of the 1960s to the Israeli contexts of the 1980s, Kahane's concept of the Jewish 'self' was being reshaped through an anti-tradition neo-biblical lens. Kahane's idea of 'transfer' expressed his neo-biblical Manichean apocalyptic political theology 'founded on divine election, and the requirement of separation from the gentile as a condition of political and spiritual sovereignty' (2021: 189). This Kahanist hermeneutics is not unlike the 'secular' Zionist disregard for diasporic Jewish learning and histories that reside outside Zionist teleology. Kahane's 'New Jew' is truly Jewish when they enact a divinely prescribed revenge against and domination over their enemies, the metaphorical Amalek that Marzel telegraphed at the opening of this chapter as 'antisemites' and 'terrorists'.

Jewish ethnocentricity and apocalyptic militancy are consistent with a racialized and thus ahistorical discourse of antisemitism and secular Zionism's sublimated political theology. Indeed, the writings of Ze'ev (Vladimir) Jabotinsky – one of the ideologues of 'secular' political Zionism and the 'forefather' of the Likud Party – were saturated with racist blood-centric language reflective of internalized antisemitism. Jabotinsky had been an influence in Kahane's trajectory. As much as Kahanism is the supposed reclaiming of a neo-biblical Jewish posture, it is entrenched in, and could have not emerged outside, the modern discourse of race. The rearticulating of Jewish self-defence beyond the secular/liberal language of national self-determination translates into an apocalyptic narrative and theo-ontological/ahistorical conceptions of Jewish un-safety. Without concrete implementation of policies to end the occupation and to redress historical injustices against Palestinians and with persistent impunity from the 'international community', the Kahanist and Kookist registers only become louder.

Forget about Tikkun Olam

Indeed, once in Israel, Kahane's religious thought diverged from Kookist romantic messianic readings that linked the redemption of the Jews with cosmological repair and redemption (Magid 2021: 189). But even in the case of Kookism, I have traced instances where an initial acceptance of 'secular' Israeli iconoclastic anti-religiosity eventually eroded, since a continuous occupation also required a broader doubling down on biblical claims to establish Jewish nativity in the land. It also eroded, as I note above, during the events of the 2005 'disengagement' from Gaza. If, within the Kookist frame, the end-time scenario relegates a special role for Jews as vessels for a universal and cosmological *tikkun olam*, for Kahane, through his selective reading of the prophet Ezekiel, redemption is ethno-centric rather than cosmological. It requires acts of 'purification' that include not only the Jewish settlement of the biblical landscape but also the removal of non-Jews, in addition to the 'self-perfection' of Jews by ridding themselves of the 'foreign' elements that have polluted Judaism through millennia of diasporic life. Such claims for 'pollution' or Hellenism purportedly licensed his criticisms of authoritative rabbinic discourse inconsistent with his Manichean vision (Magid 2021: 188–9). But it also consists of oppressive programmes and terroristic gang activities on 'Jewish streets' to introduce 'correct' Jewish practice, rather than awaiting a messianic transvaluation as envisioned by the Kookist schema. It is no longer sufficient to merely be Jewish as a matter of course, history and cultural inheritance. The authority of this secular argument has worn out in a context where the domination of Palestinians needed to be justified as 'self-defence'.

Kahanism solves Zionism's internal contradiction. For Kahane, without grounding the claim for Jewish sovereignty in biblical scripts, Zionism constitutes mere expressions of colonialism rather than divine promise and election. This is where Kahanism converges with Kookism's sacralization of the nation state as an instrument (a donkey) for Jewish redemption. Unlike Kookism, however, Kahanism sees the 'Judaizing' of the state itself as a precondition for vanquishing Amalek and Jewish exclusionary (rather than cosmological) redemption. Magid contextualizes Kahane's thinking in the latter's *The Jewish Idea* as subverting the genre of musar literature (or the tradition of Jewish ethics), referring to this genre's focus on *tikkun hamidot*, or 'individual self-perfection and ethical behavior' (Magid 2021: 164). Instead, in Kahane's nationalized 'musar', the target is 'national rejuvenation, fulfillment, and correction' (Magid 2021: 165). This process involved correcting and 'purify[ing] Torah from its diasporic defilement. Just as musar literature offers directives to amend individual character traits so that they will be more aligned with "Torah values", *The Jewish Idea* does the same for the Jewish collective body in Israel' (Magid 2021: 167). Hence, the convergence of Kookism and Kahanism entails traversing from the kabbalistic underpinning of Kookism as a form of *tikkun olam* to a perversion of *tikkun hamidot*.

Even though few studies of Israeli Judaism centralize the occupation and ongoing realities of settler colonialism, these realities are indeed critical for interpreting what Yaacov Yadgar (2020) calls the 'Jewish identity crisis' in Israel. For him, too, Israel's Jewishness needs to have a deeper content than mere demography. Hence, the convergences of Kookist and Kahanist registers expose the internal contradictions of Zionism as a modern political movement for 'Jewish' self-determination and its persistent reliance on an ontological and ahistorical conception of Jewish victimhood and/or biblical scripts. For Kahanism to capture the mainstream was not an inevitable outcome, even if still likely given the patterns of economic, legal and diplomatic impunity enjoyed by Israel's aggressive apartheid policies, which prevent the consolidation of countercurrents and relational grammars for Jewish life in Palestine.

Hebronization

According to evidence-based research (e.g. B'tselem 2021), IDF soldiers often join settlers in their violent attacks against Palestinians, demonstrating self-evident patterns of collusion; accordingly, settler violence means state violence, full stop. Once again, there is no surprise here, as religious settlers and their desire to inhabit the biblical landscape 'liberated' in 1967 were convenient for the security discourse of 'secular' Israelis such as Ariel Sharon. Sharon's long political career involved a variety of crimes against humanity, including the Sabra and Shatila massacre in 1982 and the long presence in and assault on Lebanon. But he is also remembered as an architect of the settlement in the territories occupied in 1967. The history of Jewish colonization of the 1967 territories has unfolded in violation of the Geneva Conventions and other international norms concerning laws of occupation. Sharon's construction blueprints capitalized on the messianic aspirations of those who wished to infuse 'secular' Zionism with Jewish religious significance and rekindle its frontier ethos. The patterns of collusion between settlers and the security infrastructure have not sprung out of nowhere but are rooted in a familiar choreography between illegal settlement activities; performative or genuine efforts to remove them; escalation of violence, often involving interactions with Palestinians; and then securitizing of the settlement and eventually connecting the illegal settlements (as a *de facto* annexation) to Israeli infrastructure such as sewage, electricity and health care. Fast forward to 2021 and it is the 'moderate' politician Herzog who wishes to gain some political capital by befriending Jewish terrorists from Hebron.

The colonization of Hebron, which predated the emergence of Gush Emunim, is of particular importance not only because of its central role in consolidating the settlement movement in the West Bank (what is referred to within the movement and also on other 'secular' maps as Judea and Samaria) but because of how it set the tone for Jewish 'radicalization' underwritten by state's infrastructures and subsidies (e.g. Feige 1995). The colonization of Hebron (led initially by Rabbi Moshe Levinger, a disciple of Kookism), and the origin of the settlement movement in the 1967 territories writ large, started with a Pesach celebration in 1968 and then a refusal to leave the site of the Park Hotel, where the celebration took place. The settlers were eventually relocated to a nearby military base to form the Jewish colony of Kiryat Arba, but eventually spread back into the city of Hebron by 1979 by way of colonizing Beit Hadassah and then one Palestinian home at a time. Hebron, where a once-bustling Palestinian Shuhada Street is now a ghost street designated for Jews only, is not an outlier but an expression of what is transpiring throughout the land.

Halakhic violence

In 1994 in Hebron, in the Ibrahim Mosque or the Tomb of the Patriarchs, an American-born medical doctor by the name of Baruch Goldstein massacred twenty-nine worshippers during Ramadan. Ignited by Kahanist ideology, Goldstein's attack marked the beginning of the end of the Oslo Accords, which themselves had problematically bypassed organic grassroots Palestinian resistance. Goldstein's grave in Hebron has been a site of religious pilgrimage and veneration. Similarly, Yigal Amir, who in November 1995 assassinated Yitzhak Rabin, the prime minister involved with the Oslo Accords, insists to this day that the killing of Rabin was sanctioned by rabbis who interpreted Rabin as a *moser* (one who relinquishes 'Jewish property') upon which it is necessary to execute *din moser* (Pedahzur and Perlinger 2009: 106–7). *Din,* or judgement, refers to halakhic rules. The concept of *din rodef* describes a judgement that applies to a person who threatens Jewish life, while *din moser* applies to a person intent on relinquishing Jewish property to gentiles. Both transgressions, according to the Halakha, are punishable by death.

The religious Zionist incitement against Rabin and the Oslo Accords involved a circulation of such halakhic concepts in synagogues across the country, especially in spaces associated with the settlement project. Further, broadly circulated pamphlets included rabbinic sanctioning of attacks on Palestinians and the celebration of the Goldstein massacre (Pedahzur and Perlinger 2009: 100). Amir was inspired by Goldstein to take matters into his own hands and 'save' the Jewish State from the threat of Rabin's willingness to give away land. Shortly before the assassination of Rabin, in September 1995, a group of settlers' rabbis released a halakhic rule authorizing religious soldiers to refuse orders entailing the evacuation of a settlement, thereby showing a breaking point in the instrumental relations between the 'secular' Israeli state, Kookism, and the concurrent intersection of Kookism with Kahanism.

In the aftermath of the 2005 'disengagement' from Gaza, the experience of trauma it generated among religious Zionists and the channelling of some of the 'uprooted' settlers to binational towns, commentators have identified a process of Hebronization now aimed at the *liba,* or 'heart', of Israel. This entails the targeting, through a variety of settlers' real-estate organizations, of the binational spaces remaining within the 1948 boundaries and occupied East Jerusalem. These spaces are 'binational' because the Nakba therein has not been total. In the Israeli context, such towns are referred to as 'mixed', which constitutes an expression of the racist logic of Zionism. Cities, by definition, are heterogeneous and the discourse of purity underlying *yihud* is not one unique to Hebron's Shuhada Street but rather inscribed into the anatomy of Israelism. The Hebronization of the *liba* has accelerated the convergence of Kookism and Kahanism.

Kahanism won in a place like Lyd/Lod, a binational town mostly depopulated during the Nakba of 1948. Lyd/Lod is a site where through the mechanism of *gar'inim toranim* (Torah nuclei) designed to 'Judaize' the heart of Israel, one neighbourhood and house at a time is targeted, just as in Hebron. The introduction of *gar'inim toranim* involves subsidized efforts to establish yeshivahs and Jewish learning centres in the *liba,* a process demanding an ever-expanding infrastructure of social and communal services, as well as residential options for families associated with the Yeshivah, which then translates into transforming the urban landscape, 'Judaizing' it through city planning. As in the case of the 'settlement movement', the territorially expansionist Torah nuclei would have not been enabled without the annexationist infrastructure (and collusion) of successive 'secular' governments.

Neo-Kahanism

This is how and where what Magid (2021) calls 'neo-Kahanism' manifests strongly, as it reveals the convergences of Kahane's project of nationalizing 'musar' and the Kookist messianic focus on land settlement with secular Zionists' function as useful instruments. In time, according to the Kookist formulation, 'secular' Zionists will come to recognize the religious meanings of their historical actions. In the meantime, the neo-biblical and messianic registers obscure their relational dimensions and their reliance on actual weapons, state violence and oppression as well as financial subsidies at a time of the neoliberal erosion of social safety nets; for example, the settlements in the territories occupied in 1967 are subsidized by the government, thereby fusing economic and ethnoreligious interests and incentives.

The messianic and ultranationalist gangs, whether they vandalize and terrorize Palestinians in the West Bank or in binational cities, are not Israeli realities catching up with Kahanist ideas. Instead, they exemplify how Kahanist scripts are entirely consistent with the Zionist logic designed to create a 'Jewish State'. Decades after Kahane's assassination, politicians incubated in Kahanist circles not only are openly present in the Knesset but have surfaced as leading voices. One example is Itamar Ben-Gvir, the head of Jewish Power, whose galvanizing rhetoric focuses on demonizing the 'enemy from within', which includes not only the Palestinian citizens of Israel but also non-orthodox expressions of Judaism, such as feminist reformers or legislation allowing for transportation on Shabbat. He departs from the more traditional religious Zionist Kookist preoccupation with the settlement of the West Bank by policing the 'Jewish' character of the state within the Green Line. This is apparent in his anti-democratic attacks on non-Jewish Palestinian citizens in ways that mimic Euro-American xenophobic 'strongmen' nationalism. Kahane may have been outlawed in the 1980s, but by 2021, Kahanist rhetoric had gained traction with the Israeli right and by 2022 neo-Kahanism had come to dominate the forces of the coalition in the Knesset.

This claim also rings true for the journalist Meron Rapoport (2021), who observed a large demonstration in November 2021 where Ben-Gvir took the podium to the sound of thundering applause, characterizing democracy or a 'state for all' as constituting an existential threat to the Jews. This is the same Ben-Gvir who set up a makeshift Knesset office on a sidewalk in the Sheik Jarrah neighbourhood in occupied East Jerusalem to provoke Palestinian residents under the threat of illegal displacement and incited Kahanist gangs to terrorize the streets. The tactics of the Ben-Gvir gangs, in collusion with the security forces, contributed to the escalation of violence in May 2021. By November 2021, Ben-Gvir had positioned himself as the leading voice of the 'real' Israeli right, one that promotes unabashedly Jewish ethnoreligious supremacy with no pretences to democracy. It is not democratic; it's 'Jewish' – a 'Jewish' supremacist agenda formed in broad daylight. This movement is embodied in a Ben-Gvir who, like Kahane, is only significant for his ability to perform a script whose grammar was already present, even if not inevitably, within Zionism.

To conclude, in Israel, the realities of occupation make it impossible to conceal and normalize a discussion of Jewish 'radicalization' as if the system as a whole does not authorize this through radical religious licences and teleological accounts of Jewish destiny and theo-ontological un-safety. In the case of Israel (in Palestine), what is ordinarily rendered invisible – the defining violence differentiating 'religious' and 'political' spaces – is not only visible but increasingly so. It thus becomes an instructive focus for analysis of the dynamics of religion and politics as they interact with race, racialization and other instruments of exclusion, dehumanization and erasure.

References

Abu El-Haj, N. (2001), *Facts on the Ground: Archeological Practice and Territorial Self-Fashioning in Israeli Society*. Chicago: University of Chicago Press.

Amnesty International (2022), 'Israel's Apartheid against Palestinians: A Look into Decades of Oppression and Domination', Available online: https://www.amnesty.org/en/latest/campaigns/2022/02/israels-system-of-apartheid/ (accessed 5 October 2022).

Asad, T. (1993), *Genealogies of Religion: Discipline and Reasons of Power in Christianity and Islam*. Baltimore: John Hopkins University Press.

Avnery, U. (2002), 'Barak: Israel a Villa in the Jungle', *Arab News*, 17 July. Available online: https://www.arabnews.com/node/222588 (accessed 5 October 2022).

Barakat, R. (2018), 'Writing/Righting Palestine Studies: Settler Colonialism, Indigenous Sovereignty and Resisting the Ghost(s) of History', *Settler Colonial Studies* 8/13.

B'TSelem. (2021), 'State Business: Israel's Misappropriation of Land in the West Bank through Settler Violence', November, Available online: https://www.btselem.org/publications/202111_state_business (accessed 5 October 2022).

Cohen, D. (2015), 'What Is the Temple Mount Movement?' *Middle East Eye*, 13 February. Available online: https://www.middleeasteye.net/features/what-temple-mount-movement (accessed 5 October 2022).

Declaration of Independence, Israel (1948), 14 May. Available online: https://main.knesset.gov.il/en/about/pages/declaration.aspx (accessed 25 May 2023).

Ellis, M. H. (2020), 'Holocaust Theology, the Interfaith Ecumenical Deal, and the Unintended Consequences of Jewish Christian Pilgrimage: Notes from a Jewish Theology of Liberation', in J. Rieger (ed), *Theologies on the Move: Religion, Migration, and Pilgrimage in the World of Neoliberal Capital*, 93–106, Lanham, MD: Lexington Books.

Feige, M. (1995), 'Jewish Hebron between Past and Present: A Case of Collective Memory', *Israel Studies Bulletin*, 10 (2): 5–9.

Goldberg, A., P. Ulrich and B. Klug (2021), Expert Submission to the European Commission on a Consultation on 'Strategy on Combating Antisemitism and Fostering Jewish Life in the EU'. Available online: https://ec.europa.eu/info/law/better-regulation/have-your-say/initiatives/13068-Strategy-on-combating-antisemitism-and-fostering-Jewish-life-in-the-EU/F2661357_en (accessed 5 October 2022).

Hanania, R. (2019), 'Baruch Marzel: Advocate of Ethnic Cleansing', *Arab News*, 2 July. Available online: https://www.arabnews.com/node/1519246/middle-east (accessed 5 October 2022).

Kenizor, S. (2014), 'The Telegenically Dead: Why Israel and Its Supporters Fear Gaza's Dead', *Al Jazeera*, 14 August. Available online: https://www.aljazeera.com/opinions/2014/8/14/the-telegenically-dead (accessed 5 October 2022).

Magid, S. (2021), *Meir Kahane: The Public Life and Political Thought of an American Jewish Radical*. Princeton, NJ: Princeton University Press.

Maldonado-Torres, N. (2014), 'AAR Centennial Roundtable: Religion, Conquest, and Race in the Foundations of the Modern/Colonial World', *Journal of the American Academy of Religion*, 82 (3): 636–65.

Noy, O. (2021), 'To Celebrate Hanukkah, Herzog Takes a Tour of Palestinian Suffering', *Middle East Eye*, 4 December. Available online: https://www.middleeasteye.net/opinion/israel-palestine-hanukkah-herzog-candle-hebron-suffering (accessed 5 October 2022).

Occupation of the American Mind: Israel's Public Relations War in the United States (2016), [Film] Dir. Loretta Alper and Jeremy Earp, The Media Education Foundation.

Pedahzur, A. and A. Perlinger (2009), *Jewish Terrorism in Israel*. New York City: Columbia University Press.

Persico, T. (2017), 'The End Point of Zionism: Ethnocentrism and the Temple Mount', *Israel Studies Review*, 32 (1): 104–22.

Rapoport, M. (2021), 'Itamar Ben-Gvir: With Rise of a Jewish Supremacist, Israel's Likud Is Pulled Far-Right', *Middle East Eye*, 9 November. Available online: https://www.middleeasteye.net/news/israel-jewish-supremacy-likud-ben-gvir-netanyahu-knesset (accessed 5 October 2022).

Said, E. (1978), *Orientalism*. New York: Pantheon Books.

Said, E. (1984), 'Permission to Narrate', *Journal of Palestine Studies*, 13 (3): 27–48.

Shalhoub-Kevorkian, N. (2017), 'The Occupation of the Senses: The Prosthetic and Aesthetic of State Terror', *The British Journal of Criminology*, 57 (6): 1279–300.

Shalhoub-Kevorkian, N. (2020), 'Necropenology: Conquering New Bodies, Psychics, and Territories of Death in East Jerusalem', *Global Studies in Culture and Power*, 27 (3): 285–301.

Stern-Weiner, J. (2021), *The Politics of a Definition: How the IHRA Working Definition of Antisemitism Is Being Misrepresented*. Oxford University: Free Speech on Israel.

Tatour, L. (2019), 'Citizenship as Domination: Settler Colonialism and the Making of Palestinian Citizenship in Israel', *Arab Studies Journal*, 27 (2): 8–39.

'Til Kingdom Come (2020), [Film] Dir. Maya Zinshtein, MetFim.

Wolfe, P. (1988), *Settler Colonialism and the Transformation of Anthropology*. London: Continuum.

Yadgar, Y. (2020), *Israel's Jewish Identity Crisis: State and Politics in the Middle East*. Cambridge: Cambridge University Press.

Zertal, I. and A. Eldar (2007), *Lords of the Land: The War over Israel's Settlements in the Occupied Territories, 1967–2007*. New York: Nation Books.

10

Hindu radicalization in contemporary India

Pralay Kanungo

Introduction

In December 2021 at a *Dharma Sansad* (Hindu religious parliament) held in Haridwar, a Hindu religious city on the foothills of the Himalayas, Hindu religious leaders called on followers to raise weapons against Muslims. In contrast to India's long-standing national motto *Satyameba Jayate* (truth alone triumphs), they chanted *Shastrameba Jayate* (weapons alone triumph). One Hindu seer even called for Muslim genocide, asking every Hindu to take up arms and perform ethnic cleansing (FP Staff 2021). In another *Dharma Sansad* organized in the city of Raipur, Kalicharan – a Hindu Sadhu – abused the Father of the Indian Nation, Mahatma Gandhi, and saluted his assassin, Nathuram Godse (The Quint 2021); an insensitive audience clapped (The Wire 2021).

Kalicharan, however, is not the first to denigrate Gandhi. Gandhi, a devout Hindu and an apostle of peace and non-violence, has been constantly vilified by Hindu fanatics. A group of Hindu radicals publicly enacted a mock killing of him, celebrating the pumping of bullets into Gandhi's effigy and the spilling of blood from its chest (Ahmad 2019). Radical Hindus have routinely eulogized Gandhi's assassin, Godse, in the public sphere, rationalizing his crime as just and heroic, and even campaigning to raise a temple to worship him. Godse, the 'first Hindu terrorist' in postcolonial India, has gained respectability in recent times.

Thus, over the decades, Mahatma Gandhi's liberal, tolerant, pluralist and secular India has turned Hindu nationalist. The Rashtriya Swayamsevak Sangh (RSS), the fountainhead of Hindu nationalism, also commonly referred to as Hindutva, claims India as an exclusively Hindu nation and has grown phenomenally in recent decades (Basu et al. 1993, Bhatt 2001, Kanungo 2002). Three decades ago, a large frenzied Hindu nationalist mob razed the sixteenth-century Babri Mosque in Ayodhya, reclaiming the site as birthplace of their god Ram which had been pulled down by the medieval Mughal ruler Babur (Mukhopadhyaya 1994). The politically marginalized Hindu nationalist Bharatiya Janata Party (BJP), a political affiliate of the RSS, invoked Ram as a militant national symbol of India in the 1990s (Kapur 1993) and successfully mobilized Hindus on the Ayodhya issue. The party spread its wings and gained momentum across classes, castes and regions to emerge as a dominant political power. Since 2014, the BJP, under the charismatic and populist leadership of Prime Minister Narendra Modi, has been inching towards establishing its hegemony. Today, a grand Ram temple is being constructed at the same site of demolition where the Babri Mosque once stood, under the patronage of the Indian state, without any remorse. And the story does not end there; Hindu nationalists are already reclaiming two other 'disputed' sites: Mathura (Krishna's birthplace) and Varanasi (Shiva's temple), original Hindu sites of faith that were desecrated and usurped by medieval Islamic rulers.

Prime Minister Narendra Modi, while making pledges to build an inclusive India with slogans like *Sab ka Saath, Sab ka Vikas and Sab ka Vishwas* (Together, for Everyone's Growth, with Everyone's Trust), simultaneously governs in an authoritarian fashion with a clear Hindu majoritarian orientation (Chatterjee et al. 2019). Modi's populist nationalism is firmly embedded in a large Hindu constituency, which ensures consecutive electoral victories for him as well as his political party, the BJP, at both national and sub-national level. The BJP has also elevated Yogi Adityanath, a radical Hindu monk, to high political office as the chief minister of Uttar Pradesh (UP). This is the largest Indian province with 200 million people, including 40 million Muslims. Yogi, a polarizing figure, has earned large Hindu support in the 2022 state elections, primarily for his radical anti-Muslim rhetoric and majoritarian governance. The Yogi regime is applauded for extra-judicial killings, the so-called 'encounters' of Muslim criminals; the chilling, cold-blooded murder of the Ahmed brothers, with police protection and in the full glare of media, by three young men with alleged Hindutva connections, makes a mockery of justice. Moreover, Yogi is fondly called 'Bulldozer Baba' by his Hindu admirers as he runs bulldozers over the houses and properties of illegal encroachers, targeting mostly Muslims.

Hindu nationalist India has turned Islamophobic in every sense; countering this perception, Hindu nationalists highlight Hinduphobia. The Modi government objected to the United Nations (UN) resolution that declared 15 March the 'International Day to Combat Islamophobia'. India's permanent representative to the UN observed: 'This resolution may well end up downplaying the seriousness of phobias against all other religions' (The Quint 2022). In India's view, such phobias are not restricted to Abrahamic religions only; they have also affected the followers of non-Abrahamic faiths, especially the 'anti-Hindu, anti-Buddhists, and anti-Sikh phobias' (Swarajya 2022). Such shifts in political discourses and governance practices clearly signal how conflation of Hinduism and nationalism under the current Hindu nationalist regime has created a milieu for Hindu radicalization to flourish and become entrenched. Overt and covert state patronage has emboldened Hindu radicals to create fear among minorities and occasionally unleash violence with impunity. Thus, Hindu radicalization is no longer a secret or sporadic act of violence by a few radicalized Hindu individuals or fringe Hindu groups. It has become an open and assertive demonstration of aggression and violence vis-à-vis Muslims.

In this context, this chapter deconstructs the dynamics of contemporary Hindu radicalization by looking into the complex interplay of religion, community, nation and state. At the outset, Hinduism needs to be distinguished from Hindutva (Shaban 2022); while the former is a faith/religion, the latter is a marker of identity used to make ideological claims about the Indian/Hindu nation. Hindu radicalization is an ideological and strategic component of Hindutva/Hindu nationalism, which is exclusionary and anti-Muslim.

Hindu radicalization and Muslim radicalization emerged in colonial India during the second half of the nineteenth century as a consequence of the divide-and-rule policy of colonialism, manifesting in Hindu–Muslim riots and leading to India's partition into two nations on the basis of religion – India and Pakistan. However, both genres of radicalism remained fringe and found it hard to expand their reach as Prime Minister Nehru built a strong secular India. Yet the postcolonial secular state failed to quell Hindu–Muslim communal riots, in which Muslims were major victims; besides, the democratic welfare state could not provide adequate political representation to Muslims and redress their social, economic and educational injustices. All these factors created Muslim anxiety, insecurity, marginalization and alienation, creating conditions conducive to Muslim radicalization; yet by and large, Muslim radicalization remained a low-key affair, except in Kashmir.

The ascendancy of Hindu nationalist forces, as argued in this chapter, galvanized two streams of radicalizations simultaneously. On one side, the intensification of Hindutva's anti-Muslim rhetoric and actions further escalated insecurity and alienation among Muslims, thus concretizing the prospect of Islamist radicalization. On the other, such anti-Muslim discourses, imbued with narratives of Hindu victimhood, gave a boost to Hindu radicalization. For instance, Hindu nationalists continuously rubbed the Muslim wound by chiding the Nehruvian state for 'Muslim appeasement' and unfair treatment to Hindus; simultaneously, their discourses on medieval Muslim aggression, conversion to Islam, rising Muslim populations, the general threat of global Islamist terrorism and the specific threat from neighbouring Pakistan were loud warning bells for Hindus as well. Thus, Hindutva discourse became a double-edged sword, generating fear among Muslims and anti-Muslim hatred among Hindus and propelling both streams of radicalization. After coming to power, the Hindu nationalist government emboldened and empowered Hindu radicals to terrorize Muslims both physically and psychologically in everyday life, thereby pushing Muslims towards Islamist radicalism.

Hindutva's Islamophobia and anti-Muslim violence provided ideal grounds for al Qaeda and Islamic State (IS) to draw Indian Muslims towards radicalization. While the former had earlier campaigned against 'saffron terror', in the midst of the 2020 Delhi riots, IS launched the magazine *Sawt-al-Hind* (Voice of Hind) in English, Hindi, Urdu and Bengali. The inaugural issue's opening piece, titled 'So where are you going? A Call to Muslims of India', called upon Indian Muslims to join jihad: *'O Muslims of Hind! Has the time not come for you to wake up from the deep slumber, which has overtaken all of you to the point of an intoxicated stupor? Haven't you yet realized that the idolatrous Hindus would never ever be pleased with you until you renounce the Deen of Islam in its entirety?'* Sawt Al-Hind asked Indian Muslims to shun the path of moderation and integration as 'idolatrous' Hindus would remain the perpetual enemy of Islam. Reciprocating Hindutva's hate campaign and attacking the Hindu faith, the magazine glorified Mahmud of Ghazni – a notorious 'idol breaker' for Hindus – for 'waging jihad against the *mushrikin* [polytheists] of India, destroying their idols, and spreading Islam in their lands' (Iyer and Mirchandani 2020). Thus, contemporary India continues to face the escalation of radicalization and violence by both Hindutva and Islamist forces.

Contextualizing radicalization in India

Radicalization is a multidimensional concept with multiple meanings. Admittedly, there exists no conceptual consensus on radicalization as it is a complex phenomenon, and often ambiguous; its conceptual contours, causes, discourses, manifestations, trajectories and effects are multiple and diverse (Kundnani 2012, Neumann 2013, Malthaner 2017). Conceptually and analytically, radicalization is not necessarily a religious phenomenon. However, in contemporary usage, particularly since 9/11, it has acquired a religious connotation; there has been a common and prejudicial trend to conflate Islam with violence, overlooking Islam's peaceful and non-violent traditions (Shank 2011) and vilifying Muslims as 'bad', 'violent' and 'terrorists'.

While radicalization is conceptually complex and commonly perceived as violent, it can be non-violent too (Bartlett and Miller 2012). Hinduism, which appears to be a peaceful religion, does not always celebrate non-violence (Rapoport 1984, Vidal, Tarabout and Meyer 2003, Rambachan 2017). The *Bhagvat Gita*, one of the most revered Hindu texts, carries extreme interpretations, both benign and violent. Similarly, while Buddha's preaching is anchored in peace and non-violence, Buddhist radicals in Myanmar and Sri Lanka openly espouse violence (Schonthal and Walton 2016). Whether or not violence features in radicalized movements, radicalization is commonly perceived to involve challenging and seeking to transform existing ideologies and social orders, and in an everyday sense, radicalization and violence are often used interchangeably. The religion-radicalization-violence dynamic can thus sometimes be perceived as a taken-for-granted continuum.

The meanings and trajectories of radicalization in South Asia, and more particularly in India, are diverse and are not exclusive to Muslims. The symptoms of radicalization are very much prevalent among other communities as well – religious, ethnic and marginalized. In the 1980s, radical Sikhs launched a violent movement, demanding Khalistan, a separate Sikh homeland, which the Indian state crushed by force (Singh and Shani 2021). Radical ethnic groups in India's north-eastern states have violently resisted the Indian state by demanding separate statehood, which invited a similar state response (Nag 2002, Baruah 2007).

At present, broadly, three streams of radicalization are found in India: left-wing extremist (popularly known as Maoist), Islamist and Hindutva. Left-wing radicalism, which emerged in the form of a violent peasant movement in the late 1960s and later focused on mobilizing indigenous tribal (Adivasi) communities, advocates for the annihilation of class enemies and the seizure of state power by force. This movement has affected a dozen Indian states, creating a 'red corridor' (Chakravarti 2008). Intermittently, these radicals have launched violent attacks on security forces, officials and informers. Despite confronting state repression and multiple organizational splits, left-wing extremism has managed to survive in some remote pockets. While left-wing radicalism calls for radical social and economic transformation and violent purging of the ruling class/state, Islamist and Hindutva radicalism belong to another genre of radicalism in the Indian context. Hindu radicalism represents the ideology of militant Hindu nationalism, known as Hindutva (Leidig 2020). Muslim and Hindu radicalization in India are thus primarily the by-products of a complex internal communal-national nexus, rather than manifestations of any external dynamics or global influence. Muslim radicalization is driven more by internal Hindu–Muslim communal discourses and divides rather than by Islamist ideology.

However, this is not to gloss over the role of Islamist ideology in accentuating the divide between 'us and them'. Islamist groups had reservations as postcolonial India became a secular state. Thus, they derived inspiration not from the Indian Constitution and institutions but from Islamic sources: the Darul Uloom Deoband, a conservative *madrasa*; the Jamaat-e-Islami (Islamic Society), which was committed to global Islamic revolution; and the Wahhabi movement, originating in Saudi Arabia (Haqqani 2006).

Similarly, since India did not become a Hindu state, the ideological tracts of V. D. Savarkar (Savarkar 1923) and M. S. Golwalkar (Golwalkar 1939), rather than the Constitution of India, became the holy texts for Hindutva proponents. The texts, ideologues and institutions of Hindutva and Islamist forces (though comparatively on a lower scale as a minority) continued to denigrate and demonize each other's community through hate-filled ideological propaganda, recruiting and indoctrinating foot-soldiers and inciting inter-communal violence. This has in turn led to the construction and manifestation of 'reciprocal' as well as 'cumulative' radicalization and violence (Bartlett and Birdwell 2013, Busher and Macklin 2015).

The evolution of Muslim and Hindu radicalism: Colonialism, communalism and nationalism

Islam came to the Indian subcontinent in the early eighth century with the Arabs' invasion of Sindh. From the first millennium CE onwards, different ethnic streams of invaders who were believers of Islam entered from Central Asia and Afghanistan. While many Muslim invaders returned to their homelands, some, like the Mughals, made India their home and became its rulers, making India a land of confluent and composite cultures. Islam has been part and parcel of Indian identity and culture for many centuries (Pande 1986). South Asian Islam followed an eclectic and diverse tradition as it was tempered by the tolerant preaching of liberal sects like Sufis and Barelvis and intermingling with other religions.

Despite adhering to different faiths and experiencing the occasional eruption of communal violence, Hindus and Muslims by and large lived in harmony under precolonial Muslim rule (Roy 2010); by contrast, colonialism created and instrumentalized intercommunal rivalry and sharpened the Hindu–Muslim divide. Hindus and Muslims demonstrated exemplary unity in fighting British colonialism in 1857. After crushing the mutiny, the British colonial government adopted the strategy of divide and rule by introducing a 'separate electorate' for Muslims in order to checkmate such combined resistance in future. This policy worked and the communal divide sowed the seeds of mistrust and radicalization among Hindus and Muslims. As a result, colonial India experienced a series of Hindu–Muslim riots in the early twentieth century (Pandey 1993).

Muslim leaders formed the Muslim League in 1906 to organize and mobilize Muslims; the All India Hindu Mahasabha was formed in 1915, bringing many Hindu organizations into one platform. Thus, a competitive communal politics engulfed colonial India and vicious communal discourses were disseminated. Muslim leader Muhammad Ali Jinnah advocated the 'two-nation theory' and demanded the creation of Pakistan for Muslims, arguing that Hindus and Muslims could not live together. On the Hindu side, V. D. Savarkar's exclusionary Hindutva thesis echoed similar ideas (Savarkar 1923). K. B. Hedgewar, who founded the RSS in 1925 amid Hindu–Muslim riots, claimed India as a Hindu nation as well. His mission was to organize Hindus to build a masculine, muscular militant community. Hedgewar recruited adolescent young boys and imparted *sharirik* (physical) and *boudhik* (intellectual) training every day in its daily *shakhas* (branches). While physical training was intended to enable Hindus to take on Muslims during communal riots, intellectual training demonized Muslims as 'aggressors' and 'traitors' and reinforced a sense of Hindu victimhood. Such training obviously had a clear anti-Muslim orientation and agenda. Hedgewar's successor, M. S. Golwalkar, further sharpened this anti-minority discourse by warning that Muslims and Christians should either adopt the Hindu culture and language, respect and revere Hindu religion and glorify the Hindu race and culture or risk losing citizens' rights (Golwalkar 1939: 47–8).

Mahatma Gandhi, who spearheaded India's freedom struggle, could not prevent India's partition in 1947 into two nations – India and Pakistan. It was a bloody partition forged along religious lines; while a million people were killed, seven million lost their homes and were forced to migrate, becoming refugees in two countries. Displacement and violence left a permanent scar on both communities and nations, creating fodder for future radicalization. Muslim and Hindu communalists always portrayed each other's community and nation as a permanent enemy. While independent India's adoption of secularism and modern secular political leadership took some steam out of Hindu radicalism, the Islamic state of Pakistan became fragile due to a strong state-religion nexus, thereby allowing radical Islamic clergies and political leadership to continuously espouse Hindu mistrust and hostility towards India.

Muslim radicalization in postcolonial India

After India's partition in 1947, a large number of Muslims deliberately decided to stay in India, their home for centuries. As most of the Muslim communalist leadership had left for Pakistan, Indian Muslims favoured moving along in consonance with the ethos of the new secular state; the negligible remnants of radicalization faded into oblivion for some time thereafter. However, Hindu nationalists campaigned for all Muslims to leave for Pakistan, as the rationale of the new nation was religion. They cast the loyalty of Indian Muslims to India as being under perpetual suspicion and continued to make them insecure, using slogans such as 'Go back to Pakistan'. Though Hindu nationalists were at this time still a marginal force, even then, Indian Muslims nurtured the anxiety of being a minority in a Hindu-majority India: by 1951, India had 304 million Hindus (84.1 per cent) and 35 million Muslims (9.8 per cent). Such anxiety was partly assuaged when the postcolonial Indian state became not a Hindu state but a secular and democratic state committed to the vision of *Sarva Dharma Sama Bhav* (equal treatment of all religions). The Indian Constitution guaranteed freedom of religion, non-discrimination and expansive minority rights (Articles 25–31).

Despite the adoption of such liberal constitutional measures, however, the Hindu–Muslim divide continued and became further widened by vested communal leaders from both sides. Postcolonial India witnessed major communal riots in cities like Aligarh, Meerut, Bhiwandi, Bhagalpur, Ahmedabad and Muzaffarnagar. Both majority and minority communalism instigated and played a participatory role in these riots. While Hindus were victims of the riots in some Muslim-majority areas, overall, Muslims suffered in much greater proportions due to their numerical disadvantage. Moreover, they often had to face a double disadvantage, as the security forces demonstrated a majoritarian bias; the Hashimpura episode involving the custodial deaths of thirty-eight Muslims is one such instance (Mander 2018).

Post-riots justice eluded Muslims as the Indian criminal justice system, comprising police and the judiciary, was not only biased at times but also slow, expensive and ineffective. The loss and suffering in major communal riots made younger Muslims tilt towards Islamist radicalization, which was further enhanced by the demolition of the Babri Masjid in 1992; the 1993 Mumbai riots, in which the state used disproportionate force against Muslims; the non-implementation of the follow-up Sri Krishna Commission Report; and the 2002 Gujarat genocide (Spodek 2010, Shaikh 2017, Raman 2018). Besides, whenever there was an India-Pakistan war, Indian Muslims would be humiliated as the Hindu right would label them as 'traitors' and 'fifth column' citizens. Obviously, Islamist radicals in India and Pakistan found the failure of the state to protect Muslims a potent weapon to use in attracting Muslims towards radicalization.

The socio-economic status of Muslims became another driving force for radicalization. Ironically, while the Hindu right constantly harps on Muslim appeasement in secular India, a large proportion of Indian Muslims, barring a few south Indian states, remain poor, uneducated and socially and economically disadvantaged (Sachar Committee Report 2006). The Sachar Committee Report (2006) has been an eye-opener as it reveals Muslim marginalization and exclusion in detail. Muslims have lower literacy rates and their children spend fewer years in school; their per capita income is lower than that of other marginalized communities. Muslim participation in public employment such as the civil service, police and the army is abysmally low, and they are excluded from banking and financial systems. Their political representation in national and state legislatures is low as well. While riots and biases in the criminal justice system have made Muslims insecure, this dismal picture of social and economic exclusion has further accentuated their perception of unfairness, generating another structural vector for potential radicalization (van den Bos 2020).

Insecurity, humiliation, poverty and multiple exclusions in postcolonial India have thus precipitated Muslim anger against the political class and created fertile ground for radicalization. Interestingly, Muslim radicals were not involved in the terrorist killings of top Indian leaders: Mahatma Gandhi was killed by a radical Hindu nationalist in 1948, Prime Minister Indira Gandhi by two Sikh radicals in 1984 and her son Prime Minister Rajiv Gandhi by Tamil extremists in 1991. Since Kashmir became turbulent, Islamic radicals have killed many local leaders, both Hindus and Muslims, perceived as opponents. The Indian government's National Crime Records Bureau report (2017) revealed that in 2017 jihadi terrorists killed 85; Northeast insurgents, 5; Naxalites/left-wing extremists, 138 (civilians and police/state/army personnel combined); and other terrorists, 41. Surprisingly, the Report excluded data on hate crime and lynching because the available data was considered 'unreliable' and 'vague' (The Telegraph 2019). As most hate crimes were committed by Hindu radicals, the government report prefers not to take cognizance of them. It also needs to be noted that the bulk of the killings by so-called jihadi terrorists is confined to Kashmir, suggesting that the impact of Islamist radicalization remains more local and contextual than national.

The entry of Islamist radicalization to India started in the 1980s at the behest of Pakistan. The religious rationale of partition proved erroneous, as Muslim Pakistan split in 1971 on ethnic lines and the new sovereign nation of Bangladesh was created. After losing access to India's eastern front, Pakistan continued to keep hostilities alive on the western front by making Kashmir a perpetual bone of contention. Though Pakistan lost wars against India in 1965 and 1971, it continued proxy wars through cross-border terrorism, dispatching radical Islamist militant groups to Kashmir to perpetrate violence and radicalize local Muslims. This offered justification for the Hindu nationalist rationale that Pakistan would remain India's enemy forever. Hindu nationalists escalated their vilification campaign against Pakistan and conveniently extended this enemy tag to Indian Muslims as anti-national and Pakistan's collaborators.

Hindu nationalism's campaign took an aggressive turn in the early 1980s. Militant outfits of the Sangh Parivar, like the Vishva Hindu Parishad (VHP) and Bajrang Dal (BD), intensified anti-Muslim campaigns over the conversion of some Dalits to Islam in Tamil Nadu (1983) and the withdrawal of the Muslim Women's Bill, under Muslim pressure, by the Rajiv Gandhi government. The BJP used the issue of Muslim appeasement in a national campaign to mobilize Hindus against Muslims. Sensing a favourable wind, the Sangh Parivar launched the Ram Janmabhoomi movement, reclaiming the disputed Babri Mosque at Ayodhya as the birthplace of Lord Ram. The BJP adopted the Ram temple agenda in 1989 and joined the movement. The VHP and the Bajrang Dal organized large processions, distributed *trishuls* (tridents) to Hindu youth and deployed provocative anti-Muslim slogans inviting Muslims to choose between Pakistan and the graveyard. These violent campaigns provided an impetus for Muslim radical elements to organize and retaliate.

Escalation of Islamist radicalization

As Hindu militants had escalated their anti-Muslim mobilization, the Indian government launched a political and military offensive in Kashmir to crush the demand for state autonomy and neutralize Pakistan's intervention in the state. It brazenly manipulated democratic elections in Kashmir in 1989 and escalated military deployment. This high-handed approach alienated Kashmiri Muslims and pushed some towards Islamist radicalism. Popular anger against the Indian state grew in Kashmir, and Pakistan strategically sent Islamist terrorist groups to recruit locals and expand their operation. Islamist radicals compelled Hindu Pandits to leave their homeland in

1990 (Evans 2002), and the mass exodus of Hindus from their own homeland agitated Hindus and provoked Hindu radicals.

Terrorist infiltration moved beyond Kashmir when two Pakistan supported terrorist outfits – Lashkar-e-Taiba and Jaish-e-Mohammad – attacked the Indian Parliament building in 2001. Hindu nationalists found it useful to intensify a campaign against 'Islamic terrorism' while simultaneously attacking Indian Muslims for their complicity with terrorists. Hindu nationalist campaigns became a violent spectacle in the Gujarat pogrom in 2002 in retaliation to the setting on fire of a railway compartment, allegedly by Muslim radicals, wherein fifty-seven Hindus returning from Ayodhya after performing rituals were burnt alive. The brutal genocide of more than a thousand Muslims by a radical Hindu mob and unfair and unjust treatment by a biased state gave further impetus to Islamist radicalization, as did Hindu nationalists' participation in America's post-9/11 campaign on 'war on terror', which further alienated Muslims. In 2008, Lashkar-e-Taiba stormed Mumbai's Taj Mahal hotel, killing 164 people. Even though a Pakistan-sponsored operation, Hindu radicals used this attack to discredit Indian Muslims.

Previous terrorist activities that had provided a rationale for the introduction of earlier stringent anti-terror laws, such as the 1967 Unlawful Activities (Prevention) Act (UAPA), were now deemed inadequate. In 1985, following the assassination of Indira Gandhi, India adopted the Terrorist and Disruptive Activities (Prevention) Act (TADA). Following 9/11 and the attacks on the Indian Parliament in 2001, India enacted the Prevention of Terrorism Act of 2002 (POTA). POTA's strong ideological and political agenda was demonstrated by its explicit targeting of 'Muslim militancy'; Muslims felt that they were not only being targeted but also excluded from legal due process of, and denied recourse to, judicial processes.

Radicalization can always be triggered by grievances related to discrimination and injustice. Anti-terrorist laws can be used to criminalize a community and communalize nationalism. POTA was repealed in 2004, but some of its harsher provisions were exported to UAPA (Ferreira and Gonsalves 2017). In addition, some states have their own anti-terror laws, including the Maharashtra Control of Organized Crime Act, 1999; Chhattisgarh Special Public Security Act, 2005; Jammu and Kashmir Public Safety Act, 1978; and Andhra Pradesh Public Security Act, 1992.

Following the upswing in Islamist radicalization after the Babri Masjid demolition in 1992, the turbulent decades in Kashmir and the 2002 Gujarat pogrom, radical Islamist groups like the Students Islamic Movement in India (SIMI) and Indian Mujahideen (IM) expanded their networks, drawing in more young people (Ahmad 2009, Arosoaie 2018). As intelligence agencies reported, in 2015, 200 youths were being monitored for suspicious online links with Islamic State (IS) (in 2015, 23 had travelled to Syria and Iraq, which rose to seventy in 2016), while 450 Muslims were being monitored for pro-IS leanings in 2016.

The agencies also revealed that Salafi outfits were involved in the indoctrination of Muslim youth in south Indian states and Maharashtra (Singh 2017). Interestingly, well-networked and more prosperous regions of India are more prone to IS influence than poor states like Bihar and even the Muslim majority of Kashmir (Jaishankar 2017). The poor Muslims of northern India, who often get victimized in communal riots, do not radicalize in greater numbers; this disinclination may perhaps be due to the dynamics of coping with poverty and the experience of chronic victimization during communal riots. By contrast, Muslims in southern India, who are comparatively less exposed to communal riots and have higher socio-economic and educational status, are more outraged about the future of their community under the Hindu nationalist regime.

Overall, however, the quantum of Islamist radicalization has been negligible in population terms. Islamist radicalization could not take deep roots in India, even in Kashmir, for very long. When Islamist groups, indigenous or exogenous, tried to call the shots in Kashmir, well-known clerics like Mirwaiz Farooq and politicians like Abdul Gani Lone defied their diktats and were assassinated (*The Times of India* 2021). In the past, Kashmir Muslims have even refused to bury the bodies of family members who sacrificed themselves as suicide bombers. However, peaceful and tolerant Islam in Kashmir turned militant and violent for a period of time, primarily due to the insensitive and high-handed repression of the Indian state. As Kashmir became a military zone, the demand for state autonomy turned into demand for *Azadi* (freedom/secession). Islamist radicals like Burhan Wani, a Kashmiri Muslim youth icon, drew hundreds of Kashmiri Muslims into a radical network through social media before getting killed by security forces (Peerzada 2016). Lashkar-e-Taiba often refers to *Ghazwa-e-Hind* (the holy conquest of India) as a means of liberating Kashmir from Indian control (Haqqani 2015).

Islamist radicalization has shifted since India's Hindu nationalist takeover. Majoritarian governance and everyday hate campaigns by Hindu radicals against Muslims on public platforms, in elections campaigns and on electronic and social media have become more strident. Hindu extreme discourses and actions have arguably given new impetus to Islamist radicalization. Greater numbers of Kashmiri Muslim youth have joined Islamist radical outfits after the Modi government abrogated the guaranteed constitutional status of the state under Article 370 in August 2019. Simultaneously, the Modi government took away Kashmir's statehood, deployed massive military measures to quell popular protests, blocked social media and imprisoned a large number of political leaders. All these measures have only expanded and intensified the scope of Islamist radicalization in Kashmir.

Yet Muslim anger is not confined to Kashmir alone. Muslims across India are resentful towards the current Hindu nationalist regime. They see as ominous the Modi government's adoption of the Citizen Amendment Act (CAA) and proposed introduction of the National Register for Citizens (NRC), alongside their political and economic marginalization and the routine subversion of the rule of law to inflict and deepen discrimination against Muslims. As the community's alienation deepens due to both physical and psychological insecurity, the prospects for escalating radicalization increase accordingly.

Hindu radicalization: Momentum and escalation of violence

We now turn from Muslim radicalization and its entanglement with Hindu radicalization to highlight how Hindu radicalization's momentum has become more aggressive since Narendra Modi's government came to power in 2014. Since its rise to power, India has seen strident anti-Muslim campaigns and violent actions. The Sangh Parivar has reinforced anti-Muslim narratives in the public domain through its vast organizational network and a pliable media. The vivisection of Bharat Mata (Mother India) has always been an ideological and emotional issue for Hindu nationalists, and they have continued to invoke the idea of *Akhand Bharat* (undivided India) to harbour anti-Muslim and anti-Pakistan sentiment among Hindus.

For example, Pakistan's founder, Muhammad Ali Jinnah, was brought into public controversy for no reason to portray him as a villain and Pakistan's creation as illegitimate; the purpose was to connect Jinnah, Pakistan and Indian Muslims and create a hostile perception of Indian Muslims among Hindus. Conversely, Hindutva ideologue V. D. Savarkar, who was no less responsible for partition through his exclusionary Hindutva ideology, was eulogized. School history textbooks were rewritten to reflect Hindu nationalist discourses on Hindu victimhood, partition violence, killing, displacement and the suffering of Hindus, portraying Muslims as outsiders, historical invaders and aggressors, and the chief architects of partition. Radical Hindu saints, as discussed earlier, publicly humiliated Mahatma Gandhi for his alleged role in India's partition. Gandhi-Nehru bashing became a new *mantra* (hymn) of Hindu radicalism; discourses of xenophobic nationalism replaced India's secular and composite nationalism.

Hindu radicals had never endorsed India's adoption of a secular constitution, which made freedom of religion a fundamental right, guaranteed minority rights and granted autonomy to minority institutions to preserve their language and culture. They strongly denounced India's decision to allow Muslims to be governed by their own religious laws related to marriage, divorce and inheritance, while imposing a uniform code on Hindus. Hindu nationalist leaders publicly ridiculed secularism and reiterated their commitment to implement a Uniform Civil Code (UCC) and abrogate the special constitutional status of Jammu and Kashmir under Article 370 (which they have now achieved). Hindu radicals, taking their cue from these developments, viciously attacked what they saw as the 'Muslim appeasement' policy of the Nehruvian state. Hyperbole was created around extending special favourable treatment to Muslims and the converse Hindu victimhood in Hindu-majority India in order to generate Hindu anger and mobilize Hindu radicalism.

The focus on religious conversion of Hindus to Christianity and Islam, which had been a major concern of Hindu leaders since the late nineteenth century, was ratcheted up to radicalize Hindus against minorities. Hindu nationalists reminded Hindus that in precolonial India, Muslim rulers carried out mass conversions of Hindus to Islam by force; during the colonial era, Christian missionaries converted vulnerable Hindus like Dalits and Adivasis through manipulation, coercion or fraud, and this continued in postcolonial India as well. Hindu nationalists claimed the high moral ground in portraying Hinduism as a non-proselytizing religion. At the same time, they initiated the 'reconversion' of Christians and Muslims into Hinduism (*The Financial Express* 2015). According to their logic, the ancestors of Indian Christians and Muslims were converts from Hinduism, and hence should return to their original religion, shaking off the yoke of foreign bondage.

Conversion and reconversion issues had been contentious in the past and led to routine intimidation and violence towards minorities. Sangh Parivar outfits like the Vishva Hindu Parishad and the Bajrang Dal in particular have targeted Christian missionaries, alleging that they convert various tribes and marginalized communities. Suspecting the role in conversions of Christian missionary Graham Staines, who has been serving poor leprosy patients for decades, Hindu radicals burnt him and his two sons alive in Odisha in 1999 (Kanungo 2002: 254). When a radical Hindu ascetic was killed in Kandhamal, Odisha, in 2008, Hindu radicals, suspecting a Christian conspiracy, launched a violent anti-Christian riot in 2008, killing more than forty people and making thousands of Christians homeless (Kanungo 2008); later, it was found that left-wing extremists had killed the Hindu saint. Though many states have already passed anti-conversion laws (known as Freedom of Religion Bills), making religious conversion extremely difficult, Hindu radicals continue to demand a more stringent national anti-conversion law.

While Christians have conventionally been the primary targets of Hindu radicals over conversion, in recent times, 'love jihad' became a battle cry of Hindu radicals (see also Amarasingam and Desai, this volume). This discourse alleges that Muslim men seduce Hindu women through deceptive declarations of love in order to convert them to Islam, and Hindu radical vigilantes often use violence against Muslim men on the pretext of saving Hindu women from conversion (Sarkar 2019, Strohl 2019). After frequent publicity for the alleged phenomenon of 'love jihad' in the media and public domain, many other so-called 'jihads' have followed, including 'corona jihad' (Nizaruddin 2021; see also Amarasingam and Desai, this volume); 'civil services jihad', 'land jihad' and '*redi* jihad' (street vendor jihad). Hindutva radicals invent Muslim conspiracy in multiple spheres as a pretext to unleash violence against them.

However, Hindu vigilantism has little to do with faith; it is a manifestation of hatred, intolerance and violence against a particular community, resembling the far-right radicalism now prevalent in other parts of the world. Hindu radicals do not spare ordinary Hindus either. In 2009, the cadre of Sri Ram Sene, a Hindu radical group, barged into a pub in Mangalore and assaulted the women inside for flouting traditional 'Indian' norms of decency. Hindu radicals also disrupted Valentine's Day celebrations, deeming the observance an anti-Hindu culture Western import; Hindu youths were instructed to celebrate it instead as parents' worship day. Moral policing escalated further and became violent, with Hindu radicals setting the agenda for the governance of food, clothing and social etiquette. Thus, meat shops were forcibly shut down during Hindu religious festival days (Vincent 2021); the wearing of *Hizab* (hijab) by Muslim girls in schools in Karnataka was opposed; 'Anti-Romeo squads', formed in the name of providing safety to women in public places, allegedly harassed consenting young couples. Hindu radicalization not only shows aversion towards the plurality and heterogeneity of Hindu culture but also castigates its ideological opponents. Members of Sanatan Sanstha, an obscure Hindu radical organization (which claims to be a spiritual organization with links to Hindu nationalist organizations) (Eeshanpriya 2018), were allegedly involved in the killings of rationalist Narendra Dabholkar, Kannada scholars M. M. Kalburgi and Govind Pansare, and journalist Gauri Lankesh, all four of whom were overt critics of Hindu nationalism.

Vigilantism of all kinds has been espoused to spread hatred against Muslims on social media (Mirchandani 2018, Banajee et al. 2019). Vigilantism has also crossed into violence on the question of *Go Raksha* (cow protection). As most Hindus revere the holy cow as *Go Mata* (Mother Cow), cow protection has been a key element of the Hindu agenda since the nineteenth century, particularly in north India. For the Sangh Parivar, the cow is a sacred symbol of the Hindu nation, and they want to see a national ban on cow-slaughter; many states have already adopted such a ban. As Muslims are assumed to be beef eaters and involved in cattle trading, Hindu radicals have found it convenient to bend their cow protection campaign towards anti-Muslim ends. Radical vigilante groups consisting of Hindu youth militias have patrolled the highways, physically assaulting cattle transporters on suspicion and even lynching suspects. A vigilante Hindu mob brutally killed a Muslim named Mohammed Akhlaq and injured his son because they suspected them of storing and consuming beef (*The Times of India* 2017). Later it turned out that the meat was not beef; the culprits were subsequently let off, another indication of the criminal justice system's unfairness towards Muslims.

Since the Modi government's rise to power, there has been an escalation of the Hindu nationalist obsession with reclaiming monuments, cities, localities and institutions in order to rename them with their supposedly 'lost' Hindu names. Sangh Parivar narratives have always highlighted that medieval Muslim invaders and rulers have desecrated Hindu religious places, demolished temples and built mosques and Islamic institutions; the Sangh Parivar argues these so-called symbols of slavery need to be erased and such spaces reclaimed by Hindus. Babri Mosque was the first such case of erasure and reclamation. Since then, many Hindu monuments and places have been claimed as sites of Muslim desecration, real as well as mythical, from Agra's Taj Mahal to Delhi's Qutub Minar. Cities with Muslim names have been rechristened with their 'original' Hindu names: for example, Allahabad has become Prayag Raj and Faizabad's new name is Ayodhya. The politics of reclaiming and renaming are part of a broader strategy of cultural genocide, since cultural erasure is no less important than physical elimination of Muslims (Apoorvanand 2018). Open public spaces have become communalized too; Hindu radicals, supported by the state, obstruct Muslims in their efforts to offer *Namaz* (Friday prayer) in public parks and grounds, whereas there have been no such restrictions on the use of public space for Hindu religious congregations.

The state discriminates starkly in its treatment of Hindu versus Muslim radicals. Hindu radicals like Swami Aseemanand, who confessed his involvement in the Samjouta Express bomb blast (*The Caravan* 2014), have been acquitted. Colonel Purohit, the leader of the Hindu radical group Abhinav Bharat, who was allegedly involved in the 2008 Malegaon blast (Jaffrelot 2010), is in the process of being acquitted. The ruling BJP has awarded a seat in Parliament to Pragya Thakur, a Hindu radical, who was also allegedly involved in the Malegaon blasts. By contrast, Muslims, many on the basis of unevidenced suspicion alone, have been victims of various forms of 'state terror' and have languished in jail under draconian laws on charges of terrorism. Ironically, many have ultimately been found innocent and exonerated after spending their prime years in jail.

Hindu radicalization and Muslim radicalization: Convergence and divergence

This discussion of the genesis, rationale, processes and impacts of radicalization in India has demonstrated the intricate connection between Muslim and Hindu processes of radicalization. Both are the by-products of colonial and postcolonial communal politics; both feed on each other and are conditioned more by internal rather than external forces. Both Hindu and Muslim radicalism perceive and construct the other as the enemy and invoke perceptions of victimhood, real as well as imagined. Both move as two parallel streams, disseminating narratives of fear and hatred against each other continuously; periodic communal clashes and riots nurture and harden further their respective paradigms of radicalized thought and action.

Yet there is also a significant difference between the two. Despite being a minority community with a demonstrated history of victimization and vulnerability to conditions of radicalization for the reasons outlined above, Muslims have generally shown great restraint. As Hindu radicalization has exacerbated and become violent in recent years, however, Islamist radicalization has been gaining ground. So internal push factors rather than external pull factors are the primary drivers of Islamist radicalization in India. Marginalized in a majoritarian society, often discriminated by the state and having limited internal sources at their disposal for mobilization and resistance, Muslim radicals look towards external sources for inspiration, logistics and finance, particularly from fraternal Islamist radical groups and sympathizers in India's region and beyond. Hindu radicalism, on the contrary, which was dormant in Nehruvian India, has gained legitimacy and empowerment as part of the armour of the Hindu nationalist state. Having easy access to internal resources including Hindu sympathizers and Hindu institutions for material and moral support, it enjoys both overt and covert state support.

These internal-external dynamics have tended to maximize the threat of Islamist radicalization as a part of organized global network of terror and menacing, while minimizing Hindu radicalism as sporadic, localized and less threatening. However, Hindu radicalism's ideological affinity with anti-Muslim radical right-wing individuals and networks in Europe (Nanda 2011) and other continents needs to be acknowledged; Hindu radicals also derive financial support from Hindutva's diaspora network in the United Kingdom and the United States.

Islamist radicalism, while it has gained a foothold in certain Muslim-majority regions, finds it hard to expand further due to continuous state surveillance and repression. On the contrary, Hindu radicalism has by and large escaped state surveillance, barring some critical moments such as the aftermath of Gandhi's assassination (1948), the Emergency (1975–7) and the aftermath of the Samjhauta blast (2007). The erosion of secularism, the rise of the Ayodhya movement and Hindu nationalist control of state power since 2014 have facilitated the entrenchment of Hindu radicalism. As Hindu radicalism constitutes an integral ideological and strategic component of Hindu nationalism, it has been able to grow at a rapid pace under the protection and patronage of the Hindu nationalist state, even as the same state has relentlessly acted to prevent the spread of Islamist radicalism.

Concluding remarks

Hindu radicalization, which germinated in the politics of Hindu communalism in early twentieth-century colonial India, was nurtured by the Sangh Parivar's anti-Muslim discourses and actions. Thereafter, Hindu radicalism has remained an ideological and strategic component of Hindu nationalism. The weakening of the secular state, the decline of plural and tolerant Hindu traditions and the advent of majoritarianism created a conducive milieu for the nourishment of Hindu radicalization. After Hindu nationalism became hegemonic in India, it legitimized Hindu radicals and empowered them to unleash violence on minorities at will and with impunity.

Muslim radicalization, underpinned by the aggressive manifestation of Muslim communalism before India's partition, remained subdued in postcolonial India. Constituting a minority in a secular yet Hindu-majority state, Muslims experienced an anxious insecurity, suffered during communal riots, and remained politically, economically and socially marginalized. Hindu nationalist discourses continued to claim India as a Hindu nation, demonizing Indian Muslims as an 'enemy' and questioning their loyalty and citizenship. Thus, Muslim radicalization was provided with sufficient rationale to revive and engage in occasional retaliation. Bolstered by both religious and exogenous factors, it took an Islamist turn, particularly in Kashmir, when the Indian state scuttled democratic process, escalated state oppression and became arbitrary in its application of the rule of law. Despite such social and political shifts, however, Muslim radicalization was able to make only minor headway.

When Hindu nationalists came to power in 2014, Indian Muslims became victims of majoritarian governance; Narendra Modi's celebration of nationalist masculinity sent a clear symbolic message to Muslims (Kinnavall 2019). Their physical and psychological insecurity escalated, and their religious freedom and citizenship rights, previously guaranteed under the Indian Constitution, became threatened and precarious. The state, instead of punishing those Hindu radicals who instigated and perpetrated violence against Muslims, protected and patronized them; innocent Muslims were increasingly victimized as the rule of law was manipulated to their disadvantage. Across regions and social classes, Muslims have started feeling even more anxious, angry, insecure and alienated. As a consequence, Islamic radicalization may no longer remain confined to a few Pakistan-sponsored radical/terrorist groups or to Kashmir.

Recently, Muslim violent radicalization reared its head after the spokesperson of the ruling BJP, Nupur Sharma, made insulting remarks against the Prophet Mohammad on a television programme in June 2022. The ruling party did not even take cognizance of her impropriety until some Muslim countries raised serious objections and asked for India's apology. Under pressure, the BJP suspended her from her party position. Muslims in India considered this a non-action and organized protest rallies demanding her arrest. In retaliation, Hindu nationalist organizations came out onto the streets and on social media in support of Sharma. In this charged communal atmosphere, two Muslim youths brutally beheaded a Hindu tailor in Udaipur, Rajasthan, who had circulated a social media post supporting Sharma. Brazenly, the killers circulated the video of the gruesome killing on social media, enraging Hindus across the country. Another Hindu was killed in Amaravati, Maharashtra, by a Muslim radical for the same reason. The Sangh Parivar leaders described these killings as 'Jihad against Hindus' and mobilized Hindus against Islamist terrorism (Outlook India 2022).

The insult to the Prophet Mohammad may have served as a catalyst, but the deeper motive behind such violent acts may have been the seething Muslim anger which has been fermenting against the Hindu nationalist regime for its anti-Muslim discourses, policies and actions. While Indian Muslims have generally shown tolerance, maturity and restraint, some radical individuals fail to do so. If Hindu nationalism does not retreat from its anti-Muslim hate campaigns and majoritarian governance and allows Hindu radical violence to continue unabated, then Muslim radicalization is likely to expand and escalate across a population of 200 million Muslims living under perpetual threat and humiliation.

References

Ahmad, I. (2009), 'The Secular State and the Geography of Radicalism', *Economic and Political Weekly*, 44 (23): 33–8.

Ahmad, T. (2019), 'Hindu Mahasabha "Shoots" Gandhi: Why Some Get Away and Others Don't', *The Quint*, 1 February. Available online: https://www.thequint.com/voices/opinion/hindu-mahasabha-gandhi-assassination-re-enactment-hindutva (accessed 17 July 2022).

Apoorvanand (2018), 'The Reason for Renaming Places', *The Hindu*, 13 November. Available online: https://www.thehindu.com/opinion/op-ed/the-reason-for-renaming-places/article62110680.ece (accessed 20 July 2022).

Arosoaie, A. (2018), 'Understanding the Creation and Radicalization of the Students Islamic Movement of India (SIMI) and the Indian Mujahideen (IM)', *South Asia: Journal of South Asian Studies*, 41 (3): 519–34.

Banajee, S., R. Bhat, A. Agarwal, N. Passanha and M. S. Pravin (2019), *WhatsApp Vigilantes: An Exploration of Citizen Reception and Circulation of WhatsApp Misinformation Linked to Mob Violence in India*, Department of Media and Communications, London School of Economics. Available online: http://eprints.lse.ac.uk/104316/1/Banaji_whatsapp_vigilantes_exploration_of_citizen_reception_published.pdf (accessed 26 July 2022).

Bartlett, J. and C. Miller (2012), 'The Edge of Violence: Towards Telling the Difference between Violent and Non-violent Radicalization', *Terrorism and Political Violence*, 24 (1): 1–21.

Bartlett, J. and J. Birdwell (2013), *Cumulative Radicalisation between the Far-Right and Islamist Groups in the UK: A Review of Evidence*. London: Demos.

Baruah, S. (2007), *Durable Disorder: Understanding the Politics of Northeast India*. Delhi: Oxford University Press.

Basu, T., P. Datta, S. Sarkar, T. Sarkar and S. Sen (1993), *Khakhi Shorts and Saffron Flags: A Critique of the Hindu Right*. New Delhi: Orient Longman.

Bhatt, C. (2001), *Hindu Nationalism: Origins, Ideologies and Modern Myths*. Oxford: Berg.

Busher, J. and G. Macklin (2015). 'Interpreting "Cumulative Extremism": Six Proposals for Enhancing Conceptual Clarity', *Terrorism and Political Violence*, 27 (5): 884–905.

Chakravarti, S. (2008), *Red Sun: Travels in Naxalite Country*. Harmondsworth: Penguin.

Chatterjee, A. P., T. Blom Hansen and C. Jaffrelot (eds) (2019), *Majoritarian State: How Hindu Nationalism is Changing India*. London: Hurst.

Eeshanpriya, M. S. (2018), 'Sanatan Sanstha: From Obscurity to Heart of Conspiracy' (2018), *The Hindustan Times*, 6 September. Available online: https://www.hindustantimes.com/india-news/sanatan-sanstha-from-obscurity-to-heart-of-conspiracy/story-crVNsGVfkM6v13oVGyPtMJ.html (accessed 15 June 2022).

Evans, A. (2002), 'A Departure from History: Kashmiri Pandits, 1990–2001', *Contemporary South Asia*, 11 (1): 19–37.

Ferreira A. and V. Gonsalves (2017), 'Fifty Years of Unreasonable Restrictions under the Unlawful Activities Act', *The Wire*, 9 March. Available online: https://thewire.in/author/arun-ferreira-and-vernon-gonsalves (accessed 18 July 2022).

FP Staff (2021), 'Haridwar "Dharma Sansad" Event Sparks Outrage over Hate Speeches: Here's What Happened at the Three-Day Event' (2021), *First Post*, 24 December. Available online: https://www.firstpost.com/india/haridwar-dharma-sansad-event-sparks-outrage-over-hate-speeches-heres-what-happened-at-the-three-day-event-10232871.html (accessed 1 July 2022).

Golwalkar, M. S. (1939), *We or Our Nationhood Defined*. New Delhi: Bharat Publications.

Haqqani, H. (2006), *India's Islamist Groups*, Washington, D.C.: Hudson Institute, 16 February. Available online: https://www.hudson.org/national-security-defense/india-s-islamist-groups (accessed 10 May 2023).

Haqqani, H. (2015), 'Prophecy and the Jihad in the Indian Subcontinent', Washington, D.C.: Hudson institute, 15 March. Available online: https://www.hudson.org/research/11167-prophecy-the-jihad-in-the-indian-subcontinent (accessed 16 July 2022).

Iyer, P. and M. Mirchandani (2020), *Can Communal Violence Fuel an ISIS Threat in India? An Analysis of 'Voice of Hind'*, Delhi: Observer Research Foundation Special Report, 118. Available online: https://www.orfonline.org/research/can-communal-violence-fuel-an-isis-threat-in-india (accessed 16 June 2024).

Jaffrelot, C. (2010), 'Abhinav Bharat, the Malegaon Blast and Hindu Nationalism: Resisting and Emulating Islamist Terrorism', *Economic and Political Weekly*, 45 (36): 51–8.

Jaishankar, D. (2017), 'Assessing the Islamic State Threat to India: It Is a Serious but Manageable Challenge', *The Times of India*, 11 May. Available online: https://timesofindia.indiatimes.com/blogs/toi-edit-page/assessing-the-islamic-state-threat-to-india-it-is-a-serious-but-manageable-challenge/ (accessed 6 October 2022).

Kanungo, P. (2002), *RSS's Tryst with Politics: From Hedgewar to Sudarshan*. New Delhi: Manohar.

Kanungo, P. (2008), 'Hindutva's Fury against Christians in Odisha', *Economic and Political weekly*, 13 September, 43 (37): 16–19.

Kapur, A. (1993), 'From Deity to Crusader: The Changing Iconography of Rama', in G. Pandey (ed), *Hindus and Others: The Question of Identity in India Today*, 46–73, Delhi: Oxford University Press.

Kinnvall, C. (2019), 'Populism, Ontological Insecurity and Hindutva: Modi and Masculinization of Indian Politics', *Cambridge Review of International Affairs*, 32 (3): 283–302.

Kundnani, A. (2012), 'Radicalization: The Journey of a Concept', *Race & Class*, 54 (2): 3–25.

Leidig, E. (2020), 'Hindutva as a Variant of Right-Wing Extremism', *Patterns of Prejudice*, 54 (3): 215–37.

Malthaner, S. (2017), 'Radicalization: The Evolution of an Analytical Paradigm', *European Journal of Sociology*, 58 (3): 369–401.

Mander, H. (2018), 'Hashimpura: 31 Years after Custodial Massacre of Muslims by Men in Uniform, Justice Is Incomplete', 2 November. Available online: https://scroll.in/

article/900594/hashimpura-31-years-after-custodial-massacre-of-muslims-by-men-in-uniform-justice-is-incomplete (accessed 16 July 2022).

Mirchandani, M. (2018), 'Digital Hatred, Real Violence: Majoritarian Radicalisation and Social Media in India', *ORF Occasional Paper*, Delhi: Observer Research Foundation, August: 1–30. Available online: https://www.orfonline.org/research/43665-digital-hatred-real-violence-majoritarian-radicalisation-and-social-media-in-india/ (accessed 1 June 2022).

Mukhopadhya, N. (1994), *The Demolition: India at the Crossroads*. Delhi: Indus.

Nag, S. (2002), *Contesting Marginality: Ethnicity, Insurgency and Subnationalism in North-East India*. Delhi: Manohar.

Nanda, M. (2011), 'Ideological Convergences: Hindutva and Norway Massacre', *Economic and Political Weekly*, 46 (53): 61–8.

National Crime Records Bureau (NCRB) (2017), *Crime in India—2017*, Ministry of Home Affairs. Available online: https://ncrb.gov.in/en/crime-india-2017-0 (accessed 3 October 2022).

Neumann, P. R. (2013), 'The Trouble with Radicalization', *International Affairs*, 89 (4): 873–93.

Nizaruddin, F. (2021), 'Role of Public WhatsApp Groups within the Hindutva Ecosystem of Hate and Narratives of Corona Jihad', *International Journal of Communication*, 15: 1102–19.

Outlook India (2022), 'Sangh Parivar Steps up the Heat after Kanhaiya Lal Killing in Udaipur', *Outlook India*, 11 July. Available online: https://www.outlookindia.com/national/sangh-parivar-steps-up-the-heat-after-kanhaiya-lal-killing-in-udaipur-news-208278 (accessed 14 July 2022).

Pande, B. N. (1986), *Islam and Indian Culture*. Patna: Khuda Bakhsh Oriental Public Library.

Pandey, G. (ed) (1993), *Hindus and Others: The Question of Identity in India Today*. Delhi: Viking.

Peerzada, A. (2016), 'Burhan Wani, Hizbul Poster Boy, Killed in Encounter', *The Hindu*, 8 July. Available online: https://www.thehindu.com/news/national/other-states/%E2%80%98Burhan-Wani-Kashmir-Valley%E2%80%99s-most-wanted-militant-commander-killed%E2%80%99/article60528421.ece (accessed 6 October 2022).

Raman, B. (2018), 'Reasons for Radicalization', *Outlook India*, 2 September. Available online: https://www.outlookindia.com/website/story/reasons-for-radicalization/277735/ (accessed 15 February 2022).

Rambachan, A. (2017), 'The Coexistence of Violence and Nonviolence in Hinduism', *Journal of Ecumenical Studies*, 52 (1): 96–104.

Rapoport, D. C. (1984), 'Fear and Trembling: Terrorism in Three Religious Traditions', *American Political Science Review*, 78 (3): 658–77.

Roy, A. (2010), '"Living Together in Difference": Religious Conflict and Tolerance in Pre-Colonial India as History and Discourse', *South Asia: Journal of South Asian Studies*, 33 (1): 33–60.

Sachar Committee Report (2006), 'Social, Economic and Educational Status of the Muslim Community in India', Prime Minister's High-Level Committee, New Delhi, 17 November.

Sarkar, T. (2019), 'Is Love without Borders Possible?', *Feminist Review*, 119: 7–19.

Savarkar, V. D. (1923), *Essentials of Hindutva*. Nagapur: V. V. Kelkar.

Schonthal, B. and M. J. Walton (2016), 'The (New) Buddhist Nationalisms? Symmetries and Specificities in Sri Lanka and Myanmar', *Contemporary Buddhism*, 17 (1): 81–115.

Shaban, A. (2022), 'Hinduism, Hindutva, and Ideology', in Jeffrey Haynes (ed), *Routledge Handbook of Religion, Politics and Ideology*, 341–55, New York: Routledge.

Shaikh, Z. (2017), 'Mumbai Riots 1992: Srikrishna Commission Report and Action Taken', *Indian Express*, 6 December. Available online: https://indianexpress.com/article/india/babri-masjid-demolition-mumbai-riots-1992-srikrishna-commission-report-and-action-taken-4970003/ (accessed 14 June 2022).

Shank, M. (2011), 'Islam's Non-Violent Tradition: History Is Replete with Peaceful Role Models Like "Frontier Gandhi" of Colonial India', *The Nation*, 16: 24–5.

Singh, R. K. (2017), 'Caliphate Radicalization Rising in India', *The New Indian Express*, 9 April. Available online: https://www.newindianexpress.com/thesundaystandard/2017/apr/09/caliphate-radicalization-rising-in-india-1591542.html (accessed 3 July 2022).

Singh, G. and G. Shani (2021), *Sikh Nationalism: From a Dominant Minority to an Ethno-Religious Diaspora*. Cambridge: Cambridge University Press.

Spodek, H. (2010), 'In the Hindutva Laboratory: Pogroms and Politics in Gujarat, 2002', *Modern Asian Studies*, 44 (2): 349–99.

Strohl, D. J. (2019), 'Love Jihad in India's Moral Imaginaries: Religion, Kinship, and Citizenship in Late Liberalism', *Contemporary South Asia*, 27 (1): 27–39.

Swarajya (2022), 'India Calls Out UN on Islamophobia Resolution, Underscores Phobias against Hindu, Sikh, Buddhist, and Non-Abrahamic Faiths', *Swarajya*, 16 July. Available online: https://swarajyamag.com/news-brief/india-calls-out-un-on-islamophobia-resolution-underscores-phobias-against-hindu-sikh-buddhist-and-non-abrahamic-faiths (accessed 2 July 2022).

The Caravan (2014), 'The Swami Aseemanand Interviews: The Transcript of All Four Interviews with Aseemanand', *The Caravan*, 8 February. Available online: https://caravanmagazine.in/reportage/swami-aseemanand-interviews (accessed 1 May 2022).

The Quint (2021), 'In Chhattisgarh's Raipur, Hindu Saint Kalicharan Lauds Godse for Killing Gandhi; Case Filed', *The Quint*, 27 December. Available online: https://www.thequint.com/news/india/religious-saint-kalicharan-lauds-godse-for-killing-gandhi-in-chhattisgarhs-raipur-case-filed-by-congress (accessed 1 July 2022).

The Quint (2022), '"Not Convinced": India on UN's "International Day to Combat Islamophobia" Pitch', *The Quint*, 16 March. Available online: https://www.thequint.com/news/india/united-nations-general-assembly-india-bigotry-combating-islamophobia-all-religions (accessed 10 June 2022).

The Financial Express (2015), 'VHP Justifies "Ghar Vapsi" Campaign, Says Reconversion Connects People with National Mainstream', *The Financial Express*, 3 January. Available online: https://www.financialexpress.com/india-news/vhp-justifies-ghar-vapsi-campaign-says-reconversion-connects-people-with-national-mainstream/25605/ (accessed 24 July 2022).

The Times of India (2017), 'Attacks on Muslims Since Mohammed Akhlaq's Lynching: A Timeline', *The Times of India*, 24 November. Available online: http://timesofindia.indiatimes.com/articleshow/61778337.cms?utm_source=contentofinterest&utm_medium=text&utm_campaign=cppst (accessed 1 July 2022).

The Times of India (2021), 'Mirwaiz, Lone Assassinations Proved a Nemesis for Kashmir' Separatist Movement', *The Times of India*, 22 May. Available online: http://timesofindia.indiatimes.com/articleshow/82855537.cms?utm_source=contentofinterest&utm_medium=text&utm_campaign=cppst (accessed 18 July 2022).

The Telegraph (2019), 'NCRB Report Leaves Out Lynching, Honour Killing Data for Being "Vague"', *The Telegraph*, 22 October. Available online: https://www.telegraphindia.com/india/ncrb-report-leaves-out-lynching-honour-killing-data-for-being-vague/cid/1713552 (accessed 18 July 2022).

The Wire (2021), 'FIR against Hindu Religious Leader for Derogatory Remarks Against Mahatma Gandhi', *The Wire*, 27 December. Available online: https://thewire.in/communalism/fir-against-hindu-religious-leader-for-derogatory-remarks-against-mahatma-gandhi (accessed 1 July 2022).

Van den Bos, K. (2020), 'Unfairness and Radicalization', *Annual Review of Psychology*, 71: 573–88.

Vidal, D., G. Tarabout and E. Meyer (2003), *Violence/Non-Violence: Some Hindu Perspectives*. New Delhi: Manohar.

Vincent, P. L. (2021), 'Hindutva Groups in North India Accused of Forcing Meat Shops to Shut During Navratri', *The Telegraph*, 15 October. Available online: https://www.telegraphindia.com/india/hindutva-groups-in-north-india-accused-of-forcing-meat-shops-to-shut-during-navratri/cid/1834628 (accessed 10 June 2024).

Section Four

Political mobilizations of religion on the extremist right

11

Marriage of convenience? The nexus of religious extremism and far-right militancy in Israel and the United States

Alejandro J. Beutel and Arie Perliger

Introduction

One of the deadliest far-right terrorist attacks was perpetrated by Anders Breivik, who killed 77 people and injured more than 300 on 22 July 2011. After detonating a car bomb near the office of the Norwegian prime minister in Oslo, which killed eight people, he travelled to the nearby island of Utøya and began shooting at attendees of a youth summer camp, killing an additional sixty-nine people (Erlanger and Shane 2011). On the day of the attack, Breivik released an electronic version of his ideological text, titled '2083: A European Declaration of Independence'. More than 1500 pages long, the text provided an inside look at the way in which contemporary far-right extremists are reframing the constituency they aspire to represent and integrating religious-cultural ideas into traditional far-right racist, xenophobic and nativist discourse.

For example, Breivik was less concerned about the racial diversification of Europe and more about its loss of religious homogeneity when he claimed, 'This irrational fear of nationalistic doctrines is preventing us from stopping our own national/cultural suicide as the Islamic colonization is increasing annually' (Mackey 2011). Similarly, he portrays his constituency in religious colours when emphasizing that politically correct terminology, which is becoming more prevalent in the West, 'den[ies] the intrinsic worth of native Christian European heterosexual males' (Mackey 2011).

Yet despite purported religious concerns, Breivik's motives suggest a more complicated relationship with faith, as expressed in his ideological text. For example, while Breivik points out he chose to be baptized in the Norwegian State Church at age fifteen, and identified as '100 percent Christian', he also saw himself as a 'cultural Christian' and 'not [as] an excessive religious man'. Instead, he characterized himself as 'first and foremost a man of logic', as well as 'a supporter of monocultural Christian Europe' (Gibson 2011). These statements provoked significant debate among scholars about the extent to which religion played a role in motivating the tragic events of 22 July 2011, with some suggesting the attacker's interest in religion was more sociological (i.e. related to politics and culture) rather than theological per se (Gibson 2011). The debate associated with Breivik's motives – and the broader relationship between religion and far-right movements – poses a provocative question embedded in the title of this chapter: Is the growing entanglement of far-right extremism and religion a 'marriage of convenience' or is there a potentially deeper relationship?

To begin to answer this question, we need first to understand how far-right movements and religious beliefs are increasingly converging. To do so, this chapter begins by outlining at least four ways far-right actors are integrating religious beliefs into their ideologies and discourse. It then utilizes multiple case studies from the Israeli and American far-right contexts to identify specific ways in which religious sentiments, symbols, themes and traditions are employed to (1) facilitate recruitment, (2) solidify ideological commitment and solidarity, (3) justify acts of violence by far-right actors and/or (4) gain greater social currency with wider audiences on various societal issues. The chapter will also discuss how the growing emphasis on religious identity impacts the organizational and leadership characteristics of far-right movements. We will then provide some concluding thoughts by providing a comparative analysis of Israeli- and US-far-right contexts before returning to the original question we posed on the relationship(s) between far-right movements and religion.

Four ways contemporary far-right movements incorporate religious beliefs

More than an outlier, Breivik's rhetoric illustrates a pervasive trend of integrating religious beliefs into the broader far-right ideological discourse, which has intensified in recent years. This is done in at least one of four ways.

First is an antagonistic and menacing portrayal of other religious traditions. An illustrative example is the following statement, taken from an American blog expressing far-right beliefs: 'The Muslim numbers are growing throughout the continent of Europe. They are rapidly transforming Europe into conclaves of Sharia-law strongholds' (Perliger 2020: 146). Second is the attempt to align religious narratives with far-right ideological frameworks. This is a process best reflected in the discourse of actors identifying with the Christian Identity movement (discussed later in this chapter) who justify xenophobic, antisemitic and racist beliefs and practices by providing their own unique interpretation to sections of the Old and New Testament. For instance, to justify racial segregation they commonly cite Josh. 23.12-13:

> If you do in any way go back and cleave unto the remnants of these Nations, even these that remain among you, and shall make marriages with them, and go in unto them and they unto you: Know for a certainty that there shall be snares and traps unto you, and scourges in your side and thorns in your eyes. Until ye perish off from this good land which the Lord your God has given you.

Violence against members of the LGBTQ+ community is justified by citing Lev. 20.13: 'If a man also lie with mankind as he lieth with a woman, both of them have committed an abomination, they shall surely be put to death, their blood shall be upon them.' This also includes the Ku Klux Klan (KKK) as well as antigovernment extremists from the Church of Jesus Christ of Latter-Day Saints (LDS) and African-American-centred New Religious Movements (NRMs), whose central ideological goals are secular but which nevertheless heavily reference religious traditions to legitimize their views to supporters and the wider public.

Third, far-right actors will employ religious traditions and symbols as a performative ceremonial practice aimed at solidifying shared identity. Some prominent examples of such practices are the usage of mythology and rituals used in reconstructed Germanic Heathen faiths, such as Odinism, and by neo-Nazi skinheads, as well as the adoption of Cross burning by the KKK and other white supremacist groups. The highly visible and active nature of such practices makes them an effective tool for far-right movements to enhance members' loyalty and excitement, as well as to attract new members.

Fourth, they legitimize the use of violence via religious ideological imperatives. Within the Israeli context, when Yigal Amir – a violent far-right activist who assassinated Prime Minister Itzhak Rabin in November 1995 – was interrogated by the Israeli authorities, he insisted he followed a religious legal precept known as *Din Rodef*, or 'Law of the Pursuer', that permits killing those who threaten the control of Jews in the land of Israel. Amir asserted that because Rabin led a peace process with the Palestinian leadership, which included territorial concessions by Israel, his actions met the requirements that permitted *Din Rodef* to be enacted (Pedahzur and Perliger 2009). Similarly, the 'Army of God', the most famous violent anti-abortion extremist movement in modern US history, was driven by the perception that the pro-life struggle is part of an ongoing apocalyptic war between Satan and God's children, and thus violent acts aiming to prevent the death of foetuses created in the image of God are a religious imperative.

It is also important to recognize the role of exogenous factors in the growing embrace of religious narratives and practices by far-right movements. The increasing inter-religious tensions in many Western democracies, resulting from growing demographic diversification, seem to further enhance the growing social currency of religious xenophobia, thereby placing religion at the centre of rhetoric within a growing number of far-right movements that aspire to exploit such dynamics to mobilise support. For example, like Anders Breivik, the pan-European white nationalist Identitarian Movement espouses the protection of Europe's Christian-White identity from 'Islamization' and foreign cultural influences and was triggered by changing demographics in many European countries (i.e. growing Islamic, immigrant and refugee communities) (Wilhemsen 2021). In the last few years, the movement seems to attract substantial support all over Europe, as well as to inspire some prominent violent attacks. In addition, the rise of new populist (sometimes authoritarian) political rulers, such as Donald Trump, Jair Bolsonaro, Viktor Orban and Paweł Kukiz – who in many cases promoted religious exclusivity and did not shy from questioning the loyalty of religious minorities – further amplified the role of religion in the discourse of the contemporary far right.

Jewish orthodoxy and the Israeli far right

The theological origins of the Israeli far right

Several minor Israeli far-right parties (mainly based on former leaders of 'Lehi' and 'Etzel', two militant groups who fought against the British control of Palestine in the 1930s and 1940s) populated the Israeli political system in the first years after the establishment of the state of Israel in 1948. They opposed the social-democratic characteristics of the new state and advocated for the further predominance of Jewish religious and nationalistic values over universal social and humanistic ones. Some even promoted the idea of restoring the historical Kingdom of Israel (Sprinzak 1999). However, they were never able to gain any substantial electoral traction and eventually merged into the more predominant centre and right-wing parties of the time (Heller 1989).

The event which fostered the reemergence of the Israeli far right was Israel's victory in the 1967 war. Despite lasting just six days, the results of the war fundamentally changed the course of the Israeli state and eventually restructured its political system. More relevant to our current discussion, the consequence of the war solidified the prominence of religious concepts, rhetoric and activism in the Israeli far right. Hence, it is impossible to comprehend the Israeli far right without acknowledging its strong religious identity.

The major religious stream which dominates the current Israeli far right is Religious Zionism (hence its adherents are usually referred to as Religious Zionists). Religious Zionism first emerged in the mid-nineteenth century, as it gradually departed from the more conservative ultra-Orthodox stream. The major gap between ultra-Orthodox (Haredi Jews) and Religious Zionists relates to their views regarding the circumstances that will lead to the foundation of an independent Jewish polity. While many followers of ultra-Orthodoxy believe that Jews should adopt a passive approach until the arrival of the Messiah, an event which will be followed by the establishment of a Jewish Kingdom, Religious Zionists preach a more proactive approach. They too believe that a Jewish religious kingdom will be established following the arrival of the Messiah, but the founding fathers of the Religious Zionist movement advocated that by settling the land of Israel, working the land and restoring the Hebrew language, this process could be expedited (Rubinstein 1982). Thus, in contrast to the ultra-Orthodox, the Religious Zionists have historically made efforts to find ways to bridge the gap between Jewish Orthodoxy and secular Jewish nationalist ideology. Moreover, in many ways, they have accepted the dominance of the secular nationalist streams (Lustick 1988).

Following the 1967 war, in which Israel occupied the West Bank, parts of the Religious Zionist community adopted beliefs that regarded the realization of the vision of the Greater Land of Israel by Jewish settlement in the West Bank as a decisive phase in the salvation of the People of Israel, and in the establishment of a religious Jewish state (i.e. a process of holy redemption). In other words, after the establishment of the State of Israel in 1948 and the decisive Israeli victory of 1967, they advocated that the Israeli settlement of the West Bank should be the next phase in expediting the redemption process (Rubinstein 1982, Pedahzur and Perliger 2009). Therefore, any attempt to backtrack this process, for example, by conceding lands to the Palestinians in the West Bank, was seen by them as a direct violation of God's will and should be prevented. More than seventy years after the 1967 war, this vision has become dominant in the Religious Zionist community, which comprises the decisive majority of the ideological settler population, who can be described as settlers who do not reside in the West Bank for economic and quality-of-life reasons, but for ideological motivations, and is today almost entirely ideologically homogenous.

The Religious Zionist leaders who promoted messianic activism within their communities also aspired to bring Religious Zionism to the forefront of policymaking. In the decades after the establishment of the Israeli state, the leaders of the Religious Zionism movement were comfortable in accepting the dominance of secular parties while largely focusing on ensuring the prosperity of their own cultural and social infrastructures such as schools, religious institutions and other venues. However, since the early 1980s, a growing number of Religious Zionist leaders have aimed to gain a more influential role in shaping the public and social sphere in Israel and pushing religious values to the mainstream (Zertal and Eldar 2004). For example, they have frequently challenged the liberal assumption that religion is a private matter in a democratic system and that the collective does not have the right to impose religious practices on its members. Accordingly, the post-1967 leaders of the Religious Zionist movement sought to enforce their values not only within their own community but on all Jews in Israel. Practical manifestations of their attitude can be seen in the aspirations of contemporary Religious Zionist leaders to shape state legislation in the spirit of the *halacha* (Jewish religious law), to impose religious practices in public, cultural and economic spheres; to reshape public education by forcing religious narrative into secular schools' curricula; and to prevent harm to the status of religion in the state's institutions (such as in the Israeli Defense Forces [IDF]) by any means (Pedahzur and Perliger 2004).

The Greater Land of Israel

One of the most distinct characteristics of the Israeli far right is its focus on the question of Israel's future control of the West Bank and other territories occupied during the 1967 war. Simply put, while in other democracies, the far right differentiates itself via various economic and social policy preferences, traditionally, Israeli far-right parties and movements coalesced mainly around the goal of preserving Israel's control over the West Bank. While the centre-left parties saw these territories mainly as temporary assets that eventually would be used to promote some resolution to the Israeli-Palestinian conflict, the Israeli right pushed to ensure permanent Israeli control over those territories (Aran 1987). The various far-right parties and social movements that emerged after 1967 emphasized various arguments in support of this goal. Some of them focused on security considerations and argued that the territories provide necessary strategic depth to the vulnerable Israeli state. Other parties and movements emphasized the historical connection of the Jewish people to various historical and religious sites in the territories. Moreover, as mentioned earlier, Religious Zionist movements developed a theological doctrine arguing that the Israeli victory in the 1948 and 1967 wars and the settling of Jews in the West Bank (i.e. their historical homeland) are part of a holy redemption process that will end with the coming of the Messiah and the creation of a Jewish kingdom that will be run in accordance with *halacha* (Cohen-Almagor 1992).

During the 1970s and 1980s, Religious Zionists leaders were able to mobilize most of the Religious Zionist sector (around 10 per cent of Israeli society) to support the development of Jewish settlements in the West Bank and Gaza Strip (Rubinstein 1982, Cohen-Almagor 1992). The major obstacle to the realization of the vision of the greater land of Israel – full sovereignty over territories controlled after the 1949 armistice, as well as the West Bank and Gaza Strip – was the Palestinian population residing in those areas. While initially, many of the new settlements that formed were justified via security needs, eventually, the Israeli far right developed complementary religious-ideological frameworks to justify both the aggressive confiscation of Palestinian lands by Israeli settlers and the political and social marginalization of the Palestinians (Segal 1988, Zertal and Eldar 2004). In particular, the Religious Zionist leaders legitimized the settlements by suggesting they represented a continuation of the Zionist project at large and were consistent with traditional methods used by the founders of the nation to promote Jewish sovereignty in the land of Israel (Aran 1987). Furthermore, they emphasized the analogy between the actions of contemporary settlers and the biblical story, which depicts the conquering of the land of Israel by the Hebrew people who were led by the biblical figure Joshua and followed God's orders to eradicate the native inhabitants of the land (Perliger 2015).

The Israeli far right employed several additional performative practices to emphasize the religious dimension of Jewish settlements and their part in a broader religious-historical process. To begin with, settlements were built in most cases near religious-historical sites and were styled after the biblical names of those sites. It is hard to find a biblical site – that is, a location mentioned in the biblical text – not populated by Jewish settlers. Settlements such as Shilo, Beit-El, Beit Horon, Dolev, Elkana, Elon Moreh and Gilo are some examples of this systematic effort. The importance of this practice should not be understated (Perliger and Pedahzur 2021, see also Omer this volume). The reestablishment of Jewish presence in places that Israelis associate with the biblical text and Jewish heritage was a significant part of the settlers' effort to enhance the legitimacy and positive branding of the settlements' project. This practice was especially common in the early days of the settlements and aimed both to enhance their legitimacy among mainstream Israelis and to inspire young Religious Zionists who were flocking to join the new settlements.

Relatedly, the Israeli far right also engaged in concentrated archaeological and educational efforts to produce and publicize scientific evidence of the religious and historical rights of Jews in the land of Israel, and mainly in the West Bank. The most profound example can be found in Eastern Jerusalem, which the international community still recognizes as part of the West Bank. Since the late 1980s, several far-right organizations, mostly led by settler leaders, started to purchase real estate in Eastern Jerusalem and the Old City, as well as in other locations described in biblical sources. One of those organizations, called Elad, engaged in purchasing land in an area of East Jerusalem known as 'The City of David' (which embraces the Temple Mount from the south) and sponsored a wide-scale archaeological dig with the goal of uncovering evidence of ancient Jewish presence (Shpaizman, Swed and Pedahzur 2016). Today, The City of David is one of the most extensive archaeological sites in Israel, as well as a hub of tourism and educational initiatives, which enjoy more than a million visitors a year. Hence, this strategy was successful both in strengthening the legitimacy of Jewish settlements in East Jerusalem and in exposing more Israelis to the religious rationale of the settlements project.

Religious motivations for far-right violence in Israel

The Israeli far-right engagement with political violence was always considered a somewhat peculiar phenomenon. While terrorism is often described as the 'weapon of the weak' (Crenshaw 1981, cf. Asal et al. 2018), the Jewish population in Israel has always enjoyed political and economic superiority over other ethnic groups (Smooha 2013). Moreover, outbreaks of far-right violence in Israel occurred in many cases when right-wing governing coalitions comprised the executive branch (Feige 2009). In retrospect, two dynamics usually facilitated a rise in far-right violence in Israel. The first was in retaliation to perceived Palestinian violence. During both the first and second Palestinian uprisings (1987–92 and 2001–5), Jewish far-right terrorism significantly escalated (Perliger and Pedahzur 2016). The second is in response to diplomatic peace initiatives, which included Israel's willingness to consider conceding some control of the West Bank as part of a conciliation process with the Palestinians. One of the most capable settler/far-right terrorist groups organized in Israel was formed following the Camp David Accords, implemented in 1982 by a right-wing Israeli government, in which Israel for the first time gave up territories in which Jews settled in exchange for peace with Egypt. In addition, the government accepted the principle of Palestinian autonomy in the West Bank (Sprinzak 1999).

A similar rise in far-right violence in Israel occurred after the signing of the Oslo Accords in September 1993, which further established Israel's recognition of the Palestinians' right to self-determination in the West Bank and the Gaza Strip, as well as during the implementation of the 'disengagement plan' in the summer of 2005, which included the evacuation of all Israeli settlements and military bases from the Gaza Strip (Pedahzur and Perliger 2009, Perliger and Pedahzur 2016).

Despite the perceived realpolitik reasons for the outbreak of far-right violence during peace negotiation efforts between Israel and the Palestinians, deep-rooted religious sentiments and rationalizations also facilitated the violence. More specifically, theological narratives related to the importance of vengeance and the desire to expedite the redemption of the Jewish people played an important role in the legitimization of the violence produced by the Israeli far right from the early 1980s until the end of the twentieth century (Feige 2009).

In the late 1970s and early 1980s, multiple far-right groups lamented the fact that the Temple Mount, Judaism's most revered holy site, was in the hands of non-Jews, and they believed that as long as this situation continued, the redemption of the Jewish nation would be unattainable. They further asserted that the settlement of Jews in the West Bank was pointless unless control of the Temple Mount was restored to the people of Israel. These groups utilized their own interpretation of *halachic* principles to argue that the situation in which the Temple Mount area – the historic location of the biblical Jewish Temple, also referred to as the 'Al-Aqsa compound' or *Haram al-Sharif* (Noble Sanctuary) by Palestinians and Muslims worldwide – is currently occupied by two mosques is not just disgraceful and undesirable but also a direct threat to the accomplishment of the redemption process. Hence, Jews have an obligation to act against the Muslim places of worship on the Temple Mount (Pedahzur and Perliger 2009, Perliger and Pedahzur 2016).

The most well-known of these groups was the Jewish Underground, which engaged in the early 1980s in advanced planning for bombing the Dome of the Rock (one of the two Islamic holy sites on the Temple Mount) but eventually abandoned its plan (Segal 1988). Considering the possibility that such an act would lead to an all-out war between Israel and the Arab countries and the isolation of Israel in the international arena, they approached various rabbis about whether it was permissible. But not a single prominent theological figure would give his blessings for such an action, although some provided a blessing to other violent operations of the Underground and agreed that, in principle, it is obligatory to rebuild the Jewish Temple in Jerusalem (Pedahzur and Perliger 2009).

Ironically, a much less organized and capable group was closer to achieving such a goal. The group, publicly dubbed the 'Lifta Gang' – named after the site in Jerusalem where they concealed their stockpiles of explosives and other weapons – operated during the mid-1980s and primarily focused on attacking mosques in the Jerusalem area; however, they also sought to blow up the Islamic holy sites to precipitate the redemption of the people of Israel (Sprinzak 1999). On a stormy night on 26 January 1984, they loaded four explosive charges and several grenades onto a rented minivan and proceeded through the Old City walls to the Lion's Gate entrance to the Temple Mount. They climbed the adjacent wall using ladders they had left there beforehand and descended on the other side into the Temple Mount compound. They advanced towards the Dome of the Rock, but after a few dozen metres, as they approached the stairs to the structure, a guard noticed them and blew his whistle. The surprised young men threw the explosives on the ground and took flight. When the day dawned, security forces were shocked to discover the large number of explosives left behind in the Temple Mount compound: four explosive charges, fragmentation grenades, explosive sticks and an 800-gram charge made of plastic explosives (Pedahzur and Perliger 2009).

The second theological principle which garnered popularity among violent far-right actors was that of 'vengeance'. Rabbi Meir Kahane, the founder of the Kach movement, the most militant far-right political entity in Israel's history and one that openly advocated racist and xenophobic ideology as well as supporting violent actions against Palestinians, was the first to solidify the idea of vengeance against the gentiles as religious precept. Kahane opined that harm to a Jew was considered a desecration of God's name, and thus, vengeance is a religious duty (Cohen-Almagor 1992). While Kahane was murdered in 1990 and Kach was outlawed in 1994 following a massacre against Muslim worshippers in Hebron perpetrated by one of his followers, his ideas and movement still occupy a dominant place within the Israeli far right and an influential position within Israeli political discourse more broadly. On December 21, 2022, Israel formed the most hard right government in its history, including three far-right parties consistent with Kahane's ideology (Magid 2019, Federman and Krauss 2021, cf. Kimche 2022, Keller-Lynn, 2022).

Hence, it is not surprising that numerous instances of far-right violence in Israel relied on the unique Kahanist interpretation (Afterman and Afterman 2015) of the obligation to avenge any violence against Jews. During the 1980s and 1990s, multiple Kahanist groups and individuals executed numerous retaliation attacks against Palestinians. Such attacks proliferated further during the second Palestinian uprising, which included suicide attacks and mass killing operations against Jewish targets in the West Bank and inside Israel. The most well-known of the Kahanist groups active at the time of the second Palestinian uprising was the Bat-Ayin underground, which perpetrated multiple ambushes against Palestinian passengers and vehicles on the roads of the West Bank. However, this group was most infamous for a failed attempt to detonate gas tanks and explosives at an elementary girls' school entrance in east Jerusalem in 2002 (Pedahzur and Perliger 2009).

When interrogated by law enforcement, Bat-Ayin members were open about the theological role of vengeance in their motivation to attack. They declared a desire to specifically avenge the death of Jewish infants in terrorist attacks, as well as broader belief in the religious obligation of Jewish revenge, while at the same time deterring Palestinians from continuing to attack Jewish targets. They also clarified that the girls' school was chosen, as the court verdict stated, 'with the intention of causing great suffering by murdering young girls going to learn at school' (Pedahzur and Perliger 2009).

The growing role of Jewish ultra-Orthodoxy within the Israeli far right

ultra-Orthodox parties traditionally focused on ensuring their communities' cultural, educational, and economic segregation and independence. For the most part, they refused to engage in any national policies which were not directly impacting their communities. However, over the last couple of decades, ultra-Orthodox parties have gradually adopted many of the ideological principles of the Israeli far right. This was reflected not just in their refusal since 2001 to be part of a left-centre governing coalition but also in the promotion of various far-right legislative initiatives and policies.

Until the 1990s, ultra-Orthodox political parties such as *Shas* (a Hebrew acronym for *Shom'rei Torah* [Guardians of Torah]) and *Yahdut HaTorah* (United Torah Judaism) did not believe that a secular or even a Religious Zionist government would accomplish the 'Greater Israel' vision, thereby presenting only a vague position regarding the future of the territories occupied during the 1967 war. However, since the early 2000s, following the process of hawkish radicalization among their constituencies, both parties adopted a stance similar to that of the Religious Zionist parties with regard to the territories, although in a milder and less decisive manner (Sheleg 2000, Hermann and Yaar 2001). As importantly, the leaders of ultra-Orthodox communities encouraged the formation of ultra-Orthodox settlements in the West Bank, an initiative that became so successful that today estimations put the ultra-Orthodox at 30 per cent of the settler population (Magid 2017). While many ultra-Orthodox moved to those new settlements for economic reasons, still, such a move further solidified the ultra-Orthodox community's commitment to the Greater Land of Israel idea and the settlements project.

The ultra-Orthodox parties' slide to the far right was also enabled by the exclusionary policies they consistently supported over the last two decades. They engaged in rhetoric criticizing interfaith marriages (including campaigns with strong racist tropes about Arab men who seduce Jewish women) and legislative attempts to prevent any initiative to familiarize Jewish high-school students with Arab culture, as well as serving as strong advocates for legislative efforts which aimed to prioritize the Jewishness of the state over its liberal democratic nature. Cases in point are their support for the 'Nation-State Law', which formally recognizes Israel as the national home of the Jewish people. However, it also formalizes ongoing practices, several of which are in tension with liberal democratic principles, such as the legal asymmetry between its Jewish majority and Arab non-Jewish minority (Israel Democracy Institute 2018a, Israel Democracy Institute 2018b), as well as limiting the immigration of non-Jewish persons, including individuals married to Israeli citizens (Galili 2018). The latter also reflects the growing usage of xenophobic and racist rhetoric by ultra-Orthodox parties. Their campaigns against immigrants from the former Soviet Union usually included assertions that many of them were not real Jews, that they were deliberately damaging Israel's Jewish character and that they were responsible for the increase of crime in the country and thus should be regarded as a threat to its national security (Pedahzur and Perliger 2004). Not surprisingly, ultra-Orthodox parties were also active leaders in campaigns against foreign workers, who constitute a small minority in Israel.

To conclude our discussion of the nexus of religion and far-right politics in Israel, it is evident that religious fundamentalism served as an enabling environment for the emergence of far-right (violent) actors aspiring to facilitate an apocalyptic/redemption scenario. Moreover, religious concepts and frameworks were effectively utilized to justify classic far-right policies, including ones that promote xenophobic and exclusionary policies. Lastly, religious narratives served an important role in the mobilization of potential constituencies.

Religious fundamentalism and the American far right

A diverse landscape

Notwithstanding the tremendous differences between Israel and the United States, in both countries religious doctrines and practices were closely linked with the emergence and activities of various actors on the far right of the political spectrum. Moreover, in both countries the far right is highly fragmented and includes multiple ideological streams, which leads to both organizational instability (groups frequently emerge and disappear, as well as often merge and split with each other) and operational divergence, with violent actors associated with different movements tending to favour certain tactics and targets over others (Sweeney and Perliger 2018: 54).

Despite the diverse landscape of the American far right, it can be divided into at least three major ideological streams (Perliger 2020). First are white nationalists, who advocate for the moral, cultural and/or biological superiority of the 'white' race over other collective groups of people seen as non-white, such as Jews, Blacks, Asians and Latinos, as well as others deemed 'impure' or 'parasitic' such as LGBTQI+ persons, the physically and mentally infirm, and homeless individuals. Examples of white supremacists include supporters of the Ku Klux Klan, Neo-Nazism and racist Skinheads. Second are anti-government actors, whose central organizing principle is not overt racism per se but rather intense fear and loathing of agents on behalf of government institutions, particularly the US federal government. Organizations and movements characteristic of this category include Oath Keepers, 'militia' groups, the Three Percenter movement (commonly referred to as 'III%'), tax protesters, sovereign citizens and far-right survivalists/preppers. Third are fundamentalists that purportedly organize and mobilize around religious beliefs and traditions. Some of these actors include Christian Identity churches and violent anti-abortion extremists. It is important to note that while distinct, these three categories are not mutually exclusive. For example, many scholars who identify Christian Identity as a form of white supremacy also note that during the late 1990s and early 2000s, individuals espousing its tenets were also commonly found in the anti-government movement (Barkun 1997, Berlet 2002, Levitas 2004).

The religious landscape of the US far right

Like the ideological, organizational and operational landscape of the US far right, its religious beliefs and practices are also diverse. The religious landscape can be roughly divided into at least four major categories. First is irreligion, which is defined as eschewing affiliation with organized religious practice. Typically, this is closely associated with a spectrum of beliefs that includes atheism, agnosticism, apatheism, anticlericalism and Deism (Campbell 1971). That said, irreligion should not be considered automatically synonymous with specific beliefs such as atheism, either. The white supremacist NRM Creativity explicitly rejects belief in a deity as well as an afterlife though they view being labelled 'atheist' by outsiders as a 'derogatory smear' (Creativity Alliance n.d.d.).

Second are various forms of Christianity, including extremist interpretations of Protestantism (e.g. Christian Identity and Dominionist Christianity) and Mormonism. Third are racist interpretations of reconstructed pre-Christian Germanic Heathen faiths (e.g. Odinism/Asatru). In addition to making core theological and mythological truth claims typical of many religious traditions, this category has an additional appeal for many white supremacists given its historical-geographic ties to Northern Europe, because among other things, it is seen as an 'indigenous' religion for whites.

Fourth are NRMs. Notable examples include white supremacist-inspired NRMs like Creativity, as well as African-American-centred NRMs associated with the sovereign citizen movement like some self-identified Moorish Science Temple followers. (The neo-Nazi William Luther Pierce's version of Cosmotheism, although allied in some respects, is perhaps better described as a naturalist philosophical outlook rather than an operational definition of 'religion', characterized not only by systematic beliefs and truth claims but also by the collective exercise of common rituals and depiction of symbols that express those core beliefs.)

Throughout the remainder of this chapter, when referring to the religious beliefs and practices of US far-rightists, we are discussing actors who identify with the second, third and fourth categories, namely, varieties of Christianity, racist interpretations of reconstructed pre-Christian Germanic Heathen faiths and NRMs. In the discussion that follows, space constraints do not allow us to do more than note briefly important large inactive historical organizations including the Silver Shirt Legion (Beekman 2005) and Christian Front (Gallagher 2021), which were paramilitary Christian organizations based on fascist, racist and antisemitic beliefs. Similarly recent notable micro-trends we can also only touch on here include elements of the 'alt-right' engaging with parts of the New Atheist movement (Torres 2017, 2021), some white nationalists' infatuation with Orthodox Christianity (Kelaidis 2019, Yousef 2022) and the promotion of 'uncucked' Christianity. The latter (also called 'pro-Western' Christianity), according to its proponents, 'recognises importance of genophilia [love of one's kind/tribe/relations/race], ethno-religion, identitarian religion and ethnocentrism' (Pro-Western Christianity 2013). It stands in contrast to 'cucked' Christianity, which 'promotes cuckoldry [a term co-opted from pornographic film genre with heavy racial undertones in which a white husband looks on in humiliation as one or more muscular Black men has sex with his white wife] such as mass third-world immigration, transracial adoption, diversity and "racial reconciliation" (i.e. reparations)' (Pro-Western Christianity 2013, cf. Kosse 2022).

As noted at the beginning of this chapter, violent extremist actors who embrace ideologies influenced significantly by religion tend to utilize faith traditions in at least one of four ways: to legitimate their ideologies, to mobilize sympathizers/recruit supporters, to enhance in-group cohesiveness and to justify violence and other illegal behaviours. The remainder of this section will describe how US far-right actors across each of the three major religious categories described above utilize faith traditions.

White supremacist entanglement with Christianity

Probably the best known of the Christian-oriented US far-right extremist groups is the Ku Klux Klan ('Klan'). Although the Klan is perhaps best known as a racist organization, it utilizes various Christian concepts and narratives to legitimize many aspects of its ideology and shape its performative-ritual practices. Much of its 'Klancraft' – beliefs, positions, symbols and rituals – are drawn from Christianity. For example, the Klan's primary symbol is the Blood Drop cross, also known as the Mystic Insignia of a Klansman, which contains a white cross with a red teardrop in the middle (Anti-Defamation League n.d). Johnson (2017) notes that it is meant to symbolize the 'atonement and sacrifice of Jesus Christ, as well as others who have shed their blood for the white race'. Another example is a cross burning. Although often utilized as a form of intimidation against out-group targets (e.g. African-Americans), it also has strong in-group symbolic value. To Klan members, during group meetings it also signifies sending the light of Christ out to the world (Johnson 2017).

Klan members also strengthen their in-group solidarity by performing other rituals, such as the ones described in the organization's 100-plus-year-old handbook, the Kloran (Simmons 1916). The Kloran provides a detailed guide on how to conduct Klan meetings. It describes rituals with religious symbolism, such as an introductory ceremony with a Bible opened to Romans, Chapter 25, and an invocation from the group chaplain reminding members that 'the living Christ is a Klansman's criterion for character' (Simmons 1916: 14). The Kloran also details a membership induction ceremony that contains a ten-question set of criteria for entry into a Klan chapter, including 'Are you a native-born white, Gentile American citizen?' (Q2) and 'Do you believe in the tenets of the Christian religion?' (Q4) (Simmons 1916: 26).

Another far-right movement utilizing Christian beliefs and biblical scripture is the Christian Identity movement ('Identity'). Whereas the Klan is fundamentally a political movement, albeit with strong religious elements, Christian Identity is a small, deeply racist and antisemitic offshoot of a Protestant movement known as British Israelitism, which asserts that the peoples of northern Europe are the descendants of the Twelve Tribes of ancient Israel (Barkun 1997). The Identity movement achieved the zenith of its influence within the US far right during the 1980s and 1990s, before steadily declining in the 2000s. However, one recent study asserts Identity beliefs are becoming a resurgent presence among white supremacists on the social media platform Telegram (CTEC Staff 2021).

Identity followers' core beliefs are derived from two interpretations of the biblical creation story: the One-Seedline doctrine and the Two-Seedline doctrine. One-Seedliners believe all humans, regardless of race/ethnicity, are descendants of Adam. However, northern Europeans ('Aryans') are God's true chosen people; Jews are spiritual as well as ethnic imposters and therefore not true members of the Twelve Tribes of ancient Israel (Barkun 1997). Two-Seedliners assert that only whites are the true descendants of Adam. Jews are believed to be the literal biological offspring of Eve and the serpent of the Garden of Eden, whereas other non-white races are inferior beings created by God before Adam was made, often referred to as 'pre-Adamic' and 'mud people' (Barkun 1997). The latter set of beliefs is based on a peculiar reading of Gen. 1.26 and 2.7-22.

In addition to justifying bigotry, Identity believers have also used biblical references to inspire and justify numerous acts, attempted acts and threats of ideologically motivated violence (Perliger 2020). Several far-right violent extremists appear to have been inspired by the racist tract *Vigilantes of Christendom: The Story of the Phineas Priesthood*, written by Christian Identity follower Richard Kelly Hoskins (1990). Hoskins's book called for the killing of interracial couples and other perceived enemies of the white race through 'Phineas' actions, based on his interpretation of Num. 25.6-13, Ps. 106.29-31. Examples of Phineas-inspired violence include a terrorist and bank robbery campaign by four individuals in eastern Washington State who called themselves 'Phineas Priests' (1996), a shooting attack against a Jewish day-care centre and postal worker in Los Angeles (1999), and shooting and attempted bombing of the Mexican consulate in Austin, Texas (2014) (Southern Poverty Law Center n.d.a).

Outside of referring to scripture for legitimating racist/antisemitic beliefs and justifying illegality (including violence), Christian Identity as a community is also largely characterized by social insularity and dense social networks (Perliger 2012). This insularity and ties between individual members are reinforced by the presence of a charismatic leader. In the case of the Covenant, Arm, and Sword of the Lord, a Christian Identity compound in rural Ozarks Arkansas, James Ellison was that charismatic leader. He not only recruited religiously minded individuals from the surrounding area with his preaching before slowly indoctrinating them with bigoted beliefs but he was also essential to shaping members' threat perceptions of the outside world. As a result, he was central to the community's insularity and near-violent confrontation with federal agents in 1985 (Noble 2011).

Other forms of American far-right extremism and their utilization of Christian traditions

Beyond white supremacy, varieties of Christianity have been influential upon other far-right movements like violent anti-abortion extremism and anti-government extremism. Violent anti-abortion extremists extensively cite New and Old Testament passages from the Bible to legitimize their ideologies and justify violence. The website of the Army of God (AOG), an extremist movement that advocates violence against abortion providers, is run by Reverend Donald Spitz, a Virginia-based Christian pastor. The AOG website has been an important medium to disseminate writings seeking to mobilize support and recruit individuals. The AOG website frequently posts writings from convicted anti-abortion violent extremists like Scott Roeder, Paul Hill and John Brockhoeft, as well as Christian clergy and lay activists who openly defend their actions as morally justifiable. They frequently cite biblical passages such as Gen. 9.6, Ps. 55.15 and Num. 35.33 (Army of God n.d., Hill, n.d.a., Defenders of Defenders of Life n.d., Hill n.d.b.).

This network of violent anti-abortion extremists not only cites biblical scripture but also draws inspiration from a theology known as Christian Reconstructionism ('Reconstructionism') (Jurgensmeyer 2010). Reconstructionism is part of a religious ideological umbrella called Dominion Theology ('Dominionism'). Dominionism is a spectrum of beliefs ranging from 'softer' to 'harder' ideological varieties, with Reconstructionism as its most prominent hard variety. Nevertheless, all forms of Dominionism share a common theocratic vision that asserts that 'God has called conservative Christians to exercise dominion over society by taking control of political and cultural institutions' (Clarkson 2005). This vision is based on a politically expansive interpretation of Gen. 1.26-31, in which God has vested human beings with 'dominion over all creation'. More broadly, Reconstructionists believe 'biblical law', as they understand it, supersedes secular 'man-made' law and that, when the two conflict, the former is to be obeyed over the latter. For example, Paul Hill justified his killing of George Roeder (a physician who worked in an abortion clinic) by claiming that he was conforming to 'Moral Law' which required him to 'obey God rather than the government' (Hill 2003: 4).

Reconstructionism has also been influential within larger parts of the anti-government movement. While anti-government extremism is generally not centred on religion, the movement has historically been influenced to a significant degree by religiously motivated actors. The early incarnations of the contemporary anti-government movement were significantly influenced by white supremacist Christian Identity beliefs. While the presence of Christian Identity adherents within the anti-government extremist scene has waned considerably since the 1990s (Berlet 2002), other actors espousing Christian apocalyptic and theocratic beliefs remain active and influential within the movement. In March 2010, eight members of a militia group called Hutaree were arrested for plotting a terrorist attack (all but two were later acquitted in court and those convicted received light sentences). The Hutaree's ideology was based on 'faith and most of all the testimony of Jesus', as well as referring to a biblical story about ten virgins found in Mt. 25.1-12 (Johnson 2017).

More recently, ideologues like James Wesley Rawles and former Washington State Representative Matt Shea have advocated secession from the United States and establishing a new political entity that will be based on their interpretation of biblical law (Sottile 2019, Stroop 2020). Shea also wrote a four-page document that was leaked to media outlets in 2018 called 'The Biblical Basis for War' (MyNorthwest Staff 2018). While religiously motivated actors like Rawles and Shea do not live in physically closed communities like many other Christian Identity extremists, they nevertheless live in rural parts of the United States that are geographically isolated from major population centres and tend to be strongly homogeneous in terms of culture and politics. This allows them to easily mobilize support and recruit from the local population as well as maintain internal movement solidarity (Sottile 2019).

Another Christian tradition whose followers have been heavily associated with US far-right extremism is Mormonism. To varying degrees, these extremist interpretations of Mormonism are outside of and sometimes directly at odds with the official teachings of the Church of Jesus Christ of Latter-Day Saints (LDS), the global body representing mainstream Mormonism. That said, it is also important to briefly note that the historical relationship between the LDS Church and far-right extremism is much more complicated than the expressed theological differences between the LDS Church and various types of far-right Mormon extremists (like the FLDS and Mormon Constitutionalists) may superficially suggest, which we discuss further below. For example, Harris (2017) points out that influential figures like Ezra Taft Benson, a former cabinet member of the Eisenhower presidential administration and former Apostle-President of the LDS Church, was a far-right extremist who bore significant responsibility for promoting an antigovernment 'conspiracy culture' within the Mormon Church that is common to Mormon Constitutionalists like the Bundy family.

There are at least two categories of Mormonism that are entangled with far-right extremism. First is the Fundamentalist Church of Jesus Christ of Latter-Day Saints (FLDS), a breakaway sect that formed after the mainstream LDS Church abandoned the practice of polygamy in 1890. Further differences had emerged between the FLDS and mainstream LDS when, among other things, the latter repudiated earlier teachings expressing anti-Black racism (Groat 2013, Church of Jesus Christ of Latter-Day Saints 2013) based on the belief that God had cursed the descendants of the biblical figure Cain (Gen. 9.20-25), whose curse was marked with black skin. By contrast, the FLDS has maintained those earlier racist teachings (Holthouse 2008, Southern Poverty Law Center n.d.b.). Like supporters of the Christian Identity movement, they tend to have robust mechanisms that promote strong in-group cohesion and solidarity centred on the presence of charismatic leaders like the now-incarcerated Warren Jeffs. They also live within rural-area gated communities that allow themselves to easily self-segregate from the rest of society. Moreover, consistent with many abusive cult groups, they also have internal mechanisms to punish any possible dissent and other perceived threats to leadership.

FDLS enclaves tend to be geographically located in regions where their polygamous and other socially conservative lifestyles are tolerated, condoned or materially supported, such as rural parts of Utah and Arizona (Weyermann 2012). Their geographic location also allows them to mobilize support and recruit from segments of the wider population in their regions. Finally, although thus far they have not acted violently towards minorities or other out-groups (most violence is directed inward through sexual assault and corporal punishment [Jacobson and Burton 2011]), it already has much of the physical, social and ideological infrastructure to enable that in the future (Robinson 2008). One of the missing elements has been the lack of charismatic leaders directly advocating violence towards out-groups. This is due in large part to extant interventions by authorities in jurisdictions such as Texas that have firmly enforced the law but avoided the heavy-handed mistakes seen during the 1993 federal raid against the Branch Davidian compound in Waco, Texas, that mobilized and inspired extremists into violence (Robinson 2008).

Compared to the FLDS, Mormon Constitutionalists such as Cliven and Ammon Bundy are deeply involved in the broader far-right anti-government extremist movement but follow a relatively more mainstream form of Mormonism. Mormon Constitutionalists use religious appeals both specific to Mormon texts/traditions and beyond them to legitimate their ideology to wider audiences, as well as justify any possible use of violence. For example, during the armed standoff at the Malheur Wildlife Refuge, armed participants included an individual calling themselves Captain Moroni. Moroni is an explicit reference to a figure found in the Book of Mormon (Alma 46.11–36) who fought against a tyrannical government force while carrying a flag that read, 'In memory of our God, our religion, and freedom, and our peace, our wives, and our children' (Alma 46.12). During the armed standoff at Bunkerville, Nevada, in 2014, there were supporters of anti-government extremists who also flew banners with that exact quote from the story of Moroni (Sepulvado 2016). At Bunkerville, Mormon Constitutionalists also explicitly described the US Constitution as a divine text and directly compared it to both the Book of Mormon and the Bible. By doing so, their statements are consistent with a kind of strategic ecumenism that mainstream Mormon actors have pursued the past four decades: appealing not only to other like-minded Mormons but also to other Christian denominations with whom they have sharp theological differences but similar sociopolitical views (Shupe and Heinerman 1985).

Although theologically more mainstream than the FLDS, Mormon Constitutionalists nevertheless express religious beliefs at odds with official LDS teachings to legitimate their ideology, as well as mobilize support and recruit individuals. Mormon Constitutionalists have frequently invoked themes related to the White Horse Prophecy, an apocalyptic vision purportedly made by LDS founder Joseph Smith. According to this prophecy, there will come a time of great persecution in which Mormons will 'see the Constitution of the United States almost destroyed. It will hang like a thread as fine as a silk fiber' (Sottile 2018). Although LDS Church officials have emphatically denied the authenticity of this prophecy (Kirkland 2010), far-right elements of the LDS Church repeatedly reference it in public (Sottile 2018).

Reconstructed Neo-Pagan/Heathen religions

In addition to Christianity, far-right extremists have increasingly gravitated towards a reconstructed version of pre-Christian Germanic Heathen religions. One form of Heathenry that has attracted a following among white supremacists is Odinism. Odinism (also called Wotanism or Asatru) as a contemporary belief system originated in the 1890s with the writings of Austrian mystic Guido von List. Von List's beliefs gained the attention of Henrich Himmler, who ran the Nazi Schutzstaffel (SS) and adapted it for his own organizational and ideological needs (Goodrick-Clarke 1985). After the Second World War, Odinism was transmitted to the United States and other parts of the English-speaking world through a white supremacist named Else Christensen who married a Nazi and herself had ties to the American Nazi Party. Christensen, along with later American Odinist followers like Stephen McNallen and Michael Murray, established the first Odinist organizations, such as the Asatru Folk Assembly (AFA) in the United States (Bowman 2016). These historical origins stand in stark contrast to neo-Pagan traditions such as Wicca and Druidry. Wicca, Druidry and much of neo-Paganism writ-large were reconstructed via anti-Fascist, environmental and feminist countercultures of the 1960s (McShee 2018). Inclusive forms of Heathenry such as The Troth (formerly the Ring of Troth) emerged from the same social milieu and organizations as Odinism but split off in 1987 from McNallen and the AFA, largely due to concerns about the latter's associations with white supremacist beliefs and individuals (Snook 2013).

As a result, there is a division within Heathenry, in which many prefer to be racially, ethnically and gender-identity/sexual-orientation inclusive (e.g. The Troth). However, Odinism appeals to many white supremacists because many of its leading practitioners position it as the ethnic religion of Europeans (Weber 2018). As a result, some Heathens, particularly within Odinism, take a 'folkish' position claiming that only individuals of Northern European ancestry can join the religion. On its homepage, the AFA is explicit about this point, describing the religion as 'the native, pre-Christian spirituality of Europe ... it is religion by which the ethnic European folks have traditionally related to the Divine and to the world around them' (Asatru Folk Assembly n.d.). Yet this same position can potentially legitimize extremist beliefs and provide an entryway for new recruits because it largely eschews the easily recognizable language of overt racism associated with ideologies like neo-Nazism. Many Odinist followers who claim to be non-racist defend ethnic and racial exclusivity by framing their position as akin to Native Americans practising their indigenous faiths (Snook 2013, Weber 2018).

Folkish disavowals of white supremacy are belied by the types of iconography and runic symbols they tend to emphasize – such as swastika-like spirals and the Othala rune – that happen to be closely associated with neo-Nazism (Bowman 2016). This approach to Heathenry also can easily lend itself towards justifying racist violence. This includes its emphasis on hyper-masculine interpretations specifically of Nordic gods Thor and Odin, its racialist use of the term 'Aryan', and 'an emphasis on warlike metaphors and more talk about "blood" and "the folk" than about *frith* [peaceful sanctuary/kinship], nature, spirits, direct ancestors, lore or the gods' (Bowman 2016: 19). Like any other faith tradition, engaging in religious ritual helps to strengthen social bonds between co-religionists, especially when exercised in communal social settings. However, in prison settings, where Odinism experiences some of its most rapid growth, religious membership takes on an added in-group bonding power, allowing white supremacists to congregate in a social setting characterized by intensive surveillance from prison authorities (Sanchez 2009), *de facto* racial segregation and frequent interracial violence (Weber 2018).

Other New Religious Movements

American far-right extremists are also affiliated with various forms of New Religious Movements (NRMs). One NRM is the self-described 'racial religion' Creativity, also known as the World Church of the Creator, founded by neo-Nazi Ben Klassen. Creativity followers distinguish themselves from other white supremacists via several practices. First, they produce their own core ideological texts, such as *Nature's Eternal Religion* (Klassen 1973) and *The White Man's Bible* (Klassen [1981] 2008). Second, based on these core texts, they follow tenets that outline the fundamental beliefs of the religion, such as the Sixteen Commandments (its version of the Judeo-Christian Ten Commandments), the Five Fundamental Beliefs and the Declaration of the Women's Frontier. Third, they harshly criticize other religions, particularly Judaism and Christianity. Like most other white supremacist ideologies, Creativity views Jews and Judaism as the eternal enemy of the white race. However, Creativity beliefs are also hostile to Christianity, seeing it as part of a Jewish conspiracy intended to undermine the white race. As such, Creativity positions itself 'as an alternative to the Jewish mind poison of Christianity, that has been a dagger in the spine of the White race since its inception over two thousand years ago' (Creativity Alliance n.d.a.).

As part of its beliefs and practices, Creativity also encourages its followers to engage in proselytizing for recruitment purposes. Creativity Alliance, the official organization of the Creativity religion, has several template flyers on its website that members can download to print out and publicly distribute (Creativity Alliance n.d.b.). To enhance in-group solidarity, followers are also encouraged to establish Church Primary Groups, which are local chapters that consist of at least two individuals and engage in activities that advance the beliefs of the religion (Williams and Cambeul [2009] 2020). Congregants must not remain out of contact with other members of faith for more than three months unless approved by religious leadership, failure to do that results in dismissal from the entire religion, along with ostracization and forfeiting of any property that belonged to the Creativity Alliance (Creativity Alliance 2016). Finally, the teachings of the religion easily lend themselves to being interpreted as a call to violent action. For example, the third commandment of its Sixteen Commandments states, 'Remember that the inferior colored races are our deadly enemies, and the most dangerous of all is the Jewish race. It is our immediate objective to relentlessly expand the White Race and keep shrinking our enemies' (Creativity Alliance n.d.c.). Another example is the concept of RaHoWa, or' Racial Holy War' (Creativity Alliance, n.d.d.), which has been used repeatedly by white supremacist extremists to justify violence against perceived enemies (Beutel et al. 2017).

There are also African American-centred NRMs associated with the anti-government sovereign citizen movement. The contemporary sovereign citizen landscape includes an entire category of actors, overwhelmingly African American, who identify as 'Moors'. Pitcavage (2016) points out that 'since 2009, the sovereign citizen movement has experienced a major resurgence, including among African Americans. Both Moorish and non-Moorish sovereign citizen ideas have spread rapidly within the African American community, aided by social media websites such as YouTube and Facebook. Moorish and non-Moorish sovereign ideas alike have also spread in prisons and jails across the country'.

To varying degrees, Moorish sovereign citizens have associated themselves with numerous African American-centred NRMs, including Washitaw de Dugdahmoundyah (Dew 2015), Moorish Science Temple of America (Dew 2016) and the Nuwaubian Nation of Moors (Palmer 2010, Southern Poverty Law Center n.d.c.). Like other sovereign citizens (Berger 2016), Moors believe in a set of pseudo-historical and pseudo-legal theories that collectively claim individuals are legally immune from local, state and federal authority (Southern Poverty Law Center n.d.d., Sarteschi 2021). However, Moors also have their own unique beliefs that distinguish them from other sovereign citizens. They include the idea that African Americans have special rights due to a 1787 US treaty with Morocco, that they were descended from Moors in North Africa (who in reality are a mix of Arab, Amazigh and Black ethnicities/races) and that, like Native Americans, they are also indigenous to the Americas (Pitcavage 2016).

Moorish sovereign citizens frequently appropriate certain visual motifs and nomenclature to legitimate their ideology and recruit from religious communities. For example, borrowing from the Moorish Science Temple, many of the pseudo-legal documents Moorish sovereigns use to claim their purported immunity – such as fake driver's licences, passports or birth certificates – contain the Flag of Morocco and attach suffixes like -El, -Bey or -Ali to their legal surnames (Nelson 2011, Pitcavage 2016). Although sovereign citizens overwhelmingly operate as individuals rather than in-groups (Federal Bureau of Investigation 2011), some sovereign citizen groups do exist. Washitaw de Dugdahmoundyah is an example of an African American NRM group grounded in pseudo-legal and pseudo-historical beliefs and practices consistent with sovereign citizen ideology. They engage in the kind of pseudo-legal discourse and activity that characterizes sovereign citizenry in general but is also central to exercising the core beliefs of the Washitaw religion. In turn, this helps to maintain a certain degree of in-group cohesiveness (Dew 2015).

However, this level of organization appears to be the exception rather than the norm. To the extent most sovereign citizens congregate, including most other Moorish sovereigns, it is typically in an *ad hoc* fashion revolving around events like paid seminars that peddle tax scams and other fraudulent ways to evade financial and legal troubles (Federal Bureau of Investigation 2011, Sarteschi 2021). These events are held by 'gurus', charismatic self-styled leaders who emerge as ideological entrepreneurs within the wider movement. Given the centrality of pseudo-legal and pseudo-historical thought among Moors and the wider sovereign citizen movement, these beliefs have justified a wide range of criminal activities, including producing and possessing false identification documents, tax fraud, financial scamming, traffic violations, illegal occupation of residences, false liens and other frivolous legal actions, sometimes referred to as 'paper terrorism' (Pitcavage 2016). This also includes threats and acts of physical harm, including shootings, bank robberies, murders (Pitcavage 2016) and ideologically motivated violence (MacNab 2018). One of the most recent incidents involving Moorish sovereign citizens was a six-hour armed roadside standoff on 3 July 2021 between Massachusetts State Police and eleven members of a group called Rise of the Moors (Aitken 2021, Milkovits 2021). Rise of the Moors is a group that mixes sovereign citizen beliefs with the religious tenets of the Moorish Science Temple and Islam (Milkovits 2021).

To conclude, American far-right ties with religious frameworks reflect, in many cases, the overlap between racial and religious identity in the United States, as well as the comprehension of many far-right movements of the utility of religious practices, symbols and rituals in enhancing their visibility and legitimacy. In this context, religious communities which legitimize and embrace militant rhetoric and practices provide potential violent activists both moral legitimacy (embedded in suitable interpretation of religious texts) and social support and encouragement that their violent actions are a service to their faith and the religious community they 'represent'. In addition, the above-mentioned overlap between racial and religious identity further enhances the transformation of militant religious communities to homogeneous enclaves, amplifying narrow social and political perspectives with limited exposure to countering facts or perspectives.

Comparative perspectives

This analysis of the ties between the Israeli and American far-right to religious traditions, practices and organizations/movements reflects that such linkages serve practical goals as well as nurturing wider shared ideological and cultural sentiments. From a practical perspective, ties with religious frameworks provide far-right movements access to new reservoirs of potential recruits who are already ideationally primed to embrace at least some narratives of far-right movements. Moreover, the linkage to religious institutions allows many far-right groups to try to adopt an aura of purity, righteousness, and perceived moderation, which facilitates legitimacy and high moral standing. In some cases, those ties also provide far-right actors access to tangible assets of religious movements and make it more challenging for the authorities to monitor and counter potential harmful activities given the legal and social constraints in place to protect freedom of expression and religious freedom. It is also important to acknowledge that the ties between some religious and far-right actors also evolve because of a shared ideological sphere that, in many cases, embraces sentiments of xenophobia, nativism, religious and racial/ethnic exclusiveness, and populist views. Religious actors who embrace such sentiments may not be the majority in most democracies, but some of them are and thus find it beneficial to collaborate with or facilitate otherwise secular far-right ideologies.

Both in the American and Israeli far-right contexts, religious narratives have played an extremely important role in the justification of illegal and/or violent practices. However, while in the United States many far-right groups have openly advocated violence, in Israel, at least from a decelerative perspective, most far-right movements have been more reluctant to support violence. This can be explained by the different levels of commitment to democratic principles. Specifically, while ideological tenets of the contemporary US Christian Identity, Neo-Nazi, violent anti-abortion extremism and antigovernment extremists are fundamentally incompatible with liberal democratic values, the far-right elements of the Religious-Zionist movement in Israel have always emphasized this movement's willingness to operate within the confines of the Israeli democratic procedural framework, even though its long-term objective is not compatible with the idea of a Jewish democracy. Hence, despite the American and Israeli far-right milieus' lack of success in mitigating the emergence of violent elements from within, the public in both societies has reflected somewhat differently on these acts of violence.

In Israel, the sociopolitical legitimacy of far-right Religious Zionists, including its settler element, is generally seen as legitimate and violence as an aberration of the movement. In the United States the reaction is somewhat more mixed. The very existence of overt white supremacist movements like Christian Identity, Ku Klux Klan and neo-Nazism is typically seen as illegitimate and their associated violence as a feature rather than aberration of their underlying ideologies. However, some of the key narratives associated with their violence (e.g. the 'Great Replacement' theory) have gained substantial mainstream social currency as of late, being repeated by figures such as the widely watched political commentator Tucker Carlson as well as some members of Congress (Gabbatt 2022). Moreover, compared to overt white supremacists, the underlying ideologies motivating and justifying acts of violence by other far-rightists, like anti-abortion and anti-government extremists, are often discussed in much more sympathetic terms by a wider group of people. This includes individuals in positions of social and civic influence and political power (Winter 2013, Levin 2014), even if the unlawful behaviour is ultimately condemned.

A more in-depth examination of how religious narratives facilitate far-right violence also illustrates the important role of social enclaves and the physical isolation from mainstream society as facilitators of radicalization. While religious beliefs are often perceived to cause political violence (Avalos 2005, Kimball 2008), empirically speaking, only small numbers of individuals, including those purportedly motivated by religion, have committed acts of political violence. Such explanations are also often contrasted with the less-than-pious and theologically novice backgrounds of individuals associated with religious violence (Taylor 2015, Fausset 2015).

Moreover, many of the explanations offered for the purported causes for violence by religious actors, such as dogmatism and rejection of diversity (Pratt 2017), can also be found among secular individuals too (Kossowska, Czernatowicz-Kukuczka and Sekerdei 2017, Uzarevic, Saroglou and Clobert 2017). This has led some researchers to question the link between religious belief, including fundamentalism, and violence (Williamson and Hood 2013, Wright and Khoo 2019). Instead, an emerging body of research suggests that while religious fundamentalism may play a role in the development of extreme beliefs, the turn to violence is more likely to occur among actors that not only hold strong ideological beliefs but are situated within a larger group (Hirsch-Hoefler, Canetti and Eiran 2016) that sees itself threatened by an out-group (Preston, Ritter and Hernandez 2010, Ginges et al. 2015, Beller and Kröger 2018). The probability of violence is especially elevated among actors who exist within tight-knit social networks that have limited contact with members of out-groups and have easy access to weapons as well as other logistical resources necessary to enact violence (Pedazhur and Perliger 2009, Perliger and Pedazhur 2016).

The cases described in this chapter are largely consistent with this latter body of research. It seems that in both US and Israel far-right contexts, the social networks that eventually slide into violence emerged from isolated spaces (settlements, closed compounds or socially isolated geographic areas) with limited exposure to alternative interpretations of social and political reality. Hence, long-term macro-level state policies that promote social integration may be part of the solution to counter religiously driven radicalization within the far right. Relatedly, the focus of the violence, both from the Israeli and American far right, on 'illegitimate' outsiders seems at least partially resulting from religious narratives that dehumanize and demonize out-groups.

Concluding remarks

All of this brings us back to the question asked at the beginning of the chapter: Is the relationship of religion and the far-right a 'marriage of convenience' or something more than that? The simplest and most parsimonious answer is that it depends on who is being discussed. Some cases, such as the establishment of Ben Klassen's racist and anti-theist NRM, Creativity, clearly indicate an instrumental relationship to religion. For Klassen, establishing Creativity was a religious means to an otherwise secular materialist end of advancing white supremacy. In an undated essay describing when he decided to form a new religion, he noted:

> It became abundantly clear to me that what the White Race needed was a completely new approach to the whole problem of extricating itself from the sinister Jewish conspiracy. And in order to get this new approach it seemed overwhelmingly clear that what the White Race really needed was a new religion, a new philosophy of life and a new *Weltanschauung* ... It also became overwhelmingly clear to me that to found a new [political] party based on race while trying to coexist with Jewish Christianity was impossible. Every weapon that we needed in such a struggle was already undermined and neutralized by the basic concepts of Christianity itself.
>
> (Klassen, n.d.)

In other cases, like Kahanism in Israel and Christian Identity in the United States, their respective far-right ideologies are based on systematic, deep engagement with established religious traditions, albeit unconventional interpretations of them. These two movements' relationship with religion suggests the exact opposite of a marriage of convenience. Regardless of how a particular group or movement seems to answer this question, it is clear from the cases presented in this chapter that the dynamics in Israel and the United States seem to intensify the increasing convergence of religious belief and the far right. The declining emphasis on traditional aspects of 'secular' nationalism leads far-right groups in many democracies to embrace transnational cultural-religious identities. Thus, far-right ideologues seem to increasingly embrace more regional, if not global, perspectives in the way they define 'their' constituencies. Religious affiliation, including membership in NRMs (Dawson 1998), is therefore not just a prime tool in drawing the boundaries of these new constituencies of the far right but for many potential followers, also less controversial and more attractive.

In honour of Simon Beutel. May he rest in peace and may his name be a blessed memory.

References

Afterman, A. and G. Afterman (2015), 'Meir Kahane and Contemporary Jewish Theology of Revenge', *Soundings: An Interdisciplinary Journal*, 98 (2): 192–217. https://doi.org/10.5325/soundings.98.2.0192.

Aitken, P. (2021), 'Massachusetts Police Arrest 11 Men after Standoff with Armed Group that 'Does Not Recognize Our Laws', *Fox News*, 3 July. Available online: https://www.foxnews.com/us/police-standoff-rise-of-the-moors (accessed 28 July 2022).

Anti-Defamation League (n.d.), 'Blood Drop Cross'. Available online: https://www.adl.org/education/references/hate-symbols/blood-drop-cross (accessed 9 March 2022).

Anti-Defamation League (2012), 'The Lawless Ones: The Resurgences of the Sovereign Citizen Movement'. 2nd edn. Available online: https://www.adl.org/sites/default/files/documents/assets/pdf/combating-hate/Lawless-Ones-2012-Edition-WEB-final.pdf (accessed 9 March 2022).

Aran, G. (1987), 'From Religious Zionism to Zionist Religion: The Roots of Gush Emunim and its Culture', PhD diss., The Hebrew University of Jerusalem, Jerusalem.

Army of God (n.d.), Available online: https://web.archive.org/web/20210615153621/https://armyofgod.com/ (accessed 28 June 2022).

Asal, V., B. J. Phillips, R. K. Rethemeyer, C. Simonelli and J. K. Young (2018), 'Carrots, Sticks, and Insurgent Targeting of Civilians', *Journal of Conflict Resolution*, 63 (7): 1710–35. https://doi.org/10.1177/0022002718789748.

Asatru Folk Assembly (n.d.), Available online: https://web.archive.org/web/20220309185224/https://runestone.org/ (accessed 28 June 2022).

Avalos, H. (2005), *Fighting Words: The Origins of Religious Violence*. Amherst, NY: Prometheus Books.

Barkun, M. (1997), *Religion and the Racist Right: The Origins of the Christian Identity Movement*. 2nd edn. Chapel Hill: UNC Press Books.

Beekman, S. (2005), *William Dudley Pelley: A Life in Right-Wing Extremism and the Occult*. Syracuse, NY: Syracuse University Press.

Beller, J. and C. Kröger (2018), 'Religiosity, Religious Fundamentalism, and Perceived Threat as Predictors of Muslim Support for Extremist Violence', *Psychology of Religion and Spirituality*, 10 (4): 345–55. https://doi.org/10.1037/rel0000138.

Berger, J. M. (2016), 'Without Prejudice: What Sovereign Citizens Believe', George Washington University Program on Extremism. Available online: https://extremism.gwu.edu/sites/g/files/zaxdzs2191/f/downloads/JMB%20Sovereign%20Citizens.pdf (accessed 9 March 2022).

Berlet, C. (2002), 'Hard Times on the Hard Right: Why Progressives Must Remain Vigilant', *Public Eye*, 16 (1): 1–23. https://politicalresearch.org/sites/default/files/2018-10/Public-Eye-Magazine-Spring-2002.pdf.

Beutel, A., A. Perliger, D. Johnson, A. Kalaria, E. Swanson, S. M. Choi, N. Duke and T. Gibson (2017), 'Key Concepts to Understand Violent White Supremacy', *START Center*, April. Available online: https://www.start.umd.edu/pubs/START_KeyConceptsToUnderstandViolentWhiteSupremacy_ResearchBrief_April2017.pdf (accessed 9 March 2022).

Bowman, R. (2016), 'Othala and US Heathenry's Racist Heritage', *Idunna: A Journal of Northern Tradition*, (110): 17–19. Available online: https://druidcompanion.files.wordpress.com/2017/02/idunna110-bowman-othalausheathenryracistheritage.pdf (accessed 9 March 2022).

Campbell, C. (1971), *Toward a Sociology of Irreligion*. London: Red Globe Press.

Church of Jesus Christ of Latter-day Saints (2013), 'Race and the Priesthood'. Available online: https://www.churchofjesuschrist.org/study/manual/gospel-topics-essays/race-and-the-priesthood?lang=eng#13 (accessed 28 June 2022).

Clarkson, F. (2005), *The Rise of Dominionism: Remaking America as a Christian Nation*, Political Research Associates. Available online: https://politicalresearch.org/2005/12/05/the-rise-of-dominionismremaking-america-as-a-christian-nation (accessed 5 December 2021).

Cohen-Almagor, R. (1992), 'Vigilant Jewish Fundamentalism: From the JDL to Kach (or "Shalom Jews, Shalom Dogs")', *Terrorism and Political Violence*, 4 (1): 44–66.

Creativity Alliance (n.d.a), 'Creator calendar'. Available online: https://web.archive.org/web/20210812130414/https://creativityalliance.com/about-our-church/creator-calendar/ (accessed 9 March 2022).

Creativity Alliance (n.d.b), 'Racial Loyalty News – Flyers, Stickers & Cards'. Available online: https://web.archive.org/web/20210812140147/https://creativityalliance.com/forum/index.php?action=gallery;cat=5 (accessed 9 March 2022).

Creativity Alliance (n.d.c), 'Sixteen Commandments', Available online: https://web.archive.org/web/20220120145055/https://creativityalliance.com/home/16commandments/ (accessed 9 March 2022).

Creativity Alliance (n.d.d), 'F.A.Q', Available online: https://web.archive.org/web/20210813135014/https://creativityalliance.com/about-our-church/f-a-q/ (accessed 9 March 2022).

Creativity Alliance (2016), 'Join our Church', 26 January. Available online: https://web.archive.org/web/20220405095923/https://creativityalliance.com/about-our-church/join-our-church/ (accessed 9 March 2022).

Crenshaw, M. (1981), 'The Causes of Terrorism', *Comparative Politics*, 13 (4): 379–99. https://doi.org/10.2307/421717.

CTEC Staff (2021), *Christian Identity's New Role on the Extreme Right*, Middlebury Institute of International Studies at Monterey. Available online: https://www.middlebury.edu/institute/academics/centers-initiatives/ctec/ctec-publications/christian-identitys-new-role-extreme-right (accessed 6 August 2022).

Dawson, L. L. (1998), 'The cultural significance of new religious movements and globalization: A theoretical prolegomenon', *Journal for the Scientific Study of Religion*, 37 (4): 580–95. https://doi.org/10.2307/1388142.

Defenders of the Defenders of Life (n.d.), 'Second Defensive Action Statement'. Available online: https://web.archive.org/web/20210815175614/http://www.armyofgod.com/defense2.html (accessed 28 June 2022).

Dew, S. (2015), 'Washitaw de Dugdahmoundyah: Counterfactual Religious Readings of the Law', *Nova Religio*, 19 (2): 65–82.

Dew, S. (2016), '"Moors Know the Law": Sovereign Legal Discourse in Moorish Science Religious Communities and the Hermeneutics of Supersession', *Journal of Law and Religion*, 31 (1): 70–91.

Erlanger, S. and S. Shane (2011), 'Norway Shooting and Bomb Attack Leaves at Least 92 Dead', *New York Times*, 23 July. Available online: https://www.nytimes.com/2011/07/24/world/europe/24oslo.html (accessed 28 June 2022).

Fausset, R. (2015), 'For Robert Dear, Religion and Rage before Planned Parenthood Attack', *New York Times*, 1 December. Available online: https://www.nytimes.com/2015/12/02/us/robert-dear-planned-parenthood-shooting.html (accessed 28 June 2022).

Federal Bureau of Investigation (2011), 'Sovereign Citizens: A Growing Domestic Threat to Law Enforcement', *FBI Law Enforcement Bulletin*, 1 September. Available online: https://leb.fbi.gov/articles/featured-articles/sovereign-citizens-a-growing-domestic-threat-to-law-enforcement (accessed 28 June 2022).

Federman, J. and J. Krauss (2021), 'Radical Rabbi's Followers Rise in Israel amid New Violence', *Associated Press*, 14 May. Available online: https://web.archive.org/web/20220310230929/https://apnews.com/article/israel-middle-east-violence-religion-0dcc4073d660003f4e3fa8d4ed0a9a6a (accessed 28 June 2022).

Feige, M. (2009), *Settling in the Hearts: Jewish Fundamentalism in the Occupied Territories*. Detroit: Wayne State University Press.

Gabbatt, A. (2022), 'Fox News Suddenly goes Quiet on 'Great Replacement' theory after Buffalo Shooting', *The Guardian*, 17 May. Available online: https://www.theguardian.com/us-news/2022/may/17/buffalo-shooting-fox-news-tucker-carlson-great-replacement-theory (accessed 11 June 2022).

Galili, L. (2018), 'Analysis: The Jewish Nation-State vs. Non-Jewish Immigrants from the Former USSR', *I24news*, 29 July. Available online: https://www.i24news.tv/en/news/israel/society/180499-180729-analysis-the-jewish-nation-state-vs-non-jewish-immigrants-from-the-former-ussr (accessed 28 June 2022).

Gallagher, C. R. (2021), *Nazis of Copley Square: The Forgotten Story of the Christian Front*. Boston: Harvard University Press.

Gibson, D. (2011), 'Is Anders Breivik a "Christian" Terrorist?', *Religion News Service*, 27 July. Available online: https://religionnews.com/2011/07/27/is-anders-breivik-a-christian-terrorist/ (accessed 27 June 2022).

Ginges, J., H. Sheikh, S. Atran and N. Argo (2015), 'Thinking from God's Perspective Decreases Biased Valuation of the Life of a Nonbeliever', *Proceedings of the National Academy of Sciences*, 113 (2): 316–19. https://doi.org/10.1073/pnas.1512120113.

Goodrick-Clarke, N. (1985), *The Occult Roots of Nazism: Secret Aryan Cults and Their Influence on Nazi Ideology*. New York: NYU Press.

Groat, J. B. (2013), *Mormon Church Disavows Previous Teachings on Blacks and Priesthood*. Institute for Religious Research, 21 December. Available online: https://mit.irr.org/mormon-church-disavows-previous-teachings-on-blacks-and-priesthood (accessed 28 June 2022).

Harris, M. (2017), 'Ezra Taft Benson, Dwight D. Eisenhower, and the Emergence of a Conspiracy Culture within the Mormon Church', *John Whitmer Historical Association*, 37 (1): 51–82.

Heller, J. (1989), *Lehi: Ideology and Politics, 1940–1949*. Jerusalem: Keter and Zalman Shazar Center for Jewish History.

Hermann, T. and E. Yaar (2001), 'Shas' "Dovishness": Image and Reality', in Y. Peled (ed), *Shas: The Challenge of Israeliness*, 343–89, Tel Aviv: Miskal–Yedioth Ahronoth Books and Chemed Books.

Hill, P. J. (n.d.), 'Defensive Action Statement', Available online: https://web.archive.org/web/20210615170320/https://armyofgod.com/defense.html (accessed 9 March 2022).

Hill, P. J. (n.d.b), 'Why Shoot an Abortionist?' Available online: https://web.archive.org/web/20210615163015/https://armyofgod.com/PHillwhyshootanabortionist.html (accessed 9 March 2022).

Hill, P. J. (2003), 'Mix My Blood with the Blood of the Unborn'. Available online: https://web.archive.org/web/20210626121317/http://armyofgod.com/PaulHillMixMyBlood2.pdf (accessed 9 March 2022).

Hirsch-Hoefler, S., D. Canetti and E. Eiran (2016), 'Radicalizing Religion? Religious Identity and Settlers' Behavior', *Studies in Conflict & Terrorism*, 39 (6): 500–18. https://doi.org/10.1080/1057610x.2015.1127111.

Holthouse, D. (2008), 'Racism of Raided FLDS Cult Ignored', *Southern Poverty Law Center*, 7 April. Available online: https://www.splcenter.org/hatewatch/2008/04/07/racism-raided-flds-cult-ignored (accessed 9 March 2022).

Hoskins, R. K. (1997), *Vigilantes of Christendom: The Story of the Phineas Priesthood*, 1st edn. Lynchburg, VA: Virginia Publishing Company. Available online: https://ia800902.us.archive.org/10/items/vigilantesofchristendom_201908/Vigilantes%20of%20Christendom.pdf (accessed 9 March 2022).

Israel Democracy Institute (2018a), 'Nation-State Law Explainer', 18 July. Available online: https://en.idi.org.il/articles/24241 (accessed 28 June 2022).

Israel Democracy Institute (2018b), 'Q&A about the Nation-State Law', 9 August. Available online: https://en.idi.org.il/articles/24378 (accessed 28 June 2022).

Jacobson, C. and L. Burton (2011), *Modern Polygamy in the United States: Historical, Cultural, and Legal Issues*. New York: Oxford University Press.

Johnson, D. (2017), 'Hate in God's name', Southern Poverty Law Center, 25 September. Available online: https://www.splcenter.org/20170925/hate-god%E2%80%99s-name (accessed 28 June 2022).

Jurgensmeyer, M. (2010), 'The Return of Christian Terrorism', *Religion Dispatches*, 9 April. Available online: https://religiondispatches.org/the-return-of-christian-terrorism/ (accessed 28 June 2022).

Kelaidis, K. (2019), '*Orthodoxy's Extremist Appeal*', *Orthodox Christian Laity*, 18 May. Available online: https://ocl.org/orthodoxys-extremist-appeal/ (accessed 28 June 2022).

Keller-Lynn, C. (2022), '"I've done it": Netanyahu announces his 6th government, Israel's most hardline ever', Times of Israel, 21 December. Available online: https://web.archive.org/web/20230114151012/https://www.timesofisrael.com/netanyahu-announces-his-sixth-government-israels-most-hardline-yet/ (accessed 29 October 2024).

Kimball, C. (2008), *When Religion Becomes Evil: Five Warning Signs*. New York: Harper Collins.

Kimche, J. J. (2022), 'The Rage of Meir Kahane', *First Things*, April. Available online: https://www.firstthings.com/article/2022/04/the-rage-of-meir-kahane (accessed 28 June 2022).

Kirkland, L. (2010), *Church Statement on 'White Horse Prophecy' and Political Neutrality*, Church of Jesus Christ of Latter-Day Saints, 6 January. Available online: https://

newsroom.churchofjesuschrist.org/blog/church-statement-on-white-horse-prophecy-and-political-neutrality (accessed 9 March 2022).

Klassen, B. (n.d.), 'My Own Spiritual Awakening', *The Creativity Alliance*. Available online: https://web.archive.org/web/20170112141525/https://creativityalliance.com/articles/awakenings/ben-klassen-my-own-spiritual-awakening/ (accessed 9 March 2022).

Klassen, B. (1973), *Nature's Eternal Religion*. Otto, NC: Creativity Book Publisher. Available online: https://web.archive.org/web/20211121015313/https://www.jrbooksonline.com/PDF_Books/Natures_eternal_religion.pdf (accessed 9 March 2022).

Klassen, B. ([1981] 2008), *The White Man's Bible*, 3rd edn. Otto, NC: Creativity Book Publisher. Available online: https://web.archive.org/web/20220412192325/ https://creativityalliance.com/wp-content/uploads/ebooks/HolyBooks/eBook-BenKlassen-TheWhiteMan'sBible.pdf (accessed 9 March 2022).

Kosse, M. (2022), '"Ted Cruz Cucks Again": The Insult term *cuck* as an Alt-Right Masculinist Signifier', *Gender and Language*, 16 (2): 99–124. https://doi.org/10.1558/genl.21079.

Kossowska, M., A. Czernatowicz-Kukuczka and M. Sekerdej (2017), 'Many Faces of Dogmatism: Prejudice as a Way of Protecting Certainty against Value Violators among Dogmatic Believers and Atheists', *British Journal of Psychology*, 108 (1): 127–47.

Levin, S. (2014), 'Rebel Cowboys: How the Bundy Family Sparked a New Battle for the American West', *The Guardian*, 29 August. Available online: https://www.theguardian.com/us-news/2016/aug/29/oregon-militia-standoff-bundy-family (accessed 9 March 2022).

Levitas, D. (2004), *The Terrorist Next Door: The Militia Movement and the Radical Right*. New York: St. Martin's Press.

Lustick, I. S. (1988), *For the Land and the Lord*, New York: Council on Foreign Relations.

Mackey, R. (2011), 'Online, Clues to a Suspected Attacker's Motives', *New York Times*, 23 July. Available online: https://thelede.blogs.nytimes.com/2011/07/23/scouring-the-web-for-clues-to-a-suspected-attackers-motives/ (accessed 9 March 2022).

MacNab, J. J. (2018), *Anti-Government Extremism in America: Violence Acts and Plots in the United States, 2000 to 2018*. April. Available online: http://www.seditionists.com/AGEreport.pdf (accessed 9 March 2022).

Magid, J. (2017), 'Black Is the New Orange: 30% of Settlers are Now Haredim', *The Times of Israel*, 18 July. Available online: https://www.timesofisrael.com/black-is-the-new-orange-30-of-settlers-are-now-haredim (accessed 9 March 2022).

Magid, S. (2019), 'Kahane Won', *Tablet Magazine*, 15 March. Available online: https://www.tabletmag.com/sections/israel-middle-east/articles/kahane-won (accessed 9 March 2022).

Martin, G. (2021), *Understanding Terrorism: Challenges, Perspectives, and Issues*. 7th edn, Washington, D.C.: SAGE Publications.

McShee, S. (2018), 'Why does White Supremacist Odinism Thrive in Prisons?', *The Wild Hunt*, 24 July. Available online: https://wildhunt.org/2018/07/why-does-white-supremacist-odinism-thrive-in-prisons.html (accessed 9 March 2022).

Milkovits, A. (2021), 'After the Armed Standoff with Rise of the Moors: The Spectacle Is the Point', *Boston Globe*, 6 July. Available online: https://www.msn.com/en-us/news/us/after-the-armed-standoff-with-rise-of-the-moors-the-spectacle-is-the-point/ar-AALQYht (accessed 9 March 2022).

MyNorthwest Staff (2018), 'Rep. Shea Responds to Biblical War "Manifesto" Controversy', *MyNorthwest.com*, 2 November. Available online: https://mynorthwest.com/1168964/matt-shea-Biblical-war-manifesto/ (accessed 9 March 2022).

Nelson, L. (2011), 'Sovereigns' in Black', *Southern Poverty Law Center*, 24 August. Available online: https://www.splcenter.org/fighting-hate/intelligence-report/2011/%E2%80%98sovereigns%E2%80%99-black (accessed 9 March 2022).

Noble, K. (2011), *Tabernacle of Hate: Seduction into Right-Wing Extremism*, 2nd edn, Syracuse, NY: Syracuse University Press.

Palmer, S. (2010), *The Nuwaubian Nation: Black Spirituality and State Control*. New York: Routledge.

Pedahzur, A. and A. Perliger (2004), 'An Alternative Approach for Defining the Boundaries of Party Families: Examples from the Israeli Extreme Right-Wing Party Scene', *Australian Journal of Political Science*, 39 (2): 285–305.

Pedahzur, A. and A. Perliger (2009), *Jewish Terrorism in Israel*, New York: Columbia University Press.

Perliger, A. (2012), 'Identifying Three Trends in Far-Right Violence in the United States', *CTC Sentinel*, 5 (9): 5–7. Available online: https://ctc.westpoint.edu/wp-content/uploads/2012/09/CTCSentinel-Vol5Iss9.pdf (accessed 28 June 2022).

Perliger, A. (2015), 'Comparative Framework for Understanding Jewish and Christian Violent Fundamentalism', *Religions*, 6 (3): 1033–47.

Perliger, A. (2020), *American Zealots: Inside Right-Wing Domestic Terrorism*. New York: Columbia University Press.

Perliger, A. and A. Pedahzur (2016), 'Counter Cultures, Group Dynamics and Religious Terrorism', *Political Studies*, 64 (2): 297–314.

Perliger, A. and A. Pedahzur (2021), 'The Territories in Israeli Politics', in R. Y. Hazan, A. Dowty, M. Hofnung and G. Rahat (eds), *Oxford Handbook of Israeli Politics and Society*, 533–48, New York: Oxford University Press.

Pitcavage, M. (2016), 'The Washitaw Nation and Moorish Sovereign Citizens: What You Need to Know', Anti-Defamation League, 18 July. Available online: https://www.adl.org/blog/the-washitaw-nation-and-moorish-sovereign-citizens-what-you-need-to-know (accessed 9 March 2022).

Pratt, D. (2017), *Religion and Extremism: Rejecting Diversity*. London: Bloomsbury.

Preston, J. L., R. S. Ritter and J. Ivan Hernandez (2010), 'Principles of Religious Prosociality: A Review and Reformulation', *Social and Personality Psychology Compass*, 4 (8): 574–590. https://doi.org/10.1111/j.1751-9004.2010.00286.x.

Pro-Western Christianity (2013), 'Reading List: Pro-Western Christianity', *Blogspot.com*, 1 February. Available online: https://web.archive.org/web/20220210184856/https://prowesternchristianity.blogspot.com/ (accessed 9 March 2022).

Robinson, S. (2008), 'How Dangerous Is the FLDS?', *OurFuture.org*, 22 April. Available online: https://ourfuture.org/20080422/how-dangerous-is-the-flds (accessed 9 March 2022).

Rubinstein, D. (1982), *Gush Emunim*. Tel Aviv: Hakibbutz Hameuchad (Hebrew).

Sanchez, C. (2009), 'Supreme Court Requires Prisons Give Special Consideration to Racist Pagans', Southern Poverty Law Center, 21 August. Available online: https://www.splcenter.org/fighting-hate/intelligence-report/2009/supreme-court-requires-prisons-give-special-consideration-racist-pagans (accessed 9 March 2022).

Sarteschi, C. M. (2021), 'Sovereign Citizens: A Narrative Review with Implications of Violence towards Law Enforcement', *Aggression and Violent Behavior*, 60 (101509): September–October. https://doi.org/10.1016/j.avb.2020.101509.

Segal, H. (1988), *Dear Brothers: The West Bank Jewish Underground*. Woodmere, N.Y. NY: Beit Shamai Publications.

Sepulvado, J. (2016), 'Why the Bundy Militia Mixes Mormon Symbolism with Anti-Government Sentiment', *PBS NewsHour*, 4 January. Available online: https://www.pbs.

org/newshour/nation/why-the-bundy-militia-mixes-mormon-symbolism-with-anti-government-sentiment (accessed 9 March 2022).

Sheleg, Y. (2000), *The New Religious Jews: Recent Developments Among Observant Jews in Israel*. Jerusalem: Keter Books.

Shpaizman, I., O. Swed and A. Pedahzur (2016), 'Policy Change Inch by Inch: Policy Entrepreneurs in the Holy Basin of Jerusalem', *Public Administration*, 94: 1042–58.

Shupe, A. and J. Heinerman (1985), 'Mormonism and the new Christian Right: An Emerging Coalition?', *Review of Religious Research*, 27 (2): 146–57. https://doi.org/10.2307/3511669.

Simmons, W. J. (1916), *Kloran: Knights of the Ku Klux Klan*, 5th edn, Atlanta: Ku Klux Press. Available online: https://ia903000.us.archive.org/27/items/KloranOfTheKKK_201404/Kloran%20of%20the%20KKK_text.pdf (accessed 9 March 2022).

Smooha, S. (2013), 'A Zionist State, A Binational State and an In-between Jewish and Democratic State', *Israel Democracy Institute*, 12 March. Available online: https://en.idi.org.il/articles/10497 (accessed 9 March 2022).

Snook, J. (2013), 'Reconsidering Heathenry: The Construction of an Ethnic Folkway as Religio-Centric Identity', *Nova Religio*, 16 (3): 52–76. https://doi.org/10.1525/nr.2013.16.3.52.

Sottile, L. (2018), 'Bundyville Chapter Two: By a Thread', *Longreads*, May. Available online: https://longreads.com/2018/05/16/bundyville-chapter-two-by-a-thread/ (accessed 9 March 2022).

Sottile, L. (2019), 'Bundyville: The Remnant, Chapter Four: The Preacher and the Politician', *Longreads*, July. Available online: https://longreads.com/2019/07/18/bundyville-the-remnant-chapter-four-the-preacher-and-the-politician/ (accessed 9 March 2022).

Southern Poverty Law Center (n.d.a), 'Phineas Priesthood'. Available online: https://www.splcenter.org/fighting-hate/extremist-files/ideology/phineas-priesthood (accessed 9 March 2022).

Southern Poverty Law Center (n.d.b), 'Fundamentalist Church of Jesus Christ of Latter-Day Saints'. Available online: https://www.splcenter.org/fighting-hate/extremist-files/group/fundamentalist-church-jesus-christ-latter-day-saints (accessed 12 June 2022).

Southern Poverty Law Center (n.d.c), '*Moorish Sovereign Citizens*'. Available online: https://www.splcenter.org/fighting-hate/extremist-files/group/moorish-sovereign-citizens (accessed 12 June 2022).

Southern Poverty Law Center (n.d.d). '*Sovereign Citizens Movement*'. Available online: https://www.splcenter.org/fighting-hate/extremist-files/ideology/sovereign-citizens-movement (accessed 12 June 2022).

Sprinzak, E. (1999), *Brother Against Brother*. New York: Free Press.

Stroop, C. (2020), 'Behind a Recent Stunt in Idaho Lies a Dangerous Theocratic Movement', *Religion Dispatches*, 29 June. Available online: https://religiondispatches.org/behind-a-recent-stunt-in-idaho-lies-a-dangerous-theocratic-movement/ (accessed 12 June 2022).

Sweeney, M. M. and A. Perliger (2018), 'Explaining the Spontaneous Nature of Far-Right Violence in the United States', *Perspectives on Terrorism*, 12 (6): 52–71. https://www.universiteitleiden.nl/binaries/content/assets/customsites/perspectives-on-terrorism/2018/issue-6/a4-sweeney-perliger.pdf.

Taylor, A. (2015), 'Why Are We So Surprised by the Less-Than-Pious Lives of Religious Terrorists?', *The Washington Post*, 20 November. Available online: https://www.

washingtonpost.com/news/worldviews/wp/2015/11/20/why-are-we-so-surprised-by-the-less-than-pious-lives-of-religious-terrorists/ (accessed 28 June 2022).

Torres, P. (2017), 'From the Enlightenment to the Dark Ages: How 'New Atheism' Slid into the Alt-Right', *Salon*, 29 July. Available online: https://www.salon.com/2017/07/29/from-the-enlightenment-to-the-dark-ages-how-new-atheism-slid-into-the-alt-right/ (accessed 12 June 2022).

Torres, P. (2021), 'Godless Grifters: How the New Atheists Merged with the Far Right', *Salon*, 5 June. Available online: https://www.salon.com/2021/06/05/how-the-new-atheists-merged-with-the-far-right-a-story-of-intellectual-grift-and-abject-surrender/ (accessed 12 June 2022).

Uzarevic, F., V. Saroglou and M. Clobert (2017), 'Are Atheists Undogmatic?', *Personality and Individual Differences*, 116, 164–70. https://doi.org/10.1016/j.paid.2017.04.046.

Weber, S. (2018), *White Supremacy's Old Gods*, Political Research Associates, 1 February. Available online: https://politicalresearch.org/2018/02/01/white-supremacys-old-gods-the-far-right-and-neopaganism (accessed 9 March 2022).

Weyermann, D. (2012), 'FLDS Continues Abusive Polygamist Practices in Utah and Arizona', *High Country News*, 18 June. Available online: https://www.hcn.org/issues/44.10/flds-continues-abusive-polygamist-practices-in-utah-and-arizona?b_start:int=0#body (accessed 9 March 2022).

Wilhelmsen, F. (2021). 'The Wife Would Put on a Nice Suit, Hat, and Possibly Gloves': The Misogynistic Identity Politics of Anders Behring Breivik, *Fascism*, 10 (1): 108–33. https://doi.org/10.1163/22116257-10010003.

Williams, W. and C. Cambeul (eds) ([2009] 2020), *The Creativity Alliance Handbook*, 5th edn. Oaklands Park, South Australia: Creativity Alliance. Available online: https://web.archive.org/web/20220120161216/https://creativityalliance.com/wp-content/uploads/ebooks/HolyBooks/CA-Handbook.pdf (accessed 9 March 2022).

Williamson, W. P. and R. W. Hood (2013), 'Religious Fundamentalism and Perceived Threat: A Report from an Experimental Study', *Mental Health, Religion & Culture*, 17 (5): 520–8. https://doi.org/10.1080/13674676.2013.857297.

Winter, A. (2013), 'Anti-Abortion Extremism and Violence in the United States', in G. Michael (ed), *Extremism in America*, 218–48, Gainesville: University Press Florida.

Wright, J. D. and Y. Khoo (2019), 'Empirical Perspectives on Religion and Violence', *Contemporary Voices: St Andrews Journal of International Relations*, 1 (3): 75–100. https://cvir.st-andrews.ac.uk/articles/10.15664/jtr.1482/.

Yousef, O. (2022), 'Orthodox Christian Churches are Drawing in Far-Right American Converts', *National Public Radio*, 10 May. Available online: https://wusfnews.wusf.usf.edu/2022-05-10/orthodox-christian-churches-are-drawing-in-far-right-american-converts (accessed 11 June 2022).

Zertal, I. and A. Eldar (2004), *Lords of the Land*. Tel Aviv: Kinneret Zmora-Bitan Dvir (Hebrew).

12

'Orthodoxy or Death': The embrace of Orthodox Christianity by the modern far right

Lydia Khalil

Introduction

In recent years Orthodox Christianity has gained in exposure and appeal within the far right. This includes growth in the religious appropriation of and conversion to Orthodox Christianity by a number of modern far-right movements within the Anglosphere, largely facilitated by the digital environment, globalization and Russian state influence and cultivation of the far right.

Much of the scholarship regarding the role of Christianity in the ideology and narratives of far-right extremism has tended to focus on Western Christian denominations, primarily within Catholic or Protestant traditions. The connections between Orthodox Christianity and far-right actors and movements within the Anglosphere, particularly within the online Orthosphere subculture (Sellanraa 2012, Dyga 2014), however, have remained largely unexamined in the extremism research literature due to the relatively recent emergence of the connections between Eastern Orthodox Christianity and Western far-right actors (Beutel and Perliger, this volume).

Scholars who have examined the conversion to Orthodox Christianity of far-right actors from the Anglosphere have primarily emerged out of other disciplines such as sociology and anthropology, often through the ethnographic study of specific communities, and from the disciplines of theology and history (Kelaidis 2016, 2017, 2019, Leonova 2017, 2019, Bringerud 2019, Lukasik 2021, Riccardi-Swartz 2022, Moreton 2022). There have also been journalistic accounts of the conversion by far-right actors to Eastern Orthodox Christianity (Yousef 2022) and the broader role of the Russian state and Russian Orthodox Church in cultivating the far right. Non-profit organizations who track the far right, such as the US-based Southern Poverty Law Center, have also reported on incidents and connections between far-right movements and Eastern Orthodox Christianity (Phillips 2014). Orthodoxy in Dialogue, a progressive forum for Orthodox Christian voices, has similarly tracked the rise of this phenomenon (Orthodoxy in Dialogue 2018a).

This chapter seeks to build upon this emerging set of resources and analyses to examine the specific appeal of Orthodox Christianity to two subcultures of the far right: white nationalists and the manosphere, the latter connoting a networked online space that opposes feminism and promotes patriarchy through the rhetoric of 'men's rights'. The chapter will also focus on how far-right influencers who convert to Eastern Orthodoxy interpret the theology and history of the Eastern Orthodox Church to justify and reinforce their ideological positions and narratives, specifically around male supremacism and ethnonationalism.

Conversion to Orthodox Christianity among the Western far right reveals how the harnessing of religion is a political and ideological act, not just a spiritual calling. Features of the Orthodox Christian religion – in particular, its patriarchy, hierarchy, traditionalism, anti-modernity and mysticism – are highly appealing to the far right, who draw on these features in their attempt to use religion as a means to justify exclusionary practices and ideological positions.

Orthodox Christianity

I use Orthodox Christianity to refer mostly to the Eastern Orthodox Churches that recognize the first seven ecumenical councils of Christianity and are a communion of autocephalous congregations (e.g. the Greek, Russian, Serbian, Antiochian, Romanian). These congregations shared communion with the Church of Rome until the East-West Schism of 1054 (the Eastern Orthodox Church also officially refers to itself as the 'Orthodox Catholic Church'; in this context, 'catholic' means 'universal' and not the Catholic Church of Rome). At times I also use Orthodox Christianity to include the Oriental Orthodox Churches (Coptic, Ethiopian, Armenian, Syrian, Indian and Eritrean) who left the Eastern Orthodox communion after the Third Ecumenical Council of Ephesus in 431 and the Fourth Ecumenical Council of Chalcedon in 451 over a Christological dispute that caused a schism between Byzantium and the Churches of the Oriental Orthodox communion. I do not use the term 'Orthodox Christianity' to mean small 'o' orthodoxy – an ecclesiastical term stemming from the Greek, *ortho* (straight) and *doxa* (belief) – which various Christian denominations, including the Protestants and Catholics of Western Christendom, use to denote true or traditional belief.

It is important to note at the outset that the appropriation of Orthodox Christianity by far-right converts and movements, particularly within the online Orthosphere, is often removed from the parish life and praxis of the multitude of diverse expressions of the faith by both traditional and non-traditional Orthodox Christian communities, something reflected by several denunciations of far-right appropriation by Orthodox Church figures (Phillips 2014).

Furthermore, as far back as 1872, the Eastern Orthodox Church officially decreed that phyletism – the concept that pastoral care by a particular Orthodox church can be directed only to the members of specific ethnic groups (interpreted in the modern period as racial or ethnic hatred or discrimination) – was a heresy (Alexopoulos and Johnson 2021). Eastern Orthodox leadership figures have used the doctrine of phyletism to excommunicate far-right actors who hold racist views or who promote an ultranationalist agenda.

In examining Orthodox Christianity's appeal to the far right, I do not suggest that Orthodoxy appeals *only* to converts who hold far-right ideological views. A wide variety of individuals who are attracted and have converted to Orthodox Christianity hold a myriad of political and ideological beliefs and attitudes (Herbel 2014). Similarly, those born into the faith and who come from the traditional ethnic bases of Orthodox rites espouse a range of political and ideological positions (Davis and Robinson 1996). This examination of the appeal of Orthodox Christianity to the far right is thus not intended to negate the experience of 'vernacular theology' (Bringerud 2019) or to homogenize the various lived experiences, attitudes, distinctions, levels of religiosity and differences in theological interpretation among Orthodox Christian individuals and traditions.

Moreover, the same aspects that far-right extremist converts to Orthodox Christianity find appealing about the religion – its emphasis on the communal over the individual; its enduring values and practices in the face of modernity; the rigour of its praxis combined with mysticism and mystery; its claim of an 'unbroken tradition of apostolic Christianity' (Slagle 2011), doctrinal conservatism, gender essentialism and theological justifications for traditional gender roles – are the same aspects of the faith that many other non-far-right converts also find appealing about the faith. The sense of dissatisfaction either with one's original faith or with society more generally that often drives conversion is hardly unique to far-right actors (Herbel 2014, Bringerud 2019) and is certainly not always explicitly connected to ideologically driven beliefs or justifications.

Orthodox Christianity and the far right

With these important caveats, there nevertheless remains a historical legacy of far-right, ultranationalist convergence and influence within Orthodox Christian communities and churches that modern far-right actors draw upon. From Codreanu's Legionnaires in Romania to Greece's Golden Dawn, various fascist and far-right movements have publicly embraced Orthodox Christianity as part of their exclusivist projects and have been supported by elements within their respective Orthodox Churches. They are now held up as historical examples to follow by modern-day far-right white nationalists. Some elements within Eastern Orthodox Christian communities also have a long history of antisemitism (Eisinga, Konig and Scheepers 1995), Islamophobia and reactionary politics – again, elements that are shared with the modern far right.

Some scholars have suggested that the far right's embrace of Orthodoxy is based on the systemic presence of xenophobia, racism, antisemitism and Islamophobia within Christian Orthodox communities (Kelaidis 2016, Leonova 2017, 2019). At the very least, there is a recognition of common attitudes and narratives prevalent in both Eastern Orthodox communities and far-right movements (Kelaidis 2019). This has reinforced perceptions that the Orthodox Churches are natural allies of those on the far right, insofar as there are elements with Orthodox Christian denominations who hold similar beliefs and ideas around the role of Jews in society, opposition to homosexuality and LGBTQI rights, and reactionary tendencies around multiculturalism, feminism

(Phillips 2014) and the so-called 'theology of cultural Marxism' (Dyga 2014). There are also shared concerns about secular modernism, progressivism and Islamic expansionism, all of which both far-right actors and elements within Orthodox communities present as threats to Christian civilization.

Another dimension involves the ways in which some elements of Orthodox Christian communities, particularly in diaspora settings, who have been targeted by violent Islamist extremists and jihadist movements have found common cause and shared narratives with reactionary and far-right actors and movements within the Anglosphere. This is especially the case for Oriental Orthodox sects (Lukasik 2021) and revivalist nationalist Eastern Orthodox Christian movements within the Serbian, Greek, Romanian and Russian Orthodox churches which have a history of engaging with ultranationalist, authoritarian, anti-communist, anti-Muslim and fascist ideas and movements.

There is also a geopolitical dimension to the growing appeal of and conversion to Orthodox Christianity by the modern far right. This stems in part from the cultivation of the far right by the Putin regime in Russia and its supporters in their effort to undermine state adversaries in the West (Kelaidis 2018, Butt and Byman 2020). The Putin regime has enlisted and utilized Russian Orthodoxy and religious organizations such as the Russian Orthodox Church Outside Russia (ROCOR) and the World Congress of Families (WCF) as part of this effort (Stoeckl 2020, Moreton 2022). This, alongside the resurgence of fascist and other far-right groups in predominantly Orthodox countries across Eastern Europe, has contributed to the notion that the Orthodox Church can serve as a natural ally and spiritual foundation for many different strains of the far right (Phillips 2014).

The foregoing discussion helps explain why Orthodox Christianity appeals on a number of levels to those within the far right. Below, I will provide examples of recent far-right influencers who have converted to or promoted Orthodox Christianity and focus on what I identify as two main appeals of Orthodoxy to far-right converts from the Anglosphere: first, Orthodox teachings and traditions related to patriarchy, gender essentialism, traditional gender roles and heteronormativity, and second, Orthodoxy's model for ethnically based spiritually informed communities. In the following two sections, I will discuss how the theology and praxis regarding these two issues can be construed by the far right and how they are used to justify their exclusionary practices and ideologies.

The embrace of Orthodox Christianity by white nationalists

A number of far-right converts to Orthodoxy from the Anglosphere who have been influential both offline and in the online Orthosphere have come from the United States. One of the most cited examples is the American white nationalist Matthew Heimbach, the founder of the white nationalist Traditional Workers Party (TWP) and a prominent far-right influencer who has forged networks between many US-based and international far-right and white nationalist movements (Feuer and Higgins 2016). Heimbach was a key organizer of the Charlottesville Unite the Right Rally in 2017, one of the United States's largest, most violent gatherings in recent times that brought together various white nationalists and alt-right groups. Heimbach participated in Charlottesville, waving an 'Orthodoxy or Death' banner as he scuffled with counter-protesters (Leonova 2017) and was subsequently indicted for conspiracy for his role in the violence that ensued (Heim 2016).

Prior to his advocacy of Christian Orthodoxy in Charlottesville, Heimbach became a convert to the Antiochian Orthodox Church on Lazarus Monday in 2014, along with his former father-in-law and fellow white nationalist Matthew Parrott (Southern Poverty Law Center n.d.a.). Heimbach has spoken publicly about his religious conversion and its role in his aim of creating a white nationalist movement based on Orthodox Christianity and its tenets.

Just days after his official conversion, Heimbach attended the SlutWalk protest at Indiana University Bloomington (IUB), an annual demonstration denouncing rape culture and victim-blaming, as a counter-protester. While supposedly holding a prayer vigil at the site, Heimbach engaged in an altercation with a member of the IUB Antifa and bludgeoned him with a large wooden Orthodox cross. Footage of the altercation went viral, a stark and violent illustration of Heimbach's association with Orthodoxy (Phillips 2014).

After this incident, there were multiple calls within his church for Heimbach's censure. The Antiochian Archdiocese to which he had originally converted excommunicated Heimbach and Parrott soon after, charging them with phyletism and banning them from participating in rites and receiving the sacraments in any canonical Orthodox Church. Heimbach and Parrott initially responded to their excommunication by saying they would take a step back from political involvement. However, both resumed their activities within weeks. They denied that white nationalism was a heresy within the Orthodox Church and accused the Antiochian priest and bishop who excommunicated them of being the real heretics. Heimbach also claimed that his excommunication was repealed by the Russian Orthodox Church Outside of Russia and that he had found a spiritual home within a Romanian Orthodox Church, saying, 'My spiritual father is a priest in Europe who has the support of his bishop' (Hunter 2015).

In addition to Heimbach and Parrot, another prominent TWP figure, Matthew Raphael Johnson, also converted to Orthodox Christianity. Johnson was a former academic at the University of Nebraska as well as a former priest with the noncanonical Old Calendarist Greek Orthodox Autonomous Orthodox Metropolia. He too was excommunicated and defrocked for phyletism. But that has not stopped Johnson from promoting Orthodox far-right-tinged nationalism and traditionalism. His podcast *The Orthodox Nationalist* is featured on the TradYouth website (Kelaidis 2017) and on Radio Aryan (recently renamed Radio Albion), a platform that describes itself as 'fighting for white revival' (Orthodoxy in Dialogue 2018b). Rusijournal.org, a single webpage WordPress site, presents 'Professor Johnson' as a 'Russian Orthodox medievalist' whose 'academic work is dedicated to the delegitimization of the global capitalist system and the demystification of the ideology that justifies it', alongside a range of his writings (rusijournal.org n.d.). These writings are a compendium of revisionist Russian, Serbian and Orthodox history, philosophy and theology. Johnson is also a bolsterer of Putin 'as a necessary balance to American empire and the liberal authoritarianism it enforces' (Bonald n.d.).

Concerned about the appropriation of Orthodox Christianity by far-right figures like Heimbach and Johnson, in 2018 a group of American Orthodox clergy issued 'A Statement Concerning the Sin of Racism'. The Statement declares that 'racism, antisemitism, and xenophobia are sins. Anyone within the Orthodox Church who promotes or is sympathetic to any of these must therefore repent before God for the sake of his or her own soul, and for the good of the Church' (Orthodox Christian Clergy Against Racism 2018). Johnson offered a rebuttal to this Statement titled 'The Orthodox Nationalist: A Response to the Orthodox Clergy Condemnation of Nationalism' (Johnson 2018). In his response, Johnson argues for racial and ethnic separation: '[The Statement's signatories] are forcing modern liberalism onto a church that is liberalism's antithesis. The Orthodox church's ancient position on race and Nationalism is diametrically opposed to this jejune, sentimental nonsense.' He goes on to say, 'I describe the basis for racial separatism given the violence our communities are subjected to by non-Whites daily [...]. This is a racial war because crime in Europe and America is racial. I never wanted to become a racial nationalist, it was forced upon me given the facts of life' (Johnson 2018).

These TWP members are but one example of white nationalists who have embraced Orthodoxy; many other far-right figures have also converted to and promoted Orthodox Christianity as a vehicle for their political and ideological goals. Antifascist websites have also exposed the embrace of Eastern Orthodoxy by a number of other white nationalist figures, singling out members of the neo-Nazi Iron March Forum who have converted to Eastern Orthodoxy and regularly post about Orthodoxy and reactionary sentiments (Dogpatch Press Staff 2022).

Heimbach was also not the sole Orthodox Christian to participate in the Unite the Right Rally in Charlottesville in 2017. In the weeks leading up to the rally, other far-right Orthodox figures, mostly affiliated with canonical parishes in the American South, organized on social media in support for or participated in the rally (Leonova 2017). Still other figures, like Christchurch killer Brendan Tarrant, referenced movements like the Serbian Chetniks, a group known for its genocidal violence in the Balkans and its strong association with the Serbian Orthodox Church. Dylan Roof, an American white supremacist who committed a mass shooting in 2015 targeting an African American church in South Carolina, also had connections to Eastern Orthodoxy. His spiritual advisor was an Orthodox priest (although this priest denounced Roof's actions and there is no evidence he shared or encouraged Roof's racist beliefs) (Leonova 2019).

There are also indications that some Orthodox clergy members in the West, particularly in the United States, are drifting towards far-right political ideology. Lenova (2019) cites evidence of these clergy making xenophobic remarks on Facebook and the trend of both Orthodox Christian clergy and laity posting Confederate flags superimposed with 'IC XC NIKA' (an abbreviated form of the Greek 'Jesus Christ Conquers') as Facebook profile pictures. Orthodox priests such as Reverend Mark Hodges participated in the 6 January 2021 riots on Capitol Hill in Washington, DC. Hodges was suspended from the ministry by the Orthodox Church in America's Diocese of the Midwest as a result (Stewart 2021), but he later picked up his ministry within the Russian Orthodox Church Outside Russia.

The embrace of Orthodox Christianity by far-right figures is not just an American phenomenon, however. Antipodean far-right figures have also latched onto Orthodoxy's appeal. In an Australian far-right online conference in 2020, Blair Cottrell, a well-known Australian far-right influencer who is also connected with neo-Nazi figures, also promoted Orthodox Christianity as a means to combat 'leftist infiltration of schools and local politics' and other supposedly corrupting modern influences. In the Q&A session during the 2020 online conference, Cottrell made the following comments in response to a question about how to blunt 'leftist influence' within families and local communities:

> The Greek Orthodox Church is probably your best bet. Get your kids into a Greek Orthodox Church. Hopefully we can create an [Australian] Orthodox Church of our own in the future. An Anglo Orthodox Church or something like that. It doesn't seem to exist for some reason but that's going to be extremely important in the future ... Hopefully we could create it ... I think religion is going to be a necessary aspect of healing in future.
> (Cottrell 2020)

While admitting that his own faith and relationship with God is currently lacking, Cottrell goes on to say:

> There needs to be a church of some sort that is a cultural community hub for white people. We haven't done well without it. All the evidence points to the necessity of a central church culture ... It needs to be a project in its own space. It needs to be separate from politics. It needs to be focused on community welfare.
> (Cottrell 2020)

He goes on to discuss how the Greek Orthodox Church in Australia has shared goals with the far right, for example, its staunch opposition to the legalization of same-sex marriage and its mobilization of the Church's Australian congregations to vote against this in Australia's 2017 plebiscite on the issue (Brook 2017). He praises the Greek Orthodox community for their traditional family values and patriarchal system, saying, 'They've got good girls there' (Cottrell 2020).

Cottrell also contrasts what he believes to be the 'soft' and 'feminine' version of Anglicized Christianity with what he perceives to be Orthodox Christianity's 'hard' and 'masculine' account, focusing on the visual representation of Christ's body:

> The Orthodox have got it right. They still have the most hard-line faith, in terms of Christian faith, anyway. All your modern-day Anglo Christians are about 'turn the other cheek', 'Christ loves everybody'. They are talking about the Holy Spirit as their bodies degenerate into s— because they are too lazy to do anything. People who represent Christ these days, especially white people, are full of s— and they don't know what they are talking about. If you look at the images of Christ in the Greek Orthodox literature, he doesn't look like a pansy, he doesn't look like a soft c—, like he's made to look in the majority Anglicized Christianity. He's got a stern hard look.
> (Cottrell 2020)

Cottrell attempts to reference (but can't quite recall accurately) Lk. 12.51, a passage that quotes Jesus as saying, 'Do you think that I have come to give peace on earth? No, I tell you, but rather division', in an attempt to use Christian teachings to justify the need for violence and division.

The Orthosphere

The take-up of Orthodox Christianity by Western far-right figures globally has also been spurred and facilitated by the digital environment, where far-right online subcultures have both merged and emerged. The clearest manifestation of this is the emergence of the Orthosphere and the 'Orthobro' phenomenon.

The Orthosphere has been described as an online subculture that puts an 'Orthodox glaze' over internet meme and troll culture inherent to the manosphere and far right (Malone 2021). The Orthosphere network is a loose collection of online bloggers and content creators who reject liberalism, postmodern relativism and materialism. While specific beliefs and goals within the Orthosphere can differ, it is united by a reactionary anti-feminist, anti-LGBTQI, anti-democratic, anti-globalist and often antisemitic agenda informed by the traditionalist movement's conviction that the world is corrupted by modernity (Sedgwick 2004, Teitelbaum 2020).

Their ideology centres on the defence of 'traditional authority, traditional morality, the monarchy, the patriarchal family, the *ethnos*, and the Church' (Sellanraa 2012). According to the Orthosphere website *Throne and Altar*, the Orthosphere's goal is 'defending the legitimate authority of God, tradition, fathers, and kings against the diabolical partisans of freedom and equality' (Bonald n.d.).

The Orthosphere is populated for the most part by an Anglosphere-derived array of male American, British and Australian reactionaries who elaborate on the ideological frameworks informing their critique of modern liberalism and defence of traditionalism. Many are converts to Eastern Orthodox Christianity. But others are traditionalist Catholics or ultraconservative Protestants whose ideas are nevertheless heavily influenced by the history and example of Byzantium and Orthodox Christianity.

The Orthosphere has an anachronistic understanding of Orthodox Christian history and the historical and theological schisms within Christianity. It is also mostly, although not exclusively, removed from ecclesiastical authority, pastoral oversight of priests and other church leaders and the lived experience of Orthodox Christian communities (Malone 2021). In some cases, Orthosphere actors align with the Russian Orthodox Church against the Ecumenical Patriarchate of Constantinople and other Eastern and Oriental Orthodox rites, a preference that evidences the influence over and cultivation of the transnational far right by the Russian Orthodox Church and the Russian state (Malone 2021, Riccardi-Swartz 2022).

Participants in the Orthosphere are self-described 'Christian reactionaries' who believe that modernity, as a basic anchor-point of contemporary Western civilization, has become 'corrosive' to traditionalist values and identities (Dyga 2014). In turn, the Orthosphere has been promoted as a new space to promote far-right ideas in the West that rely on the assertion and reinforcement of strong traditionalist moral, philosophical and spiritual doctrines.

Described as an 'exotic hothouse of alternative rightist tendencies' (Dyga 2014), the Orthosphere's rejection of modernity and contemporary society is a rejection of what its proponents call 'The Cathedral [...] the framework of educational institutions, the media-entertainment complex, major political parties' and accompanying progressive discourse and legislative overreach regarding social, political and cultural issues that frame 'everything traditionalists value as mere "social constructs" to be deconstructed at will' (Dyga 2014).

While their discourse is steeped in the language of spirituality and morality, self-described 'Orthos' acknowledge they are a political and ideological project. According to the Orthosphere *Throne and Altar* blog site:

> We recognize that the societies of the West are radically disordered, and it is our desire that they move toward a more proper order, one which acknowledges Christianity. Although we are Christians, our primary concern here is not with how individual souls are to be saved from the wrath of God, but rather with how society ought to be ordered.
>
> (Bonald n.d., see also Dawson, this volume)

One subset of the Orthosphere is the 'Orthobros', young to middle-aged men of the alt-right who have recently converted to Eastern Orthodoxy, either from other Western European Christian denominations or who have had no prior religious affiliation. These men spend their time challenging what they perceive as the prevailing modern secular and atheistic zeitgeist and what they view as evidence of the degeneracy of secular Western democratic countries. Their answer to addressing the supposed degeneracy of modernity is to valorize a return to the Byzantine Empire's Orthodox cultural and religious traditions – which they see as embodied in contemporary terms by Putin's Russia or the American far-right Trumpian movement – in order to 'save' civilization from the destruction wrought by the Enlightenment values responsible for modernity (Colavito 2017).

Orthobros not only take aim at social and political liberalism but also direct much of their commentary towards 'dunking on' Catholicism and Protestantism, re-enacting a contemporary manifestation of the historical legacy of competition and conquest between Rome and Constantinople, culminating in Christianity's Great Schism of 1054. Yet their embrace of modern digital technologies also sees them create content and perform online, championing the superiority of Eastern Orthodox Christianity by referencing and using a 'fashwave aesthetic' (Smith IV 2018) and the tropes, behaviours, memetic irony (Keen, Crawford and Suarez-Tangil 2020) and language of far-right online troll culture.

Orthobros and the manosphere

The Orthobros both emerge from and merge with the online manosphere. The manosphere (Ging 2019) is another online subculture that incorporates incels (involuntary celibates), men's rights advocates and pick-up artists (PUAs) who oppose feminism and espouse hateful attitudes towards women and often the LGBTQI community. The manosphere promotes an anti-feminist, grievance-fuelled masculinity that is pervaded with entitlement and bigotry (Sugiura 2021). Discourse within the manosphere can often also overlap with far-right sentiments, sharing similarly racist, antisemitic, anti-globalization, anti-immigration, homophobic views and authoritarian tendencies. Participation in the manosphere has been seen as a stepping-stone into other extreme far-right movements (Romano 2018), and there are multiple links between the manosphere and white supremacist and neo-Nazi movements (Southern Poverty Law Center n.d.b), an unsurprising feature given these movements' shared characteristics of misogyny and notions of male supremacy. The element within the manosphere that is more concerned with reinforcing patriarchal norms as a means to rectify the perceived societal takedown of cisgender men through feminism (Clark-Flory 2020) is the common point of intersection with the Orthosphere's promotion of a similar agenda.

Prominent 'Orthobro' figures include Jay Dyer, Roosh V, Brother Augustine and Norwegian Nous, all of whom associate with the far-right dimension of the manosphere and embed the promotion of patriarchy and authoritarianism within their discussion of Orthodox Christian theology and praxis. Websites like Patristic Faith feature their writings along with other Orthobro influencers. The conversion of prominent manosphere influencer Daryush Valizadeh, known online as 'Roosh V', is a prominent example of how the Orthosphere and the manosphere intersect. In his former life as a PUA, he advocated and justified rape, saying, 'No means no – until it means yes' (Southern Poverty Law Center n.d.c) and 'Make rape legal if done on private property' (Wellman 2015). Since his conversion, Valizadeh has publicly renounced his PUA identity in a statement on his blog and declared his baptism into ROCOR (Valizadeh 2021a).

Although Valizadeh may have renounced his PUA identity, his male supremacist views are still prevalent in his persona as a born-again Orthodox Christian. Though he now decries pick-up artistry, saying he used to 'make women God' and now shuns discussion and advocacy of casual sex, he has not explicitly renounced his previous male supremacist and misogynistic writings. Declaring that 'the manosphere had hit a dead end' (Valizadeh 2021b), he has instead found an alternative vehicle for his ideas through his involvement in the Orthosphere and its interpretation of Orthodoxy as a reactionary revolt against modernity and a pathway towards restoring male stature and authority.

Roosh V's conversion is not unique, nor is it a deviation from his radical trajectory as a male supremacist and reactionary. It is representative of a broader trend within the far right and the manosphere that has seen many far-right adherents embrace Eastern Orthodox Christianity as a bulwark to religiously justify their extremist ideologies.

Patriarchy, heteronormativity and anti-feminism in Orthodox Christianity

To understand the specific appeal of Christian Orthodoxy's patriarchal structures and gender norms for far-right actors within the Orthosphere, manosphere and white nationalist movements, it is necessary to understand their doctrinal and cultural underpinnings. Patriarchy applies quite literally to Orthodox Christian sects: they are all headed by male bishops, called Patriarchs, who are the head of each autocephalous church within the Orthodox communion (Kizenko 2013). Women are excluded from the critical fraternities of the priesthood, the monastery and from other clerical roles (e.g. acolytes or deacons), and thus from any official clerical leadership role.

Women in the Orthodox Church are more restricted in official positions than even those within the Catholic Church, where women may now serve as readers and assist as altar servers, as well as assisting priests in administering Holy Communion. There is no such dispensation for women in the Orthodox Churches. Referencing 1 Tim 2.12 – 'But I suffer not a woman to teach, nor to usurp authority over the man, but to be in silence' – women, as a rule, are not to raise their voice in Orthodox Churches, which excludes them from making readings from the Bible and delivering homilies (although there can be exceptions and variations within parishes).

Priesthood within the Orthodox Church remains an exclusively heteronormative male domain. Priests must (with rare exception) be married, cisgender and heterosexual. The clergy hold significant institutional power within the rigid hierarchy of the Orthodox churches. Obedience and the subsuming of personal desire are spiritual goals in Orthodox Christianity. Within the Orthodox Christian tradition, this obedience is understood to be first and foremost to God, but the priest is the earthly representative of God and therefore the congregation is expected to obey the priest's instructions and his divinely guided interpretation of scripture. Since only men can become priests in Eastern Orthodox churches, ultimate obedience to and authority on earth is therefore given to men alone.

Within the more intimate domestic sphere, men are enjoined as heads of household to be the 'priests', with the accompanying power and authority over their family. Marriage, again heteronormatively legitimated only between a man and woman, is viewed as a microcosm of the broader church and its relationship to the divine. Through marriage, men, representing Christ, are the divinely ordained heads of households, and women, representing the Church, as guided and nurtured through Christ's love and sacrifice, form the foundation of the Christian community.

The patriarchal role of men is reflected clearly in the marriage vows of Orthodox Christian rites where the authority of the husband is codified. Marriage vows include commands expressed in the Pauline epistle Eph. 5.22: 'Wives, submit to your husbands, as to the Lord.' Husbands are enjoined to 'love their wives as Christ so loved the Church', and wives to 'obey your husbands'. Unlike many Western Christian denominations, in which such enjoinments of women's obedience to men are no longer part of the wedding vows or can be excluded according to the preferences of the betrothed, marriage rites and vows made in Orthodox churches, like all other rites, cannot be altered. Such beliefs and praxis reinforce male authority within the Orthodox Christian tradition and the Orthosphere, white nationalists and other far-right converts tend to emphasize the hierarchy and privilege such authority grants to men, rather than the deeper, genderless teachings of spiritual discipline and obedience.

They also ignore the teaching of many Church fathers who emphasize the message embedded within the marriage vows of loving mutual responsibility rather than hierarchal gender-based roles, ignoring the part of the Pauline epistle in which men are commanded to 'love their own wives as their own bodies; he who loves his wife loves himself. For no one ever hated his own flesh, but nourishes and cherishes it, just as the Lord does the church. For we are members of His body' (Eph. 5.28-30). Orthodox Christianity includes those who advocate for a reformed interpretation of the marriage vows and the Church's teachings around gender roles (Vrame 2008). And in practice there are deviations from, variances in individual attitudes and nuances and negotiations around the issue of priestly and male obedience within parishes and families. However, despite these differences in orthopraxy, obedience to the priest and to male heads of household continues to prevail within mainstream interpretation and the institutional position of the Orthodox churches on gender roles (Vrame 2008, Bringerud 2019).

Such restrictions on women and insistence on the primacy of men are not only evident in Orthodox belief and praxis around the priesthood and marriage but also reflected in the gendered organization of physical space of the churches (McDowell 2013); while not always strictly adhered to in some parishes, traditionally men and women sit on separate sides of the church during services. Women are expected to dress modestly and cover their hair while in attendance at church (as is common in many other religious traditions). Women are not only barred from formal positions within the Orthodox Church; due to their purported 'nature and sexuality and bodily functions' (Keinänen 2010), their participation in official ceremonies is also restricted. The Orthodox Church follows ancient Judaic practices around the sanctity of the tabernacle, which restricts women from entering the altar behind the *iconostasis* and does not allow them to receive communion while menstruating or for a set period after childbirth. This explicit exclusion and proscription of women is appealing to elements of the far right because it reinforces the privileges of men and emphasizes essentialist gender roles and norms. Humility and modesty are important practices that shepherd the believer towards holiness within Orthodox Christianity, but these values are especially emphasized for women. Because their modesty is strongly emphasized and their official role in church life is limited, this codifies and theologically justifies that position that women should hold a secondary or separate status (Vrame 2008).

For reactionary right actors and male supremacists, such canonical proscriptions against women's participation, the emphasis on their obedience and the preservation of exclusively male roles are highly appealing. Far-right converts focus on this model of divinely sanctioned male power. This religious exposition provides justification for their anti-feminist and male supremacist political and ideological goals. Eastern Orthodox Christianity offers them a useful bulwark against other Western Protestant and Anglican denominations which have expanded the role of women in the clergy and official leadership positions. This is a very palatable construct for far-right male converts, who tend to gloss over the differences in orthopraxy within Orthodox Christian communities, the negotiations around these constructs among many Orthodox Christianity adherents, and the 'vernacular theology' that has allowed women substantive roles and meaningful experiences within the Church (Keinänen 2010, Kizenko 2013, Bringerud 2019).

It is also attractive to the far right because not only does the Orthodox Christian tradition believe that gender roles and authority are divinely ordained but because within the Orthodox Church it is easier to derive additional authority as a member of the clergy. Becoming a priest in Eastern Orthodox churches does not require celibacy as does the Catholic Church; in fact, priests are required to be married with families. Bishops, however, must be celibate and rise up through the ranks of monks.

For Orthodox converts from the manosphere in particular, Orthodox Christianity offers them two avenues of power and agency. For those more motivated by the hierarchy of men over women and restoring male authority, they can turn to the Orthodox priesthood and the authority of the male head of household. For those who are obsessed with their own celibacy, such as incels, they can find power in the Orthodox tradition of monasticism and the emphasis on virginity and celibacy. Rather than a source of shame or enfeeblement, virginity and asexuality are symbolic of holiness within the Orthodox tradition (Bringerud 2019). The two most revered and holy figures in Orthodox Christianity – Jesus (God) and his mother Mary (the *Theotokos*, or the God bearer) – are virgins in Orthodox theology. The figures who hold the highest authority in the church are celibate monks and bishops. Orthodox Christianity offers a model of masculinity removed from sexual prowess or procreation which can be highly appealing for the incel faction of the manosphere. In Orthodox Christianity, a man who does not engage in sexual activities is considered to be a more pure and holy representative of the Father; such men can 'become representatives for the ultimate human potential for godliness' (Bringerud 2019). Sexual relations are also prohibited before marriage, and sexual desire is viewed as something to be conquered and overcome as an aspect of discipline and obedience in Orthodoxy. This aligns with the manosphere's preoccupations around controlling their sexuality and sexual desire (similar to the abstinence from sex promoted by far-right movements) as a means to male empowerment (Burnett 2021).

Ethnicity, anti-globalization and anti-Western expression

Eastern Orthodoxy is also a mode of Christianity where spirituality is suffused with identity, ethnicity and cultural heritage. The Orthodox communion's autocephalous, decentralized churches are traditionally organized along national or ethnic lines. The declaration of phyletism as a heresy did not prohibit the churches from solidifying their own ethnic characters. From their very descriptors – for example, the *Greek* Orthodox Church, the *Russian* Orthodox, *Serbian* Orthodox or *Coptic* Orthodox Church – their religious praxis is inexorably tied to their ethnic and national cultures, histories and identity. It is beyond the scope of this chapter to go into a detailed examination of Church history and the complex relationship between nationality and Orthodox Christianity. I note here, however, that ethnic identity is deeply embedded in and informs religious rituals and practices (Oddie 2012). Religious identity and national identity and politics are often deeply intertwined (Bringerud 2019).

The Byzantine Empire was a theocracy of Orthodox Christianity (Papanikolaou 2003), but it was after the fall of Constantinople and under the Ottoman Empire's millet system that ethnicity and Orthodox religion became more intertwined. Under the Ottoman Empire, the Orthodox Church was used as an administrative unit.

Patriarchs became not only the spiritual leaders of their congregations but were made political and civil leaders who had jurisdictional authority over Christians under the Ottomans (Ware 1997, Papadakis 1988). This allowed Christianity to survive under Ottoman rule, but it also made it 'nearly impossible to separate the civic from the spiritual' (Bringerud 2019).

When the Ottoman Empire collapsed, giving rise to smaller nation-state, many of them united behind a vision of Orthodox Christianity as a marker of national identity (Ware 1997). This led to the development of 'political Orthodox Christianity', which connotes religious practice in the service of ethnopolitical identity (Skedros 2016). During the emergence of nation-states among communities in the former territories of Byzantium and the Ottoman Empire, Orthodox Christianity, intertwined with ethnicity, was used as a means of nation-building. To practice and defend Orthodox Christianity was simultaneously to practice and defend one's ethnic and/or national identity (Bringerud 2019).

This history is now being referenced and aspired to by far-right converts to Orthodox Christianity, and particularly by white supremacists, as a historical and alternative model of nationality and citizenship to the current model of pluralistic nationality in Western democracies based on allegiance to a set of ideas and principles rather than to national or ethnic sameness. The far right has valorized the historical development of Eastern Orthodoxy along ethnic lines, and the enmeshment of Orthodoxy and nationalism, as a model to oppose what they see as the corrupt and degenerate pluralism and multiculturalism of Western democracies and to 'protect' the white nation. As Katherine Kelaidis (2017) writes, 'While this system of ecclesiastical governance predates by centuries modern concepts of race and nationalism, for a nationalist steeped in the rhetoric of racial separatism, it is impossible not to see a reflection of separatist beliefs' and an 'endorsement of their views.'

Orthodox Christianity's history of religious practice tied to ethnically based communities also appeals to far-right actors who desire the creation of their own exclusivist ethnically based communities. Whether Orthodox converts or not, many on the far right believe, as one anonymous poster on a far-right forum writes:

> At the end of the day, the countries who have Orthodox populations have remained more racially and culturally sound than the nations with no religion or, worse, Protestantism. The Orthodox base is a major reason why Greeks, Russians and Serbs understand the Jewish question far better than any member of your college Atheists club.
>
> (cited in Phillips 2014)

Similarly, the American far-right Orthodox convert Matthew Heimbach, discussed above, has used the history of the Christian Orthodox church to justify and promote his separatism and white nationalism (Hunter 2015), arguing that Orthodoxy can be used as a model for the ethnic self-determination of all races, not just the white race:

> I converted to the Orthodox Church because it theologically in my opinion is the superior Church. Through apostolic succession the Church has remained true to

the principles of the disciples and the founding of our Faith. White nationalism can be labelled [...] [as] an extension of an overall umbrella that respects our regional and ethnic heritage. [...] As an Orthodox Christian I believe in the separation of races into ethnically based Church's [sic]. That is why even in Orthodoxy there is for instance a Greek, Russian, Romanian, Serbian, etc. Orthodox Church. Regional and racial identity is a fundamental principle of Christianity, much to the dismay of Leftists. I believe black Christians should be in their black Church's [sic], with black priests, having black kids, going to black Christian schools, etc.

(Heimbach 2013)

Heimbach (2013) not only seeks to appropriate Orthodoxy for the protection of white identity in general but considers the preservation of what he sees as a very specific regional subcultural identity: 'Southerners have a very distinct culture, and to be able to dream of an autocephalous Dixie Church would be amazing.' He has acknowledged the significant inspiration he has derived for his views from Corneliu Zelea Codreanu, a Romanian fascist figure who in 1927 founded the Legion of the Archangel Michael (also known as the Legionnaires), a violent ultranationalist and antisemitic organization that mixed fascism with a mystical Romanian Orthodox revolutionary message. Codreanu and the Legionnaires utilized religious symbolism, Orthodox Christian theology and morality to shape a movement meant to counteract the modernization, democracy and 'Judeo-Bolshevism' they believed were tarnishing an otherwise rural and morally pure nationality in Romania (Haynes 2008).

Concluding remarks

The conversion by white nationalists, male supremacists, manosphere influencers and other far-right extremist actors to Orthodox Christianity fulfils a broader need or a 'spiritual hunger' and meaning that mere ideology and political advocacy seemingly cannot satisfy for this cohort (Burton 2019). Yet while Orthodoxy may fill a spiritual yearning, it can also be used to justify, actualize and sustain the political and ideological positions of the far right. Traditionalist religions like Orthodox Christianity are being conscripted by the far right because they assess their political efforts to be insufficient or faltering. They need a spiritual movement to sustain their political and ideological battles. In this way the far right's embrace integrates the spiritual and the political. It is emblematic of the recognition by far-right converts to Christian Orthodoxy that religion can play an important role in the creation of social categories and identities, including ethnic and racial constructions, the acceptance and justification of gender norms, and the reinforcement of ideological beliefs.

In addition to Orthodox Christianity's appeal as a model for exclusivist ethnically based communities and the structure of strong patriarchy to uphold male authority and 'family values', its perceived value lies in its attractiveness for the far right as an anti-democratic, anti-liberal bulwark against the decadence and weakness of liberal modernity. It is this combined appeal of the solace of the traditional and the exoticism of the unfamiliar – something at once old and new that hearkens back to a perceived historical authenticity that can nevertheless be practised and lived in the modern era – that make of conversion to Orthodoxy a countercultural, even revolutionary, form of expression and resistance for far-right actors. Far-right converts have made and are likely to continue to make a deep ideological and cultural investment in what they perceive as Orthodox Christianity's timelessness, tradition and authentic expression of Christianity – unblemished due to its stubborn and staunch opposition to change and modernity – coupled with its commitment to hierarchy, patriarchy and its example of community based on ethnic identity.

References

Alexopoulos, S. and M. E. Johnson (2021), *Introduction to Eastern Christian Liturgies*. Collegeville, MN: Liturgical Press.

Bonald (n.d.), *Throne and Altar*. Available online: https://bonald.wordpress.com (accessed 6 October 2022).

Bringerud, L. (2019), *Whose Tradition? Adapting Orthodox Christianity in North America*, PhD diss., Memorial University of Newfoundland. Available online: https://research.library.mun.ca/13907/ (accessed 6 October 2022).

Brook, B. (2017), 'Claims Parishioners Were "Screamed at" by Anti-Same-Sex Marriage Priest Who Demanded His Flock All Vote No', *news.com.au*, 6 September. Available online: https://www.news.com.au/lifestyle/gay-marriage/claims-parishioners-were-screamed-at-by-antisamesex-marriage-priest-who-demanded-his-flock-all-vote-no/news-story/b800c05f41b435322e87ab15faaf8adc (accessed 6 October 2022).

Burnett, S. (2021), 'The Battle for "NoFap": Myths, Masculinity, and the Meaning of Masturbation Abstention', *Men and Masculinities*, 25 (3): 477–496. https://doi.org/10.1177/1097184X211018256.

Burton, T. I. (2019), 'A Notorious Pickup Artist Found God. Lots of Angry White Radicals Do', *Washington Post*, 31 May. Available online: https://www.washingtonpost.com/outlook/a-notorious-pickup-artist-found-god-lots-of-angry-white-radicals-do/2019/05/30/8f009d24-8237-11e9-9a67-a687ca99fb3d_story.html (accessed 6 October 2022).

Butt, S. and D. Byman (2020), 'Right-Wing Extremism: The Russian Connection', *Survival*, 62 (2): 137–52, https://doi.org/10.1080/00396338.2020.1739960.

Clark-Flory, T. (2020), 'The Manosphere's Existential Crisis Is Building the Future of the Far Right', *Jezebel*, 13 October. Available online: https://jezebel.com/the-manospheres-existential-crisis-is-building-the-futu-1844673454 (accessed 6 October 2022).

Colavito, J. (2017), 'Orthodox Christian Occult Conspiracy Theorist Boards Trump Train, Calls for Rejection of the Enlightenment and the Establishment of Autocracy', *JasonColavito*, 10 February. Available online: https://www.jasoncolavito.com/blog/orthodox-christian-occult-conspiracy-theorist-boards-trump-train-calls-for-a-rejection-of-the-enlightenment-and-the-establishment-of-autocracy (accessed 6 October 2022).

Cottrell, B. (2020), 'XYZ Conference Night 5 with Speaker Blair Cottrell', *XYZ Conference*, 4 July. Available online: https://www.bitchute.com/channel/JVQ25NiUKd9s/ (accessed 6 October 2022).

Davis, N. and R. Robinson (1996), 'Religious Orthodoxy in American Society: The Myth of a Monolithic Camp', *Journal for the Scientific Study of Religion*, 35 (3): 229–45, https://doi.org/10.2307/1386553.

Dogpatch Press Staff (2022), 'The Fascist Fringe of Fury Fans: The Eastern Orthodox Connection', *Dogpatch Press*, 9 March. Available online: https://dogpatch.press/2022/03/09/fascist-fringe-eastern-orthodox/ (accessed 6 October 2022).

Dyga, E. (2014), 'The Future of Australian Conservatism', *Quadrant Online*, 14 October. Available online: https://quadrant.org.au/magazine/2014/10/future-australian-conservatism/ (accessed 8 October 2022).

Eisinga, R., R. Konig and P. Scheepers (1995), 'Orthodox Religious Beliefs and Antisemitism: A Replication of Glock and Stark in the Netherlands', *Journal for the Scientific Study of Religion*, 34 (2): 214–23. Available online: https://www.jstor.org/stable/1386766 (accessed 6 October 2022).

Feuer, A. and A. Higgins (2016), 'Extremists Turn to a Leader to Protect Western Values: Vladimir Putin', *New York Times*, 3 December. Available online: https://www.nytimes.com/2016/12/03/world/americas/alt-right-vladimir-putin.html (accessed 6 October 2022).

Ging, D. (2019), 'Alphas, Betas, and Incels: Theorizing the Masculinities of the Manosphere', *Men and Masculinities*, 22 (4): 638–57.

Haynes, R. (2008), 'Work Camps, Commerce, and the Education of the "New Man" in the Romanian Legionary Movement', *The Historical Journal*, 51 (4): 943–67, http://www.jstor.org/stable/20175210.

Heim, J. (2016), 'This White Nationalist Who Shoved a Donald Trump Protester May Be the Next David Duke', *Washington Post*, 12 April. Available online: https://www.washingtonpost.com/local/this-white-nationalist-who-shoved-a-trump-protester-may-be-the-next-david-duke/2016/04/12/7e71f750-f2cf-11e5-89c3-a647fcce95e0_story.html (accessed 6 October 2022).

Heimbach, M. (2013), 'Matthew Heimbach at American Freedom Conference – Comments Section', *Occidental Dissident*, 16 July. Available online: http://occidentaldissent.com/2013/07/13/matthew-heimbach-at-american-freedom-conference/comment-page-2/ (accessed 6 October 2022).

Herbel, O. (2014), *Turning to Tradition: Converts and the Making of the American Orthodox Church*. Oxford: Oxford University Press.

Hunter, R. (2015), 'My Interview with Matthew Heimbach', *Orthodox in the District: Living the Ancient Faith in the Nation's Capital*, 26 June. Available online: https://ryanphunter.wordpress.com/2015/06/26/my-interview-with-matthew-heimbach/ (accessed 6 October 2022).

Johnson, M. (2018), 'The Orthodox Nationalist: A Statement Concerning the Necessity of Racism', *Radio Albion*, 7 March. Available online: https://www.radioalbion.com/2018/03/the-orthodox-nationalist-statement.html (accessed 6 October 2022).

Keen, F., B. Crawford and G. Suarez-Tangil (2020), *Memetic Irony and the Promotion of Violence within Chan Cultures*. Lancaster: Centre for Research and Evidence on Security Threats (CREST). Available online: https://crestresearch.ac.uk/resources/memetic-irony-and-the-promotion-of-violence-within-chan-cultures/ (accessed 14 October 2024).

Keinänen, M. L. (2010), 'The Home, the Sacred Order and Domestic Chores in PremodernRussian Orthodox Karelia', in M. L. Keinänen (ed), *Perspectives on Women's Everyday Religion*, 119–54, Stockholm: Acta Universitatis Stockholmiensis. Available online: https://www.diva-portal.org/smash/get/diva2:332100/FULLTEXT01.pdf (accessed 6 October 2022).

Kelaidis, K. (2016), 'How Orthodox Christianity Became the Spiritual Home of White Nationalism', *Religious Dispatches*, 30 November. Available online: https://religiondispatches.org/how-orthodox-christianity-became-the-spiritual-home-of-white-nationalism/ (accessed 6 October 2022).

Kelaidis, K. (2017), 'White Supremacy and Orthodox Christianity: A Dangerous Connection Rears Its Head in Charlottesville', *Religious Dispatches*, 18 August. Available online: https://religiondispatches.org/white-supremacy-and-orthodox-christianity-a-dangerous-connection-rears-its-head-in-charlottesville/ (accessed 6 October 2022).

Kelaidis, K. (2018), 'The Potentially Explosive Russian Church Intrigue Revealed by Mueller Investigation', *Religious Dispatches*, 29 August. Available online: https://religiondispatches.org/the-potentially-explosive-russian-church-intrigue-revealed-by-mueller-investigation/ (accessed 6 October 2022).

Kelaidis, K. (2019), 'Orthodoxy's Extremist Appeal', *Orthodox Christian Laity*, 18 May. Available online: https://ocl.org/orthodoxys-extremist-appeal/ (accessed 6 October 2022).

Kizenko, N. (2013), 'Feminized Patriarchy? Orthodoxy and Gender in Post-Soviet Russia', *Signs*, 38 (3): 595–621, https://doi.org/10.1086/668516.

Leonova, I. (2017), 'Deafening Silence', *Public Orthodoxy*, 16 August. Available online: https://publicorthodoxy.org/2017/08/16/deafening-silence/#more-3323 (accessed 8 October 2022).

Leonova, I. (2019), 'Orthodox and White?', *The Wheel*, 17. Available online: https://static1.squarespace.com/static/54d0df1ee4b036ef1e44b144/t/5d40a034c1dd0200013aee6b/1564516409084/Wheel17_Ch5_Leonova.pdf (accessed 6 October 2022).

Lukasik, C. (2021), 'Economy of Blood: The Persecuted Church and the Radicalization of American Copts', *American Anthropologist*, 23 (3): 565–77, https://doi.org/10.1111/aman.13602.

Malone, V. (2021), 'Welcome to the Orthosphere (Orthobros Gone Wild)', Street Level Apologist – Vocab Malone YouTube Channel, 5 August. https://www.youtube.com/watch?v=abW2Aa2oSKg (accessed 6 October 2022).

McDowell, M. G. (2013), 'Seeing Gender: Orthodox Liturgy, Orthodox Personhood, Unorthodox Exclusion', *Journal of the Society of Christian Ethics*, 33 (2): 73–92.

Moreton, B. (2022), 'The U.S. Christians Who Pray for Putin', *Boston Review*, 11 March. Available online: https://bostonreview.net/articles/the-u-s-christians-who-pray-for-putin/ (accessed 6 October 2022).

Oddie, M. (2012), 'The Relationship of Religion and the Ethnic Nationalism in Bosnia-Herzegovina', *Occasional Papers on Religion in Eastern Europe*, 32 (1), https://digitalcommons.georgefox.edu/ree/vol32/iss1/3.

Orthodox Christian Clergy against Racism (2018), 'A Statement Concerning the Sin of Racism', *Orthodox Clergy Blogspot*, 27 February. Available online: https://orthodoxclergy.blogspot.com/2018/02/a-statement-concerning-sin-of-racism.html (accessed 6 October 2022).

Orthodoxy in Dialogue (2018a), 'White Supremacy in the American Orthodox Church: An Open Letter to the Assembly of Canonical Orthodox Bishops of the United States of America', 22 January, *Orthodoxy in Dialogue*. Available online: https://orthodoxyindialogue.com/2018/01/22/white-supremacy-in-the-american-orthodox-church-an-open-letter-to-the-assembly-of-canonical-orthodox-bishops-of-the-united-states-of-america/ (accessed 6 October 2022).

Orthodoxy in Dialogue (2018b), 'A Response to the Orthodox Clergy Condemnation of Nationalism by Matthew Raphael Johnson', *Orthodoxy in Dialogue*, 10 March. Available online: https://orthodoxyindialogue.com/2018/03/10/a-response-to-the-orthodox-clergy-condemnation-of-nationalism-by-matthew-raphael-johnson/ (accessed 8 October 2022).

Papadakis, A. (1988), 'The Historical Tradition of Church-State Relations Under Orthodoxy', in P. Ramet (ed), *Eastern Christianity and Politics in the Twentieth Century*, 37–58, Durham, NC: Duke University Press.

Papanikolaou, A. (2003), 'Byzantium, Orthodoxy, and Democracy', *Journal of the American Academy of Religion*, 71 (1): 75–98, http://www.jstor.org/stable/1466304.

Phillips, J. (2014), 'East of Eden', *SPLC Intelligence Report*, 21 November. Available online: https://www.splcenter.org/fighting-hate/intelligence-report/2014/east-eden (accessed 6 October 2022).

Riccardi-Swartz, S. (2022), *Between Heaven and Russia: Religious Conversion and Political Apostasy in Appalachia*. New York: Fordham University Press.

Romano, A. (2018), 'How the Alt-Right's Sexism Lures Men into White Supremacy', *Vox*, 26 April. Available online: https://www.vox.com/culture/2016/12/14/13576192/alt-right-sexism-recruitment (accessed 6 October 2022).

Rusijournal.org (n.d.), 'The Russian Orthodox Medievalist'. Available online: https://www.rusjournal.org/ (accessed 6 October 2022).

Sedgwick, M. (2004), *Against the Modern World: Traditionalism and the Secret Intellectual History of the Twentieth Century*. New York: Oxford University Press.

Sellanraa, S. (2012), 'The Rise of the Orthos', *The Brussels Journal*, 21 January. Available online: https://www.brusselsjournal.com/node/4904 (accessed 6 October 2022).

Skedros, J. C. (2016), 'You Cannot Have a Church without an Empire: Political Orthodoxy in Byzantium', in G. E. Demacopoulos and A. Papanikolaou (eds), *Christianity, Democracy, and the Shadow of Constantine*, 219–31, New York: Fordham University Press.

Slagle, A. (2011), *The Eastern Church in the Spiritual Marketplace: American Conversions to Orthodox Christianity*. DeKalb: Northern Illinois University Press.

Smith IV, J. (2018), 'This Is Fashwave, the Suicidal Retro-Futurist Art of the Alt-Right', *MIC*, 13 January. Available online: https://www.mic.com/articles/187379/this-is-fashwave-the-suicidal-retro-futurist-art-of-the-alt-right (accessed 6 October 2022).

Southern Poverty Law Centre (SPLC) (n.d.a), 'Matthew Heimbach', Available online: https://www.splcenter.org/fighting-hate/extremist-files/individual/matthew-heimbach (accessed 6 October 2022).

Southern Poverty Law Centre (n.d.b), 'Male Supremacy'. Available online: https://www.splcenter.org/fighting-hate/extremist-files/ideology/male-supremacy (accessed 6 October 2022).

Southern Poverty Law Centre (n.d.c), 'Daryush "Roosh" Valizadeh'. Available online: https://www.splcenter.org/fighting-hate/extremist-files/individual/daryush-roosh-valizadeh (accessed 6 October 2022).

Stewart, C. (2021), 'Priest with Ties to Area Parish Suspended after Urging, Joining U.S. Capitol Protest', *Dayton Daily News*, 21 January. Available online: https://www.daytondailynews.com/news/priest-with-ties-to-area-parish-suspended-after-urging-joining-us-capitol-protest/X4OZS43MG5EORKAXGULZCTRFJM/ (accessed 6 October 2022).

Stoeckl, K. (2020), 'The Rise of the Russian Christian Right: The Case of the World Congress of Families', *Religion, State and Society*, 48 (4): 223–38.

Sugiura, L. (2021), *The Incel Rebellion: The Rise of the Manosphere and the Virtual War Against Women*. Bingley: Emerald Publishing.

Teitelbaum, B. (2020), *The War for Eternity: The Return of Traditionalism and the Rise of the Populist*. London: Allen Lane Press.

Valizadeh, R. (2021a), 'Why I Left the Armenian Church for ROCOR', *RooshV.com*, 31 May. Available online: https://www.rooshv.com/why-i-left-the-armenian-church-for-rocor (accessed 6 October 2022).

Valizadeh, R. (2021b), 'The Rise of the Orthosphere', *RooshV.com*, 12 July. Available online: https://www.rooshv.com/the-rise-of-the-orthosphere (accessed 6 October 2022).

Vrame, A. (2008), 'Four Types of "Orthopraxy" Among Orthodox Christians in North America', in A. Papanikolaou and E. Prodromou (eds), *Thinking through Faith: New Perspectives from Orthodox Christians Scholars*, 279–307, Crestwood, NY: St. Vladimir's Seminary Press.

Ware, T. (1997), *The Orthodox Church*. London: Penguin.

Wellman, A. (2015), '"Make Rape Legal on Private Property": Shock "Call" from Self-Styled Pick-up Guru', *Mirror Online*, 19 February. Available online: https://www.mirror.co.uk/news/uk-news/roosh-v-make-rape-legal-5193802 (accessed 6 October 2022).

Yousef, O. (2022), 'Orthodox Christian Churches Are Drawing in Far-Right American Converts', *National Public Radio*, 10 May. Available online: https://www.npr.org/2022/05/10/1096741988/orthodox-christian-churches-are-drawing-in-far-right-american-converts (accessed 6 October 2022).

13

Preparing for Day X: Looking into Germany's extreme right-wing radicalization

Frederic Heine and Tina Magazzini

Introduction

Over the past decade Germany has not been spared from the increase in religiously inspired violent attacks that have taken place in Europe more generally. Yet these violent incidents have not yielded death tolls of the same magnitude from such attacks as those experienced by other European countries in Western Europe (Sealy and Magazzini 2025). Overall, Germany experienced fewer than twenty domestic casualties as a result of Islamist terrorist attacks between 2001 and 2022 (Brost et al. 2022). In 2022 the country reported zero attacks classed as 'jihadist', although thirty persons suspected of involvement in terrorist offences were arrested that same year, (Europol 2023).

In parallel, however, an increasingly worrisome phenomenon has been that of far-right extremism targeting religious minorities. The shooting at a shisha-bar in Hanau in February 2020 was only the most sensational of a series of attacks against minorities, and right-wing violence has long been downplayed and understudied, despite being identified by academics and practitioners as the most important form of radicalization in Germany. In line with the focus of this volume, this chapter examines right-wing attacks in Germany aimed at religious communities and racialized minorities. Such attacks have been acknowledged as the main domestic threat in recent years by both the domestic intelligence service (Bundesamt für Verfassungsschutz, the main agency gathering intelligence on extremism) and by Germany's former interior minister Horst Seehofer (VOA 2020), reinforced by the fact that by international comparison Germany represents 'the country in Western Europe with the highest level of RTV (Right-Wing Terrorism and Violence)' (Ravndal et al. 2020: 17).

In order to explore the development of Germany's far-right violent radicalization, we first look into the ways in which radicalization and extremism are employed in the German context, making the case for including far-right violent radicalization within the frame of religiously inspired radicalization. We then focus on two case studies which can be seen as landmarks in this type of violence: the attack on the synagogue in Halle on 9 October 2019, and the shootings of February 2020 in Hanau. We then try to unpack the main drivers of these attacks by grouping them in terms of the macro-, meso- and micro-dynamics at play (Magazzini et al. 2024). What emerges is a complex picture in which unresolved aspects of Germany's past are intertwined with the fears and 'othering' of newer generations towards newcomers.

In so doing, we draw significantly on conceptual and empirical research conducted within the framework of the EU Horizon 2020 GREASE project on radicalization, secularism and the governance of religion, drawing on both desk research and ten semi-structured interviews with twelve individuals conducted in 2020. The Hanau attack on 19 February 2020 occurred during fieldwork, with only two interviews conducted after the event. While the fieldwork was conducted in order to answer a broader set of questions, including appropriate strategies of deradicalization, in this chapter we are interested specifically in the question of how practitioners explained the escalation of right-wing terrorism in Germany against the backdrop of their specific practical expertise. We found that the combination of their specific sensitivities and perspectives, when viewed in the context of existing literature and also the specifics of the cases in question, add up to a tentative 'bigger picture' of the causes that lie beneath the escalation of violence.

Data was collected from interviewees selected to reflect a range of stakeholders with different perspectives and experiences on issues of radicalization, prevention and deradicalization. Key stakeholders therefore include researchers/analysts (Interviews 2, 3, 4), law enforcement (Interview 9), state administration (Interviews 7, 8) and civil society organizations (CSOs) (Interviews 1, 3, 5, 6, 10), including two organizations run by and for religious/ethnic minorities (Interviews 5, 10). In the German case, the perspective of civil society organizations is particularly prominent since there is a long tradition and great variety of civil society organization involvement in countering the far right.

Conceptualizations of radicalization and extremism

The notion of 'radicalization' has enjoyed alternate success in Germany, while the most widely employed term traditionally used to describe both right- and left-wing radicalism was 'extremism'. The concept of 'extremism' sought to capture different political movements and ideologies under one umbrella term, and it was employed until recently in official policies to describe a tendency towards a totalitarian ideology, in opposition to a (fictional) 'democratic centre' represented by the German constitution (Jesse and Mannewitz 2018). With 'extremism' being framed in opposition to the democratic-constitutional state, it is not surprising that this notion has mostly been used by the German Federal Office for the Protection of the Constitution (Bundesamt für Verfassungsschutz – hereafter VS) (Wippermann 2010), an intelligence agency that gathers information on political threats to the constitution and reports to the Ministry of the Interior.

Even though from its inception in 1950 the VS used the term 'radical' and only started to use 'extremism' in 1973 (Wippermann 2010), the rationale for the shift was that using 'radical' posed the problem that political ideologies came under the radar of the VS simply because they sought to tackle social issues at their 'roots', whereas 'extremism' had an alleged clearer definition of being 'on the fringes' of politics and in opposition to the constitution. In this context, 'Islamism' entered the debate as a 'new' threat to the German constitution in the early 2000s and has been framed as another expression of extremism in national debates, while the notion of radicalization gained currency at the international level in the aftermath of 9/11.

However, the VS's usage of 'extremism' has generated its own set of critiques: on the one hand, it has been argued that opposition to the constitution per se, in the absence of political violence, can end up framing as 'extreme' those groups or individuals who simply oppose a narrowly defined political centre, but who should not be placed under security surveillance. The fact that it is the VS itself that defines which views are 'extreme' has serious practical implications: the label 'extreme', like the label 'radical', still allows for vast discretion on the part of the VS. For example, members of the left-wing party Die Linke was deemed 'extreme' and kept under observation by the VS from its formation in 2007 until 2014, yet the right-wing populist party AfD (Alternative for Germany) was only recently – in the state of Thuringia (2019) and then federally (2019) – included in the list of groups deemed to hold 'extreme views'. This should not, however, be interpreted as a sign that far-right violence is a novel phenomenon:

> Right wing extremism is the core of all forms of extremism in Germany. It is historically the core, it's the sort of extremism that I would call domestic. Ironically the term of 'homegrown' radicalization, usually used for Muslim individuals radicalized in Germany, is very fitting for right-wing radicalization, for the neo-Nazi substance that we have and have always had, also in 60s, 70s, 80s, from the Munich Oktoberfest bombing and the whole cover-up around that. We have a profound tradition of right-wing extremism after the war and outright terrorism also, which at the time was in line with the Red Army Faction, just not reported on.
> (Interview 1, CSO)

Applying the notion of 'religiously inspired radicalization' to the far right

It is in part because of the shortcomings of the 'extremism' framework in Germany that scholars and practitioners have in recent years embraced the concept of radicalization, even though differences exist between state institutions and civil society, as well as between state institutions in different federal states.

Perhaps the most significant difference is that the intelligence and law enforcement agencies tend to approach radicalization through the prism of extremism, with the key operational criteria being a 'law and order' position interested in the occurrence of violence and crime (law enforcement) or the 'protection of the constitution' (domestic intelligence service), while academia and civil society actors tend to adopt a 'pedagogical preventive position'. An analyst from a civil society organization commented:

> In my experience, there's a lot of horseshoe theory, equating right and left-wing extremism and exculpating the centre, which is something that academia and civil society don't share, that they don't buy into. For instance, the centre study

[cf. Zick et al. 2019] shows very well that racism is very spread in the centre. And that the difference between right-wing extremism and left-wing is very stark.

A key debate around radicalization involves the opposition between a conservative, law-and-order-focused concept that identifies with the political-cultural centre of society, and a more left-wing concept that emphasizes the continuities between political centrist discourses and radicalized movements and actions, thereby problematizing the political centre.

However, as the result of the escalation of right-wing terrorism, there has been an increased recognition of the need for collaboration between state institutions and civil society actors, leading to an approximation of conceptualizations over recent years (Interviews 2, 3, 6, 8, 9). Even though no consensus has been reached on a definition of radicalization that can be applied uniformly, recent academic scholarship employs the notion to describe processes that can lead from affinity with certain ideas to terrorist acts (Neumann 2013a, Malthaner 2017, Zick 2017, Quent 2019). Radicalization is sometimes discussed in relationship to extremism, with some authors defining radicalization as a 'process through which individuals or groups become extremists' (Neumann 2013b, Knipping-Sorokin Stumpf and Koch 2016, Abou-Taam et al. 2019). Within these traditions, scholars make differences between 'cognitive radicalization', or radicalization of beliefs, and behavioural radicalization (Neumann 2013b, Malthaner 2017). The key element of behavioural radicalization is that of violence, with recent research suggesting a differentiation between radicalization without violence, into violence, and within violence (Abay Gaspar et al. 2018), without normatively problematizing all aspects of radicalization without violence per se.

However, in civil society, the notion of radicalization – associated with a particular emphasis on individual events – is not without its critics:

> I don't call it radicalization, actually, I call it 'violent extremism'. Because the radicalization concept is problematic. One thing that could be helpful for European discourse is the German concept of 'hatred': the precise term is 'group-focused enmity' [Gruppenbezogene Menschenfeindlichkeit cf. Zick et al. 2008], hostility and aggression towards groups. […] If I were to explain what that is, it is about aggressive prejudices towards foreigners, anti-diversity, antisemitism or anti-LGBT opinions and attitudes; elements of social Darwinism, hostility towards those perceived as weak. […] But all extremist ideologies resemble each other and coincide in basic traits: devaluation of a group of others, strong black and white thinking, and this is the core of it.
>
> (Interview 1, CSO)

In official documents, state institutions tend to use the notion of 'politically motivated crime' to refer to radicalization, and always differentiate between right-wing, left-wing and Islamist-motivated crimes (which is the terminology used by the police) and ideologies (the term used by the VS). While there has been a recent shift towards the concept of 'hate crime', the counterterrorism apparatus is still largely organized around the concept of the perpetrator acting 'for a cause' rather than 'against someone' (such as a minority, a religious community, etc.), which would require adopting the perspective of the victim as the defining criteria for the categorization of the act. Some members of minority groups challenge the usefulness of this approach, claiming that it is important to acknowledge the religious identity of the victims of Islamophobic attacks:

> The right-wingers have a very clear ideological goal of Islam as an enemy to be fought. […] I'm emphasizing this not because I'm somehow 'greedy' for a role as a victim. But the main targets of the racist attacks taking place are Muslims; the main target is Islam. That's a fact. Pegida [Patriotic Europeans Against the Islamicization of the Occident] could only grow as much as it did by claiming to 'prevent the Islamization of the occident'. The AfD has in its main programme that Islam is not a religion but an ideology and has therefore to be fought. […] And right-wingers and far-right terrorists have in recent years launched many attacks on Muslims and their buildings.
> (Interview 10, religious-ethnic minority CSO)

However, perhaps because of the focus on the motivation of the perpetrator rather than the victim groups, many interviewees did not use the term 'religiously attributed or inspired radicalization' in reference to right-wing extremist attacks on religious minorities, and opinions were mixed: some thought that the religious identity of the victims was a central motivation for becoming a target, while for others, religion itself was only used instrumentally by the attackers: 'The core, the motivation of it, is a certain view of others – foreigners, of difference – and a great deal of anxiety and aggression' (Interview 1, CSO).

All interviewees agreed that, regardless of the role of Islam in far-right violent radicalization, the conflation of ethnic and religious categories runs rife. Such conflation can be found in the bestseller *Deutschland schafft sich ab* [Germany is abolishing itself] by Thilo Sarrazin (2010), a politician formally member of the SPD, which puts forward a racist genetic argument that claims a general intellectual inferiority of Muslims. There is a conflation between religious identity and a supposed genetic/racial category, one that casts all migrants from the Middle East as Muslims. Many interviewees also mentioned a strategic dimension of this conflation:

> Religion has been instrumentalized by the far right as a fundamental pillar of cultural identity. This is very artificially constructed, with the European Christian supposed identity constructed against the Muslim invaders, towards the others, the extremist ones, etc. […] This is very instrumental, with the idea to reach conservative people, with the aim to portray religion as an expression of fundamentally different and incompatible cultures, so that Europe is seen as a Christian-Judean cultural space – although the Judean is often left out – in which Muslims supposedly cannot be integrated. There is a dichotomy constructed, and this works through the association between Muslims and migration, between invasion and Islam.
> (Interview 4, researcher/analyst)

But regardless of how central 'religion' is to the ideology and motivation of different perpetrators, it certainly plays a central role in socio-political discourses and ideologies of both identity and security. Religion is mobilized to identify targets for attacks and to make religious minorities the primary victims of such attacks. This means that when categorizing such attacks as 'hate-crimes', minority religious identity is an important marker of being targeted by right-wing terrorism.

The German case: A brief background

Germany has seen an increase in its Muslim population and the visible presence of Islam both politically and socially in recent decades, as have other countries in Western Europe. In 1970 almost 95 per cent of the population were members of one of the two dominant Christian churches, 1.3 per cent were Muslim and just 3.9 per cent identified as non-religious, according to official statistics (Sealy and Modood 2021). In 2020, Christians still made up the majority of the population, but this majority has now decreased to 66 per cent (Sealy and Modood 2021). Muslims now account for 6.9 per cent of the population, Buddhists and Jews 0.3 per cent each, and the proportion of those who identify as non-religious has risen to 26.3 per cent. This change is the result of gradual secularization and migration, but also reflects the unification of West Germany with the former ideologically atheist East Germany in 1990 (Sealy and Modood 2021).

Religious diversity, and the growing significance of Islam in particular, has increasingly become perceived as a threat by a large proportion of the German population, with 55 per cent of non-Muslims in Western Germany and 66 per cent in Eastern Germany saying they saw Islam as a threat and perceived a failure of Muslims to integrate (Cesari 2013). Indeed, it seems that Germans' opinions of non-Christian religions are notably worse than in other parts of Western Europe, with political parties displaying overt distrust, if not hostility, towards Muslims (Großbölting 2016: 240).

Against this background, a new wave of far-right mobilization against Islam swept through the country beginning in October 2014. The 'PEGIDA' movement – Patriotic Europeans Against the Islamization of the Occident – originated in Dresden, Saxony. The movement held increasingly large weekly 'Monday demonstrations', growing from just a few to 25,000 participants in January 2015, after the Charlie Hebdo attacks in Paris. The movement rapidly spread to other cities in Germany, with offshoots such as 'LEGIDA' in Leipzig and 'KAGIDA' in Kassel. Politically, it was the AfD (Alternative for Germany), founded in 2013, that capitalized on the spread of Islamophobic attitudes. Electorally, the party has been very successful, particularly in Eastern Germany, where it exceeded 20 per cent in all states (except Berlin) in recent years. In federal elections, the party achieved 12.6 per cent of the vote in 2017. Since 2020, one of the three internal factions of the party, 'The Wing', is classified as being right-wing extremist according to the VS, which monitors this faction in part because of its open support for the narrative of the 'great replacement' theory (Litschko 2020a).

An important element in strengthening – and radicalizing – the AfD was likely the heightened and divisive public discourse, moral panic and accompanying narratives around the refugee intake in 2015 (notably, following the rise and growth of PEGIDA). Since 2014, there has been an increase in the proportion of the population that agrees with degrading sentiments about asylum seekers from an already very high level of 44 per cent in 2014 to an even higher level of 54 per cent in 2018–19 (Zick, Küpper and Berghan 2019). While both the government and civil society have taken measures to welcome Ukrainians fleeing the war in 2022, such migration – seen as less 'problematic' than that of other groups, such as refugees fleeing the Taliban's 2021 takeover of Afghanistan, for instance – reveals how attitudes are shaped largely in response to the ethnoreligious identity of minorities, rather than their legal status. These developments suggest a radicalization of substantive segments of German society and in particular a strengthening of 'New Right' attitudes, which are traditional far-right ideological elements couched in a modernized language, such as 'the governing parties deceive the people' (22 per cent agreement), and 'Germany is being infiltrated by Islam' (25 per cent agreement) (Zick, Küpper and Berghan 2019).

In the mid-2010s attacks by 'lone operators' with links to IS became more prominent in Germany (Burke and Feltes n.d., Dienstbühl 2019). On the other hand, violence and terrorism from those with a right-wing extremist background are on the rise. While this is a transnational phenomenon in Europe, North America, Australia and New Zealand (Ahmed et al. 2020: 142), it is particularly pronounced in Germany (O'Connor 2020, Ravndal et al. 2020).

There is a long history of right-wing terrorism in both the Federal Republic of Germany as well as in the former German Democratic Republic (East Germany, henceforth GDR). The terrorist attack that caused the highest death toll, with thirteen fatalities and many more injured, took place in 1980 at the Munich Oktoberfest. The perpetrator, Gundolf Köhler, was a known neo-Nazi and member of the Wikingjugend and the Wehrsportgruppe Hoffmann, two far-right paramilitary groups. However, Köhler was declared a lone actor with private motivations in a rushed investigation. In 2014, prosecutors reopened the case and reviewed the evidence – part of which had been destroyed by the police to clear space. The case was closed in July 2020, concluding that the motivation for the attack was right-wing extremism, but with no conclusive evidence for the involvement of others in the attack (Baur 2020). Less than three months after the incident, a leading member of the Wehrsportgruppe Hoffmann murdered the Jewish publisher and rabbi Shlomo Levin and his partner Frida Poeschke in their home (Heymann and Wensierski 2011).

A growing far-right subculture emerged in the 1980s. But a particularly serious episode of radicalization happened after German reunification in the 1990s, when a combination of high unemployment and a political authority vacuum in the former GDR created opportunities for the emergence and establishment of far-right structures (Interviews 1 and 6). Racist violence escalated in 1991–2, including arson attacks and bombings, claiming at least five lives. In Rostock-Lichtenhagen, a city on the German Baltic coast, during a siege on an asylum-seeker shelter that lasted several days, a residential building that hosted over one hundred workers from Vietnam was besieged for days (22–26 August 1992) by a crowd of 3000, with organized neo-Nazis among them. On the third day of altercations, the police, unable to clear the crowd, withdrew to ensure the safety of law enforcement. The residential building was then attacked and set on fire by the mob, with the residents still inside, among shouts of 'we will get you all'. The firefighters, called by a neighbour, were unable to access the building because of the crowd. Those inside the burning building meanwhile managed to escape through the roof to a neighbouring building. The mood in this phase was described as reminiscent of a pogrom (Quent 2019: 176–8).

Out of this environment, three neo-Nazis – Uwe Böhnhardt, Uwe Mundlos and Beate Zschäpe – who had grown up in Jena in the environment of a nascent far-right subculture radicalized further. In 2011 it was revealed that from 1999 to 2011 a series of attacks was committed by the previously unknown National Socialist Underground (NSU) comprising this trio (and possibly their supporters). The series of attacks included nine targeted killings of people with a migrant background – often shopkeepers and restaurant owners of Turkish, Kurdish and (in one case) Greek origin – the murder of a policewoman, another forty-three attempted killings and three bomb attacks (Quent 2019). However, law enforcement, led by the special investigating mission called 'Soko Bosporus', primarily focused their investigation on the social milieu of the victims, assuming the killings had been carried out by non-Germans. The media called the murder series 'Dönermorde', or 'kebab' murders, and speculated about migrant milieus and 'walls of silence' that allegedly made investigation impossible (Virchow, Thomas and Grittmann 2015). After the uncovering of the NSU, a long trial against the group's surviving key member Zschäpe proceeded until 2018. This was followed by an extensive public debate over right-wing terrorism and the failures and flaws of the security apparatus, including allegations of cover-ups and destruction of evidence by the domestic intelligence service, which was criticized for its failure to investigate these allegations and to humanize the victims (Nebenklage NSU-Prozess 2020).

The escalation of extreme right-wing attacks

Against this background of right-wing radicalization in Germany, we turn now to what we argue is the further escalation of far-right radicalization and terrorism in recent years. The year 2019 alone saw two incidents that can be both seen as watershed moments in the German context – and during our fieldwork in 2020, another, even deadlier, attack shattered Germany.

The first incident was a deadly attack on a synagogue in Halle, Sachsen-Anhalt, on Yom Kippur (9 October) in 2019. While the failure of the perpetrator, Stephan Balliet, to break into the synagogue protected the fifty-one worshippers inside from harm, he killed a forty-year-old female passer-by, and later entered a kebab shop where he killed another victim, uttering the words '*Döner, nehm wa*' ('kebab, we'll take that') on his video stream. Balliet filmed and live-streamed his attack and published two English-language manifestos online, in which, among other things, he uses memes from incel culture, refers to his manifesto as a 'spiritual guide for discontented White Men' and unequivocally states, 'Kill all Jews'. He debates whether to attack a mosque, an antifascist centre or a synagogue, and reasons that even if he killed 'one hundred golems' it would make no difference since 'they' are shipping greater numbers to Europe, so that the only solution is 'to cut the head of the ZOG [Zionist occupation government]' (Önnerfors 2019). In the live-stream video of his attack, he further declares – again in English – that feminism is at fault for the mass migration because of sinking birth rates, and that behind all problems is 'the Jew' (Schwarz and Gensing 2019). One CSO interviewee commented, 'Stephan B. didn't have a very elaborate ideology, but rather fragments of memes.' Key to this was a variation on the great replacement narrative, which, according different segments of the online alt-right, is 'just migration because people want to be better off, […], an invasion, […], or on the most extreme fringes, the Jews started wars in the Middle East to trigger migration flows, which they use so that in Europe [and the] US races mix, and mixed races are more easily controlled' (Interview 3).

The significance of this attack cannot be overstated. Despite the failure of Balliet to achieve his primary goal – to 'kill as many non-Whites as possible, Jews preferred' – he did take the lives of two individuals. Except for the Munich shooting in 2016, discussed below, this was the first significant right-wing terror attack clearly inspired by an international wave of right-wing attacks. The style and language of the manifestos and the livestream followed the pattern of attacks in Pittsburgh (October 2018), Christchurch (March 2019), Poway (April 2019) and El Paso (August 2019), placing the attack in the context of a 'global community' (Interview 3). In the wake of the attack, many commentators, particularly Jewish, expressed anger at the failures of the security institutions to prevent the attack, and at the lack of compassion and adequate reactions from politicians and civil society (Kapitelmann 2019, Salzborn 2019, Schneider 2019).

The latest attack of those outlined in this chapter took place in Hanau, Hessen, in 2020 and was the deadliest of the three, claiming ten lives and that of the attacker, Tobias Rathjen. He opened fire at people on the streets around and inside a kiosk and two shisha bars, killing nine people out of racist motives (saying their names: Ferhat, Gökhan, Hamza, Said Nessar, Mercedes, Sedat, Kaloyan, Fatih, Vili became a political statement against invisibilization of the victims (#SayTheirNames 2020)), before fleeing to his home, where he killed his mother and then himself. The attacker left a manifesto in German and a video in English. The manifesto contains an idiosyncratic paranoid conspiracy theory of a secret service that is reading his mind and controlling world affairs. But arguably the most staggering element of the manifesto is his proclamation that the populations of more than twenty-five countries – mostly North African and Middle Eastern countries, including Israel, and Asian and South Asian countries – 'must be completely annihilated'. These are seen as 'ethnic groups, races or cultures' that are 'destructive in every respect'. After this 'coarse cleansing', a 'fine cleaning' should be conducted in other countries in Africa, South and Central America. He also states that since not all people with a German passport are 'purebred', half of the German population should also be annihilated. He specifically (but not exclusively) mentions Islam as a destructive race/culture: 'Very few races have emerged positively; other races and cultures have not only made no contribution here but are destructive – especially Islam' (Rathjen, cited in Caniglia et al. 2020: 4–5).

Rathjen's idiosyncratic conspiracy theory also has some similarities with antisemitic conspiracies, especially when he speaks of a 'shadow government' that is more powerful than the president of the United States, a 'very small "elite"' in possession of secret knowledge (Rafael 2020). Ultimately, in his own words, his attack has been motivated by the dual motives of racist and conspiracy thinking: on the one hand, to raise awareness of the alleged secret organization, and on the other, to deliver a blow against the 'degeneration of our volk' (Rafael 2020). But unlike the Halle attack, and despite the video message in English, there are few traces of the specific milieus of the alt-right or references to previous attacks. Expert Alexandra Kurth has described the manifesto as clearly being that of a right-wing extremist, but an 'unread' one, with his own 'genius' at the centre of his world view (cited in Leimbach 2020). However, racism and conspiratorial narratives clearly demonstrate the influence of the far right's narratives and world view, including racism, Islamophobia, antisemitism, a preoccupation with birth rates, a narrative aligned to the 'great replacement' and a *völkisch* nationalist world view. The strategic elements of his attack – targeting places where he could expect to find ethnic and religious individuals to be his prime victims, his video message and his manifesto – also clearly echo attacks like that of Christchurch terrorist Brenton Tarrant.

Shisha bars had been the specific targets of racist vitriol by many regional and local AfD politicians, who agitated against them as supposed hotspots of crime, such as Dimitri Schulz, a member of the regional parliament in Hessia (Rathjen's state), who had posted about a 'gang-rape in shisha bar!'. However, the primary reason for targeting shisha bars was simply their alignment with the visible presence of a migrant and diaspora subculture, as made clear by Hamburg AfD politician Olga Peterson, who complained about the increase of 'shisha bars, Turkish shops, kebab shops' in her neighbourhood, asking sentimentally, 'How many of [these] can my hometown bear still?' (Beutin 2020). Initially, however, the police did not classify the Hanau attack as bearing a right-wing extremist motivation, focusing instead on Rathjen's idiosyncratic conspiracy theories as the main driver (Litschko 2020b). In the attack's highly politicized aftermath, numerous actors – in particular ethnic and religious minorities and civil society organizations – expressed their anger and frustration at the perceived inaction by the authorities on right-wing extremist terrorism (Kohrs 2020, Litschko 2020b, #SayTheirNames 2020).

The three attacks discussed here have arguably been the most significant acts of right-wing terrorism and violence in Germany in recent years. However, there are several incidents predating these attacks that indicate an escalation leading to these events that are also worthy of mention. On 22 July 2016, the fifth anniversary of the right-wing terror attacks in Oslo and Utøya, eighteen-year-old David Sonboly shot and killed 9 people, all from ethnic minority background in a Munich shopping area, injuring five and killing himself. Bavarian law enforcement agencies concluded that this was a shooting rampage, stating revenge for mobbing as the motive for the attack. Independent consultants disagreed (e.g. Quent 2017), and after new evidence emerged, including a direct link to a shooting in the United States, new investigations concluded in October 2019 that Sonboly's attack had indeed been 'politically motivated' right wing terrorism (Ahmed et al. 2020: 147, Fuchs and Stroh 2020). Like Halle, the deed fits the pattern of a lone-actor terrorist who radicalized online and related deeply to likeminded individuals transnationally.

It is also noteworthy that a series of attacks planned by German right-wing terrorist groups have been disrupted. In 2018, members of the Revolution Chemnitz group were arrested for attempting to attack politicians, journalists and economic elites. In February 2020, twelve members of the unnamed 'Group S' planned attacks on mosques and discussed further attacks on refugees and politicians in ten different federal states using semi-automatic weapons (Connolly 2020). Perhaps the most alarming incident was the arrest of thirty members of the Nazi/prepper group Nordkreuz, which included police and military personnel, who were planning a large-scale attack on people they deemed responsible for the 2015 decision to accept refugees from Syria. Investigators found the names and addresses of 25,000 local politicians, weapons and 2,000 body bags that had all been sourced from police and official military supplies (Ravndal et al. 2020). The notorious case of Franco Albrecht, a German military officer who posed as a refugee and planned a right-wing terrorist attack under a false flag, has attracted international coverage (Bennhold 2021). His far-right views had been known in his unit, as he had written a master's thesis where he tried to prove a Jewish world conspiracy. Although his thesis was rejected on the grounds of antisemitism and pseudo-scientific argumentation, he was simply allowed to submit another one and to carry on. His plans were uncovered in part by a chance discovery and led to a series of investigations. He has now been found guilty of the planning of a severe state-threatening act of violence and sentenced to five and a half years of prison, the first military personnel in Germany's post-war history to be convicted and sentenced for such a crime (Ramelsberger 2022). However, investigations into possible supporters have been scarce. According to the Federal Ministry of the Interior, the Nordkreuz group and the wider chatgroups and regional groups of which it formed a part (and of which Franco Albrecht had been a member) still exist and some of its members still legally possess weapons (Schmidt 2021, Potter 2022).

In December 2022, another plot from the far right was uncovered, this time coming from the milieu of the so-called 'Reichsbürger' (Reich citizens), a community of over 20,000 members who deny the legitimacy of the German state based on conspiracy theories and veiled antisemitism. A group that formed around Heinrich XIII 'prince' Reuss, comprising sixty-three individuals against whom investigations are ongoing (among them former AfD member of parliament and judge Birgit Malsack-Winkemann, as well as current and former members of police and military services), was planning to initiate broad unrest through acts of terrorism – including arresting and 'delivering judgement' to members of the government for their handling of the pandemic. The ultimate goal was a coup d'etat, installing a shadow government under the rule of Heinrich Reuss (Fischermann et al. 2023). Like Franco A. and Nordkreuz, a key reference point was the triggering of a 'day x', a goal shared not only by these actors but also by neo-Nazi groups, Q-Anon, and transnationally operating accelerationist terrorist groups and individuals (Rafael 2022).

Macro-, meso- and micro-drivers of radicalization

Within the literature on radicalization processes, three analytical dimensions are frequently distinguished: a macro-level focus on social structure and political culture, a meso-level focus on specific groups and elements of society and their social formation, and, at the micro level, a focus on the individual features of radicalization. These distinctions reflect the evolution of the field of radicalization studies. Beginning with an older tradition of research on political violence in the context of social movement studies focusing on the collective (meso) level, radicalization studies in the aftermath of 9/11 shifted focus to concentrate thematically on jihadist radicalization and conceptually on micro-level individual processes of radicalization (Potter 2022: 378–82), while a critical macro-level approach has emphasized various macro-structural conditions that can influence radicalization pathways and trends (Eckert 2013, Malthaner 2017). These concepts have mostly developed around jihadist radicalization, and only more recently have they been applied to radicalization on the far right (Quent 2019, Logvinov 2019). Indeed, mechanisms of radicalization on all these levels can be quite similar across ideological differences (Quent 2019).

Building on these insights, we now turn to the way in which the drivers of far-right radicalization and the recent escalation we have discussed above are constructed through the lens of our 'practical experts' (practitioners, radicalization experts and law enforcement officers), whose combined sensitivities and analyses can help us develop a 'bigger picture' frame in which to consider the recent escalation of far-right violence in Germany.

Social change and affective crises: Macro-factors

On the macro level, an often-mobilized explanation for radicalization relates to ongoing changes in economic structures and increasing levels of inequality, resulting in part from globalization (researcher/analyst, interview 4). This is particularly heightened because of the current economic crisis, which has worsened during the Covid-19 pandemic:

> In times of economic insecurity, we always see that extreme ideas get stronger. [...] So, people start to feel that they are going to lose out, that they experience an existential threat. And so, people look for things that offer support [...] And right-wing and religious extremism, partly also left-wing extremism, offer that support, and easy answers. And they offer identities. And identities lead to groups, and people feel more secure as members of a group.
>
> (Interview 5, CSO)

This statement emphasizes that such dynamics involve issues of perception, rather than of actual social class or of economic insecurity as such. Indeed, the average AfD voter has an income in line with or slightly above the national average yet nevertheless feels disadvantaged (Herschinger et al. 2018: 150). The economic position of the perpetrators of these attacks themselves is mixed, and none seemed to have been particularly impacted by a crisis. Balliet had started a chemistry degree at Martin Luther University Halle-Wittenberg, but dropped out after two terms, was unemployed and lived with his mother. Rathjen, on the other hand, held a business degree and was working for various financial firms, although he too, aged forty-three, still lived with his parents (Crawford and Keen 2020).

Another macro-societal change that intersects with the micro level is that of shifting gender roles:

> One root cause is [...] [a] crisis of masculinity. Men cannot be the sole breadwinner anymore, they do not find a job with which they can support their family alone, it is not so easy anymore to find a partner [...]. If you look at the perpetrators, [they are] often socially isolated, and informed by ideas of male supremacy, of a right or claim to privilege. And to cope with their damaged ego, this is lived through omnipotence fantasies. So that's the original cause, I would say.
> (Interview 3, researcher/analyst)

The manifestos of both Stephan Balliet and Tobias Rathjen included strong misogynistic elements. Balliet's manifesto featured clear references and ideological proximity to the incel movement: he describes feminism as the cause of the downfall of the West, which is the legitimation for the 'great replacement' (Kemekenidou 2019), imitating a similar argument by Breivik (Kaiser 2020). Tobias Rathjen's manifesto also stated, under the heading 'the topic of women', that he hadn't had romantic relationships with women for many years and betrays a feeling of entitlement to women and their bodies similar to that of the incel community, even though he does not explicitly refer to their ideology (Jasser et al. n.d.). Still, the 'aggrieved entitlement' (Kimmel 2017) of white men can be listed as a key development that forms a bridge to mainstream discourses and culture which nurture male entitlement (Jasser et al. n.d.), and a gateway for online radicalization into the alt-right (Interview 3, researcher/analyst).

This 'crisis of masculinity' (an often contested term within gender and masculinity studies) (Bereswill and Neuber 2011, Jordan and Chandler 2019, Beck 2021: 94) on the one hand reflects socio-structural and cultural changes in many countries in the global north, including processes of increased gender equality, deindustrialization and socio-economic precarity, all of which undermine the ability to live up to ideals of masculinity that are still culturally dominant (Sauer 2017). On the other hand, the inability to meet masculinity expectations may be experienced as deeply subjective and problematic, filtering down to the micro level, whereas specific narratives that maintain an ideology of male supremacy and entitlement become radicalizing factors at the meso level.

An additional macro element is widespread racism, Islamophobia and antisemitism, and the related concept of 'group-focused enmity' (GFE) (Zick et al. 2008). While the question of whether Muslims, Jews or 'foreigners' are the central target group depends on the particular strand of right-wing extremism, anti-Muslim racism has increasingly come to occupy a central role in society, building on Germany's struggle to inclusively govern its religious diversity (Interviews 5, 10, ethnic-religious CSOs). The refugee influx in 2015–16, and 'the constant admonitions in the media that "we are close to a collapse of the functioning of society and state"' (Interview 10, CSO) critically amplified these issues, fostering feelings of insecurity and the 'othering' of migrant minorities. Significantly, groups within the federal army and police forces also radicalized, for example the 'uniter' network (researcher/analyst, interview 3; Flade 2021).

From crisis to existential threat: The meso level

On a meso level, our interviewees highlight three central issues: the role of narratives that have the ability to transform the experiences of macro-level crises to an existential threat, the circulation of these within mainstream culture, and the organizational and networking capacities of actors on the far-right spectrum. One key turning point, according to one researcher/analyst interviewee, was in 2010,

> with Thilo Sarazzin's book *Germany is doing away with itself*, which was a key text in making social Darwinism and racist thoughts socially acceptable. This was *the* bestseller of the last fifty, sixty years and penned by an SPD [Social Democratic Party] politician, seemingly from the centre-left. The ideas of the book are not new; they go back to the thirties, the idea of the death of the people [*Volkstod*]. And this central paranoia of the right-wing [...] had been made socially acceptable by Sarazzin. [...] This connection of the extension of what is say-able, and the much broader reach of right-wing ideas through social media, is the main cause of recent escalation of radicalization.
>
> (Interview 2)

As this interviewee points out, Sarazzin's book rehashes the narrative of an existential threat that is much older, originating in the idea of the *Volkstod*/white genocide. His 'hybrid racism' (*Butterwege*) combines pseudo-biological racism – the argument that different ethnic groups, with supposedly different genetic profiles, have differential levels of intelligence – with cultural racism, enabling him to argue that Muslims' supposed disadvantages in educational achievements are due to their 'Islamic-cultural background' (Sarrazin, cited in Canan 2014). He then claims that due to differing 'birth rates' between Muslims and non-Muslims, there is a threat of declining intelligence across society; combining racism and eugenicism, he calls this 'conquest by fertility' (Sarazzin 2010: 326, own translation).

A more extreme, conspiratorial version of the same narrative circulates around far-right networks as the 'The Great Replacement', a term coined and popularized by Renaud Camus in 2011. In this version, the same fear that the white, secularized Christian population of Europe will be replaced by non-white others is espoused, but as part of a greater plan orchestrated by 'replacism'. Different variations of the theory emphasize different puppeteers: one variant builds on the theory of 'Eurabia', involving the Islamization of Europe as planned and executed by Gulf states and aided by the European political establishment, a theory that influenced Norwegian right-wing terrorist Anders Breivik. A version of this was also used by the New-Zealand Terrorist Brenton Tarrant in his aptly named manifesto 'The Great Replacement'. Apart from portraying Muslims as 'Islamic invaders', Tarrant's manifesto, like Sarazzin's, specifically claims 'birth rates' as the central issue (Tarrant, cited in Nilsson 2022).

In the case of the Hanau attacker, the combined obsession with birth rates, the supposedly inferior intellect of people of colour and Muslims, and the centrality of Islamophobia mirror Tarrant's key theses; however, explicit references to the 'great replacement' are absent. Rathjen's manifesto thus resembles Sarazzin's book; Rathjen's self-presentation and language in this document, in which he considers nothing less than the *annihilation of the entire populations of large regions of the globe*, uses the matter-of-fact language of an accountant, rather than a hateful mass murderer, calling to mind in some ways the 'banality of evil' that Hannah Arendt observed in Eichmann's self-presentation. In yet another version, however, the 'great replacement' is ultimately a Jewish conspiracy. This is the variation we see in Balliet's manifesto: rather than targeting Muslims, which he calls 'Golems' – suggesting they are being controlled by Jews – his aim was to target Jews to 'cut off [sic] the head of ZOG', or the 'Zionist Occupation Government', a term circulating as early as the 1970s among North American neo-Nazis. Balliet also combined Islamophobia and antisemitism with antifeminism, since he understood feminism as responsible for the low birth rates.

As these currents show, such narratives of existential threat combine elements of global discourses – from the transnational 'alt-right' (Nagle 2017) and 'New Right' originating in France (with strong echoes in Germany) to the post-9/11 'counter-jihad' movement vilifying Islam and celebrating transnational antisemitic neo-Nazis – with the more localized national circulation of far-right narratives, including Sarazzin's theses.

From loser to hero: The micro level

At the micro level, radicalization is primarily based on individual factors of psychosocial development. From this perspective, the ideological content of extremist ideologies can appear secondary:

> Every aspect of psychological mental health in a wider sense makes you vulnerable to recruiting factors. Whether you end up buying into conspiracy theories, or get sucked into a right-wing extremist militia, for some young people it is almost irrelevant, or does not make a difference. We need to develop strategies to take care of everybody, every young person, on a very broad level.
>
> (Interview 1, CSO)

But it is not generic mental health or suffering that makes individuals susceptible to radicalization. One indicator of this is that almost invariably, the perpetrators of far-right violent extremism are white men. In discussing the phenomenon of radicalizing 'angry white men', Kimmel (2017) identifies 'aggrieved entitlement' as a key element. Individual grievances are experienced in high contrast to a sense of identity-based (such as gender, ethnicity and religion) entitlement to social privileges, conveyed by mainstream culture and intergenerational communication. This contrast is often experienced as individual failure: notably, Balliet repeatedly berates himself in the livestream as a 'loser'. Narratives that blame others for these grievances are attractive because they relieve the ego from the sense of failure, and instead feed into a sense of betrayal by a society that should have worked, in the eyes of angry white men, to their advantage, making them particularly susceptible to conspiratorial narratives.

In this context, radicalization also offers an experience of heroic superiority: being part of a select elite that sees things clearly and has the courage to act, so that, ultimately, the act of extreme violence and power over others can instill a sense of remasculinization (Jensen and Larsen 2021). The point about individual radicalization processes indirectly ties to the question of the 'lone actor' violent extremist. The term refers to a concept that is often used to describe the kinds of attacks such as those of Kassel, Hanau and Halle: they are 'classical cases of individual perpetrators, lone actors that radicalized themselves' (Interview 9, law enforcement), as police often frame these cases. The concept of the lone actor in the context of Germany has often been used in distinction to jihadist terrorism, in which links with terror organizations such as IS are often more emphasized. This is partly because of a difference in tactics: the confession to the crime is a key propaganda tactic for many jihadist terror groups, whereas for right-wing extremism (as NSU and Franco Albrecht), the tactic is sometimes to not reveal responsibility in order to either to continue to reap terror (NSU) or to frame refugees (Albrecht) in order to destabilize civil society and eventually provoke a civil war, a far-right extremist strategy sometimes termed 'accelerationism' (Beauchamp 2019).

However, the 'lone actor' concept is heavily debated since it seems to decontextualize the specific terrorist act and perpetuator from any ideological or networked context. This has problematic consequences not only for the investigation and prosecution of potential links and networks but also for its role in creating a public perception of white male terrorists as dangerous individuals in contrast to Muslim terrorists as part of a threatening population.

Referring to the attacks in Munich in 2016 and Halle, an interviewee reflected:

> Those were perpetrators that were acting alone – even though their ideas and their rationale to act came from digital network cultures, from international communities, organized right-wing extremists [...], but the planning and execution of those deeds is fundamentally done alone. But that does not mean that it should be understood as 'lone actor terrorism' – they don't do it for themselves, they act for the community.
>
> (Interview 2)

Indeed, the view that lone actors 'self-radicalize' is unsubstantiated; rather, their radicalization can be traced to 'various social networks' (Hamm and Spaaij 2017: 59) which can be on- or offline, although post-9/11 there has been a clear shift from radicalization in organized extremist groups to affinity with anonymous online sympathizers (Hamm and Spaaij 2017: 74, see also Schuurman et al. 2019). This form of provoking terrorism is called 'stochastic terrorism', involving 'the use of mass media to provoke random acts of ideologically motivated violence that are statistically predictable but individually unpredictable' (Hamm and Spaaij 2017: 84). This works particularly through 'dangerous speech' (Benesch 2014: 5): narratives that make violent acts appear consequential, understood by the audience as a call to violence even if not explicitly called for. 'Dangerous speech' designates specific groups as foreign, or out-groups, to exclude them, claiming that they pose an existential threat to the in-group (see also Ahmed et al. 2020). This is precisely the radicalizing function of the great replacement narrative.

On the basis of the insights provided by the 'practical experts' we interviewed, alongside critical engagement with the scholarly literature, we argue that the recent escalation of German far-right violent radicalization can be attributed to a number of factors that, combined, increase the stochastic likelihood of far-right terrorism. On the macro level, the perception of increased competition for (artificially) scarce economic resources, discourses of masculinist and white supremacy, and a flawed political-discursive approach to Germany's increasing religious and ethnic diversity have contributed to some individuals' sense of insecurity and precarity, increasing their susceptibility on a micro level towards radicalization through increased receptivity towards far-right messaging. Meso-level factors also come into play, seemingly providing explanations for and framing of individual experiences and grievances that are in turn related to macro-level transformations. Such explanations appear attractive because they allow blame-shifting and reinforce a sense of entitlement. When these 'explanations' identify not only a culprit but also a more profound existential threat, and when they circulate with increased reach and intensity online, radicalization and stochastic terrorism are a likely consequence.

Concluding remarks

The recent escalation of right-wing radicalization has laid bare a very significant problem for the German state in relation to right-wing extremism. As argued by the head of a civil society organization:

> We have always advocated that the vehemence and meticulousness towards religious forms of extremism, especially after 9/11, must necessarily be extended to right-wing radicalism. We have warned that right-wing radicalism can flourish in the shadow of the fight against Islamism. Unfortunately, our warnings were not taken seriously and today we are experiencing exactly this consequence. [...] Today we are starting to see the beginning of an acknowledgement, and after Hanau it is clear at least that we have racism in the middle of our society, which is fuelled and cultivated by right-wing extremists.
> (Interview 10, religious/ethnic CSO)

The state has responded actively to these developments but is still in a transition phase. A key distinction is that, in relation to civil society engagement in preventing right-wing extremism, Germany can build on a long tradition, whereas the intelligence, security and law enforcement agencies have demonstrated very serious shortcomings in the past. This was particularly evident during the NSU terror wave, where flawed and prejudiced investigations left major wounds. Double standards persist in the treatment of terrorist incidents, with the state and media downplaying right wing terrorism, while Muslims and Islam are constantly regarded with a 'generalised suspicion' (Interview 10) of being involved in violence, terrorism or extremism. Finally, some individual members of law enforcement are themselves subjects of right-wing radicalization, with some having used police data to compile death lists and arsenals in preparation for 'Day X', a 2017 plot allegedly involving members of the German military and including the far-right Hannibal/Nordkreuz network. (Former) police and military were also involved in the plot of the 'Reichsbürger'. There is a heightened focus and prosecution of such cases now, but increased scrutiny remains necessary.

Nevertheless, there are some reasons for cautious optimism. There is a notable shift in the political debate; even the domestic intelligence service now accepts right-wing radicalization as the biggest threat to security, shifting the focus of counterterrorism from Islamist terrorism to right-wing terrorism after two decades. Some law enforcement agencies in federal states have also made changes from 2011 onwards, publishing comprehensive strategies, increasing capacities against online radicalization and improving their approach and sensibilities to hate crime and its victims, even though there is still arguably a lot of room for improvement, particularly in relation to anti-Muslim hate crimes (ethnic-religious CSO, interview 10). There is also an emerging public discourse and increasing understanding of the position of minorities, not least in relation to their efforts to make themselves heard. At the same time, of course, the continuing rise of the AfD and the concomitant 'societal radicalisation' in Germany give cause for serious concern.

Germany can look to a long history of civil society engagement, and some of the core institutional problems – including the absence of a democracy promotion law that would enable civil society projects to become sustainable – now seem solvable under a renewed political willingness to build on these strengths (the new coalition government has recently brought a democracy promotion bill to its first parliamentary hearing [BMFSFJ 2023]). There are also signs that the distance between civil society and state actors is increasingly being bridged, both conceptually and in terms of practical cooperation. This means, despite significant challenges, at least in one respect the situation is better than in the 1990s. As one interviewee stated:

> I was commissioner for integration [*Auslaenderbeauftragte*] [in the 1990s] [...]. Back then, there were no civil society structures at all. This time it is different, if there has been some [far-right] presence locally here, some events, there's always a big societal outcry, because we have civil society actors, and state agencies that take these things seriously. Particularly the municipalities have learned a lot and built resilience and have prevented further escalation and dealt pretty well with the situation in 2015.
>
> (CSO, interview 6)

Overall, however, there seems to still be a certain tone-deafness on behalf of public figures and institutions in reaction to attacks. A more empathetic reaction would be beneficial, would signal unequivocally that an attack on Germany's minorities is an attack on all citizens, and would portray that the German state does not make implicit distinctions between 'autochthonic' Germans and those with a migration background. This would require including migrant and Muslim organizations more prominently in the public debate and taking them seriously as 'part of the solution' (ethnic-religious CSO, interview 5) without applying double standards that see them simultaneously framed as suspects in relation to extremism. It is perhaps now the role of politics to facilitate, through institutional funding and long-term support, the taking of the lead by civil society and migrant organizations in its approach to countering right-wing radicalization by addressing its root causes.

References

Abay Gaspar, H., C. Daase, N. Deitelhoff, J. Junk and M. Sold (2018), *Was ist Radikalisierung? - Präzisierungen eines umstrittenen Begriffs*. Frankfurt am Main: Leibniz-Institut Hessische Stiftung Friedens- und Konfliktforschung (HSFK).

Abou-Taam, M., A. Dziri, E. Lehnert, D. Meiering, S. Teune and N. Foroutan (2019), 'Radikalisierung von Gruppen: Brückennarrative als verbindende Erzählstrukturen', in C. Daase, N. Deitelhoff and J. Junk (eds), *Gesellschaft Extrem: Was wir über Radikalisierung wissen*, 91–129, Frankfurt: Campus.

Ahmed, R., S. Albrecht, M. Fielitz, J. Junk, M. Kahl, H. Marcks, D. Mullis, M. Quent and M. Sold (2020), 'Eine neue Welle des Rechtsterrorismus/Transnationale Sicherheitsrisiken', in Bonn International Center for Conversion, Leibniz-Institut Hessische Stiftung Friedens- und Konfliktforschung, and Institut für Friedensforschung und Sicherheitspolitik an der Universität Hamburg (eds), *Friedensgutachten 2020: Im Schatten der Pandemie: letzte Chance für Europa*, 141–57, Bielefeld: transcript.

Baur, D. (2020), 'Ulrich Chaussy über Oktoberfestattentat: "Wer hat da vertuscht und warum?"', *Die Tageszeitung: taz*, 9 July. Available online: https://taz.de/!5698681/ (accessed 18 July 2020).

Beauchamp, Z. (2019), 'Accelerationism: The Obscure Idea Inspiring White Supremacist Killers around the World', *Vox.com*, 18 November. Available online: https://www.vox.com/the-highlight/2019/11/11/20882005/accelerationism-white-supremacy-christchurch (accessed 2 October 2022).

Beck, D. (2021). 'Diskursive Brückenschläge: Medien, Maskulismus, Rechtsextremismus', *ZRex – Zeitschrift für Rechtsextremismusforschung*, 1 (1): 90–107.

Benesch, S. (2014), '*Countering Dangerous Speech: New Ideas for Genocide Prevention*', United States Holocaust Memorial Museum Working Paper. Available online: https://www.ushmm.org/m/pdfs/20140212-benesch-countering-dangerous-speech.pdf (accessed 24 June 2020).

Bennhold, K. (2021), 'Day X (podcast)', *New York Times*, 19 May. Available online: https://www.nytimes.com/2021/05/19/podcasts/far-right-german-extremism.html (accessed 6 October 2022).

Bereswill, M. and A. Neuber (2011), 'Einleitung', in M. Bereswill and A. Neuber (eds), *In der Krise? Männlichkeiten im 21. Jahrhundert*, 7–17, Münster: Westfälisches Dampfboot.

Beutin, L. G. (2020), 'Blauer Hass gegen Shisha-Bars', *nd-aktuell.de*, 22 February. Available online: https://www.nd-aktuell.de/artikel/1133241.hanau-blauer-hass-gegen-shisha-bars.html (accessed 22 July 2022).

BMFSFJ (2016), 'Bericht der Bundesregierung über Arbeit und Wirksamkeit der Bundesprogramme zur Extremismusprävention', Berlin, Report Number: 1BR60). Available online: https://www.bmfsfj.de/resource/blob/117610/354cf0b045adc89e2a07968851334c8d/bericht-der-bundesregierung-zur-exemismuspraevention-data.pdf (accessed 21 September 2024).

BMFSFJ/BMI (2016), 'Strategie der Bundesregierung zur Extremismusprävention und Demokratieförderung', Berlin. Available online: https://www.bmfsfj.de/bmfsfj/service/publikationen/strategie-der-bundesregierung-zur-extremismuspraevention-und-demokratiefoerderung-109024 (accessed 21 September 2024).

BMFSFJ (2023), 'Gesetz zur Stärkung von Maßnahmen zur Demokratieförderung, Vielfaltgestaltung, Extremismusprävention und politischen Bildung

(Demokratiefördergesetz)', 16 February. Available online: https://www.bmfsfj.de/bmfsfj/service/gesetze/gesetz-zur-staerkung-von-massnahmen-zur-demokratiefoerderung-vielfaltgestaltung-extremismuspraevention-und-politischen-bildung-demokratiefoerdergesetz-207726 (accessed 18 May 2023).

BMI (2019), 'Gegen Rechtsextremismus und Hasskriminalität. Bundesregierung beschließt Maßnahmenpaket [online]', *Bundesministerium des Innern, für Bau und Heimat*. Available online: http://www.bmi.bund.de/SharedDocs/pressemitteilungen/DE/2019/10/kabinett-beschliesst-massnahmen-gg-rechtsextrem-u-hasskrim.html?nn=9390260 (accessed 6 October 2022).

Brost, L., Kahl, M., Morgenstern, T. and M. Sold (2022), Islamismus und islamischer Terrorismus in Deutschland seit 2001: Aktivitäten – Strukturen – Merkmale. Hamburg: IFSH Research Report #11, available online: https://ifsh.de/file/publication/Research_Report/011/Research_Report_011_DE_V4_web.pdf (accessed 3 November 2024).

'Bundesverfassungsschutz erklärt AfD zum Prüffall' (2019), *Deutsche Welle*, 15 January. Available at: https://www.dw.com/de/bundesverfassungsschutz-erkl%C3%A4rt-afd-zum-pr%C3%BCffall/a-47086892 (accessed 21 September 2024).

Bundesamt für Migration und Flüchtlinge (2020), Aktuelle Zahlen. Mai 2020. https://www.bamf.de/SharedDocs/Anlagen/DE/Statistik/AsylinZahlen/aktuelle-zahlen-mai-2020.pdf?__blob=publicationFile&v=5 (accessed 2 July 2020).

Burke, P. and J. Feltes (n.d.), 'CT Overview: Germany', *Counter Terrorism Ethics*. Available online: http://counterterrorismethics.com/the-counter-terrorism-landscape-in-germany/ (accessed 16 July 2020).

Butterwegge, C. (2010), 'Die Entsorgung des Rechtsextremismus', *Blätter für deutsche und internationale Politik*, 2010 (1): 12–15.

Caiani, M., D. Della Porta and C. Wagemann (2012), *Mobilizing on the Extreme Right: Germany, Italy, and the United States*. Oxford: Oxford University Press.

Canan, C. (2012), 'Über Bildung, Einwanderung Und Religionszugehörigkeit', in M. Haller and M. Niggeschmidt (eds), *Der Mythos Vom Niedergang Der Intelligenz: Von Galton Zu Sarrazin: Die Denkmuster Und Denkfehler Der Eugenik*, 135–53, Wiesbaden: Springer VS.

Caniglia, M., L. Winkler and S. Métais (2020), 'The Rise of the Right-Wing Violent Extremism Threat in Germany and Its Transnational Character', 20, Brussels: European Strategic Intelligence and Security Center. Available online: http://www.esisc.org/publications/analyses/the-rise-of-the-right-wing-violent-extremism-threat-in-germany-and-its-transnational-character (accessed 21 September 2024).

Cesari, J. (2013), *Why the West Fears Islam: An Exploration of Muslims in Liberal Democracies*. New York: Palgrave Macmillan.

Connolly, K. (2020), 'Germany's Muslims Call for Protection after "Far-Right Terror Plot" Arrests', *The Guardian*, 17 February. Available online: https://www.theguardian.com/world/2020/feb/17/germanys-muslims-call-for-protection-after-far-right-terror-plot-arrests (accessed 24 June 2020).

Crawford, B. and F. Keen (2020), 'The Hanau Terrorist Attack: How Race Hate and Conspiracy Theories Are Fueling Global Far-Right Violence', *CTC Sentinel*, 13 (3): 1–8.

Deutscher Bundestag (2020), 'Gesetz gegen Rechtsextremismus und Hasskriminalität beschlossen', *Deutscher Bundestag*. Available online: https://www.bundestag.de/dokumente/textarchiv/2020/kw25-de-rechtsextremismus-701104 (accessed 6 October 2022).

Dienstbühl, D. (2019), *Extremismus und Radikalisierung kriminologisches Handbuch zur aktuellen Sicherheitslage*. Stuttgart München Hannover Berlin Weimar Dresden: Boorberg.

Dilmaghani, F., S. J. Kramer and M. Quent 2020, 'Verfassungsschutz: Wir brauchen einen Masterplan gegen Rechtsextremismus', *Die Zeit*, 21 February.

DPA (2016), 'Chemnitz: Deutschland nur knapp großem Terroranschlag entkommen', *Wirtschaftswoche*, 10 October.

Eckert, R. (2013), 'Radikalisierung - Eine soziologische Perspektive', *Aus Politik und Zeitgeschichte*, 63 (29–31): 11–17.

Eckert, R. (2015), 'Rechtsterrorismus und Sicherheitsbehörden', in U. Wenzel, B. Rosenzweig and U. Eith (eds), *Rechter Terror und Rechtsextremismus: aktuelle Erscheinungsformen des Rechtsextremismus und Ansätze der politischen Bildungspraxis*, 31–52, Schwalbach/Ts: Wochenschau-Verlag.

Europol (2023), European Union Terrorism Situation and Trend Report 2023, Available at: https://www.europol.europa.eu/cms/sites/default/files/documents/European%20Union%20Terrorism%20Situation%20and%20Trend%20report%202023.pdf (accessed 3 November 2024).

Fischermann, T., C. Fuchs, A. Geisler, J. Grunert, Y. Musharbash, C. Schmidt, M. Steinhagen, A. Hoepfner and A. Ehmann (2023), 'Reichsbürger: Countdown To the Coup', *Die Zeit*. Available online: https://www.zeit.de/2023-05/reichsbuerger-coup-plans-prince-reuss-english (accessed 25 May 2023).

Flade, F. (2021), 'The Insider Threat: Far-Right Extremism in the German Military and Police', *CTC Sentinel*, 15 (4): 1–10.

Fuchs, I. and K. Stroh (2020), 'Anschlag in München - Innenministerium bewertet Tat neu', *Süddeutsche.de*. Available online: https://www.sueddeutsche.de/muenchen/anschlag-muenchen-2016-rechtsextremismus-polizei-neubewertung-1.4655637 (accessed 4 January 2020).

Fürstenau, M. (2019), 'Verfassungsfeinde und staatliche Gefahren', *Deutsche Welle*, 22 May.

Großbölting, T. (2016), *Losing Heaven: Religion in Germany since 1945*, trans. A. Skinner, New York: Berghahn Books.

Hamm, M. S. and R. F. J. Spaaij (2017), *The Age of Lone Wolf Terrorism*. New York: Columbia University Press.

Heitmeyer, W. (ed) (2011), 'Gruppenbezogene Menschenfeindlichkeit (GMF) in einem entsicherten Jahrzehnt', *Deutsche Zustände: Folge 10*, 15–41, Berlin: Suhrkamp Verlag.

Heitmeyer, W. (2012), 'Rechtsextremismus und gesellschaftliche Selbstentlastung', *Aus Politik und Zeitgeschichte*, 62 (18–19): 22–7.

Herschinger, E., K. Bozay, O. Decker, M. von Drachenfels, C. Joppke and K. Sinha (2018), *Radikalisierung der Gesellschaft? - Forschungsperspektiven und Handlungsoptionen*, PRIF report, Frankfurt am Main: Leibniz-Institut Hessische Stiftung Friedens- und Konfliktforschung (HSFK). Available online: https://www.hsfk.de/fileadmin/HSFK/hsfk_publikationen/prif0818.pdf (accessed 24 June 2020).

Heymann, T. von and P. Wensierski (2011), 'ERMITTLER: Im rechten Netz', *Spiegel Online*, 43. Available online: https://www.spiegel.de/spiegel/print/d-81136824.html (accessed 31 December 2019).

Jasser, G., M. Kelly and A. K. Rothermel (2020), 'Das Manifest des Hanau-Attentäters zwischen Rechtsextremismus und Frauenhass: Frauenfeind, aber kein Incel', *Belltower News. Netz für digitale Zivilgesellschaft*. Available online: https://www.belltower.news/das-manifest-des-hanau-attentaeters-zwischen-rechtsextremismus-und-frauenhass-frauenfeind-aber-kein-incel-97509/ (accessed 26 June 2020).

Jensen, S.Q. and J.F. Larsen (2021), 'Sociological perspectives on Islamist radicalization – bridging the micro/macro gap', *European Journal of Criminology*, 18 (3): 426–443.

Jentsch, U. and E. Sanders (2020), 'Weder Schläfer noch Wolf - Rechter Terror zwischen NSU und AfD', *NSU Watch*.

Jesse, E. (2018), 'Grundlagen', in *Extremismusforschung: Handbuch für Wissenschaft und Praxis*, 23–58, Sonderausgabe für die Bundeszentrale für Politische Bildung. Bonn: bpb, Bundeszentrale für Politische Bildung.

Jesse, E. and T. Mannewitz (2018), *Extremismusforschung: Handbuch für Wissenschaft und Praxis*. Sonderausgabe für die Bundeszentrale für Politische Bildung. Bonn: bpb, Bundeszentrale für Politische Bildung.

Jordan, A. and A. Chandler (2019), 'Crisis, What Crisis? A Feminist Analysis of Discourse on Masculinities and Suicide', *Journal of Gender Studies*, 28 (4): 462–74. https://doi.org/10.1080/09589236.2018.1510306.

Kaiser, S. (2020), 'Hass gegen Frauen: Rechtsextrem und Sexist', *Die Zeit*, 23 February. Available online: https://www.zeit.de/politik/deutschland/2020-02/hass-frauen-rechtsterrorismus-motive-taeter-hanau-feminismus (accessed 24 June 2020).

Kapitelmann, D. (2019), 'Antisemitischer Terror: Hässliche Worte, hässliche Taten', Die Tageszeitung: taz, 12 October. Available online: https://taz.de/!5629067/ (accessed 26 June 2020).

Kemekenidou, P. (2019), 'Der White Noise des Terrors', *Gender Equality Media e.V.* 25 October. Available online: https://genderequalitymedia.org/halle-balliet/ (accessed 5 July 2020).

Kimmel, M. (2017), *Angry White Men: American Masculinity at the End of an Era*. New York: Nation Books.

Knipping-Sorokin, R., T. Stumpf and G. Koch (2016), *Radikalisierung Jugendlicher über das Internet? Ein Literaturüberblick*. Hamburg: Deutsches Institut für Vertrauen und Sicherheit im Internet.

Kohrs, C. (2020), 'Anschlag in Hanau - Vertreter der Muslime fordern Taten', *Süddeutsche.de*. Available online: https://www.sueddeutsche.de/politik/mazyek-zentralrat-der-muslime-altug-hanau-anschlag-1.4809229 (accessed 25 February 2020).

Leimbach, A. (2020), 'Extremismusforscherin über Hanauer Attentäter: "Seine politischen Bezüge sind rechtsextrem"', *hessenschau.de*, 20 February. Available online: https://www.hessenschau.de/gesellschaft/extremismusforscherin-ueber-hanauer-attentaeter-seine-politischen-bezuege-sind-rechtsextrem,hanau-attentaeter-rechtsextrem-100.html (accessed 26 June 2020).

Litschko, K. (2020a), 'Geheimdienstchef über "Flügel" "Das ist offener Rassismus"', *Die Tageszeitung: taz*, 12 March. Available online: https://taz.de/!5667643/ (accessed 18 July 2020).

Litschko, K. (2020b), 'Reaktion auf BKA-Papier zu Hanau: "Furcht vor Verharmlosung"', *Die Tageszeitung: taz*, 30 March. Available online: https://taz.de/!5675606/ (accessed 12 June 2020).

Logvinov, M. (2019), 'Dynamiken der Radikalisierung und Logik der Gewalt', in *Rechte Hassgewalt in Sachsen: Entwicklungstrends und Radikalisierung*, 219–35, Göttingen: V&R unipress.

Magazzini, T., Eleftheriadou, M. and A. Triandafyllidou (2024), The Non-radicalisation of Muslims in Southern Europe. Migration and Integration in Italy, Greece, and Spain. Palgrave.

Malthaner, S. (2017), 'Radicalization: The Evolution of an Analytical Paradigm', *Archives Européennes de Sociologie: European Journal of Sociology*, 58 (3): 369–401.

'Nach Schuss in Porz: Ex-CDU-Politiker Hans-Josef Bähner drohen bis zu zehn Jahre Haft', (2020), *Kölner Stadt-Anzeiger*, 28 May. Available online: https://www.ksta.de/

koeln/nach-schuss-in-porz-ex-cdu-politiker-hans-josef-baehner-drohen-bis-zu-zehn-jahre-haft-36767526 (accessed 16 July 2020).

Nagle, A. (2017), *Kill All Normies: Online Culture Wars From 4Chan and Tumblr to Trump and The Alt-Right*. Winchester, UK: John Hunt Publishing.

Nebenklage NSU-Prozess (2020), 'Presseerklärung: Ein Mahnmal des Versagens des Rechtsstaates', *NSU Nebenanklage*. Available online: https://www.nsu-nebenklage.de/blog/2020/04/30/30-04-2020-presseerklaerung-ein-mahnmal-des-versagens-des-rechtsstaates/ (accessed 3 July 2020).

Neumann, P. (2013a), 'Radikalisierung, Deradikalisierung und Extremismus', *Aus Politik und Zeitgeschichte*, 63 (29–31): 3–10.

Neumann, P. (2013b), 'The Trouble with Radicalization', *International Affairs*, 89 (4): 873–93.

Nilsson, P. E. (2022), 'Manifestos of White Nationalist Ethno-Soldiers', *Critical Research on Religion*, 10 (2): 221–35.

O'Connor, F. (2020), 'Far-Right Lone Actor Terror Attack in Hanau: A Mirror of Contemporary German Politics?', *Right Now!* (blog). Oslo: C-REX—Centre for Research on Extremism. Available online: https://www.sv.uio.no/c-rex/english/news-and-events/right-now/2020/far-right-lone-actor-terror-attack-in-hanau.html (accessed 16 June 2024).

Önnerfors, A. (2019), 'The Germany Synagogue Terrorist's Manifesto Highlights Threat of Neo-Nazism', Centre for Analysis of the Radical Right, 24 October. Available online: https://www.radicalrightanalysis.com/2019/10/24/the-germany-synagogue-terrorists-manifesto-highlights-threat-of-neo-nazism/ (accessed 4 January 2020).

Potter, S. (2022), 'Rechtsextreme Prepper: Das "Nordkreuz"-Verfahren wurde eingestellt, doch das Netzwerk ist weiterhin aktiv', *Belltower.News*. Available online: https://www.belltower.news/rechtsextreme-prepper-das-nordkreuz-verfahren-wurde-eingestellt-doch-das-netzwerk-ist-weiterhin-aktiv-127719/ (accessed 25 July 2022).

Quent, D. M. (2017), *Ist die Mehrfachtötung am OEZ München ein Hassverbrechen? Gutachten über die Mehrfachtötung am 22. Juli 2016 im Auftrag der Landeshauptstadt München*. Jena: Institut für Demokratie und Zivilgesellschaft.

Quent, M. (2019), *Rassismus, Radikalisierung, Rechtsterrorismus wie der NSU entstand und was er über die Gesellschaft verrät*. 2., überarbeitete und erweiterte Auflage. Weinheim Basel: Beltz Juventa.

Rafael, S. (2020), 'Rechtsterroristische Anschläge mit 10 Opfern: Zur Ideologie des rechtsextremen Attentäters von Hanau', *Belltower.News*. Available online: https://www.belltower.news/rechtsterroristische-anschlaege-mit-10-opfern-zur-ideologie-des-rechtsextremen-attentaeters-von-hanau-96085/ (accessed 21 July 2022).

Rafael, S. (2022), 'Update Reichsbürger-Razzien: Das breite Netzwerk der revolutionsbereiten Reichsbürger*innen', *Belltower.News*. Available online: https://www.belltower.news/update-reichsbuerger-razzien-das-breite-netzwerk-der-revolutionsbereiten-reichsbuergerinnen-144131/ (accessed 25 May 2023).

Ramelsberger, A. (2022), 'Urteil gegen Offizier: Franco A. war zur Terrortat entschlossen', *Süddeutsche.de*, 15 July. Available online: https://www.sueddeutsche.de/politik/franco-a-urteil-begruendung-1.5622060 (accessed 25 July 2022).

Ravndal, J. A., S. Lygren, A. R. Jupskås and T. Bjørgo (2020), *RTV Trend Report 2020. Right-Wing Terrorism and Violence in Western Europe, 1990–2019*. Oslo: C-REX–Center for Research on Extremism.

Salzborn, S. (2019), 'Antisemitismus nach dem Halle-Anschlag: War da was?', *Die Tageszeitung: taz*, 5 December. Available online: https://taz.de/!5642816/ (accessed 19 December 2019).

Sarrazin, T. (2010), *Deutschland schafft sich ab: wie wir unser Land aufs Spiel setzen*. 4. Aufl., München: Deutsche Verlags-Anstalt.

Sauer, B. (2017), 'Social-Theoretical Reflections on European Right-Wing Populism. The Analytical Potential of the Category Gende', *Politische Vierteljahresschrift*, 58 (1): 3–22.

'#SayTheirNames: Warum so viele die Namen der Opfer von Hanau teilen [online], 2020', *jetzt.de*. Available online: https://www.jetzt.de/politik/hanau-unter-saytheirnames-machen-menschen-auf-die-opfer-des-anschlags-aufmerksam (accessed 6 October 2022).

Schneider, R. C. (2019), 'Antisemitismus: Diese lächerlichen Mahnwachen vor Synagogen', *Die Zeit*, 16 October. Available online: https://www.zeit.de/2019/43/antisemitismus-juden-rechtsextremismus-halle-deutschland (accessed 26 June 2020).

Schmidt, C. (2021), 'Nordkreuz-Gruppe: Rechtes Prepper-Netzwerk besteht trotz Terrorermittlungen fort', *Die Zeit*, 2 July. Available online: https://www.zeit.de/politik/deutschland/2021-07/nordkreuz-rechtsterrorismus-tag-x-2017-ermittlungen-bundestag-kleine-anfrage (accessed 7 April 2022).

Schuurman, B., L. Lindekilde, S. Malthaner, F. O'Connor, P. Gill and N. Bouhana (2019), 'End of the Lone Wolf: The Typology That Should Not Have Been', *Studies in Conflict & Terrorism*, 42 (8): 771–8.

Schwarz, K. and P. Gensing (2019), 'Angriff in Halle: Stream Voller Hass', *tagesschau.de*, 10 September. Available online: https://www.tagesschau.de/inland/halle-taeter-101.html (accessed 24 June 2020).

Sealy, T. and T. Modood (2021), 'Germany: Federal Corporatism' in Triandafyllidou, A. and T. Magazzini, Routledge Handbook on the Governance of Religious Diversity.

Sealy, T. and T. Magazzini (2025), 'The governance of religious diversity and the challenge of (violent) radicalization in Western Europe' in Grossman, M. and H. Hellyer, Rethinking Religion and Radicalization, Bloomsbury: 57–75.).

Virchow, F., T. Thomas and E. Grittmann (2015), *"Das Unwort erklärt die Untat" Die Berichterstattung über die NSU-Morde – eine Medienkritik*. Frankfurt am Main: Otto Brenner Stiftung, No. 79.

Voice of America (2020), 'Germany Sees Right-Wing Extremism as Top Security Threat', *VOA*, 9 July. Available online: https://www.voanews.com/a/europe_germany-sees-right-wing-extremism-top-security-threat/6192511.html (accessed 6 October 2022).

Wippermann, W. (2010), *Politiologentrug. Ideologiekritik der Extremismus-Legende*. Berlin: Rosa-Luxemburg-Stiftung, No. 10–2010.

Zick, A. (2017), 'Extremistische Inszenierungen: Elemente und Pfade von Radikalisierungs- und Deradikalisierungsprozessen', in N. Böckler and J. Hoffmann (eds), *Radikalisierung und extremistische Gewalt: Perspektiven aus dem Fall- und Bedrohungsmanagement*, 15–36, Frankfurt am Main: Verlag für Polizeiwissenschaft.

Zick, A., C. Wolfe, B. Küpper, E. Davidov, P. Schmidt and W. Heitmeyer (2008), 'The Syndrome of Group-Focused Enmity: The Interrelation of Prejudices Tested with Multiple Cross-Sectional and Panel Data', *Journal of Social Issues*, 64 (2): 363–84. https://doi.org/10.1111/j.1540-4560.2008.00566.x.

Zick, A., B. Küpper and W. Berghan (2019), *Verlorene Mitte - feindselige Zustände: Rechtsextreme Einstellungen in Deutschland 2018*. Bonn: Dietz, JH.

14

Mapping conspiritual radicalization: The intersection of conspiracy movements, spirituality and radicalization

Vivian Gerrand

Introduction

While significant research has been undertaken into religiously inspired or attributed radicalization to violent extremism, relatively little attention has been paid to the ways in which 'conspirituality' – a portmanteau term used to describe the intersection of conspiracy theories and contemporary forms of spirituality (Ward and Voas 2011) – may also feature in trajectories of radicalization. This chapter explores how conspiracy thinking has been mobilized by alternative/new religious movement (NRM) influencers during the Covid-19 pandemic to the detriment of democracy and public health strategies. Mapping radicalization trajectories towards militant forms of conspiritual thinking and wellness, I identify the ways in which the conducive environment of Covid-19-heightened vulnerabilities has intersected with the unique selling points of conspiracist spiritual and wellness groups, often with an agenda that leverages existing individualized spiritual beliefs, pandemic-related anxieties, traumatic legacies, loss of trust in institutions and hesitancy surrounding vaccines.

Rather than viewing such radicalization trajectories in isolation or as exceptions, I explore here the ways in which conspiracist or conspiritualist radicalization trajectories mobilize cherry-picked versions of spirituality to construct polarizing in- and out-group dynamics that bear similarities to those of religiously inspired or attributed extremist groups. To enhance understanding of how spiritually inspired or attributed forms of radicalization to conspiracy thinking have increased their reach and influence during the pandemic, I draw on qualitative digital ethnographic case studies of radicalization to conspiritual thinking and militancy as observed through the social media and encrypted messaging applications of three popular, trusted alternative health and wellness influencers – Dr Christiane Northrup, Pete Evans and JP Sears – to explore these issues.

Understanding conspirituality in the Covid-19 context

While 'religion' is understood to typically refer to traditional institutionalized belief systems, and 'spiritual' denotes an individual's 'free relationship with the sacred', the terms 'religion' and 'spiritual' are used in this chapter with mindfulness of their ambiguous and contested nature (Palmisano and Pannofino 2020). Recent studies complicate their boundaries, arguing for novel articulations of how religion and spirituality are mobilized and intertwined within a post-secular esoteric, holistic spiritual milieu. This holistic spiritual milieu, particularly in the West, has seen an expansion of individualized, hybrid and self-empowered 'lived experience' epistemologies not matched by a growth in institutional religions (Halafoff, Shipley et al. 2020, Griera et al. 2022, Roginski and Rocha 2022). Indeed, the New Age spiritual movement is often referred to as a New Religious Movement (NRM) (Lewis and Tøllefsen 2016).

Online environments have enabled access to a smorgasbord of new religious and conspiritual influences and influencers who have become trusted sources of information in the face of prevalent distrust in governments and institutions. Characterized by suspicion of elite global control and New Age consciousness, conspirituality was already a significant political and spiritual philosophical movement prior to the Covid-19 pandemic (Campbell 1972, Griera et al. 2022).

Spiritual and wellness communities, long-time proponents of complementary and alternative healing practices, were not immune to conspiracy thinking well before the arrival of Covid-19. The introduction of divisive QAnon ideology into these communities through prominent lifestyle influencers has led some to radicalize along conspiritual trajectories of militancy (Beres, Remski and Walker 2020, Kelly 2020, Khalil 2020), including recruitment into violent extremism (Berger, Aryaeinejad and Looney 2020, Avis 2020). Covid-19 intensified engagement with this movement, which has attracted new adherents through the promotion of the idea that the pandemic was an opportunity for awakening, planetary ascension and transformation, in pointed contrast to the characterization of government public health and biomedical strategies adopted to address the crisis as a threat to freedom, mental and physical well-being.

Messaging within conspiritual networks encouraged alternative health and spiritual practices, intuition, magic and bodily autonomy (Halafoff, Shipley et al. 2020, Parmigiani 2021) as a mode of resistance to public health measures such as mask-wearing, lockdowns and vaccines, which have been viewed as instruments of 'deep state' control and surveillance together with 5G technologies (Amarasingam and Argentino 2020, Halafoff, Weng et al. 2020, Kelly 2021). This messaging intersected with the accelerationist narratives of far-right political actors, which also promoted anti-vaccine sentiment through the notion, for example, that the Covid-19 vaccine rollout was part of a plot to sterilize 'White' populations (Richards 2022).

Spirituality, wellness and radicalization in an environment of grievances

Public health measures critical to stopping the global spread of Covid-19 led to job loss, uncertainty, trauma and increased time spent online in many countries.

In addition to ushering in an era of expanded internet dominance, the impacts of the pandemic in Australia, the United States, Canada, Europe and elsewhere have deepened existing socio-economic atomization and inequalities, and with them vulnerabilities to novel kinds of social influence in an environment of heightened sense of grievance and fear. Combined with the multimodal affordances (Eisenlauer and Karatza 2021) of clear and encrypted internet platforms, this has hastened the targeted 'sale' of particular brands of social division (Dexter, Fox Koob and Estcourt 2021). Their appeal rests in offering simple solutions to a highly complex set of problems or in identifying a ready-made scapegoat. They have also appealed to the need for belonging in ways that, rather than promoting solidarity across different groups experiencing common challenges, have instead focused on creating and profiting from antagonistic communities.

Perceptions that public health measures are authoritarian have been accompanied by a parallel growth in conspiracy-oriented ideologies, which have infiltrated and connected unexpected demographics, including stay-at-home mothers (Dickson 2020, Kelly 2020), Indigenous communities (Yunkaporta 2022), extreme-right actors (Richards 2022) and yoga practitioners (Beres, Remski and Walker 2020). Uniting them was a search for alternative explanations that might help make sense of what was happening, especially in situations of lockdown for those who were effectively housebound because of mobility and travel restrictions and unable to undertake their normal activities.

This became particularly acute in countries like Australia, for example, when public health measures shut down allied health responses to the pandemic, leaving patients desperate and practitioners forced to go underground to treat them. That these health services were deemed non-essential while other orthodox Western health practitioners, touted as heroes by politicians and the media, were able to continue working alienated sections of the spiritual and complementary and alternative health community who were deeply invested in managing Covid-19 on their own terms. This further amplified distrust in and resentment towards biomedical institutions such as big pharmaceutical companies and governments. It prompted an elevation within these communities of conspiracy-thinking about the pandemic, in particular the introduction of the QAnon conspiracy – a divisive social movement originating in the United States that advocates resistance to so-called 'global elites' who are seen as manipulating populations for their own ends.

These dynamics fostered increased crossover between the far right and a radical action orientation that is now discernible in wellness and spiritual epistemic communities. A small minority of conspiritualists has radicalized to what I term (along with Beres, Remski and Walker 2020) militant wellness (Gerrand 2020b). 'Militancy' is conjoined here with wellness to refer to the ways in which some cohorts within conspiritual and wellness demographics now position themselves as being in a state of combat or conflict, usually with public health measures imposed by governments. Militancy refers to both posture and action orientation. While the specific influencers analysed below, for example, have not undertaken overt violent actions consistent with those of terrorists, they have adopted militant stances that draw on a repertoire of extremist bonding icons (Wignell, Tan and O'Halloran 2017) explicitly linked to violence or the threat of violent action such as guns, MAGA caps and Neo-Nazi symbols.

Extremist groups with divergent ideologies have undergone accelerated cross-pollination in the Covid-19 crisis (Khalil 2020). Scholars have begun to pay attention towards developing syncretic trends (Argentino, Amarasingam and Conley 2022) and common philosophical emphases among extremist groups such as an investment in purity and black and white thinking (Gerrand 2020a, Cassam 2021). In this sense, the Covid-19 pandemic has enabled mostly far-right extremist actors to mobilize and recruit within diverse demographics.

In contemporary usage, the term 'radicalization' tends to refer to the process whereby individuals 'come to view violence as a legitimate method of solving social and political conflicts' (Bermingham et al. 2009). Without a particular set of enabling cultural, socio-economic, historical and political conditions, however, extreme ideologies in themselves are unlikely to lead people towards violent action. As in other democracies that have imposed vaccine mandates, demonstrations in Australia during the longest of its six lockdowns during 2020 and 2021 have included anti-democratic extremists seeking to capitalize on pandemic-induced grievances, including credible threats against government and public health officials' lives (Hunter 2021, McKenzie and Lucas 2021, Mason 2021, Roose 2021, Cecco 2022). A range of countries saw healthcare workers, vaccination centres and ordinary citizens complying with public health orders also become targets of hate (Kelly 2021, Pasqualetto 2021, Karvelas 2021). Alt-right groups have converged with anti-mask, anti-vaccine and anti-lockdown protestors at medical facilities with healthcare workers also experiencing physical assault (Beres, Remski and Walker 2021, Kennedy 2021, Pasqualetto 2021).

Such incidents highlight the deleterious social consequences of the turn towards militancy on the part of a cohort of conspiritual, far-right and wellness activists. While the targeted violence displayed in their behaviour is specific to the context of the pandemic, it is not unique in its antagonistic impulse to define, attack and remove an enemy, an impulse shared by all exclusivist violent groups, and one that threatens democracy.

That the activists themselves claim to be dissenting in defence of their freedoms is critical (Beres, Remski and Walker 2021). Within the Australian context – in which emergency measures were used to pursue a 'Covid-zero' strategy for much of 2020 and 2021 – this conducive environment of grievances arguably peaked during Melbourne's sixth lockdown (for a timeline of Melbourne's Covid-19 lockdowns, see Boaz 2021). Unlike the rest of Australia, Melbourne had had a uniquely long lockdown in 2020 that lasted from July to October of that year. While this lockdown proved damaging to mental health and livelihoods and in some cases breached human rights (Glass 2020), it nevertheless produced the desired outcome of zero Covid cases, freeing the city to reopen once the lockdown had ended. During the 2021 lockdown, by contrast, many in the community were already at breaking point both financially and psychologically (Teixeira da Silva 2021) without the economic support experienced for closed businesses through the Australian federal government's Jobkeeper and Jobseeker schemes that had protected livelihoods and people from poverty in 2020.

When vaccine mandates were introduced in the middle of this third long lockdown, the conducive environment of grievances peaked. The absence of supports and increased strain on the community increased the vulnerability of some to the influence of alternative health and far-right influences who appeared to be listening sympathetically to community concerns about the impact of long lockdowns and fears about new-generation vaccines being mandated.

Throughout the pandemic, alternative spiritual and wellness communities had striven to address many of these concerns, providing an interpretative lens that brought certainty and comfort – a distinctive feature of religious thought – to these communities at a time of crisis (Carone and Barone 2001). The introduction of vaccine mandates produced an intersection of social influence and grievance that led many to join encrypted messaging applications (used by those whose content had been deplatformed from mainstream outlets) where they could find solace in likeminded cohorts and access unmoderated and frequently conspiratorial content from around the world, priming some of the city's inhabitants for civil unrest. Combined with the closure of particular industries (such as construction) previously accustomed to favourable treatment during the pandemic as industries considered essential to keep the economy going during lockdown periods, there was little to keep the anger of some of the city's inhabitants off the streets.

Represented in the media as 'Neo-Nazi' demonstrations, the civil street protests that ensued served as recruitment grounds for disgruntled members of the community, putting them in touch, many for the first time, with far-right agendas and organizations. The fact that much of the media reported the demonstrations as being uniformly sympathetic to neo-Nazi ideology only served to enhance far right groups' notoriety and prominence within the mainstream (Brown, Mondon and Winter 2021, Thomas 2021) and strengthen the pipeline from vaccine hesitancy and anger over lockdowns to adherence to conspiracy-led militancy. Prominent lifestyle influencers began to don MAGA hats, switching from 'left-wing' to 'right-wing' seemingly overnight in ways that have confounded easy analyses of their ideological dispositions.

Adherents to conspiracy and extreme wellness movements are readily dismissed as unstable. Yet the motivations driving their trajectories of radicalization are both highly complex and context-dependent, requiring detailed and critically empathetic analysis of the narratives, networks and nuances that inform their pathways into militant radicalization (Kruglanski, Belanger and Gunaratna 2019, McAleer 2019, Gerrand 2020b).

To begin this part of the discussion, I turn now to an analysis of the trajectories of Dr Christiane Northrup, Pete Evans and JP Sears, three conspiritual influencers who were both popular and prominent prior to the pandemic and who have all adopted conspiracy-based ideologies that have led them to radicalize to militancy. Observing discursive shifts in their social media content since the outset of the Covid-19 pandemic, and comparing this content with their pre-pandemic material, the analysis will consider their unique selling points and their intersection with conspiracy, polarizing content and incitement to violent action, covering selected content between May 2020, when Mikki Willis's film *Plandemic* (2020) was released, and March 2022. Digital ethnography methods, combined with multimodal analysis (Kress 2009), are used to examine the narratives and networks of each of these wellness community influencers to conceptualize and map such trajectories. Digital ethnography enables insight into the sociocultural dimensions of human interactions online, including how algorithmic environments may drive radicalization (Little and Richards 2021).

A multimodal approach is used to qualitatively assess the narratives contained within the content on these platforms. Multimodal analysis is central to the success of this method as it pays attention to the role of image, sound and gesture and the meaning made from their interaction with text, enhancing critical discourse analysis (Machin 2013). The posts and their accompanying engagements in the comments section are coded for their promotion of unique selling points: simplicity and certainty (black and white thinking), bodily autonomy and survival of the fittest, individualization of responsibility (it's your fault if you fall ill), invocation to militancy and violence (direct or indirect), intuition over the biomedical model, and invocation of terrain theory and purity.

My understanding of these trajectories is also informed by my long-term investment in alternative health approaches and connection to wellness communities over a twenty-year period as a yoga practitioner. As a researcher of radicalization who is also an 'insider' within such communities, friendships with allied health workers and people who have turned to conspirituality in the pandemic have granted me informal access to the nuances of the religiously guarded attachment to bodily autonomy, magical thinking, intuition and both bodily and cognitive sovereignty.

Throughout the pandemic, I have maintained close relationships with friends who are on the vaccine-hesitant spectrum. In addition, over a seven-month period from September 2021 until March 2022, I have regularly monitored the Telegram accounts of local and global anti-lockdown, anti-vaccine mandate groups whose adherents' concerns overlap in many areas with those of the three conspiritualist influencers examined below. In particular, my analysis is informed by the activities of anti-lockdown groups that generated hundreds of new notifications from anti-vaccine groups during Melbourne's third long lockdown, which lasted from August until October 2021.

The unique selling points of conspirituality and militant wellness

The pandemic has provided an ideal environment and opportunity for extremist actors to mobilize around shared holistic understandings of health, often underpinned by terrain theory (Gainty 2021), that bond them while conflicting with public health measures. In an analysis of the self-presentation strategies of four alternative health influencers who adopted conspiritual thinking in the pandemic, wellness researcher Baker (2022) found that some influencers also monetize their audiences through a range of alternative health modalities – from supplements to retreats – for economic, political and social profit.

Wellness adherents may have little trust in government institutions and pharmaceutical companies, but readily place their trust in parasocial relationships with macro- and micro-influencers (Baker 2022) with whom they share an investment in bodily autonomy, purity, superiority and vaccine hesitancy. Time spent online in closed groups following the stories of people who have experienced negative side effects from Covid-19 vaccinations, for example, may position vaccines as a social harm. Algorithmic design that recommends and reinforces familiar content (Gillespie 2019) may then work to entrench emotional silos in which heightened focus on the potential rare side effects of coronavirus vaccines eclipses the much more common damaging health consequences of contracting Covid-19.

By failing to bridge different perspectives and information sets, such spaces reproduce the kind of content that drives exclusivist forms of resilience to the detriment of democracy and social cohesion (Grossman et al. 2016) – evident in the rise of conspiracy thinking during the Covid-19 pandemic which led in part to the United States's riots on Capitol Hill in January 2021 and to ongoing social unrest in Europe, North America and Oceania. Antisocial forms of resilience have been the subject of considerable sociological research (e.g. Aly et al. 2016, Grossman 2021) as efforts to prevent violent radicalization have proliferated. Increased attention has also been paid to the growth of QAnon (Amarasingam and Argentino 2020), wellness influencers (Baker 2022) and conspiritual movements (Halafoff, Weng et al. 2020, Bertuzzi 2021). The specific trajectories of militant wellness by which people in wellness communities radicalize to violent extremism, becoming an in-group that must expel an outgroup to secure its legitimacy through violent action (Berger 2017, 2018), remain poorly understood.

Wellness influencer JP Sears, the creator of YouTube video series *AwakenWithJP* (2013–present), identified some of the unique selling points of conspirituality and militant wellness in an Instagram post from October 2021 in which he claims to have tested positive to sovereignty. The post was captioned 'This infection feels pretty damn good. Let me know if you've tested positive' and continues:

> JUST TESTED POSITIVE FOR SOVEREIGNTY
> Symptoms include:
> Critical thinking
> Bodily autonomy
> Speaking your truth
> The gift of discernment
> Standing up against tyranny
> Advocating for your children
> Socially distancing from the system

These themes emerge consistently in the analysis of the radicalization trajectories of the three influencers covered here. Content within local and international anti-lockdown and anti-vaccine mandate Telegram groups such as Vic Freedom Movement (in Victoria, Australia), Anti Vaxx Daily News and the Italian *Io non mi vaccino* (I won't be vaccinated), affirms this attachment to sovereignty and bodily autonomy on the part of these group's adherents. It also confirms the importance of regarding oneself to be a 'critical thinker', doing one's 'own research' in the pursuit of truth in order to protect children and reject the perceived 'tyranny' of 'the system'. To these characteristics, one may add certainty, purity, belonging, magical thinking, simplicity (mythologized past), essentialist understandings of gender, the promise of 'great collective awakening', atomization and superiority, 'survival of the fittest' and the concept of trickle-down wellness (Gerrand 2020b).

The next section maps the trajectories of holistic health influencers who have both adopted and encouraged conspiracy thinking in the pandemic, culminating in an embrace of the right, alt- and far right – for example, shifting in the US context from supporting the Democrats to supporting the Republican Party (which has itself shifted further towards the far right in recent years) in order to understand the ways in which the messaging of conspiritual and alternative health influencers has driven disinformation conducive to radicalization (Center for Countering Digital Hate 2021a).

Christiane Northrup

Self-healing is a highly personal and individual process. Self-healing requires personal disarmament, refusing to be at war any longer with a part of your body or your life that's trying to tell you something. Let war end with you.

(Northrup [1994] 2020: 1570)

The following excerpt is from an interview with Christiane Northrup by Jeff Witzeman in the documentary *Signposts on the Road to Ascension* (2021).

JW *There's an illusion with you that oh, Chris Northrup – she's come to this place now where she's on this plateau and she doesn't have to feel anymore.*

CN *Oh my God. You know, there are parts of me ... and so I've learned to love them, ok. Here's an example. Alright, let's see. Do I get to pick the firing squad to kill these demons? Now, if you were a New Age person and you read books like 'You cannot afford the luxury of a negative thought', you would be afraid that that thought is going to somehow lead you to 'oh oh oh cancel cancel cancel – I had a bad thought, I wanted to harm that person ...'*

No. I like those thoughts. I listen to Zev Zelenko [anti-vaccine doctor] say: 'I am all for love and forgiveness and if anyone comes near one of my children, I will have no problem putting a bullet in their head.' I want people to own that part of themselves because that is righteous anger. It is a cause of health.

Alternative health practitioner and conspiritualist Dr Christiane Northrup has become iconic within militant wellness spaces in the pandemic. A qualified physician in obstetrics and gynaecology known for her bestselling books such as *Women's Bodies, Women's Wisdom* ([1994] 2020) and *The Wisdom of Menopause* ([2001] 2021), Northrup's alignment with QAnon-adjacent ideology in the coronavirus pandemic and her anti-vaccine messaging claiming that Covid-19 vaccines are more dangerous than Covid-19 have had significant influence over her large number of followers.

Northrup's publications have drawn on a blend of individualized hybrid pseudoscientific and scientific spiritual beliefs that are rooted in occult, pagan and energy-based medicine privileging emotion and intuition. Northrup views healing as 'a highly personal and individual process'; her *Women's Bodies* draws upon complementary and alternative holistic medical practices that promote a shift 'from external control to self-care', culminating in a twelve-step 'Women's Wisdom Program for Flourishing and Healing', the final step of which is to 'actively pursue pleasure and purpose' (Northrup [1994] 2020).

Prior to the Covid-19 pandemic, Northrup had dedicated much of her life to supporting women through holistic health methods and encouraging them to put themselves first. Northrup told women to listen to their bodies, express their needs, face uncomfortable feelings, view age as 'just a number' and to live according to your values (Northrup 2013). Dr Northrup had published best-selling books on holistic health to support processes such as menopause through alternative methodologies, including shifting the psychology around ageing to see it as a 'gift' rather than a burden. Northrup had become a prominent voice within alternative health circles and is a trusted source of information for people – especially women – who felt let down by Western medical approaches to health. Earlier in her life, Northrup had been a more mainstream progressive figure, reportedly donating to the US Democratic Party.

The pandemic prompted a shift in Northrup's political stance and, in keeping with Mikki Willis's documentary film *Plandemic* (2020), upheld the idea that the novel coronavirus was fabricated to consolidate the power of elites. Since the Covid-19 pandemic, Northrup has promoted conspiracies such as the extreme and unfounded idea that the Covid-19-vaccinated can harm the unvaccinated through 'shedding' and has urged unvaccinated partners to leave their vaccinated partners (Remski 2021a). The Center for Countering Digital Hate (2021b) has identified Northrup in their list of most influential medical misinformation proponents, the Disinformation Dozen. More recently, Northrup has adopted explicitly militant rhetoric, as is evident from the excerpt above from her 2022 interview above with filmmaker Jeff Witzeman about undertaking collective violent action through a 'firing squad' in the name of righteous anger, which she claims is a 'cause of health'. Northrup's shift from progressive, alternative health practitioner invested in holistic approaches to women's health and sexuality to 'matriarch of pastel-Q', Trump-supporting 'light worker' (Remski 2021b) is illustrative of trajectories of conspirituality more broadly (Dickson 2020).

Northrup's new social media accounts appear to have understood the need to mask her militant rhetoric: a recent post on her new Instagram page featured her playing a harp while talking about her views on gun laws. As a post-menopausal gynaecologist playing a harp, her image would likely have led content moderators to regard her as harmless, enabling her to continue to promote her militant messaging.

Following the take-down of her most popular social media account, Northrup migrated to alternative tech platforms with minimal content moderation. Nevertheless, her most controversial content no longer appears on her Facebook and Instagram accounts after one account with 150,000 followers was removed. Frequent posts on these accounts remind followers to access Northrup's unmoderated content on alternative tech platforms, including the far-right favourite Gab.

Pete Evans

The wholefoods cookbooks, condiments and wellness products of Australian celebrity chef Pete Evans had enjoyed broad appeal and fame until the Covid-19 pandemic (LeClerc 2022). In the pandemic, however, Evans's focus on wellness led him from being a proponent of edgy dietary advice to one of extremist narratives and practices that attracted warnings and fines from health authorities (Therapeutic Goods Administration 2021). In November 2020, beside the bowls of lush superfood ingredients that had made Evans a household name, the celebrity chef posted a meme online that led to his publisher and major sponsors ending their relationship with him (Quinn and Carmody 2020).

According to Evans, the cartoon featured 'a caterpillar and a butterfly having a chat over a drink'. However, it also juxtaposed two potent symbols of division. One of the insects wore a red MAGA (Make America Great Again) hat, while the other displayed the ancient Norse Sonnenrad, the black sun Nazi occult symbol (Anti-Defamation League n.d.) flaunted by the far-right terrorist in Christchurch as part of his manifesto before he murdered fifty-one people in 2019 (Wilson 2020). Evans's ambiguous attempt to walk back this invocation of violence by claiming the innocence of insects talking failed to convince, and he was soon de-platformed for violating Facebook and Instagram's terms of service.

The commonly held view that Evans was simply unhinged at the time of posting the symbol fails to account for the overlap of his radicalization with that of many others. Indeed, the respective radicalization pathways explored here illuminate some key features of how conspiritualist thinking and its crossover with QAnon and far-right conspiracies have infiltrated some quarters of the wellness industry (Halafoff, Weng et al. 2020, Khalil 2020).

Crisis, trauma and uncertainty create psychosocial conditions that increase vulnerability to black and white conspiracy thinking and extremism. In wellness circles, and within the far right (but also in other extremist organizations), there is also often a high value placed on purity, which then sets the scene for spiritual ascension (Baker 2022). Accompanied by the fantasy of a return to a simple, mythologized past – what sociologist Zygmunt Bauman (2017) terms a 'retrotopia' – this desire for purity was mobilized in Nazi Germany to perpetrate genocide. Hitler's radical embrace of environmental protections, early anti-smoking and associated *volkisch* lifestyle campaigns for Aryan 'blood and soil' contributed to his racial hygiene movement, which sought to romance an (imagined) neo-paganism connection with nature and the 'pure' or biologically and culturally unadulterated Aryan body (Koehne 2012). Operating at another time of crisis (post-Spanish flu pandemic and the ensuing Great Depression), Hitler sought to control and purify the German nation by pursuing the Third Reich.

Clearly, the cleansing of one's physical body and so-called 'ethnic cleansing' are not one and the same. But does a desire to purify one's body sometimes make someone susceptible to other ideas that promote purity? In Nazi Germany, doctors were tasked with 'cleansing' their national community of perceived threats following the racialized principles of eugenics. As Susan Bachrach writes in her article on the Nazi doctrine of 'racial hygiene': 'Racial hygiene measures began with the mass sterilization of the "genetically diseased" and ended with the near-annihilation of European Jewry' (2004: 147).

Unlike in Nazi Germany, in which national public health was given priority, understandings of well-being outside the context of public health crises are today often limited to individual health. The wellness industry tends to promote health as a personal responsibility. If you're sick, it's your fault. In this atomized view of humanity – one that has driven neoliberal policies for decades – poverty is also a moral failing (Gerrand 2020a). Within the Australian context, however, Evans soon found parliamentary allies among fringe politicians who had been courting the anti-lockdown movement with respect to vaccine resistance and government overreach. One of these allies was Liberal Party MP turned Independent Craig Kelly, who had sought to cultivate vaccine hesitancy in the community via indiscriminate text messages to Australians on the electoral role with links to the Therapeutic Goods Association's list of Covid-19 vaccine side effects.

JP Sears

Star comic wellness influencer JP Sears, who reaches mass audiences on YouTube through his YouTube channel *AwakenWithJP* (2013–present), embodies militant wellness. Sears has moved from producing 'ultra-spiritual' satire that once provided refreshing relief from wellness gurus who took themselves too seriously to the promotion of anti-masking, anti-government messaging, anti-vaccination, unproven health supplements and 'freedom'-badged merchandise. Sears's brand of awakening entails both 'waking up' and enlightenment and, during the pandemic, also served to signify his commitment to retailing the 'truth' and seeing through the 'mainstream narrative', which he critiques in comic videos that convey an increasingly radical far-right agenda. It is important to note that Sears's brand of freedom does not include freedom to be gender diverse. Sears's posts have escalated from gender essentialism in 2020 to overt transphobia in 2022, an anti-gender stance that misinformation researchers Little and Richards (2021) have found can readily 'lead users from transphobic videos to far-right rabbit holes' on social media platforms.

Since early 2020, Sears has used social media platforms to satirize the 2020 US election, encourage his followers to question Biden's victory and promote the idea of an incipient civil war, all while advertising a range of alternative health products such as 'Primally Pure' deodorant (Gerrand 2020b). Unlike earnest conspiritualists such as Dr Christiane Northrup, JP Sears has yet to have his accounts de-platformed from popular social media platforms Facebook and Instagram. He enjoys the largest following on mainstream social media platforms of the influencers analysed in this chapter. Sears's use of satire has enabled him to continue to post controversial topics through the lens of humour that has enabled his communications of medical misinformation and conspiracies about the 2020 US election to escape the attention of content moderators.

On Instagram in the lead-up to the 2020 US election, Sears boasted that he had bought a gun as part of taking his spirituality 'more seriously'. Rather than triggering an alarm for content moderators to the violent potential of advertising such a purchase, it fits within Sears's broader comic narrative appeal to his long-time followers, many of whom responded to the post with clapping and thumbs-up emojis. The Instagram post of Sears holding a gun was carefully juxtaposed against a resort-like poolside location. Sears wore a cloak, slippers and bathing suit, his ludic attire masking the perception that he could be inciting hatred or violence and playing to his persona as a comedian. This technique of disguising radicalizing content has been used by a range of actors on the far-right spectrum to retain popular accounts.

Like comedy, the posting of everyday mainstream content can readily garner significant audiences on Instagram with the right hashtags. When interspersed with occasional violent material, this can work as a deliberate 'slow red-pill' strategy of recruitment (Citarella 2021). In the case of Sears, comedy throughout the pandemic has done the work of normalizing anti-government attitudes. Now, it is deftly wielded (insofar as it has not led to take-downs) to model the crossing over into violent action orientation. The crossing over in the image referenced above looks like a life-enhancing carnivalesque game of dress-ups, rather than something that could easily end life.

In January 2022, Sears posted a video captioned 'Why I was wrong about guns' in which he reflects on how his views on gun ownership have changed *(AwakenWithJP,* Episode 61). The video, titled 'Why we need more guns', includes excerpts from a pre-pandemic recording made in which Sears satirizes Republican-voting gun owners as backward and gullible. These excerpts contrast with his current view that the US Constitution's Second Amendment right to bear arms is central to protecting the Constitution's other amendments: above all, freedom.

Sears has since become a staunch supporter of anti-vaccine mandate protests in North America, giving a speech in praise of freedom at a 'Defeat the Mandates' rally in January 2022. Held on the steps of Capitol Hill in Washington, Sears's speech included praise for those responsible for the 6 January insurrection a year earlier. Resonant with the militancy of Northrup's stated willingness to kill to defend children's rights and slay 'demons', Sears's militancy has shifted from comic to overt. The implications of this shift are clear, yet Sears has still managed to maintain his popular social media accounts, while Northrup's and Evans's accounts were de-platformed.

Conclusion

This chapter has considered the radicalization trajectories of three conspiritual influencers in the context of the Covid-19 pandemic. The conspiritual radicalization trajectories of Dr Christiane Northrup, Pete Evans and JP Sears appeal to individualized forms of spirituality and investment in bodily autonomy, control and purification at a time of crisis. The militant radicalization trajectory of each one of these influencers highlights some of the key ways in which the crossover between the far right and radical action orientation has occurred in wellness and spiritual epistemic communities. While the influencers analysed here have not undertaken overt violent actions consistent with those of terrorists, they have adopted militant stances that draw on a repertoire of (violent) extremist bonding icons (Wignell, Tan and O'Halloran 2017) such as guns, MAGA caps and Neo-Nazi symbols.

The fact that popular alternative health and spiritual influencers Evans and Northrup pursued conspiracy-based messaging strategies that led to a loss of mainstream credibility and lucrative commercial publishing contracts indicates the extent to which these influencers were acting with conviction. Both had cultivated the trust of their followers of holistic health and spiritual promotion and dietary advice over decades. The radicalization trajectory of JP Sears, conversely, recalls those of pandemic profiteer micro-influencers who have achieved prominence from the adoption and promotion of anti-vaccine, Q-Adjacent content. Evans and Northrup lost status with the broader community in their conspiritual radicalization trajectories. Their shift from celebrities to de-platformed conspiracists transmogrified these once famous figures, reducing their reach and influence within the mainstream cultures where they had attracted large followings.

In the case of all three influencers, spirituality is individualized, and health and wealth are considered personal concerns, rather than attributes of particular cultures, histories, structures and systems. Many spiritual and wellness adherents no longer regard public health as a collective responsibility. These same attitudes were acutely manifest in anti-mask, anti-lockdown and anti-vaccine mandate demonstrations with their cries for 'freedom' from public health pandemic orders. Conspiritual trajectories of radicalization remind us that, like religion, spirituality, health and wellness may be co-opted by conspiracy thinking and powerful vested interests. To address the ongoing ramifications of such radicalization trajectories, it is important to acknowledge that there is usually a kernel of truth in conspiracy-thinking. Genuine concerns about the exploitative nature of large, profit-before-people agricultural, fossil fuel, pharmaceutical and tech industries often animate conspiracies such as that of QAnon. Instead of dismissing them, the conspiritual milieu's engagement with these concerns highlights the nature of the perceived threat being experienced. It also presents compelling evidence for the urgent need to listen to anxieties and respond pro-socially to multisystemic grievances in order to restore trust in governments and institutions (Gerrand 2020c) if we are to avert the proliferation of conspiritual militant radicalization.

References

Aly, A., S. Macdonald, L. Jarvis and T. M. Chen (2016), *Violent Extremism Online: New Perspectives on Terrorism and the Internet*. Abingdon: Taylor & Francis.

Amarasingam, A and M. Argentino (2020), 'The QAnon Conspiracy Theory: A Security Threat in the Making?' *CTC Sentinel*, 13 (7): 37–44.

Ammerman, N. T. (2013), 'Spiritual but Not Religious? Beyond Binary Choices in the Study of Religion', *Journal for the Scientific Study of Religion*, 52 (2): 258–78.

Anti-Defamation League (n.d.), 'Sonnenrad'. Available online: https://www.adl.org/resources/hate-symbol/sonnenrad (accessed 6 October 2022).

Argentino, M., A. Amarasingam and E. Conley (2022), 'One Struggle': Examining Narrative Syncretism between Accelerationalist and Salafi-Jihadists, London: International Study for the Centre of Radicalization.

Avis, W. (2020), *The COVID-19 Pandemic and Response on Violent Extremist Recruitment and Radicalization*, K4D Helpdesk Report 808, Brighton, UK: Institute of Development Studies. Available online: https://opendocs.ids.ac.uk/opendocs/handle/20.500.12413/15322 (accessed 6 October 2022).

AwakenWithJP (2013–present), [Video series] Dir. JP Sears. USA: YouTube. Available online: https://www.youtube.com/user/AwakenWithJP (accessed 6 October 2022).

Bachrach, S. (2004), 'In the Name of Public Health – Nazi Racial Hygiene', *The New England Journal of Medicine*, 351: 417–20. Available online: https://www.nejm.org/doi/full/10.1056/nejmp048136 (accessed 6 October 2022).

Baker, S. A. (2022), 'Alt. Health Influencers: How Wellness Culture and Web Culture Have Been Weaponised to Promote COVID-19 Conspiracy Theories and Far-Right Extremism', *European Journal of Cultural Studies*, 25 (1): 3–24.

Bauman, Z. (2017), *Retrotopia*. London: Polity Press.

Beres, D., M. Remski and J. Walker (2020), 'Om-ed and Dangerous: Militant Wellness' with Sarah Hightower', *Conspirituality* Podcast, 15 October. Available online: https://conspirituality.net/wellness/21-om-ed-and-dangerous-militant-wellness/ (accessed 6 October 2022).

Beres, D., M. Remski and J. Walker (2021), 'Fascism Down Under!!! With Dr Izzy Smith', *Conspirituality* Podcast, 16 September. Available online: https://conspirituality.net/wellness/69-fascism-down-under-w-dr-izzy-smith/ (accessed 6 October 2022).

Berger, J. M. (2018), *Extremism*. Cambridge, MA: MIT Press.

Berger, J. M. (2017), *Extremist Construction of Identity: How Escalating Demands for Legitimacy Shape and Define In-Group and Out-Group Dynamics*. The Hague: The International Centre for Counter-Terrorism.

Berger, J. M., K. Aryaeinejad and S. Looney (2020), 'There and Back Again: How White Nationalist Ephemera Travels between Online and Offline Spaces', *The RUSI Journal*, 165 (1): 114–29.

Bermingham, A., M. Conway, L. McInerney, N. O'Hare and A. F. Smeaton (2009), 'Combining Social Network Analysis and Sentiment Analysis to Explore the Potential for Online Radicalisation', *2009 International Conference on Advances in Social Network Analysis and Mining*, 231–6, https://doi.org/10.1109/ASONAM.2009.31.

Bertuzzi, N. (2021), 'Conspiracy Theories and Social Movements Studies: A Research Agenda', *Sociology Compass*, 15 (12), December. https://doi.org/10.1111/soc4.12945.

Boaz, J. (2021), 'Melbourne Passes Buenos Aires' World Record for Time Spent in COVID-19 Lockdown', *ABC News*, 3 October. Available online: https://www.abc.net.au/news/2021-10-03/melbourne-longest-lockdown/100510710 (accessed 6 October 2022).

Brown, K., A. Mondon and A. Winter (2021), 'The Far Right, the Mainstream and Mainstreaming: Towards a Heuristic Framework', *Journal of Political Ideologies*, 28 (2): 152–79. https://doi.org/10.1080/13569317.2021.1949829.

Campbell, C. (1972), 'The Cult, the Cultic Milieu and Secularisation', in *A Sociological Yearbook of Religion in Britain* (5), London: SCM Press.

Carone, D. A. and D. F. Barone (2001), 'A Social Cognitive Perspective on Religious Beliefs: Their Functions and Impact on Coping and Psychotherapy', *Clinical Psychology Review*, 21 (7): 989–1003.

Cassam, Q. (2021), *Extremism: A Philosophical Analysis*. London: Routledge.
Cecco, L. (2022), '"Queen of Canada": The Rapid Rise of a Fringe QAnon Figure Sounds Alarm', *The Guardian*, 23 August. Available online: https://www.theguardian.com/world/2022/aug/23/queen-of-canada-qanon-rise-conspiracy-alarm (accessed 14 June 2024).
Center for Countering Digital Hate (2021a), 'Pandemic Profiteers. The Business of Anti-Vaxx', 1 June. Available online: https://counterhate.com/research/pandemic-profiteers/ (accessed 6 October 2022).
Center for Countering Digital Hate (2021b), 'The Disinformation Dozen: Why Platforms Must Act on Twelve Leading Online Anti-Vaxxers', 21 March. Available online: https://counterhate.com/research/the-disinformation-dozen/ (accessed 6 October 2022).
Citarella, J. (2021), 'There's a New Tactic for Exposing You to Radical Content Online: The "Slow Red-Pill"', *The Guardian*, 15 July. Available online: https://www.theguardian.com/commentisfree/2021/jul/15/theres-a-new-tactic-for-exposing-you-to-radical-content-online-the-slow-red-pill (accessed 6 October 2022).
Dexter, R., S. Fox Koob and D. Estcourt (2021), 'The Price of "Freedom": How Anti-Lockdown Protest Leaders Make Money from the Movement', *Sydney Morning Herald*, 12 December. Available online: https://www.smh.com.au/national/the-price-of-freedom-how-anti-lockdown-protest-leaders-make-money-from-the-movement-20211130-p59de5.html (accessed 6 October 2022).
Dickson, E. J. (2020), '"Pastel QAnon" Is Infiltrating the Natural Parent Community', *Rolling Stone*, 14 December. Available online: https://www.rollingstone.com/culture/culture-news/qanon-pastel-antivax-natural-parenting-community-freebirth-1098518/ (accessed 6 October 2022).
Eisenlauer, V. and S. Karatza (2021), 'Multimodal Literacies: Media Affordances, Semiotic Resources and Discourse Communities', *Journal of Visual Literacy*, 39 (3–4): 125–31. https://www.tandfonline.com/doi/full/10.1080/1051144X.2020.1826224.
Gainty, C. (2021), 'Germ Theory Denialism Is Alive and Well – and Taking the Nuance out of Scientific Debate', *The Conversation*, 5 July. Available online: https://theconversation.com/germ-theory-denialism-is-alive-and-well-and-taking-the-nuance-out-of-scientific-debate-163408 (accessed 6 October 2022).
Gerrand, V. (2020a), 'Can Social Networking Platforms Prevent Polarisation and Violent Extremism?' *Open Democracy*, 13 November. Available online: https://www.opendemocracy.net/en/global-extremes/can-social-networking-platforms-prevent-polarisation-and-violent-extremism/ (accessed 6 October 2022).
Gerrand, V. (2020b), 'Pete Evans, Militant Wellness and Nazism', *Overland*, 2 December. Available online: https://overland.org.au/2020/12/pete-evans-militant-wellness-and-nazism/ (accessed 6 October 2022).
Gerrand, V. (2020c), 'Resilience, Radicalisation and Democracy in the COVID-19 Pandemic', *Open Democracy*, 2 April. Available online: https://www.opendemocracy.net/en/global-extremes/resilience-radicalisation-and-democracy-covid-19-pandemic/ (accessed 6 October 2022).
Gillespie, T. (2019), *Custodians of the Internet: Platforms, Content Moderation, and the Hidden Decisions That Shape Social Media*. New Haven: Yale University Press.
Glass, D. (2020), *Investigation into the Detention and Treatment of Public Housing Residents Arising from a COVID-19 'Hard Lockdown' in July 2020*. Melbourne, Vic: Office of the Victorian Ombudsman, 17 December. Available online: https://www.ombudsman.vic.gov.au/our-impact/investigation-reports/investigation-into-the-detention-and-

treatment-of-public-housing-residents-arising-from-a-covid-19-hard-lockdown-in-july-2020/ (accessed 6 October 2022).

Griera, M., J. Morales i Gras, A. Clot-Garrell and R. Cazarín (2022), 'Conspirituality in COVID-19 Times: A Mixed-Method Study of Anti-Vaccine Movements in Spain', *Journal for the Academic Study of Religion*, 35 (2): 192–217.

Grossman, M. (2021), 'Resilience to Violent Extremism and Terrorism: A Multisystemic Analysis', in M. Ungar (ed), *Multisystemic Resilience: Adaptation and Transformation in Contexts of Change*, 293–311, Oxford: Oxford University Press.

Grossman, M., M. Peucker, D. Smith and H. Dellal (2016), *Stocktake Research Report: A Systematic Literature and Selected Program Review on Social Cohesion, Community Resilience and Violent Extremism 2011–2015*, Melbourne: State of Victoria. Available online: https://amf.net.au/entry/stocktake-research-report-victoria-university-australian-multicultural-foundation/ (accessed 6 October 2022).

Halafoff, A., H. Shipley, P. D. Young, A. Singleton, M. L. Rasmussen and G. Bouma (2020), 'Complex, Critical and Caring: Young People's Diverse Religious, Spiritual and Non-Religious Worldviews in Australia and Canada', *Religions*, 11 (4): 166. https://doi.org/10.3390/rel11040166.

Halafoff, A., E. Weng, C. Rocha, A. Singleton, A. Roginski and E. Marriott (2020), 'The Pandemic Has Provided Fertile Conditions for Conspiracy Theories and "Conspirituality" in Australia', *ABC Religion and Ethics*, 13 October. Available online: https://www.abc.net.au/religion/covid-conspiracies-and-conspirituality/12760976 (accessed 6 October 2022).

Hunter, F. (2021), 'Police Responded to "Specific Threats" against Politicians over Weekend', *The Age*, 22 November. Available online: https://www.smh.com.au/national/police-responded-to-specific-threats-against-politicians-over-weekend-20211122-p59b4p.html (accessed 6 October 2022).

Karvelas, P. (2021), 'A Melbourne Vaccination Hub Has Closed Its Doors due to Increased Violence in the City', Australian Broadcasting Corporation, 23 September. Available online: https://www.abc.net.au/radionational/programs/drive/a-melbourne-vaccination-hub-has-closed-its-doors-due-to-increas/13555586 (accessed 6 October 2022).

Kelly, A. (2020), 'Mothers for QAnon', *The New York Times*, 9 October. Available online: https://www.nytimes.com/2020/09/10/opinion/qanon-women-conspiracy.html (accessed 6 October 2022).

Kelly, C. (2021), '"Wellness Warriors": How Victoria's Vaccine Mandate Sparked Divisions in Progressive Brunswick', *The Guardian*, 27 November. Available online: https://www.theguardian.com/australia-news/2021/nov/27/wellness-warriors-how-victorias-vaccine-mandate-sparked-divisions-in-progressive-brunswick (accessed 6 October 2022).

Kennedy, J. (2021), 'Sydney Nurse Speaks out about Alleged Assault at Dundas COVID-19 Testing Site', *ABC News*, 11 August. Available online: https://www.abc.net.au/news/2021-08-11/nurse-at-covid-testing-clinic-allegedly-punched-in-face/100369452 (accessed 6 October 2022).

Khalil, L. (2020), 'Cross-Promotion', *Global Network on Extremism and Technology*, 22 July. Available online: https://gnet-research.org/2020/07/22/cross-promotion/ (accessed 6 October 2022).

Koehne, S. (2012), 'Hitler's Faith: The Debate over Nazism and Religion', *ABC Religion and Ethics*, 18 April. Available online: https://www.abc.net.au/religion/hitlers-faith-the-debate-over-nazism-and-religion/10100614 (accessed 14 June 2024).

Kress, G. (2009), *Multimodality: A Social Semiotic Approach to Contemporary Communication*, London: Routledge.

Kruglanski, A., J. Bélanger and R. Gunaratna (2019), *The Three Pillars of Radicalization: Needs, Narratives, and Networks*. New York: Oxford University Press.

LeClerc, T. (2022), 'Consumption, Wellness, and the Far Right', *M/C Journal*, 25 (1). https://doi.org/10.5204/mcj.2870.

Lewis, J. R. and I. B. Tøllefsen (eds) (2016), *The Oxford Handbook of New Religious Movements*, Volume 2, Oxford: Oxford University Press.

Little, O. and A. Richards (2021), 'TikTok's Algorithm Leads Users from Transphobic Videos to Far-Right Rabbit Holes', *Media Matters*, 10 May. Available online: https://www.mediamatters.org/tiktok/tiktoks-algorithm-leads-users-transphobic-videos-far-right-rabbit-holes (accessed 6 October 2022).

Machin, D. (2013), 'What Is Multi-Modal Critical Discourse Studies?', *Critical Discourse Studies*, 10 (4): 347–55.

Mason, P. (2021), 'The New Alliance between Anti-Vaxxers and the Far Right Is a Deadly Threat', *New Statesman*, 4 October. Available online: https://www.newstatesman.com/science-tech/2021/09/the-new-alliance-between-anti-vaxxers-and-the-far-right-is-a-deadly-threat-2 (accessed 6 October 2022).

McAleer, T. (2019), *The Cure for Hate: A Former White Supremacist's Journey from Violent Extremism to Radical Compassion*. Vancouver: Arsenal Pulp Press.

McKenzie, N. and C. Lucas (2021), 'Far-Right Protester Charged by Counter-Terror Police Amid Talk of Killing Daniel Andrews', *The Age*, 18 November. Available online: https://www.theage.com.au/politics/victoria/far-right-protester-charged-by-counter-terror-police-amid-talk-of-killing-daniel-andrews-20211117-p599qx.html (accessed 6 October 2022).

Northrup, C. ([1994] 2020), *Women's Bodies, Women's Wisdom. Creating Physical and Emotional Health and Healing*. Carisbad, CA: Hay House.

Northrup, C. ([2001] 2021), *The Wisdom of Menopause*. 4th edn, New York: Random House.

Northrup, C. (2013), 'What I Know Now', *Prevention*, 65 (1): 54–8, January.

Palmisano, S. and N. Pannofino (2020), 'Frenemies: Spirituality and Religion', in S. Palmisano and N. Pannofino (eds), *Contemporary Spiritualities. Enchanted Worlds of Nature, Wellbeing and Mystery in Italy*. London: Routledge.

Parmigiani, G. (2021), 'Magic and Politics: Conspirituality and COVID-19', *Journal of the Academy of Religion*, 89 (2): 506–29.

Pasqualetto, A. (2021), 'Attacchi no-vax ai centri vaccinali. L'ultimo assalto a Imperia: "Danni e scritte con gli spray"', *Corriere della Sera*, 19 August. Available online: https://www.corriere.it/cronache/21_agosto_19/attacchi-no-vax-centri-vaccinali-l-ultimo-assalto-imperia-danni-scritte-gli-spray-c578309c-00cf-11ec-bffe-529df168f627.shtml (accessed 6 October 2022).

Plandemic: The Hidden Agenda Behind Covid-19 (2020) [Film] Dir. Mikki Willis. USA: Skyhorse.

Quinn, K. and B. Carmody (2020), 'Dumped by Sponsors, What Happens to Pete Evans now?', *Sydney Morning Herald*, 17 November. Available online: https://www.smh.com.au/culture/tv-and-radio/dumped-by-sponsors-what-happens-to-pete-evans-now-20201117-p56f7j.html (accessed 6 October 2022).

Remski, M. (2021a), 'The Conspirituality Report. Christiane Northrup Encourages Anti-Vaxxers to Shun Pro-Vax Partners. Intervening in Followers' Sex Lives Is a Cultic Technique', *Medium*, 20 April. Available online: https://matthewremski.medium.com/

christiane-northrup-encourages-anti-vaxxers-to-shun-pro-vax-partners-1ee1021a870 (accessed 6 October 2022).

Remski, M. (2021b), 'The Conspirituality Report. Algorithmic Charisma: The Online Theatre of Soft-Q Influencers'. *Medium*, 30 March. Available online: https://matthewremski.medium.com/algorithmic-charisma-5aa26778a8e4 (accessed 6 October 2022).

Richards, I. (2022), 'Neoliberalism, COVID-19 and Conspiracy: Pandemic Management Strategies and the Far-Right Social Turn', *Justice, Power and Resistance*, 5 (1–2): 109–26.

Roginski, A. and C. Rocha (2022), 'The Body as Evidence of Truth: Biomedicine and Enduring Narratives of Religious and Spiritual Healing', *Journal for the Academic Study of Religion*, 35 (2): 168–91.

Roose, J. (2021), ''It's Almost Like Grooming': How Anti-Vaxxers, Conspiracy Theorists, and the Far-Right Came Together over COVID', *The Conversation*, 21 September. Available online: https://theconversation.com/its-almost-like-grooming-how-anti-vaxxers-conspiracy-theorists-and-the-far-right-came-together-over-covid-168383 (accessed 6 October 2022).

Signposts on the Road to Ascension (2021), [Film] Dir. J. Witzeman. USA: JW Films.

Teixeira da Silva, J. A. (2021),'Corona Exhaustion (CORONEX): COVID-19-Induced Exhaustion Grinding down Humanity', *Current Research in Behavioural Sciences*, 2. https://doi.org/10.1016/j.crbeha.2021.100014.

Therapeutic Goods Administration (2021), 'Peter Evans Chef Pty Ltd fined $79,920 for Alleged Unlawful Advertising', *Therapeutic Goods Administration Media Release*, 25 May. Available online: https://www.tga.gov.au/news/media-releases/peter-evans-chef-pty-ltd-fined-79920-alleged-unlawful-advertising (accessed 6 October 2022).

Thomas, E. (2021), 'What's Wrong with Calling the Melbourne Protests "Far Right"?', in *The Strategist*, Canberra: Australian Strategic Policy Institute. Available online: https://www.aspistrategist.org.au/whats-wrong-with-calling-the-melbourne-protests-far-right/ (accessed 6 October 2022).

Ward, C. and D. Voas (2011), 'The Emergence of Conspirituality', *Journal of Contemporary Religion*, 26 (1): 103–21.

Wignell, P., S. Tan and K. O Halloran (2017), 'Violent Extremism and Iconisation: Commanding Good and Forbidding Evil?', *Critical Discourse Studies*, 14 (1): 1–22.

Wilson, J. (2020), 'The Neo-Nazi Symbol Posted by Pete Evans Has a Strange and Dark History', *The Guardian*, 24 November. Available online: https://www.theguardian.com/world/2020/nov/24/the-neo-nazi-symbol-posted-by-pete-evans-has-a-strange-and-dark-history (accessed 6 May 2022).

Yunkaporta, T. (2022), 'Black-Pilled: Conspirituality, Backlash, and Indigenous Online Radicalization', *ABC Religion and Ethics*, 11 May. Available online: https://www.abc.net.au/religion/tyson-yunkaporta-indigenous-online-radicalisation/13877124 (accessed 6 October 2022).

Index

Afghanistan 43–4, 119, 121–4, 147
  mujahideen in 121, 132
Albania 10, 77–83, 92–3
  Balkan Investigative Reporting
    Network 81
  counter-terrorism operations 81
  foreign terrorist fighters (FTFs) in
    80–3, 93
  Muslim Community of Albania
    (KMSH) 80, 82
  national strategies (whole-of-society-
    approach) 82
  religious harmony/tolerance 82
  unofficial mosques 80, 82
Albrecht, Franco 257, 262
Amir, Yigal 170, 199
Anglicized Christianity 233
Anglosphere 13, 227, 230, 234
anti-abortion extremists 21, 199, 207, 210, 212, 217
anti-Black racism 211
anti-conversion laws 149, 186
anti-government extremism 207, 210, 212, 215, 217
anti-immigrant 58, 61
anti-Muslim 11, 42, 45, 47, 49, 58, 61, 128, 139, 176–7, 182, 185, 190, 264.
  See also Muslims
  violence in India 145–7
  violence in Sri Lanka 141–5
anti-Salafi campaigns 62
antisemitism 157, 162–3, 166–7, 229, 257
Army of God (AOG) movement 199, 210
Arya Samaj organization 145
Asatru Folk Assembly (AFA) organization 213
Asatru/Wotanism. *See* Odinism
Australia 41, 233, 273–4
authoritarian/authoritarianism 105–6, 176, 232, 236, 273
autocephalous congregations 228, 237, 239, 241

Ba'asyir, Abu Bakar 121, 125–6
Balliet, Stephan 254, 258–9, 261
Bangladesh 182
Bat-Ayin underground, West Bank 205
behavioural radicalization 27, 29, 64, 250.
  See also cognitive (ideological) radicalization
Belgium 10, 57–9, 61–3, 65
  ban of religious signs/symbols 67
  Belgian Muslim Executive (BME) 65
  Brussels attacks 66
  moderate secularism in 65–8
  Muslim Executive, selection of 66
Ben-Gvir, Itamar 158, 171
Berger, J. M. 14, 28, 30, 79, 140–1
The Bible (biblical law) 209–12
Black Lives Matter (BLM) movement 47
Book of Mormon 212
Bosnia and Herzegovina (BiH) 9, 77–9, 83–7, 92–3
  foreign terrorist fighters (FTFs) in 84–5
  Interreligious Council (IRC) 87
  mujahideen in 83–4
  Operation Ruben in Republika Srpska 86–7
  para-jamaats 85, 87, 93
  parallel congregations 85
  policy strategies and impacts 85–7
  resilience-building initiatives 86
Breivik, Anders 197–9, 259–60
British Israelitism movement 209
Buddhists 139, 141–3, 145, 151, 178
  Sangha (Buddhist monastic community) 142
Bulgaria 9, 77, 87–93
  Act to Limit the Wearing of Clothing Partially or Completely Covering the Face 91
  Bulgarian Criminal Code 90
  foreign terrorist fighters (FTFs) in 90, 92

National Plan for Combating Terrorism 90
Project Law for Revision of the Denominations Act 91
Roma community 87–9, 93
Salafi interpretations of Islam 88–9
Strategy for Countering Radicalization and Terrorism (2015) 90
terrorist attack in 2012 87–8, 90
Byzantine Empire 235, 239

Cameron, David 62
Camp David Accords (1982) 203
Castex, Jean 69
Chechen–Russian conflict 9, 102–3, 106–8, 112–13
Christian Identity movement 198, 207, 209–11, 217–18
Christianity 12–13, 44, 87, 145, 197, 207–8, 214
    Anglicized Christianity 233
    Christian Reconstructionism 210
    Eastern Orthodox Christianity 13, 227–9, 232, 234–6, 238–40
    Greek Orthodox Church 233, 239
    Oriental Orthodox Churches 228
    Orthodox Christianity (*see* Orthodox Christianity)
    pro-Western Christianity 208
    Romanian Orthodox Church 231, 241
    Russian Orthodox Church 227, 230–1, 234
    Serbian Orthodox Church 232
Christians 19, 67, 87, 124, 126, 141, 144, 150, 159, 180, 185–6, 197, 208, 240, 252
    anti-Christian riot in India (2008) 186
    Christian missionaries 150, 185–6
    Christian reactionaries 234
    influential upon far-right movements 210–13
Church of Jesus Christ of Latter-Day Saints (LDS) 199, 211–13
Church Primary Groups 214
Codreanu, Corneliu Zelea 13, 229, 241
cognitive (ideological) radicalization 27, 29, 64, 123, 250. *See also* behavioural radicalization

Commission on Race and Ethnic Disparities in 2021 (Sewell Report) 45–7
communal violence 124, 139, 143, 146, 179
conspiracy thinking 13–14, 271–3, 277–8, 280, 283
conspirituality 13–14, 271
    in Covid-19 context 272
    and militant wellness 13–14, 276–8
    public health measures, Covid-19 272–6
conspiritual thinking 13, 271, 276
Cottrell, Blair 233
counter-extremism 7, 41, 43, 49, 51–2, 64, 66
counter-radicalization 7, 62, 70, 87
counter-terrorist/-terrorism 7, 22, 49–50, 63, 66, 79, 81, 90, 92–4, 123, 125, 128
Covid-19 pandemic 13–14, 47, 52, 141, 258, 271
    conspirituality in Covid-19 context 272
    corona jihad (#CoronaJihad) in India 147–9
    public health measures 272–6
    social media influencers in context of 278–83 (*see also specific influencers*)
Creativity Alliance organization 214
Creativity (racial religion) 214, 218
Crenshaw, Martha 7, 20
critical race and religious studies 41–2

dangerous speech, violence 262
Dharmapala, Anagarika 142
domestic intelligence service 63, 247, 249, 254, 264
Dominionism (Dominion Theology) 210
Dutthagamini 142

Eastern Orthodox Christianity 13, 227–9, 232, 234–6, 238–40
Egypt 162, 203
    Egyptian Muslim Brotherhood 121, 131
Elad organization 202–3
Elara, Chola king 142
ethnic groups 141, 178, 203, 228, 255, 260

ethnonationalism 9–10
ethno-religious relations 9, 12, 83, 92–3
Europe 8, 22, 26, 48–9, 198–9, 213, 232, 247, 260
    Muslims in 24, 43–4, 52
    refugee crisis 43, 58, 91
    South-Eastern Europe (*see* South-Eastern Europe)
    Western Europe (*see* Western Europe)
Evans, Pete 280–3
everyday religion 25, 28, 31. *See also* lived religion

far-right extremism (far-right extremist movements) 5, 11, 45, 57–8, 197–8
    American far right (*see* The United States, religious fundamentalism and American far right)
    analysis of American *vs.* Israeli 216–18
    anti-abortion violent extremists 210
    far-right white nationalists 13, 207–8, 228–30
    in Germany (*see* Germany)
    and Islamophobia 48–9
    Israeli far right (*see* Israel, Jewish orthodoxy and Israeli far right)
    and Orthodox Christianity (*see* Orthodox Christianity)
    and religious beliefs 11–13, 198–9
    and religious minorities 247
    and Western Christian denominations 13, 227, 237
Fashion Bug, violence against 143
felt/experienced mobilization of religion 6
foreign fighters 9, 57, 80, 84–5, 89, 92, 102, 122, 126–7, 129, 132
foreign policy 43–4, 61
foreign terrorist fighters (FTFs) 77–8, 80–1, 84–5, 88, 92, 127
fourth wave of modern terrorism. *See* religious terrorism
France 10, 52, 57–8, 62–3, 68, 71, 261
    ban of religious signs/symbols 69
    Charlie Hebdo attacks, Paris 61, 252
    French Council of the Muslim Faith (Conseil français du culte musulman, CFCM) 62, 69
    French National Action plans 62
    laïcité policy 61, 69–70
    prevent radicalization 62
    Prevent to Protect strategy (2018) 63
    secularist statism in 68–70
functional definition of religion 4.
    See also substantive definition of religion
Fundamentalist Church of Jesus Christ of Latter-Day Saints (FLDS) 211–12

Gandhi, Mahatma 175, 180–1, 185
gar'inim toranim (Torah nuclei) 170
Gaza Strip 165, 202–3
Germany 10, 52, 57–63, 65, 247, 252–4
    Alternative for Germany (AfD) 249, 252, 258, 264
    ban of religious signs/symbols 67
    behavioural radicalization 64
    Bundesamt für Verfassungsschutz (VS) 248–50, 252
    conceptualizations of radicalization and extremism in 248–9
    crisis of masculinity 259
    from crisis to existential threat 260–1
    Die Linke party 249
    EXIT strategy 64, 70
    extreme right-wing attacks 247–8, 254–7, 262
    German Democratic Republic (GDR) 253
    German Islam Conferences (*Deutsche Islam Konferenz,* DIK) 65–6, 68
    Heathen faiths/Heathenry 12, 199, 207–8, 213–14
    moderate secularism in 65–8
    National Socialist Underground (NSU) 254, 262–3
    prevent radicalization 63
    psychosocial development 261–3
    religiously inspired radicalization 249–52
    religious population of 252
    social change and affective crises 257–9
Global North 43–5, 49, 259
Godse, Nathuram 175
Goldstein, Baruch 169–70
Golwalkar, Madhav Sadashivrao 179–80

governance of religious diversity 8–10, 58, 71
　comparative modes of governance 59
　conceptualizing (violent) radicalization 61–4
　desk-based research 58–9
　moderate secularism 10, 59, 61, 64–8
　secularist statism 10, 59, 64, 68–70
　state governance of religion and violent radicalization 60–1
GREASE project. *See* Horizon 2020 GREASE project
great replacement theory 48, 140, 217, 252, 255–6, 259–60, 262
Greek Orthodox Church 233, 239
group-focused enmity (GFE) 259

Hanafi Sunni Islam 88
hate crimes 45, 63, 111, 182, 250, 252, 264
Hebraism 161, 166
Hebronization 169–70
Hedgewar, Keshav Baliram 180
Heimbach, Matthew 230–2, 240–1
Hellenism 168
Hellenization 165
Her Majesty's Government (HMG) 47
Herzog, Isaac 158–60, 169
Hezbollah 88
Hinduism 13, 176, 178, 185
Hindus 10–11, 139, 175, 177, 190
　Hindu radicalism 179–80, 184–7
　vigilantism 186–7
Hitler, Adolf 48, 158, 280
Hodges, Mark 232
homegrown terrorism 21–2, 24, 26–7, 88, 128
Horizon 2020 GREASE project 4, 8, 59, 248
Hoskins, Richard Kelly, *Vigilantes of Christendom: The Story of the Phineas Priesthood* 209
Hutaree group 211

Ibrahim, Anwar 131
improvised explosive device (IED) 122, 125, 128
India 10–11, 52, 139, 141, 151
　accusation against Nizamuddin Auliya mosque, Delhi 148
All India Hindu Mahasabha (1915) 179–80
anti-CAA protests 148
anti-Christian riot (2008) 186
anti-Muslim violence in 145–7
anti-terrorist laws 183
Arya Samaj organization 145
assassination of leaders 181, 183
Babri Mosque in Ayodhya, destruction of 146, 175–6, 182–3, 187
Bajrang Dal (BD) 182, 186
Bharatiya Janata Party (BJP) 146–7, 149, 175–6, 182, 187, 189
Citizenship Amendment Act (CAA) 146–7, 184
contextualizing radicalization in 178–9
convergence and divergence of (Hindu/Muslim) radicalization 188
corona jihad (#CoronaJihad) 147–9
cow protection (ban on cow slaughter) 187
Dharma Sansad (Hindu religious parliament), Haridwar 175
evolution of Muslim/Hindu radicalism 179–80
Hindu radicalization 184–7, 189
Hindutva/Hindu nationalism 10–11, 141, 145–6, 151, 175–8, 180, 182
Indian Mujahideen (IM) 183
Islamist radicalization 182–4, 188–9
jihad against Hindus 189–90
Kashmir 181–5, 189
Khalistan movement 119, 178
Khilafat movement 145
left-wing radicalism (Maoist) 178
love jihad (religious conversions) 146, 149–51, 186
Muslim radicalization in postcolonial 180–2
National Crime Records Bureau report (2017) 182
National Register of Citizens (NRC) 147–8, 184
Prevention of Terrorism Act of 2002 (POTA) 183
Ram Janmabhoomi movement 146, 182

Rashtriya Swayamsevak Sangh (RSS) 146, 150, 175
renaming cities 187
Sachar Committee Report (2006) 181
Sangh Parivar 182, 185–7, 189
Sewa International (RSS international wing) 146
socio-economic status of Muslims 181
Students Islamic Movement in India (SIMI) 183
terrorist activities in 183, 187
Uniform Civil Code (UCC) 185
vigilantism 186–7
Vishva Hindu Parishad (VHP) movement 150, 182, 186
Indonesia 10, 120–6, 131–2
arrests of terrorism suspects 123
Bali bomb attacks (2002) 122, 124–5
Darul Islam (DI) movement 120–2, 131
Detachment 88/Densus 88 125
Gerakan Merdeka Aceh (GAM, Free Aceh Movement) 119
Indonesian nationalist movement 120
Jamaah Ansharusy Syariah (JAS) 126
Jemaah Ansharut Daulah (JAD) 119, 123, 126, 130–1
Jemaah Anshrut Tauhid (JAT) 125–6
Jemaah Islamiyah (*see* Jemaah Islamiyah (JI))
jihad in Ambon and Poso 124
Laskar Jihad group 124
lone-actor attacks in 123
Negara Islam Indonesia (NII, Islamic State of Indonesia) 120
Partai Keadilan Sejahtera (PKS, Prosperous Justice Party) 131
Pesantren al-Mukmin 121
pesantren (Islamic boarding school) 121
post-Suharto Indonesia 121–2, 131
terrorist attacks in 125–6
training camp in Aceh 125–6
in-groups 14, 28, 30, 79, 105, 140–1, 151, 208, 211, 214–15, 262, 271, 277.
See also out-groups
institutional/institutionalized racism 46–7, 51

Iraq 29, 44, 57, 66, 77, 80, 84, 88, 113, 122–3, 127, 129, 183
Islam 6–7, 11, 14, 17, 19, 25, 42, 44, 62–3, 66, 68, 79–80, 83–4, 87, 89, 102, 104, 106–7, 145, 177–9, 185, 252
Hanafi Sunni Islam 88
South Asian Islam 179
Sufi Islam 102–3, 108
Sunni Islam 128
Islamic State (IS) movement 9, 45, 57, 79–80, 88–90, 101–2, 110–11, 113, 119–20, 122–3, 126–8, 131, 144, 177, 183
Sawt-al-Hind (Voice of Hind) magazine 177
and siege of Marawi 128–30
support for IS in Malaysia 127–8
Islamic State of Iraq and Syria (ISIS) 29, 119
Islamic State of Iraq and the Levant (ISIL) 119
Islamism 9, 60, 69, 104, 249
Islamophobia 7, 19, 41–2, 48–51, 151, 176–7, 229, 251–2, 261
Islamophobic fabrication 50
normalization of Islamophobia after 9/11 43–5
Israel 11–12, 88, 158
apartheid 163
'The City of David' 203
Gush Emunim (Block of the Faithful) movement 158, 165, 169
Haram al Sharif/Temple Mount 157, 159–60, 162, 166, 203–4
Israeli Defence Force (IDF) 158
Israeli-Palestinian conflict 201
Jewish orthodoxy and Israeli far right 200–6
analysis of American *vs.* Israeli 216–18
Greater Land of Israel 201–3, 206
religious motivations 203–5
theological origins 200–1
ultra-orthodoxy 205–6
King David Accords (1979) 162
Likud Party 160, 167
Ne'manei Har Habayit (Temple Faithful) 160
Otzma Yehudit political party 158

radicalization and self-defence 163–4
settler colonialism 164–5
Third Temple 157, 159–61, 166
yihud (Judaization) 160, 166, 170

Jaish-e-Mohammad terrorist group 183
Jemaah Islamiyah (JI) 119, 124, 127, 130–2
  emergence of 122
  origins of 120–1
  splinter bombings 125
Jerryson, Michael, emergency mindset 11, 140
Jewish Underground group 162, 204
Jewish
  din rodef/din moser 170, 199
  ethnocentric/ethnocentricity 160, 164–6
  halacha (Jewish religious law) 201–2, 204
  halakhic rules 169–70
  Hasbarah and discursive violence 162–3
  Jewish orthodoxy and Israeli far right (*see* Israel, Jewish orthodoxy and Israeli far right)
  Jewish settlements 168, 200, 202–3
  Jewish un-safety 163, 167
  Kahanism and politics of Jewish purity 167
  subverting Jewish tradition 158–60
Jews 12, 57, 60–1, 67, 80, 157, 160, 162–9, 171, 199–207, 209, 214, 229, 255, 259, 261
jihadist terrorism 19, 23, 90, 124, 262
  homegrown jihadists 24, 26 (*see also* homegrown terrorism)
  ideological explanation of 22–3, 26–7, 29
  interpretive mistakes 24–30
  jihadist radicalization 25, 258
  Western jihadists 21, 25–7
jihad(i)/jihadism 3, 5, 7, 17, 19–23, 52, 84, 89, 104, 119, 124, 126, 144
  in Ambon and Poso (Indonesia) 124
  Salafi-jihadist ideology 26–7, 29, 62
Jinnah, Muhammad Ali 180, 185
Johnson, Boris 48

Johnson, Matthew Raphael 231–2
  'The Orthodox Nationalist:
    A Response to the Orthodox
    Clergy Condemnation of
    Nationalism' 232
  The Orthodox Nationalist podcast 231
Judaism 13, 166, 168, 171, 203, 214

Kahane, Meir 158, 163, 165–6, 168, 171, 204
  The Jewish Idea 168
  Judeo-pessimism 163, 166
Kahanism 12, 158, 163, 165–8, 170, 205, 218. *See also* neo-Kahanism
Kalicharan (Hindu Sadhu) 175
Kartosuwirjo, Sekarmadji Maridjan 120
Klassen, Ben 214, 218
Köhler, Gundolf 253
Komando Jihad organization 121
Kook, Avraham Isaac 164–5
Kookism 164–8, 170–1
Kook, Zvi Yehuda 164–5
Ku Klux Klan (KKK) 199, 207–9, 217

Laqueur, Walter 7–8
Lashkar-e-Taiba terrorist group 183–4
Laskar Jihad group 124
Laskar Jundullah group 124
Legion of the Archangel Michael (Legionnaires) 241
LGBTQ+ community, violence against 198–9
liberal-democratic societies 20, 27
Lifta Gang group 204
lived religion 25. *See also* everyday religion
lone actor extremists 21, 49, 123, 253, 256, 262

Majelis Mujahideen Indonesia (MMI, Indonesian Mujahideen Council) 125
majoritarian/majoritarianism 10–11, 139–40, 143, 146, 176, 181, 189
Malaysia 10, 119, 121–2, 126–8, 131–2
  arrests of terrorism suspects 127–8
  Special Branch counterterrorism police unit 128
  support for IS in 127–8

manosphere 228, 234–6, 239
marriage of convenience 11–13, 166, 198, 218
Marzel, Baruch 157–8, 160, 167
May, Theresa 62
militant wellness movement 13–14, 276–8
moderate secularism 10, 59, 61, 64–8, 71
Modi, Narendra 10, 176, 184–5, 187
Moors/Moorish sovereign citizens 141, 215–16
Mormon Constitutionalists 211–12
Mormonism 207, 211–12
mujahideen (Islamic holy warriors) 84, 121, 124, 132
multiculturalism 6, 52
Murtopo, Ali 121
Musa, Ahmed 88–9, 91
muscular liberalism 64
Muslims 7, 10, 12, 19, 29, 42, 45, 49–50, 62, 64, 68–9, 84, 93, 104, 109, 159, 263
   American Muslims 44
   British Muslims 43, 51
   European Muslims 24, 43–4, 52
   Indian Muslims 10, 148–50, 177, 180–1, 183–5
   Indonesian Muslims 120
   Muslim organizations 9, 65–7, 69, 80, 92, 264
   Muslim radicalization in India 177, 179–80, 182–4
   Russian Muslims 9, 102, 110
Muzakkar, Abdul Kahar 120
Myanmar 139–40, 178

National College for Teaching and Leadership (NCTL) 50
national identity 6, 9, 239–40
Nazi Germany 280–1
Nehru, Jawaharlal 177, 185
neo-biblicalism 158, 160–1, 165–7
neo-Kahanism 170–2. *See also* Kahanism
neo-Nazism 213, 217, 232–3, 236, 253–4, 257, 261, 275
neo-Paganism 213–14, 280
Netanyahu, Benjamin 158
new atheism 19
New Atheist movement 208

New Religious Movements (NRMs) 12–13, 25, 68, 199, 207–8, 214–16, 271. *See also specific religions*
new terrorism 7
New York Times (NYT), Trojan Horse podcast 42, 50–1
Nordkreuz group 257, 263
normalization 41–2
   of Islamophobia after 9/11 43–5
   of racism 46–8
normative secular bias 5, 15, 18
Northrup, Christiane 282–3
   Women's Bodies, Women's Wisdom 278–9

Odinism 199, 207, 213–14
ontological antisemitism 157, 167
Orientalism 164
Oriental Orthodox Churches 228
Orthobros 234–6
Orthodox Christianity 13, 208, 227–9, 241–2
   ethnicity, anti-globalization and anti-Western expression in 239–41
   and far right 229–30
   holy figures in 239
   patriarchy, heteronormativity and anti-feminism in 236–9
   political Orthodox Christianity 240
   priesthood 237, 239
   by white nationalists 230–4
Orthosphere 13, 227–8, 230, 234–6
   Throne and Altar website 234–5
Oslo Accords (1993) 170, 203
Ottoman Caliphate 145
Ottoman Empire 78, 87, 89, 239–40
out-groups 14, 28, 30, 140–1, 212, 218, 262, 271. *See also* in-groups

Pakistan 119, 121–2, 132, 147, 180–3, 189
Palestine 158–9, 163, 166, 168, 200
   Hebron 158–9, 170, 204
Palestinians 162–70, 203–5
   Nakba (Palestinian catastrophe of 1948) 162, 165, 170
Parrott, Matthew 231
Patriarchs (male bishops) 237, 240
patriarchy/patriarchal system 236–9

Patristic Faith website 236
PEGIDA (Patriotic Europeans Against the Islamization of the Occident) movement 252–3
The Philippines 10, 119, 121–2, 124, 127–30
  Abu Sayyaf Group (ASG) 129–30, 132
  Camp Abubakar 121
  IS and siege of Marawi 128–30
  New People's Army (NPA) 130
  Philippines Armed Forces 129
  suicide bomb attacks 130
  Sulu Archipelago 128–30
  terrorist attacks in 125
phyletism 228, 231, 239
politically motivated crimes 63, 250
political Orthodox Christianity 240
political violence 27–8, 30, 57, 217, 258
politicized social identity 28
politico-ideologically motivated violence 41
polygamy/polygamous 211–12
preventing and countering violent extremism (P/CVE) programmes 70–1, 90
Protestants 150, 207, 209, 227–8, 234, 238
Putin, Vladimir 230, 232, 235

Al-Qaeda 43, 57, 79, 84, 88, 90, 119, 122–3, 126–7, 131–2, 140, 177
QAnon ideology 272–3, 277–8, 280, 283

Rabin, Itzhak, assassination of 199
race/racism/racialization 41–2, 49, 52, 197–8, 213, 260
  denial of racial exclusion 45–8
  institutional/institutionalized racism 46–7, 51
  racial hygiene 280–1
  racial separatism 232, 240–1
  scientific racism 48
  systemic racism 42, 46–7, 51
radicalized individuals, components of 105
RaHoWa (Racial Holy War) 214–15
Rahula, Walpola, *The Heritage of the Bhikku* 142
Rapoport, David 7, 17
Rathjen, Tobias 48, 255–6, 258–60
Rawles, James Wesley 211

Reconstructionism 210
religio-political texts 28–9
religiosity 3–5, 9, 11, 14, 18–20, 22, 24–7, 30, 89, 164, 229
religious affiliation 4, 12, 60, 77, 87, 126, 207, 219
religious beliefs 3, 5, 7–8, 12, 23, 208
  far-right movements and 198–9, 217–18
religious conversions 87, 149–51, 185–6, 227–9, 231–2, 236, 239, 241–2
religious diversity 4–5, 12, 60, 68–71, 82, 85, 87, 252, 259
  institutional accommodation of 65
  radicalization and governance of 8–10, 58
religious fundamentalism 8, 206–18
religious identities 4, 9, 11–12, 42, 45, 63, 79, 198, 200, 216, 219, 239, 251–3
religiously attributed radicalization 5, 9, 57–9, 62, 64, 77–87, 92–4, 251, 271
religiously motivated radicalization 25, 41, 83, 87, 92
religious minorities 9–10, 12, 30, 42–3, 46–9, 60–1, 63, 69, 71, 83, 87, 91, 139, 247, 251, 253, 264
religious motivations (in religious terrorism) 18, 23–5, 31, 92, 113, 203–5
religious narratives 8, 198–9, 201, 206, 217–18
religious normative bias 18–19
religious terrorism 5, 17–18, 20–1, 23, 26, 30–1
Religious Zionism 160, 200–2, 205, 217
Roma community 87–9, 93
Romanian Orthodox Church 231, 241
Roof, Dylan 232
Roy, Olivier 8–9, 24
Rushdie, Salman 43
  The Rushdie Affair 43, 51
Rusijournal.org webpage 231
Russia
  Chechnya 101, 103, 107
  conceptualizing radicalization 104–6
  domestic politics and legislation 108–9
  empirical study 106–7

foreign politics 109–10
hate crimes in 111
Muslims in 9, 102, 110
North Caucasian Federal District of Russia 102
North Caucasus 101–4, 106–13
Russian Federation with Muslim populations 103
Russo-Chechen wars 9, 102–3, 106–8, 112–13
second-class citizens in 110–11
socio-economic and psychological factors 110–13
terrorist attack at Orthodox Churches 101–2
Russian Orthodox Church 227, 230–1, 234
Russian Orthodox Church Outside Russia (ROCOR) 230, 232
Rwandan genocide of 1994 30

Salafism 8, 25, 49, 62, 66, 80, 83–5, 88–9, 103–4, 107–9, 112–13, 124
Salafi jihadism/jihadist 26–7, 29, 62, 130–2
Wahhabism 62, 103, 108
Sarrazin, Thilo, *Deutschland schafft sich ab* (Germany is abolishing itself) 251, 260–1
Saudi Arabia 66, 124
Savarkar, Vinayak Damodar 179–80, 185
Hindutva: Who Is a Hindu? 145
scientific racism 48
Sears, JP 281–3
sectarian/sectarianism 19, 71, 119, 128
secular bias 20
dominant secular bias 21–3
normative secular bias 5, 15, 18
secularization of Western society 21, 26
secular/secularism 4, 8, 10, 12, 27, 32, 59, 66, 157, 160–1, 168, 180, 219
moderate secularism 10, 59, 61, 64–8
secularist statism 10, 59, 61, 64, 68–71
secular Zionism 157, 161, 165, 167, 169
security threats 68, 70, 77
self-radicalization 123
Serbian Orthodox Church 232
settler colonialism 159, 165–8
Sewell Report 45–7
Sharma, Nupur 189

Sharon, Ariel 169
Shea, Matt, 'The Biblical Basis for War' 211
Sixteen Commandments of Creativity 214
social identity theory 28, 30
social media 47, 139, 232, 279, 281–2
corona jihad (#CoronaJihad) in India 147–9
digital ethnography methods with multimodal analysis 275–6
rumours on sterilization in Sri Lanka 143–4
spread of religious ideas 215
Sonboly, David 256
Southeast Asia 10, 119, 121, 126, 178.
 See also India; Indonesia; Malaysia; Myanmar; Sri Lanka; The Philippines
radicalization and social networks in 122–4
South Asian Islam 179
South-Eastern Europe 9, 77–8, 94.
 See also Albania; Bosnia and Herzegovina (BiH); Bulgaria
Southern Poverty Law Center 227, 231, 236
sovereign citizen movement. *See* Moors/Moorish sovereign citizens
Soviet Union, dissolution of 43, 102
Sri Lanka 11, 139–41, 151, 178
anti-Muslim violence in 141–5
Anuradhapura period (377 BCE–1017 CE) 142–3
Bodu Bala Sena (BBS) 143
Liberation Tigers of Tamil Eelam (LTTE) 119, 144
Mahavamsa (historical poem) 142
Moors of Sri Lanka (Muslims) 141
population of 141
rumours on (sterilization) social media 143–4
Sinhala-Buddhist nationalism 142–3, 151
Sinhala nationalist movements 11, 144, 151
Sinhalese community 140, 142–5
suicide bomb attacks (2019) 144
'A Statement Concerning the Sin of Racism,' American Orthodox clergy 232

state-religion connections 58–9, 64–5, 67–9
stochastic terrorism 262–3
strategic mobilization of religion 6
substantive definition of religion 4. *See also* functional definition of religion
Suharto 120–1, 131
Sukarno 131–2
Sungkar, Abdullah 121, 125
Syria 57, 77, 80, 82, 84, 88–9, 113, 122–3, 127, 129–30, 183
systemic racism 42, 46–7, 51

Tablighi Jamaat, Islamic reformist movement 148–9
Taliban 43, 132, 253
Tambiah, Stanley J. 140
Tarrant, Brendan 232, 256, 260
Thailand 119, 149
Thalib, Jafar Umar 124
tikkun hamidot 168
tikkun olam 165, 167–8
Toronto 18 jihadist group 28
Traditional Workers Party (TWP) 230–2
transcendence/transcendent 4, 8, 29
transnational networks 10–12, 110, 132, 145, 253, 261
Trojan Horse Affair in UK 42, 49–51
The Troth (Ring of Troth) 213
Trump, Donald 48, 279

ultranationalism 12, 171, 229
Ultra-Orthodox (Haredi Jews) 200, 205–6
The United Kingdom (UK) 10, 44–5, 52, 57–9, 61–3
  ban of religious signs/symbols 67
  Commission on Countering Extremism (CCE) 63
  democratic constellation in 65, 68
  moderate secularism in 65–8
  Muslim Council of Britain 66
  Muslim organizations in 66
  Prevent strategy 62–4, 70
  Trojan Horse Affair in 42, 49–51
The United States 11, 41, 43–4, 52, 59, 167, 211–12, 256, 273
  religious fundamentalism and American far right 206–16
    analysis of American *vs.* Israeli 216–18

Christianity influential upon far right movements 210–13
    diverse landscape 206–7
    NRMs 214–16 (*see also specific religions*)
    reconstructed neo-Pagan/Heathen religions 213–14
    religious landscape 207–8
    white supremacist with Christianity 208–10
  Unite the Right Rally in Charlottesville (2017) 230, 232

Valizadeh, Daryush (Roosh V) 236
vernacular theology 229, 238
Von List, Guido 213

Wahhabism 62, 103, 108
  Salafism (*see* Salafism)
Wahid, Abdurrahman 124
war on terror 42, 44–5, 66, 164, 183
Washitaw de Dugdahmoundyah group 215
Wehrsportgruppe Hoffmann group 253
West Bank 164, 169, 171, 200–5
Western Europe 9–10, 48, 57–9, 62, 65, 70, 88, 235, 247, 252. *See also* Belgium; France; Germany; The United Kingdom (UK)
white nationalist movements 13, 199, 207, 228–34, 236, 240–1
white supremacy 12, 48–9, 213–14, 232, 236, 240
  with Christianity 208–10
Wikingjugend group 253
Willis, Mikki, *Plandemic* 275, 279
Witzeman, Jeff 278–9
World Church of the Creator. *See* Creativity (racial religion)
World Congress of Families (WCF) 230

Yogi Adityanath (Bulldozer Baba) 176

Zionism 12, 157–62, 164–8, 170–1
  Religious Zionism 160, 200–2, 205, 217
  secular (political) Zionism 157, 161, 165, 167, 169